Flyfisher's Guide to™
NEW YORK

Titles Available in This Series

Saltwater Angler's Guide to Southern California

Saltwater Angler's Guide to the Southeast

Flyfisher's Guide to the Florida Keys

Flyfisher's Guide to Idaho

Flyfisher's Guide to Northern California

Flyfisher's Guide to Montana

Flyfisher's Guide to Michigan

Flyfisher's Guide to Wyoming

Flyfisher's Guide to Northern New England

Flyfisher's Guide to Washington

Flyfisher's Guide to Oregon

Flyfisher's Guide to Colorado

Flyfisher's Guide to Pennsylvania

Flyfisher's Guide to Minnesota

Flyfisher's Guide to Utah

Flyfisher's Guide to Texas

Flyfisher's Guide to™
NEW YORK

Eric Newman

Wilderness
Adventures
Press, Inc.™

Belgrade, Montana

This book was made with an easy opening, lay flat binding.

© 2002 Eric H. Newman

Cover photograph © 2002 Gregory Cuda
Author Photograph ©2002 Frederic Thorner
Photographs contained herein © 2002 Eric H. Newman, or as noted:
Fish Illustrations © 2001 R.D. Dye

Maps, book design and cover design © 2002 Wilderness Adventures Press, Inc.
Flyfisher's Guide to™

Published by Wilderness Adventures Press, Inc.
45 Buckskin Road
Belgrade, MT 59714
800-925-3339
Website: www.wildadv.com
email: books@wildadv.com

Printed in the United States of America

Library of Congress Cataloging-in-Publication Data
Newman, Eric H., 1958 -
    Flyfisher's guide to New York / by Eric H. Newman.
        p. cm.
    Includes index.
    ISBN 1-885106-92-0 (pbk. : alk. paper))
    1. Fly fishing—New York (State)—Guidebooks.   2. New York (State)—Guidebooks.
    I. Title.

    SH529 .N48 2002
    799.1′24′09747—dc21
                                                                                    2001006520

Table of Contents

Acknowledgments

In addition to having a great subject to write about, I was very lucky to have the help and support of family, friends and colleagues while working on this book. Recognizing them here is only a small measure of my appreciation.

First, thanks to my parents, Gus and Winnie Newman, my sister Debi, brother-in-law Jeff and nephews Jack and Matt, who all provided much love and support (and, in the case of my parents, frequent use of their car).

My long-time friend David Ader first got me interested in flyfishing and he and Pippa have been enthusiastic about this project from the start, as have my friends Bob Grill and Rick Zopatti.

Fred Thorner kindly introduced me to the people at Wilderness Adventures Press. He and Linda, along with their son Eric, also offered fishing information, publishing tips and general encouragement. Encouragement and advice also came from Trout Unlimited colleagues and friends Susanne Weiser, John Crow, Mike Parks, Jerry Hoffnagle and Wayne Tusa.

Finally, everyone at Wilderness Adventures Press—Chuck and Blanche Johnson, Darren Brown, Marcia Rueter Leritz, and Peter Riess—has been unfailingly professional and a pleasure to work with.

In addition, this book couldn't have been written without help from many people across the state. Trout Unlimited colleagues and other avid anglers from every part of New York were very generous with their time and knowledge, and a wealth of fishing information was provided by tackle shop owners, professional guides, DEC staff and tourism bureaus. At the risk of omitting a few individuals, I've set out their names below. I'm sure there are some mistakes in this book, but they aren't the fault of the people listed here.

Ron Allen, Bob Angle, Nancy Arena, Ed August, Michael Austin, Ed Bartholomew, Joe Battaglia, Jim Bell, Gil Bergen, Fran Betters, Ron Bierstine, Dave Brandt, Peter Brown, Peter Burns, Al Carpenter, Sr., Al Caucci, Mike Chocul, Herb Clark, Herb Colby, Carl Coleman, Ann Cooper, Scott Cornett, Jeff Covell, Greg Cuda, Paul Dahlie, Tim Damon, Bert Darrow, Peter Davidson, George Dechant, Dave Delillo, Mike DeTomasso, Pat Doldo, Bill Donato, David Duff, Lisa Dull, John Dwyer, Rick Eck, Bill Emerich, Bob Ewald, Shahab Farzanegan, Fred Fioli, Keith Fitzpatrick, Mike FlahertyMark Francatto, Walt Franklin, Bill Fries, John Gaulke, Nat Gillespie, Chuck Godfrey, Julie Gosselin, Dick Graves, Brad Hammers, Bruce Handey, Bob Harman, William Hilts, Lynne Hoppe, Jim Hotaling, Carolyn Harding, Kevin Henebry, Peter Hetko, Peter Hunkin, Betsy Jacobson, Diane Johnson-Jaeckel, Don Jones, Phil Koons, Greg Koslowski, Mike Lagree, Roy Lamberton, Traci Larossa, Mark Libertone, Steven LaMere, Mark Malenovsky, Mike Mayhood, Renata Mazzio, Norm McBride, Rob McCormick, Russ McCullough, Bob Meade, Steve Metzler, Bill Miller, Pat Miura, John Morette, Bill Mishanec, Milt and Pat Nehrke (and the members of the Cohocton TU Chapter), Keith Nehrke, Bill Newcomb, Laurie Nichiporuk, Ray Ottulich, Ron Pierce, Rich Preall, Mike Pyrek, Nick Rash, Kevin Riley, Craig Robbins, Ron Robert, Hank Rope, Dave Rossie, Victor Sasse, Dave Savko, Sam Scafidi, Anne Marie Schaummann, Al Smith, Bob Smith, John Spisinger, Jim Stachowski, Irwin Stone, Leslie Supernant, Paul Terrell, Dave Thompson, Don Traver, Jacob Trimmer, John Vargo, Joe Verdone, Don Walker, Clarence Ware, Les Wedge, Randy Weidman, Judd Weisberg, Bill Wellman, Pat White, Chris Williamson, Gary Wilsey, Don Winter Jerry Wolland, Dan Yando, Mike Zak, Dan Zielinski, Ken Ziobro

Introduction

AND HOW TO USE THIS BOOK

New York State offers an amazing array of places to flyfish: narrow spring creeks and enormous flows like the Delaware and Susquehanna, mountain ponds in the Adirondacks and virtual oceans in Lake Ontario, Lake Erie and Lake Champlain. These waters host almost every freshwater fish that will take a fly.

This book focuses primarily on trout and salmon, but smallmouth, some muskellunge and carp, and even the occasional bowfin (see Lake Champlain) are covered too. Saltwater angling in New York demands a book of its own; however, you will find river fishing for migratory shad and striped bass in these pages. There is an emphasis on moving waters, but plenty of pond fishing is included.

Before we get to the fishing, a few words on how to use the information here.

Geography

New York is divided into 62 counties (including the five boroughs/counties that make up New York City). In turn, each county is divided into towns, plus some cities. And within the towns are villages or hamlets (usually including one with the same name as the town). Throughout this book, "town" refers to the full geographic entity, not just the village of the same name, while "village" means a place of commercial or residential development (even though some may technically be hamlets or settlements).

Names

Stream and pond names in New York can be confusing. There are several Salmon Rivers, a bunch of Clear Creeks (two feeding Cattaraugus Creek alone) and a smattering of Trout Brooks and Cold Brooks, just to name a few. On the other hand, a single stream or pond may have several different names used by anglers, on maps, or in regulations. The book tries to flag these points of confusion whenever possible. The same goes for roads: I've typically listed both names and numbers. Some pronunciation guides are offered too, to make names like Chautauqua and Genegantslet easier to say.

Art Flick, and all the entomologists who followed him, made fly tying and fishing more productive, but using common names for insects is the rule throughout this book. There are a few flies better known in Latin—the *Isonychia*, the *Potomanthus*, the Trico (short for *Tricorythode*), and the *Callibaetis*—so you will find those names used here.

Finally, the New York State Department of Environmental Conservation, which has primary responsibility for the state's fish and game (along with many other duties), is referred to frequently as the DEC. It should not be confused with the DEP—the New York City Department of Environmental Protection—which is mentioned often in the South section of this book. That city agency manages the reservoirs and dams so important to fishing in the Delaware and Croton Watersheds.

Sections

New York has streams running in all directions, borders two Great Lakes plus Lake Champlain, and hosts major drainages in the Hudson, Delaware, Susquehanna, St. Lawrence and Genesee rivers. As a result, the state isn't easily divided into self-contained fishing regions. The four sections in this book—South, Central, North and West (with subsections in each)—group geographic areas, waters and types of fishing that tend to belong together, but you may occasionally find a nearby stream in another section or subsection. A few hub cities are near sectional boundaries; the listings indicate when the fly shops and accommodations there serve more than one region.

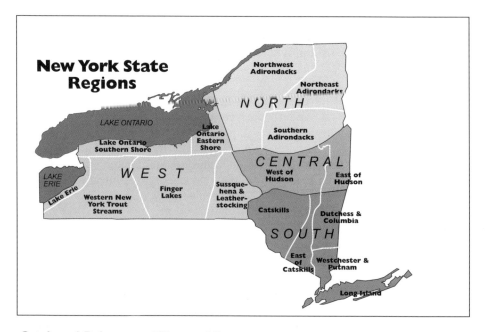

Catch and Release and Thermal Stress

Catch and release sustains good fishing, particularly on wild trout streams. I strongly support it and urge anyone using this book to do the same. That said, the catch limits are given here along with other regulations for the streams and lakes. This is a personal choice, but if you decide to keep fish—even fish other than trout—please do it sparingly.

Anglers can also help our trout fisheries by paying attention to temperatures. The mortality rate for released trout soars when they are taken from warm water. And even if you're planning to keep them, hooking struggling fish huddled at an underground spring isn't very sporting. Experts differ on the precise cutoff point, but it is good idea to carry a thermometer (always a useful accessory) and to stop fishing when the water is 70 degrees or higher.

Access

Anglers have a lot of public access on New York streams. This includes extensive easements under the state's program of Public Fishing Rights, which acquires access to sections of stream banks on private landholdings. (Look for the bright yellow signs that say "Public Fishing Stream.") We all like to get into that secret spot, but private property should be respected. If fishing on a PFR section, stay within the easement area. If you're in doubt about whether land is posted, ask permission to fish—many landowners will say yes, especially to fly anglers. And please be sure to leave all property at least as clean as you found it.

Maps

The editors at Wilderness Adventures Press and I worked together to make the maps helpful and accurate. Still, they are only guides—if an access point on the map turns out to be posted, or looks unsafe, common sense requires traveling to another spot. And, while boat accesses and river miles are offered on a number of waterways, anyone planning a float trip will need navigational maps and information, along with safety equipment, before setting out.

Changes

I've tried hard to make everything here accurate at the time of publication, but bear in mind that the information in the book is subject to change. Regulations are revised (every two years now in New York), as are stocking practices. Nature makes changes too: floods and ice scour stream bottoms and insect and trout populations rise and fall. Away from the stream, tackle shops, restaurants and hotels move or close. If you find anything is different from what's given here—or you just have some information or experience you'd like to share—feel free to write the author care of the publisher or via email at: ehn@bigfoot.com.

Though conditions are always changing, the challenges and the joys of fly fishing remain constant. I hope this book will help anglers experience a little more of both.

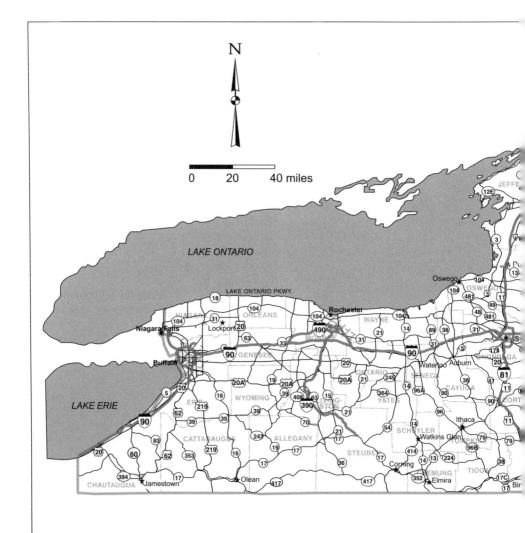

New York
Major Roads and Hub Cities

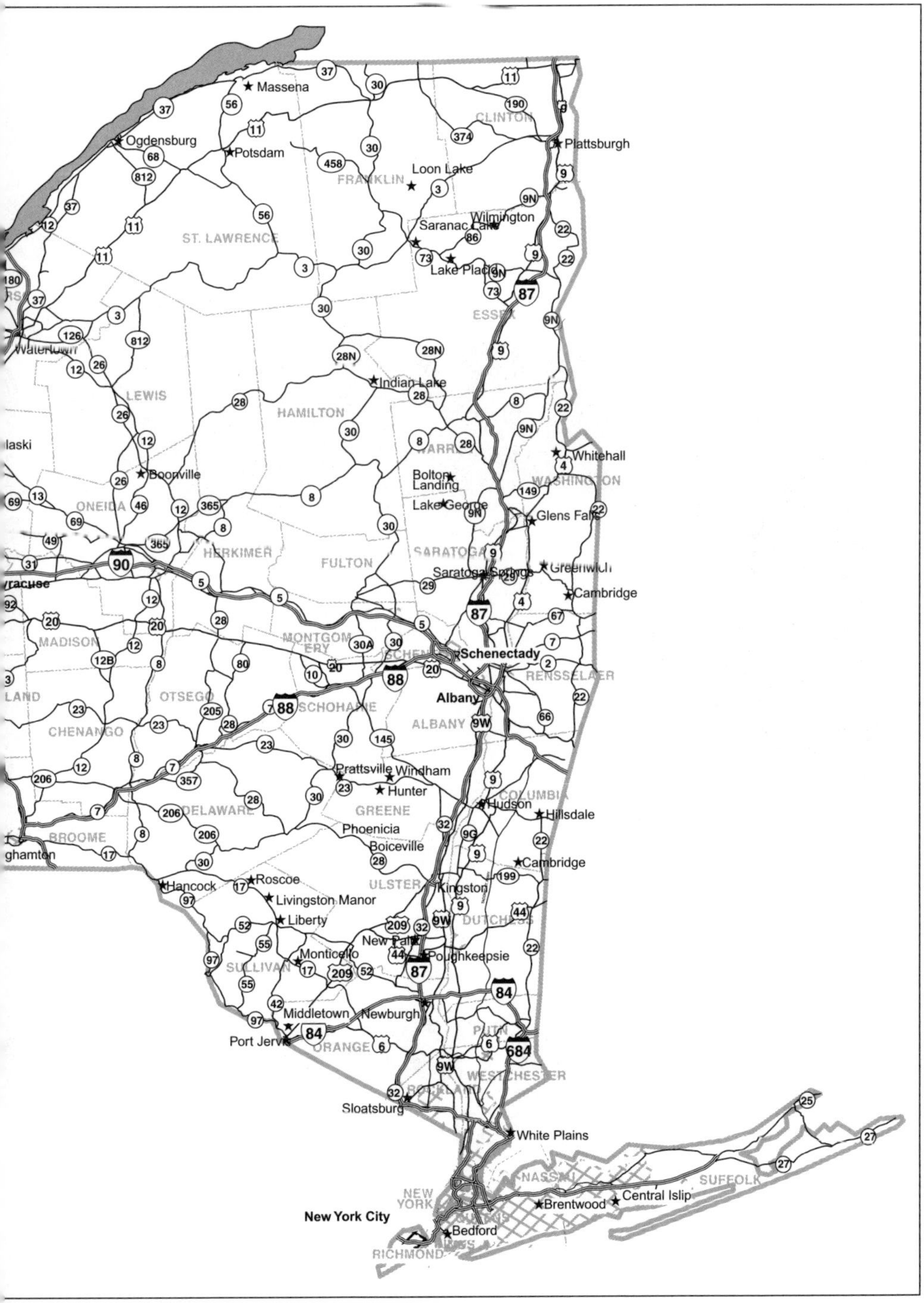
Massena
Ogdensburg
Potsdam
Plattsburgh
CLINTON
FRANKLIN
Loon Lake
Wilmington
Saranac Lake
Lake Placid
ST. LAWRENCE
ESSEX
Watertown
LEWIS
Indian Lake
HAMILTON
Whitehall
WARREN
Bolton Landing
WASHINGTON
Boonville
Lake George
Glens Falls
ONEIDA
HERKIMER
FULTON
SARATOGA
Saratoga Springs
Greenwich
Cambridge
Syracuse
MADISON
MONTGOMERY
Schenectady
RENSSELAER
Albany
OTSEGO
SCHOHARIE
ALBANY
CHENANGO
Prattsville
Windham
Hunter
COLUMBIA
Hudson
Hillsdale
DELAWARE
GREENE
Phoenicia
Boiceville
BROOME
Binghamton
Cambridge
Hancock
Roscoe
Livingston Manor
ULSTER
Kingston
Liberty
DUTCHESS
New Paltz
Monticello
Poughkeepsie
SULLIVAN
Middletown
Newburgh
Port Jervis
ORANGE
PUTNAM
WESTCHESTER
ROCKLAND
Sloatsburg
White Plains
NASSAU
SUFFOLK
NEW YORK
New York City
Brentwood
Central Islip
Bedford
RICHMOND

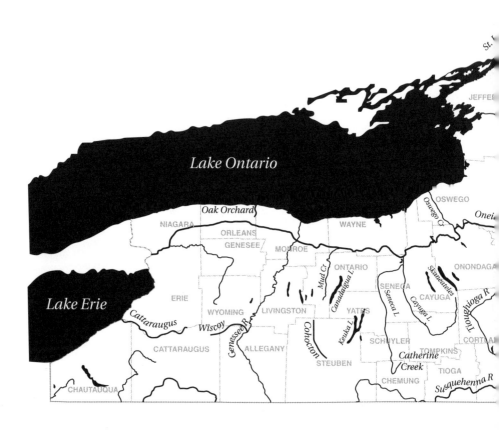

New York State
With Major Rivers and Lakes

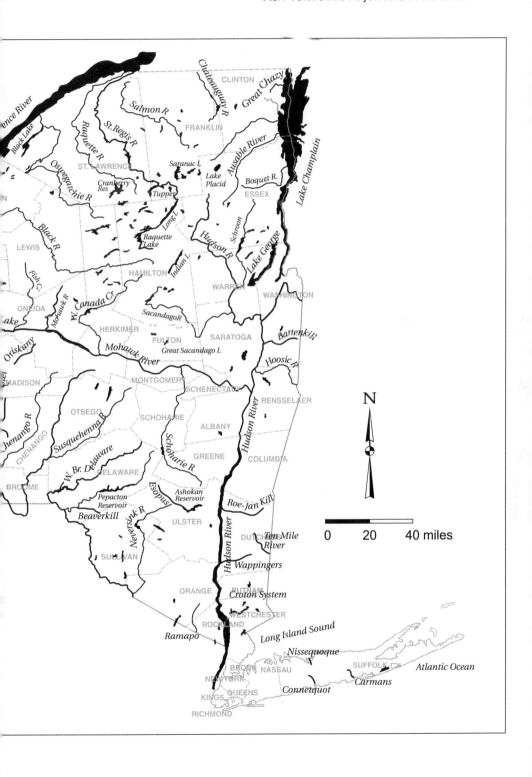

Regulations and License Information

New York angling is subject to a three-tiered set of regulations: general regulations, watershed regulations for Lake Erie, Lake Ontario, Lake Champlain, the Finger Lakes and their tributaries and regulations for specific waters by county. (In addition, there are some special regulations for a few border waters, for the Catskill and Croton watersheds that provide New York City's water supply and for fishing within some state or local parks.) There are good reasons to adjust rules to specific waters and species, but it can make things confusing. Regulations at the time of publication are provided with the individual water descriptions, but anglers are advised to always check the current published regulations before fishing.

New York State recently adopted a two-year regulation cycle; current regulations are in effect to September 30, 2002 (note that this leaves the last two weeks of the 2002 trout season subject to change). Set out below are the general angling regulations (some warmwater species are omitted) and license fees for New York State through September 30, 2002, followed by contact information for the Department of Environmental Conservation.

General Angling Regulations

Species	Season	Daily Limit/Size
Trout (brook, brown and rainbow and hybrids; splake)	April 1 - October 15	5/Any size
Lake Trout	April 1 - October 15	3/21"
Landlocked Salmon	April 1 - October 15	3/15"
Kokanee	April 1 - October 15	10/Any size
Coho, Chinook, Pink Salmon, Steelhead	Watershed Regulations	See individual Water Descriptions & Published Regulations
Black Bass Largemouth & Smallmouth	3rd Saturday in June - November 30	5/12"
Muskellunge	3rd Saturday in June - November 30	1/30"
Tiger Muskellunge	1st Saturday in May - March 15	1/30"
Walleye	1st Saturday in May - March 15	5/15"
Northern Pike	1st Saturday in May - March 15	5/18"

Licenses and Fees

Freshwater anglers age 16 or older are required to have a fishing license. One-year licenses are valid from October 1 to September 30 (note that a new license is required for the last 15 days of the standard trout season). Resident licenses are only available to those domiciled in New York for the preceding 30 days.

Many sports and tackle shops sell licenses—county and town clerks issue them as well. Licenses can also be obtained by mail (check, VISA or Mastercard accepted). A printable application for the mail-in license can be found on the DEC Web site. For residents only, licenses can also be obtained by telephone (fishing only) during business hours at 518-402-8845. Payment for telephone licenses must be made by credit card.

RESIDENT

Senior (65+/Military Disability)	$5.00
Fishing - Season	$14.00
Fishing - 3 day	$6.00

NON-RESIDENT

Fishing - Season	$35.00
Fishing - 5 day	$20.00
Combination - Hunting, Fishing, Deer-Hunting, Bowhunting, and Muzzleloading	$225.00

A special New York City permit is required to fish the reservoirs in the water supply system in the Catskills and both the reservoirs and streams in the Croton watershed.

DEC Contact Information

The Department of Environmental Conservation, which oversees fishing and hunting in New York State (as well as managing state parks and wildlife areas, establishing and enforcing environmental laws and many other activities) is headquartered in the state capitol in Albany. It also has nine regional offices (with some sub-offices) and maintains several fishing hotlines with updated fishing information.

DEPARTMENT OF ENVIRONMENTAL CONSERVATION OFFICES

Main Office: 50 Wolf Road, Albany, New York, 12233

Division of Fisheries Office: 625 Broadway, Albany, NY 12233; 518 402-8920

Home Page: www.dec.state.ny.us

Fisheries Home Page: www.dec.state.ny.us/website/dfwmr/fish/index.html

REGIONAL OFFICES

Region 1 (Long Island) Loop Road, Building 40, Stony Brook, NY 11790; 631-444-0354

Region 2 (New York City) 1 Hunters Pt. Plaza, 4740 21st Street, Long Island City, NY 11101; 718-482-4900

Region 3 (Lower Catskills and Croton) 21 South Putt Corners Road, New Paltz, NY 12561; 845-256-3000

Region 4 (Upper Catskills, mid Hudson Valley) 1150 Westcott Road, Schenectady, NY 12306; 518-357-2234

Region 5 (Eastern Adirondacks) Route 86, P.O. Box 296, Ray Brook, NY 12977; 518-897-1200

Region 6 (Western Adirondacks) 317 Washington Street, Watertown, NY 13601-3787; 315-785-2262

Region 7 (Susquehanna, Leatherstocking, Eastern Finger Lakes) 615 Erie Boulevard, West Syracuse, NY 13204; 315-426-7400

Region 8 (Western Finger Lakes, Southern Ontario Shore) 6274 E. Avon-Lima Road, Avon, NY 14414; 716-226-2466

Region 9 (Erie Tributaries, Western New York), 270 Michigan Avenue, Buffalo, NY 14203; 716-851-7000

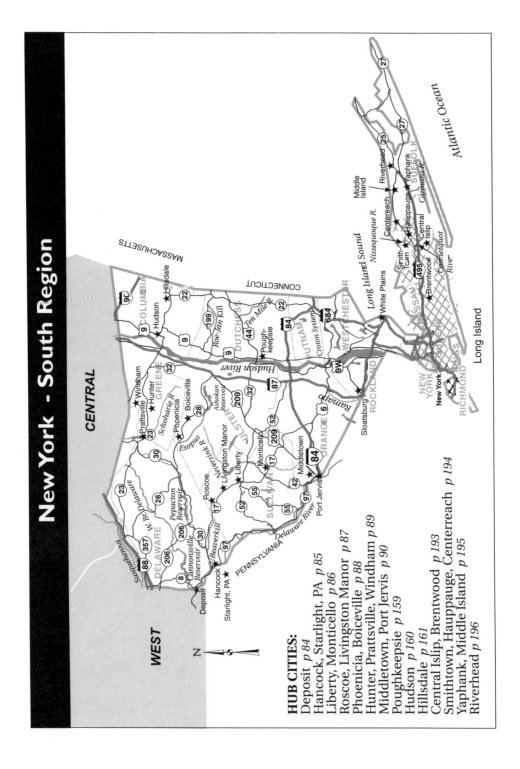

New York - South Region

HUB CITIES:
Deposit *p 84*
Hancock, Starlight, PA *p 85*
Liberty, Monticello *p 86*
Roscoe, Livingston Manor *p 87*
Phoenicia, Boiceville *p 88*
Hunter, Prattsville, Windham *p 89*
Middletown, Port Jervis *p 90*
Poughkeepsie *p 159*
Hudson *p 160*
Hillsdale *p 161*
Central Islip, Brentwood *p 193*
Smithtown, Hauppauge, Centerreach *p 194*
Yaphank, Middle Island *p 195*
Riverhead *p 196*

South Region

The large Catskill streams are naturally the best known fishing in this section. They deserve the attention they get, but anglers have lots of other waters to choose from in the southern part of the state. In the Catskills, small streams offer a nice contrast to the bigger waters. And, the area east of the Catskills has some streams too often ignored. Across the Hudson, there is good fishing, not to mention beautiful scenery, in Columbia and Dutchess Counties, and excellent tailwater fishing in the Croton Watershed. Long Island, though better known for saltwater species, offers flyfishing for trout in some fine spring creeks and ponds.

CATSKILLS

No region of the country has the rich flyfishing history of the Catskills, and few can match the Catskills' abundance of good trout streams set closely together.

The water here is pretty evenly divided between freestone streams and tailwaters—and a number of the rivers have both kinds of fishing. Wading is the primary fishing method, but the Delaware system offers the opporunity for Western-style float trips.

There is a good deal of natural reproduction in these streams, and with proper attention there could be more. The Beaverkill/Willowemoc system in particular is being studied to improve habitat. It, like many streams in the region, suffered terribly from devastating floods—and some overzealous clean up work—in 1996.

The best-known Catskill streams—the Beaverkill and Willowemoc and the Delaware System—justly receive most of the attention. But anglers should not neglect famous but less visited streams like the Neversink, the Esopus and the Schoharie. Small streams in the Catskills can also provide good fishing. And even on the Beaverkill and Delaware, some good sections are lightly fished.

THE DELAWARE RIVER

Understanding Delaware Flows

The Delaware River is a group of three connected but distinct streams—the West Branch, the East Branch and the Main Stem—that make up an entire river system. Individually they are top-notch trout waters, and together they offer some of the best fishing in the East. They are separate fisheries, but understanding their related flows is important to understanding the fishing in the river.

The lower East and West branches of the Delaware flow from reservoirs and meet at Hancock, New York to form the main Delaware River, often called the Main Stem. The Delaware flows 75 miles from Hancock to the end of the New York portion at Port Jervis, then continues 255 miles to Delaware Bay. After a series of disputes among the four bordering states—New York, Pennsylvania, New Jersey and Delaware—rules were established for the flows in the river, administered by the Delaware River Basin Commission.

The complex rules effectively require New York City—which operates the Cannonsville Reservoir on the West Branch and the Pepacton Reservoir on the East Branch—to supply sufficient fresh water to the downstream communities, including Philadelphia. (If too little fresh water flows downstream, the supply near the river's mouth becomes spoiled by seawater.) When required, the city fulfills this obligation primarily with releases into the West Branch from the Cannonsville Reservoir, reserving most of the Pepacton Reservoir water for its own needs.

In addition to the releases required by the agreement, New York City provides some minimum flows to protect trout habitat. These are not always enough to avoid dangerous conditions for the trout, however. A coalition of conservation groups, anglers, business owners and watershed communities are hoping to get a flow regime that better protects fish. With the competing demands for the water and the involvement of the multi-state commission, this will necessarily take time.

For anglers, as well as fish, flow changes can have a temporary but dramatic impact on the fishing, particularly on the West Branch and Main Stem. When flows are increased, the cold water moves downstream at about one mile per hour. Fish may take up to a full day to adjust, and hatches can be delayed or fail to materialize at all. High water can also make wading difficult. Conversely, minimum flows can mean low water and spooky trout, and make a float trip impossible. Combined with warm weather, low flows can leave the Upper Main Stem and the West Branch itself warmer than desirable for trout fishing. For these reasons, it is always useful to check current Delaware flows and temperatures with local tackle shops, by phone or online, or at the USGS Web site before traveling to the Delaware.

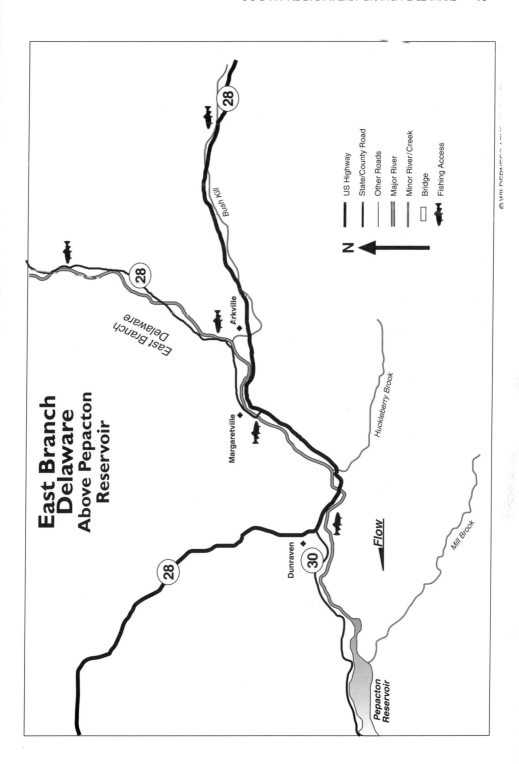

EAST BRANCH DELAWARE

The East Branch of the Delaware is a hard stream to characterize. A small free-stone stream above the Pepacton Reservoir, it becomes a tailwater below. But the upper half of the tailwater often looks more like a spring creek, and the lower half—after the Beaverkill enters—essentially reverts to a freestone stream.

The East Branch rises in the northeast corner of Delaware County, not far from the Schoharie Reservoir, and meanders 20 miles, passing through the town of Margaretville on its way to the Pepacton Reservoir. The river is a small to medium-sized freestone stream in this section. Five thousand brown trout are stocked each year and there is good natural reproduction. As a smaller freestone stream, this section is best fished early—generally until the middle of June. After April, you are likely to have a section of the stream to yourself.

It is below the Pepacton Reservoir that the East Branch fishing really shines. For most of its length, there are stocked and wild browns, with good natural reproduction. Rainbows from the Delaware's Main Stem are also mixed in. The East Branch below the Pepacton Reservoir has two distinct sections. The first 14 miles, from the Reservoir at Downsville to the junction with the Beaverkill in the village of East Branch, is cold-release tailwater (though its slow, weedy flow can resemble a spring creek). After the waters of the Beaverkill flow in at the town of East Branch, the remaining 12 miles are really a freestone stream, with water that warms considerably in summer.

The hatches encompass virtually all of the major mayflies and caddis. Good early season hatches include the Hendricksons, which come off here in early to mid-May. Judd Weisberg, who guides extensively on the East Branch, considers Sulphurs and Blue Winged Olives the most important hatches , in part because of their duration. Along with emergers, comparaduns and parachutes to imitate Blue Winged Olives, he likes the Delaware Adams—an old Walt Dette pattern with an olive body and hackle palmered the length of the fly. For the caddis, a complete range of colors and sizes is important—especially imitations for the small black caddis in early season and the prolific light and dark grannom (Shad Fly) of May.

Streamers can also work in the East Branch. When water comes over the top of the dam, reservoir alewives come downstream, mostly in March and April. At other times a standard Black-Nosed Dace can take big browns. Al Carpenter, whose shop is on the banks of the stream, has fished here since the 1930s, reports that the largest East Branch catch he knows of, a 10-pound, 29-inch brown, was taken in 1992 near the airport in Downsville on a Matuka streamer.

Because the upper half of the East Branch runs slow and clear most of the time, stealth is essential. Charge into a low, clear pool, even a long way from rising fish, and your chances of taking fish are virtually nil. Carpenter advises anglers to stalk like a blue heron—enter a pool slowly and give the fish plenty of time to calm down and start rising freely before casting. (Long leaders and fluorocarbon tippets will also help.) The bridges at Corbett and Shinhopple, among other slow pools, offer this kind of challenging fishing.

If you don't have that much patience, look for narrower, faster stretches and drift a nymph through the feeding lanes. Any of the standard nymphs should work if properly presented—including a Hare's Ear or Pheasant Tail. Carpenter recommends a simple green dubbed nymph—there is no name for it—to imitate the plentiful caddis larva in the stream. There are some good riffles near the top of the stream at the Fireman's Park in Downsville and at the many mid-stream islands on the river.

Riffles created by islands are good spots for nymphing the East Branch.

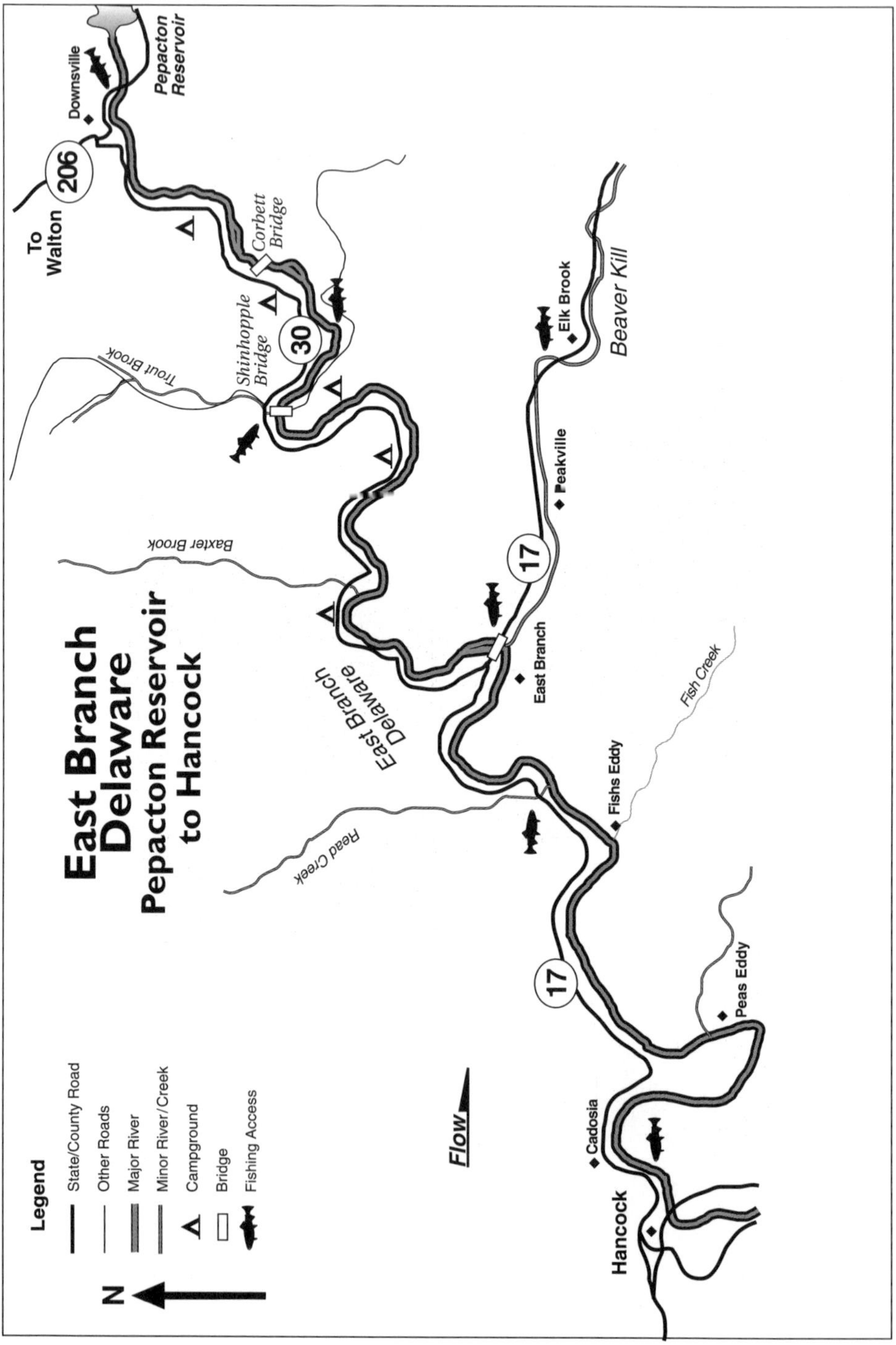

East Branch
Delaware
Pepacton Reservoir
to Hancock

Legend

State/County Road
Other Roads
Major River
Minor River/Creek
Campground
Bridge
Fishing Access

N

Flow

Downsville
Pepacton Reservoir
To Walton
206
Corbett Bridge
Shinhopple Bridge
30
Trout Brook
Baxter Brook
East Branch Delaware
Read Creek
Elk Brook
Beaver Kill
Peakville
17
East Branch
Fish Creek
Fishs Eddy
Peas Eddy
17
Cadosia
Hancock

Be sure to carry a thermometer when fishing here; you will want to look for water in the 52 to 65 degrees range. In spring this will generally be lower downstream, moving up as the feeders and air temperatures warm. In the middle of summer, the first 6 miles from the dam to Shinhopple will offer the best fishing.

Near the village of East Branch, the Beaverkill enters and for the remaining 12 miles the East Branch fishes like a typical freestone stream. There are more stocked browns in this lower stretch. Though no rainbows are stocked here, they do make their way in from the Delaware. This far from the reservoir, the cold-release water has warmed, so the water temperature and level fluctuates with the rain and the Beaverkill flows. As a result, this section is best fished in May and June and again in fall. The area near Fishs Eddy, where Fish Creek enters, is good. Also, try the deep, wide bend pool off Route 17 in Cadosia, close to the river's end.

Access on the East Branch is readily available. There is a decent amount of parking, and substantial sections on both sides of the river are marked as public fishing easements. Route 30 provides access on the western bank down to the village of East Branch (River Road provides access to the eastern bank), while Local 17 (not the highway) runs along the stream after the Beaverkill enters.

The East Branch upstream of the Pepacton Reservoir may be fished from April 1 to September 30; 5 fish per day of 9 inches or better may be kept. Below the reservoir to the Shinhopple Bridge, the same April 1 to September 30 season applies, and no fishing for any species is permitted outside this season. Two fish of 12 inches or more may be taken.

Below Shinhopple Bridge to the stream's end at Hancock there is an extended trout season from April 1 to November 30. However, after October 15 this lower section is catch and release only. Up to October 15, the same two trout/12 inch limit applies.

Stream Facts: East Branch Delaware

Seasons/Regulations
- Above Pepacton Reservoir: April 1 to September 30 (5 fish per day, 9 inch minimum).
- Pepacton Reservoir to Shinhopple Reservoir: April 1 to September 30 (2 fish per day, 12 inch minimum) no fishing out of trout season permitted.
- Shinhopple Bridge to end of stream (in Hancock): April 1 to November 30; 2 fish/12 inch limit to October 15, catch and release only after October 15.

Fish
- Mostly brown trout, stocked and some wild; a few wild rainbows (more as you approach Main Stem of Delaware River). Some brook trout in tributaries, primarily above Shinhopple.

River Characteristics
- Freestone stream above Pepacton Reservoir. Tailwater below, with runs, riffles and wide, slow-moving pools; 20-40 feet wide in upper half, 40-60 feet wide in lower half. Mostly easy wading.

River Flows
- Modest cold releases for most of season. Water warms after Beaverkill enters. First 6 miles to Shinhopple fishes best in most summers.

East Branch Delaware River—Major Hatches

INSECT	J	F	M	A	M	J	J	A	S	O	N	D	FLIES
Little Black Caddis 16-18													Elk Hair Caddis, Goddard Caddis, Bead-Head Pupa
Blue Winged Olive 14-24													Comparadun, Parachute, CDC Emerger, Compara-Emerger, Pheasant Tail Nymph
Quill Gordon 12-14													Quill Gordon Dry, Quill Gordon Wet
Light & Dark Hendrickson 12-16													Light and Dark Hendrickson, comparadun or parachute, dark brown Hendrickson Nymph
Light & Dark Grannom (Shad Fly) 14-18													Elk Hair Caddis, Lafontaine Deep Pupa & Emergent Pupa, X-Caddis, Bead-Head Pupa
Green, Gray, Tan Caddis 12-18													Elk Hair Caddis, Lafontaine Deep Pupa & Emergent Pupa, X-Caddis, Bead-Head Pupa, Delaware Adams
Sulphur 16-20													Comparadun, Parachute, CDC Emerger, Compara-Emerger, Pheasant Tail Nymph, Hare's Ear Nymph
March Brown 10-12													Comparadun, Extended-Body Dry Flies, Hare's Ear Nymph
Gray Fox 12-14													Comparadun, Extended-Body Dry Flies,
Green Drake 10-12													Coffin Fly Spinner, Comparadun, Extended-Body Dry Flies, Zug Bug
Light Cahill 12-16													Cream Variants, Comparaduns, Cahill Wet F y, Light Hare's Ear Nymph
Slate Drake (Isonychia) 12													Comparadun, Extended-Body Dry Flies, Leadwing Coachman, Zug Bug
Trico 22-26													Trico Spinner, Griffith's Gnat
Midges 20-28													Brassie, Serendipity, Midge Dry, Griffiths Gnat
Streamers													Alewife imitations, Black-Nosed Dace

WEST BRANCH DELAWARE

Large wild trout, abundant hatches and cold water releases make the West Branch of the Delaware among the best trout streams in the state. These same ingredients make it among the most demanding fisheries as well. First-time visitors to the tailwater section of the West Branch will often come away frustrated and even the best anglers are sometimes humbled. Patience and skill are necessary to hook and land these fish. The long section above the Cannonsville Reservoir has some good fishing that is often neglected.

Above the Reservoir

The West Branch begins as a tiny trickle in the town of Stamford, which effectively marks the beginning of the entire Delaware River. This upper stretch is a small stream for its first 15 miles but picks up tributaries along its way and widens around Delhi, where it becomes a medium-sized stream for its remaining 20-mile run to the reservoir. There are a number of informal pullouts, as well as some dedicated access on Route 10, which parallels this portion of the river.

Just below Delhi, the Little Delaware River enters. This is a pretty good small trout stream in its own right, with a stocking of about 700 fish and some wild browns. Public access is available on the Little Delaware in various spots along Route 28, and from Route 6 farther upstream. It is open until October 15.

Water coming over the Cannonsville Dam—prelude to the "alewife hatch."

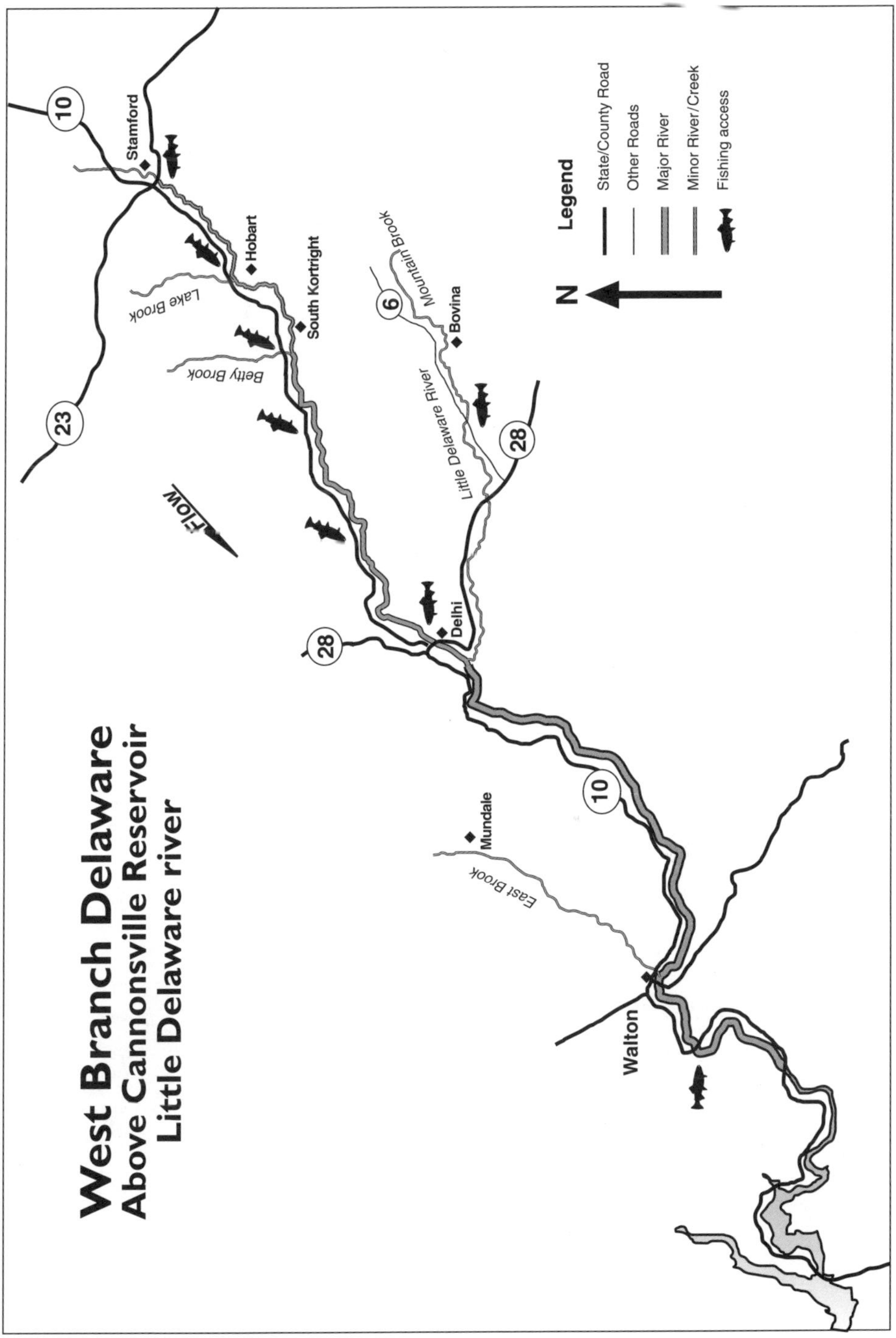

West Branch Delaware
Above Cannonsville Reservoir
Little Delaware river

Legend

State/County Road	
Other Roads	
Major River	
Minor River/Creek	
Fishing access	

Stamford

Hobart

South Kortright

Lake Brook

Betty Brook

Mountain Brook

Little Delaware River

Bovina

Delhi

Mundale

East Brook

Walton

FLOW

N

© WILDERNESS ADVENTURES PRESS, INC.

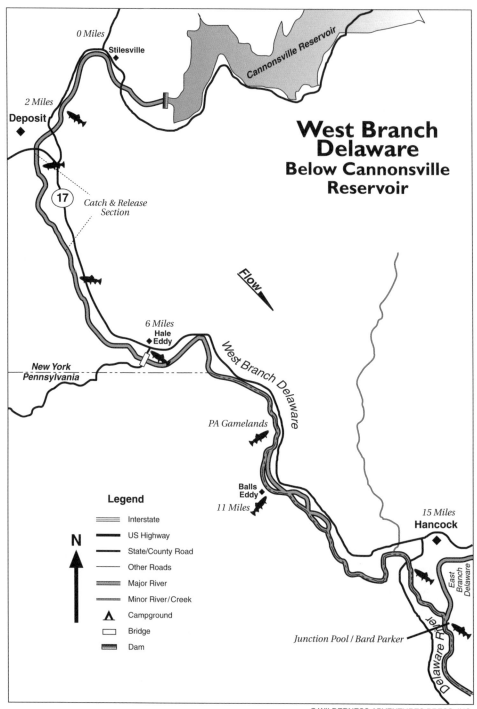

West Branch
Delaware
Below Cannonsville
Reservoir

0 Miles
Stilesville

Cannonsville Reservoir

2 Miles
Deposit

17

Catch & Release
Section

Flow

6 Miles
Hale
Eddy

West Branch Delaware

New York
Pennsylvania

PA Gamelands

Balls
Eddy

11 Miles

15 Miles
Hancock

East
Branch
Delaware

Legend

Interstate
US Highway
State/County Road
Other Roads
Major River
Minor River/Creek
Campground
Bridge
Dam

N

Junction Pool / Bard Parker

Delaware River

This upper section of the West Branch is stocked with brown trout—over 15,000 fish are put in on a nearly 30-mile stretch each year. There is good holdover and some natural reproduction. Close to the reservoir, large browns ascend the upper West Branch to spawn in the fall, but the entire stream above the reservoir is subject to a shortened season of April 1 to September 30. Regulations permit 5 fish per day, 9 inches or longer.

West Branch Delaware Below Cannonsville

Below Cannonsville Reservoir, the West Branch becomes a world-class tailwater. The releases generally keep the West Branch at ideal trout temperatures for its entire 15-mile run from the dam to its junction with the East Branch in Hancock and provide fertile habitat for mayfly, caddis, stoneflies and midges.

The fish here are entirely wild and good-sized: browns and less numerous rainbows in the 10- to 15-inch range are common, and fish up to 24 inches are caught. The size doesn't fully indicate their powe; even a 12-inch wild fish here can break off a 5X tippet.

Locating these West Branch fish is not as simple as on a small stream. Changing releases and mobile fish are among the factors that make the fishing here so challenging. And the river is wide, with substantial portions that don't hold many fish. Focus on pools and riffles, where most of the trout are found.

Access is pretty good on the West Branch. Most of it is on the east shore from the dam to the Hale Eddy Bridge, and on the west shore (Pennsylvania) below that. Except when the water is unusually high, you can wade well up and down from the entry points. Access to the last couple of miles before Hancock is difficult. Though wade fishing is popular, a float trip is a good way to fish the West Branch, particularly for anglers new to the river. There are three main floats: Stilesville (near the reservoir) to Hale Eddy, Hale Eddy to Balls Eddy and Balls Eddy to the confluence in Hancock.

The hatches here are abundant and often multiple. The mayflies run the gamut from early season Quill Gordons and Hendricksons through summer varieties of Sulphurs and Blue Winged Olives to the small Olives and Tricos and larger Cahills and *Isonychia* (Slate Drakes) of late summer and early fall. Caddis are abundant here, too, rounded out by midges almost year round and sporadic stonefly hatches.

Knowing which fly to use here can be difficult, with small and large mayflies or mayflies and caddis coming off at the same time. Even during a solo hatch, fish may key on nymphs under the surface, emergers or duns. Anglers need to focus on the type of rises to determine the insect and/or the stage. Regular Delaware anglers often carry small binoculars to make this easier. There are whole books devoted to this topic, but a general rule of thumb is that splashy rises are to caddis, rises with a small bubble mean a trout taking duns, rises without an air bubble—especially where the bulge of a fish's back is visible—signify fish feeding just below the surface.

For dry fly fishing on the West Branch, a flush-floating imitation is essential. The comparadun, which Al Caucci developed along with Bob Nastasi, is a very effective low riding dun. Parachutes will also work, but they are not as sturdy. Caucci, who has studied the Delaware intensively and conducts a school on the West Branch, notes that finicky, wild fish tend to key on flies that are vulnerable; during a hatch this often means emergers. A CDC emerger with a Zelon shuck in the right colors is a good fly. Caucci also developed the simple but effective compara-emerger with a Zelon shuck, dubbed body and down-winged deer hair.

Nymphs needn't be quite as specific, but anglers should bear in mind that a particular nymph will not drift in large numbers until a hatch is imminent. Ordinary terrestrials are not much of a factor here, but dense migrations of cinnamon or black flying ants hit the water sporadically. When they do, anglers need a few winged ants in their boxes, as the fish will take little else.

Whatever fly you are using, a drag-free presentation is crucial. Al Caucci finds that a common mistake of visiting anglers is throwing a straight cast, which promptly causes the fly to drag. Even if the drag isn't visible to the angler, it is to the fish, and they won't touch the offering. He recommends slack line casts quartered downstream as the proper way to fish most pools and runs on the West Branch. You may want to put a small strike indicator a foot or two up from your dry fly to better watch for drag. A 9-foot, 5-weight rod with a fast action is the right equipment for this river.

For anglers, the larger, early season flies, such as the Hendricksons, can be easier to fish. They are more visible and the fish seem to lose some of their famous caution at this time. At the other end of the size spectrum are the tiny Blue Winged Olives and Tricos. West Branch fish will often take bunches of these in gulps; timing your cast to these rises is important. In summer and fall, there are sporadic hatches of the large *Isonychia*. The adults are only briefly on the water, but they are big enough to draw strikes. For the nymph, a Zug Bug is a good imitation.

In addition to the insects, there are a considerable number of crayfish in the stream. Some local anglers use an imitation that is essentially a brown Woolly Buggers with a bit of orange. These need to be fished slowly on the bottom. For getting crayfish and other streamers deep, and covering a lot of water, any of the sinktip lines with long weighted sections—such as the Teeny Nymph lines, Cortland QD or Scientific Anglers Mastery Express—are ideal.

Though they don't live in the stream, alewives from the reservoir can also be important food. When the reservoir is full they wash over the top (and when it is very low, they sometimes get pulled through the valves—though often not in one piece.) This occurrence, called the "alewife hatch," triggers aggressive feeding by large fish. The local tackle shops and guides each have their own favorite alewife pattern, often with a good deal of silver sparkle. The important features are a widebody and a dark top, white underside and some silver flash (a bit of blue is helpful too). A black and white Deceiver or similar Clouser Minnow would work. The alewife imitations will also work as attractors even when there is no "hatch."

Just like the fishing, regulations on the West Branch are quite complicated. Upstream of Cannonsville Reservoir the season is April 1 to September 30 (5 fish per day, 9-inch minimum). Below the reservoir to the point at which the West Branch becomes the New York-Pennsylvania border (1.7 miles below the Hale Eddy Bridge, about 10 miles downstream of the dam) the season is April 1 to September 30, and to protect spawning trout, all out of season fishing is strictly prohibited (even for chubs or other fish with no closed season). In most of this 10-mile stretch, 2 fish per day of 12 inches or greater can be taken. However, there is a two-mile catch and release section starting where the Route 17 Quickway crosses the stream.

Where the West Branch becomes the New York/Pennsylvania border to the stream's end at the beginning of the Main Stem, it is open to year round trout fishing. However, fish may only be kept—2 per day, 12 inches or more—between the first Saturday after April 11 and September 30. The rest of the year, this last part of the river is catch and release only.

A brave angler wet wading at the Hale Eddy Bridge.

Stream Facts: West Branch Delaware

Seasons/Regulations
- Above Cannonsville Reservoir: April 1 to September 30 (5 fish per day, 9-inch minimum)
- Cannonsville Reservoir to Route 17 Quickway Crossing: April 1 to September 30 (2 fish per day, 12 inch minimum), no fishing out of trout season permitted.
- Route 17 Quickway Crossing to point 2 miles downstream: April 1 to September 30; catch and release and artificial lures only; no fishing out of season permitted.
- From end of catch and release section to Pennsylvania border (1.7 miles downstream from Hale Eddy bridge) April 1 to September 30, two fish per day, 12-inch minimum.
- From Pennsylvania border to end of river: year round, 1st Saturday in April to September 30, 2 fish, 12 inches or longer, rest of year catch and release-artificial lures only.

Fish
- Mostly brown trout; fewer wild rainbows (more as you approach Main Stem of Delaware River).

River Characteristics
- Tailwater with runs, riffles and wide, slow-moving pools; 20-50 feet wide in upper half, 40-100 feet wide in lower half. Mostly easy wading, unless water is unusually high. Float trips possible at most water levels.

River Flow
- Generally, higher in spring, lower in summer and fall, but depend heavily on weather and releases under complex regulations—check before traveling.

West Branch Delaware River—Major Hatches

INSECT	J	F	M	A	M	J	J	A	S	O	N	D	FLIES
Early Black\Brown Stone 12-14													Elk Hair Caddis, Stonefly Nymphs
Little Black Caddis (Chimarra) 16-18													Elk Hair Caddis, Goddard Caddis, Bead-Head Pupa
Blue Winged Olive 14-24													Comparadun, Parachute, CDC Emerger, Compara-Emerger, Pheasant Tail Nymph
Blue Quill 16-18													Blue Quill Dry, Pheasant Tail Nymph
Quill Gordon 12-14													Quill Gordon Dry, Quill Gordon Wet
Light & Dark Hendrickson 12-16													Light and Dark Hendrickson, Comparadun or Parachute, dark brown Hendrickson Nymph
Light & Dark Grannom (Shad Fly) 14-18													Elk Hair Caddis, Lafontaine Deep Pupa & Emergent Pupa, X-Caddis, Bead-Head Pupa
Green, Gray, Tan Caddis 12-18													Elk Hair Caddis, Lafontaine Deep Pupa & Emergent Pupa, X-Caddis, Bead-Head Pupa
Sulphur 16-20													Comparadun, Parachute, CDC Emerger, Compara-Emerger, Pheasant Tail Nymph, Hare's Ear Nymph
March Brown 10-12													Comparadun, Extended-Body Dry Flies, Hare's Ear Nymph
Gray Fox 12-14													Comparadun, Extended-Body Dry Flies,
Green Drake 10-12													Coffin Fly Spinner, Comparadun, Extended-Body Dry Flies, Zug Bug
Light Cahill 12-16													Cream Variants, Comparaduns, Cahill Wet Fly, Light Hare's Ear Nymph
Slate Drake (Isonychia) 12													Comparadun, Extended-Body Dry Flies, Leadwing Coachman, Zug Bug
Trico 22-26													Trico Spinner, Griffith's Gnat
Flying Ants, Red & Black 16-22													Ant patterns with deer hair, zelon or hackle tip wings
Midges 20-28													Brassie, Serendipity, Midge Dry, Griffith's Gnat
Alewife 4-10, 4XL-6XL													Black and White Deceiver or Clouser, Local Patterns

DELAWARE MAIN STEM

The New York section of the Delaware River runs 75 miles from Hancock to Port Jervis. Along the way, anglers can find outstanding fishing for trout, smallmouth bass and shad. Wading and shore fishing are possible, but the size of the river and the limited access make a float trip the ideal way to target any of these species.

Trout

Generally, the trout water of the Upper Delaware runs from its start at the junction of the East and West branches in Hancock about 25 miles downstream to Callicoon. Beyond Callicoon, the water is warmer and more heavily populated with smallmouth bass, though some good trout continue to be taken as far down as Cochecton/Damascus, five miles south. The second half of the trout stretch, roughly Hankins to Callicoon, is more vulnerable to high temperatures during lower releases in summer. In these conditions, trout anglers should move upstream to the first 10 miles below Hancock.

The trout in the Upper Delaware are wild rainbows, with a handful of browns mixed in. The rainbows were an accidental stocking. Reportedly, a train carrying rainbow fingerlings broke down on the banks of the Main Stem around the turn of the century. Without refrigeration, the fish would not survive, and the engineer decided it was better to put them in the Delaware than see them perish.

Despite those inauspicious beginnings, the rainbows have thrived here. They are particularly strong and in contrast to the species' usual reputation, extremely selective. Their picky feeding is largely due to the abundance of food in the Delaware; as with the West Branch, the hatches here cover virtually every aquatic insect, often in heavy numbers. In addition to the plentiful food, the frequent slow pools give the fish a very good look at whatever imitation an angler is using.

The fish are also mobile, moving up or down the river, including well into the West Branch, to find cooler water. A radio telemetry study conducted jointly by the DEC and Trout Unlimited found that some Delaware rainbows traveled over 50 miles in a single year.

Because the river is big and the fish move, the best way to get to the trout is by floating the river, ideally from a guided drift boat. While guided float trips are not inexpensive—running about $300 per day—they will give you access to all the best spots and best fish in a given segment of the river. Drifting will also cut down on the need for long, difficult casting, and an experienced guide will be able to decode the complex hatches on the river.

You can also put in a canoe, (a number of the local outfitters will rent boats, with shuttle service generally available). The upper Main Stem does not have serious rapids, but some knowledge of the river, its hazards, and its safety regulations is essential. Whether you float yourself or go with a guide, figure on traveling about one mile per hour (faster if the water is high), with added time for anchoring or beaching the boat to fish. Popular floats for trout include Shehawken (opposite

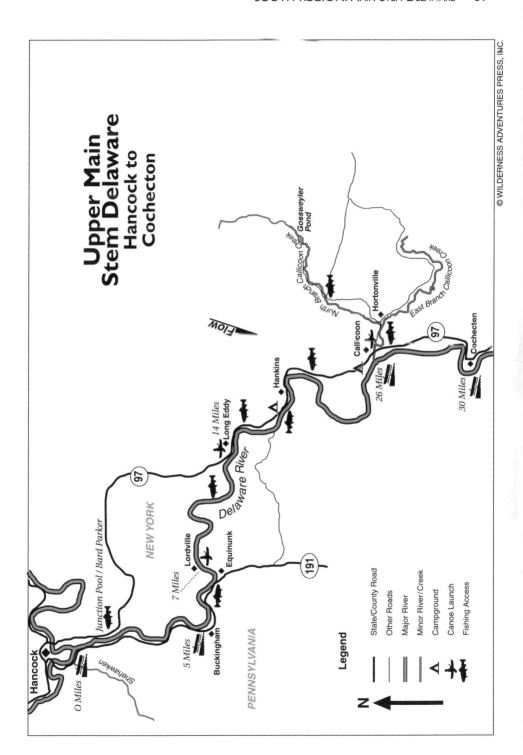

Upper Main
Stem Delaware
Hancock to
Cochecton

Flow

Gossweyler
Pond

Callicoon Creek

North Branch Callicoon Creek

Hortonville

East Branch Callicoon Creek

Callicoon

97

26 Miles

Cochecton

30 Miles

Hankins

14 Miles
Long Eddy

97

Delaware River

NEW YORK

Lordville

7 Miles

Equinunk

191

5 Miles

Buckingham

Junction Pool / Bard Parker

Hancock

O Miles

Shehawken

PENNSYLVANIA

Legend

State/County Road

Other Roads

Major River

Minor River/Creek

Campground

Canoe Launch

Fishing Access

N

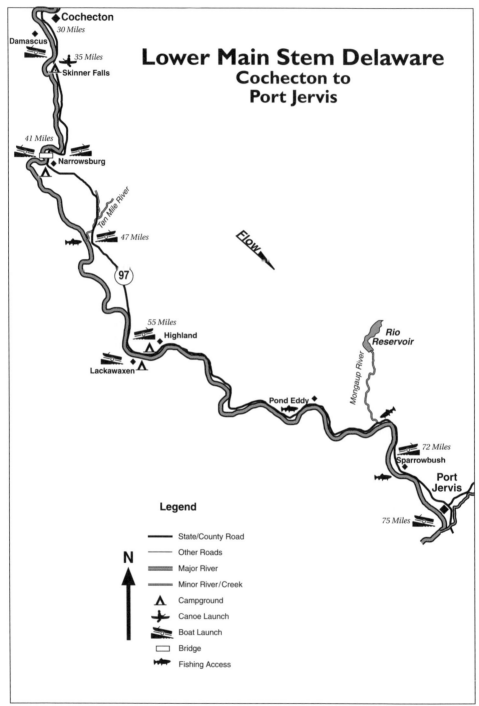

Lower Main Stem Delaware
Cochecton to
Port Jervis

Cochecton
30 Miles
Damascus
35 Miles
Skinner Falls

Flow

41 Miles
Narrowsburg

Ten Mile River

47 Miles

97

55 Miles
Highland

Lackawaxen

Pond Eddy

Rio
Reservoir

Mongaup River

72 Miles
Sparrowbush

Port
Jervis

75 Miles

Legend

N

——— State/County Road
——— Other Roads
——— Major River
——— Minor River/Creek
Δ Campground
Canoe Launch
Boat Launch
Bridge
Fishing Access

© WILDERNESS ADVENTURES PRESS, INC.

Hancock) to Buckingham, Buckingham to Lordville, Lordville to Long Eddy and Long Eddy to Callicoon. Guides sometimes use private sites in addition to these public ramps.

For anglers on foot, one of the best places to fish the upper Delaware is in Hancock, off Route 97, just below the confluence of the East and West branches. On the east bank of the river at this point—variously known as Junction Pool, Bard Parker or the Sewage Treatment Plant—there is an ample parking lot with good wading access. You won't have this pool to yourself, but there is generally enough room to move about, especially when the water is at moderate levels. Rainbows inhabit this pool year round, and there is usually something hatching during the season. Except early in the season, the pool usually demands long casts, as the cooler water from the West Branch is on the far bank (where the access is private).

Wading is also possible at any of the public boat launches between Hancock and Callicoon. These include the boat ramp on the western shore at Buckingham and another Pennsylvania access at Equinunk, along with the canoe launch on the east bank at Lordville. Farther down, there are four east bank access points closely set at Long Eddy, Basket Creek, Kellums and Hankins, then a long gap to the access at Callicoon. In general, crowds will diminish as you head south on the river.

The challenge of fishing on foot is not limited to the relatively sparse access points. The river is often wider than your best cast, and often too deep to wade across. The changing releases and temperatures, combined with the mobility of the rainbows, means you can't count on finding trout where you are fishing. Carry a thermometer and be ready to drive to another access if the water is too warm (or, in early season, too cold). Don't waste much time on water that isn't likely to hold fish—the trout are primarily found in pools and riffles.

The hatches in the Main Stem are similar to those in the West Branch, though generally a bit earlier since the water warms as it heads downstream. The early season large flies include Hendricksons, March Browns and Gray Fox, along with smaller Sulphurs and some early season Blue Winged Olives. As anywhere, but especially with wild fish, the larger flies are easier to see and the fish seem less cautious when feeding on them. Still, good, low riding dry fly imitations are important. For nymphs, beadheads with Gold-Ribbed Hare's Ear or Pheasant Tail dressings are useful in riffles.

As summer wears on, except when large releases are taking place, the fish will move upstream toward cool water and feed on a mix of smaller Sulphurs, Blue Winged Olives and Tricos. The small Olives and Tricos can be extremely demanding fishing. For the Olives, an emerger/cripple pattern or a nymph fished in the film is often more productive than a dry fly. The Tricos hatch at night and land in the mornings; it is the latter spinner fall that is most productive.

One way to avoid the difficulties of fishing with tiny flies in summer and fall is to use Light Cahills and *Isonychia* instead. These larger flies hatch more sporadically but are very attractive to trout. Again, low riding dry flies are called for. And even though the *Isonychia* usually hatch out of the stream, emergers are known to work for this insect on the Delaware. Another large fly for summer is the White Fly, which hatches along the Upper Delaware for 2 to 3 weeks beginning in mid-August. A size 10-12 White Wulff or comparadun will work. The White Fly skitters over the water much like a caddis, and Rick Eck of River Essentials recommends swinging a large white soft hackle with partridge tail and collar during the White Fly hatch.

One insect that is not present on the West Branch but is important on the Main Stem is the hellgrammite. This large dark nymph—anywhere from one to two inches long—lives up to three years; an imitation like Murray's Hellgrammite (a Woolly Bugger body with an ostrich herl tail) makes an excellent searching pattern. For streamers, the alewife hatch is not much of a factor in the main river, but there are chubs and fall fish. Large white Zonkers and coneheaded minnow imitations are a good bet. Crayfish and leech patterns are also useful. In either case, one of the long sink tip lines will help cover the big water. A 6-weight line is ideal for streamers, and a fast-action 5-weight generally is enough for smaller flies.

The Main Stem forms the boundary between New York and Pennsylvania, so special "border water" regulations apply. A current license from either Pennsylvania or New York is valid on either side, and trout fishing is open all year. However, only one trout a day over 14 inches may be taken between the first Saturday after April 11 and September 30. For the rest of the year (September 30 to that first Saturday after April 11) the entire Main Stem in New York is catch and release only for trout. As always, and especially in a blue-ribbon wild trout fishery, catch and release at all times is strongly recommended.

The productive Bard Parker pool at the beginning of the Main Stem.

Smallmouth

As noted, after Callicoon (or even higher up in summer) the smallmouth population increases and the trout fishing declines. The smallmouth in the Delaware are all wild and average 9-12 inches, although 14- to 20-inch fish are caught. While sometimes mixed in with trout, their preferred habitat is not identical. Look for smallmouth in broken water: rapids, current breaks and pocket water behind boulders. The fish will generally be found in water temperatures between 65 and 75 degrees. The peak time for Delaware smallmouth fishing is July through October. Smallmouth are particularly averse to bright light, so in summer, mornings and evenings are best, especially for topwater action.

On top, smallmouth here will hit poppers in white or black as well as brighter colors like orange and chartreuse. Subsurface, a black or olive Zonker is effective, as is a Clouser Minnow in dark/light to imitate small fish or in crayfish colors of brown and orange. A Zonker with a nymph tied to the bend is an effective rig. The Hellgrammite nymph also works for smallmouth. Though adult mayflies are not a staple for smallmouth, when the White Fly hatches in late August the fish will feed on the surface. A White Wulff pattern in size 10 or 12 will work for smallmouth as well as trout.

The gear for Delaware smallmouth should be a 6- or 7-weight rod; a floating line will generally be enough. Leaders should be at least 4 pounds, up to 9 feet for nymphing and as little as 4 to 6 feet for surface flies and streamers.

As with trout, a drift boat trip is ideal for Delaware smallmouth. (You may pick up trout—often big ones—in the lower part of the river at the mouths of the larger feeders, including the Mongaup on the New York side and the Lackawaxen in Pennsylvania.) For wading anglers, there are about 10 access points between Callicoon and Port Jervis. After Callicoon, heading downstream they are Damascus (PA), Skinner Falls, Narrowsburg (the area around the bridge is particularly good for smallmouth), Ten Mile River, Lackawaxen (PA, at Zane Grey Museum), Highland, Sparrowbush and Port Jervis. Pond Eddy (private boat access) to Sparrowbush (above Port Jervis) is a popular smallmouth float. (Kitatinny Canoes, 800-356-2852 or www.kittatinny.com, rents canoes and rafts on this section of the Main Stem and offers its own access points and shuttle service.) Be aware that there are several class II rapids between Cochecton/Damascus and Port Jervis.

The Border Water regulations for the Main Stem allow smallmouth fishing all year, with 5 fish of 12 inches or more allowed.

Shad

In addition to trophy rainbows and smallmouth, the Delaware River is one of the best places to flyfish for shad. Properly called the white shad or the American shad, these fish ascend the river to spawn each spring, creating a brief but intense fishing opportunity. As many as 800,000 shad enter the mouth of the Delaware each year, although probably no more than half make it to the New York portion of the river. They are sometimes called the poor man's salmon due to the spawning run. Unlike salmon, they do not necessarily spawn in their native rivers.

Male shad, called bucks, enter the river first at Philadelphia and as the water warms, move upstream. The bucks in the Delaware generally run 2 to 4 pounds. Their female counterparts, known as "roes" for the eggs they carry, run up to six pounds and follow the males by about a week. The first shad generally make it to Port Jervis, the lower end of the New York Delaware, by late April or Early May and stay until early June.

Timing and water temperature are the key factors in finding shad. Water that holds between the low fifties and upper sixties is ideal. Fishing, especially flyfishing, when they are not present in large numbers is usually futile. Also, shad tend to have already spawned when the water temperature hovers near 70, and by then the fish have little fight left in them. The USGS Web site gives water temperatures for a few of the rivers it covers, including the main stem Delaware at Callicoon. Add a couple of degrees for the temperature farther down at Port Jervis, and remember that water temperature will fluctuate considerably from day to night in early spring.

Shad can be caught as far upstream as the East and West branches of the Delaware, where trout anglers are sometimes surprised to find them on the end of the line, but they are better fighters earlier in their travels when they are fresh, or "bright," from the ocean. Callicoon to the end of the Delaware's New York run is a good segment to focus on if you are targeting shad.

Kevin Riley holds a shad "buck" from the Delaware.

The vast majority of shad anglers use spinning gear with traditional Shad Darts, but they can be caught on a fly rod. A relatively stiff rod in 6- to 8-weight is best. A sink tip or long, weighted leader on a floating line is most often used. A reel with a sensitive drag is important, not to avoid breaking tippets but to keep the hook from pulling out of the shad's paper-thin mouth. Remember that spawning fish generally aren't feeding, so their choice of lies is not affected by the need for food. Shad avoid faster water; look for them at current breaks and in shallow edges when the water is high and fast. As with other species in the Delaware, floating is the ideal way to fish for shad. Remember that the Lower Main Stem is a little rougher for floating.

All Delaware shad anglers have flies they swear by and at a given time some may work better than other, but putting the moving fly in front of the shad is the key to taking fish. Usually flies have a marabou or calf tail and a tinsel body, in various combinations of black, orange and chartreuse. A common technique is to swing the fly through likely holding spots. Guide Kevin Riley likes to tease shad into striking with the "hammer pull." Keep the tip of the line low to the water and pointed nearly downstream. It may help to keep the rod butt against your stomach. Pull in 6 to 12 inches of line crisply, then let it slip back downstream with the current (a marabou tail provides the best action for this technique). If you can manage it without burning your finger, hold the line under your rod hand when you strip—the shad's take is usually subtle.

Stream Facts: Delaware Main Stem

Seasons/Regulations
- Trout: First Saturday after April 11 to September 30, 1 fish per day, 14-inch minimum; remainder of year open, catch and release only.
- Smallmouth: All year, 5 fish, 12-inch minimum.
- Shad: All year, 6 fish per day.

Fish
- Mostly wild rainbow trout, a few browns from tributaries, wild smallmouth and spawning shad.

River Characteristics
- Wide tailwater, trout water down to Callicoon (above in summer). Runs, riffles and wide, slow-moving pools. Mostly easy wading, unless water is high. For floating, water becomes rougher below Cochecton/Damascus.

River Flows:
- Cold releases from East and West branches year round, volume varies widely depending on downstream demands for water (check before traveling).

Delaware River Main Stem—Major Hatches

INSECT	J	F	M	A	M	J	J	A	S	O	N	D	FLIES
Early Black\Brown Stone 12-14				▬									Elk Hair Caddis, Stonefly Nymphs
Little Black Caddis (Chimarra) 16-18				▬▬									Elk Hair Caddis, Goddard Caddis, Bead-Head Pupa
Blue Winged Olive 14-24				▬▬▬▬▬▬▬▬▬▬▬▬▬▬									Comparadun, Parachute, CDC Emerger, Compara-Emerger. Pheasant Tail Nymph
Blue Quill 16-18					▬▬								Blue Quill Dry, Pheasant Tail Nymph
Quill Gordon 12-14					▬▬								Quill Gordon Dry, Quill Gordon Wet
Light & Dark Hendrickson 12-16					▬▬								Light and Dark Hendrickson, comparadun or parachute, dark brown Hendrickson Nymph
Light & Dark Grannom (Shad Fly) 14-18					▬								Elk Hair Caddis, Lafontaine Deep Pupa & Emergent Pupa, X-Caddis, Bead-Head Pupa
Green, Gray, Tan Caddis 12-18					▬▬▬▬▬▬▬▬▬▬								Elk Hair Caddis, Lafontaine Deep Pupa & Emergent Pupa, X-Caddis, Bead-Head Pupa
Sulphur 16-20						▬▬▬▬▬							Comparadun, Parachute, CDC Emerger, Compara-Emerger. Pheasant Tail Nymph, Hare's Ear Nymph
March Brown 10-12						▬▬							Comparadun, Extended-Body Dry Flies, Hare's Ear Nymph
Gray Fox 12-14						▬▬							Comparadun, Extended-Body Dry Flies,
Green Drake 10-12						▬							Coffin Fly Spinner, Comparadun, Extended-Body Dry Flies Zug Bug
Light Cahill 12-16						▬▬▬▬▬▬▬							Cream Variants, Comparaduns, Cahill Wet Fly, Light Hare's Ear Nymph
Slate Drake (Isonychia) 12						▬▬		▬▬					Comparadun, Extended-Body Dry Flies, Leadwing Coachman, Zug Bug
Brown Drake 10-12							▬▬						Extended-Body Brown Drake,
Trico 22-26								▬▬▬▬					Trico Spinner, Griffith's Gnat
White Fly 12-14								▬▬					White Wulff, White Soft Hackle
Flying Ants, Red & Black 16-22						▬▬▬▬▬▬							Winged Ant Patterns
Midges 20-28	▬▬▬▬▬▬▬▬▬▬▬▬▬▬▬▬▬▬▬▬												Brassie, Serendipity, Midge Dry, Griffith's Gnat
Helgrammites (Dobson Fly)	▬▬▬▬▬▬▬▬▬▬▬▬▬▬▬▬▬▬▬▬												Murray's Helgrammite, Black Wooly Bugger

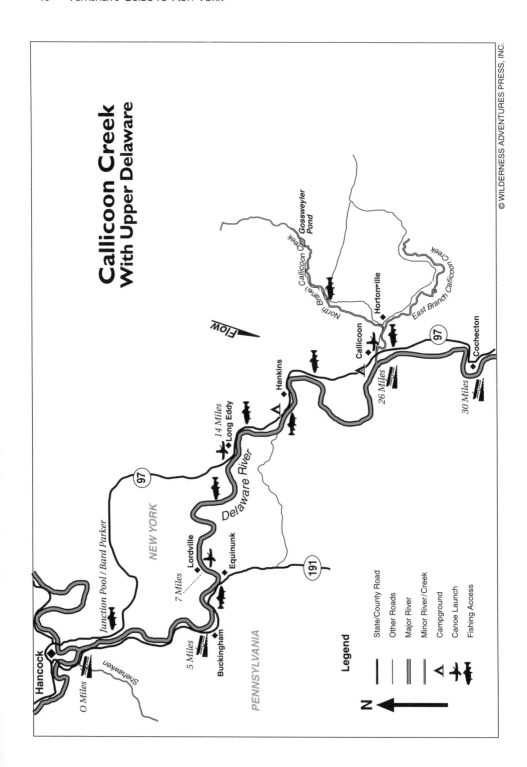

Callicoon Creek
With Upper Delaware

© WILDERNESS ADVENTURES PRESS, INC.

CALLICOON CREEK

Callicoon Creek, which joins the main stem of the Delaware River at the town of the same name, holds trout in its main stem and eastern and northern branches.

The East Branch is stocked heavily with brown trout—about 3,000 in just a few miles. However, it is subject to high temperatures in summer, and is mostly a put-and-take fishery.

The North Branch up to the impoundment outside Callicoon Center (Gossweyler Pond), about 6 miles in all, is better trout water. Wild browns in the 8- to 12-inch range live in the North Branch and some large wild rainbows from the Delaware spawn here in spring. About 2,400 brown trout are stocked here as well. Access is available through easements along most of the North Branch up to Callicoon Center from North Branch Road.

After the branches join at Hortonville, the stream runs roughly another mile or so to the Delaware. This section is also stocked with about 700 browns, and undoubtedly sees some wild fish from the Delaware.

All parts of the Callicoon are open for trout fishing from April 1 to October 15 without special regulations.

The Beaverkill

The Beaverkill is rich in flyfishing history. From Theodore Gordon and George LaBranche at the turn of the century, to A.J. McClane and Lee Wulff in more recent decades, the river has been at the center of American flyfishing. Not only famous anglers but famous flies are connected to the Beaverkill: the Hendrickson, the Lady Beaverkill, and the Coffin Fly were all developed on these waters.

Of course, anglers are generally more eager to fish in the present than the past. On that score, the Beaverkill, despite a few conservation issues, still fishes well, with a wide and prolific array of hatches and a large supply of stocked fish, supplemented by occasional wild trout.

Renowned fly tier Poul Jorgensen throws out the first cast on opening day at Junction Pool.

The Beaverkill begins near Alder Lake in Ulster County and quickly enters Sullivan County. The upper Beaverkill, before it merges with Willowemoc Creek, is excellent water but almost entirely private. The only public access here is at the Covered Bridge State Campground off Route 152, and the last portion above the entrance of the Willowemoc. (Guests at the Beaverkill Valley Inn in Lew Beach also have access to the upper Beaverkill.) Anglers at the campground report that there is a good population of wild brook trout there, but they tend to disperse when the stocking is done in spring.

The main section of the river runs about 13 miles from its junction with the Willowemoc in Roscoe to its end, where it flows into the East Branch of the Delaware in the village of East Branch. The first three miles of the river, from the Beaverkill/Willowemoc junction in Roscoe to what is called Trestle Pool is undoubtedly the most famous and most heavily fished section of the Beaverkill. This stretch contains the Junction Pool itself (home to the legendary Beamoc, the two-headed trout unable to decide which stream to enter), which often yields large trout, and the first 2.5-mile catch and release section, including a series of named pools and runs.

Each of the famous spots here is marked with a plaque explaining a bit of its history. As for the fishing, this stretch contains runs, riffles and slow pools that offer a wealth of hatches and excellent fishing, especially before the water warms in late June. Cairn's Pool is the most popular spot. The varied habitat it contains in its several hundred yards provides good hatches of virtually every fly that lives in the Beaverkill. Often, it seems like every angler in the Beaverkill is here, too, drawn by its deserved fame and the proximity of Old Route 17 that parallels the stream. For fishing almost as good but generally less crowded, try Barnhardt's Run and Pool about a mile upstream. You'll need to park at Hendrickson's Pool and wade upstream. Angler's with disabilities can find Project Access sites at Ferdon's Pool (and at Junction Pool upstream).

The hatches throughout this upper section are dense and run across the spectrum of mayflies, with substantial caddis hatches as well. In early season, the Quill Gordons and Hendricksons offer great fishing in late April and early May. Also among large flies, March Browns are especially dense, as are *Isonychia* and Green Drakes later in the season. Early season small black caddis are abundant, as are both the light and dark grannom (Shad Fly) that hatch in mid-May and carpet the water (and everything else). Fishing caddis dries is especially tricky with so many naturals on the water—a vulnerable emerger pattern is often a better bet.

Except for Cairn's Pool, some hatches are better in one pool than another. Local anglers report that Barnhardt's is particularly good for Hendricksons and Green Drakes. For the latter, it is generally the white-bodied evening spinner stage of this hatch (dubbed the Coffin Fly by legendary local tier Walt Dette) that is fished. Extended-body flies tied with foam or natural materials are most commonly used. However, some tiers have taken to using long streamer hooks, creating the abdomen with thin strips of Tyvek, a thin, buoyant material from Dupont often used in synthetic white envelopes.

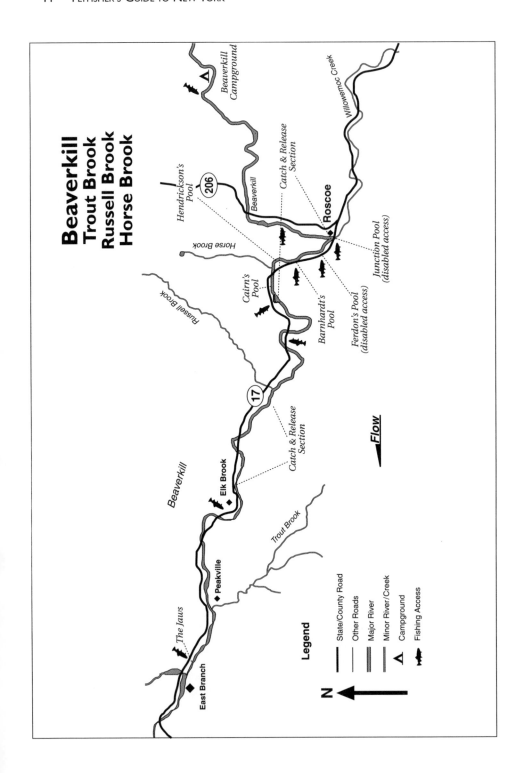

Another particularly good spot in this upper catch and release segment is Horse Brook Run, named for the tributary that enters here. The run has faster water and offers excellent fishing for March Browns from late May on, and for the *Isonychias* that emerge at roughly the same time and again in September.

Fly type is important on the Beaverkill. According to Jim Bell, of Trout Unlimited's Beamoc Chapter, the river's slower water demands low-riding dry fly imitations such as parachutes and comparaduns. However, he finds that standard ties like Quill Gordons (when they are hatching), the Usual and the Wulff series work well in the riffles. With two prime hatching periods a year, the *Isonychia* nymph is an excellent searching pattern, particularly in rocky water—a Zug Bug or Prince Nymph is usually close enough. Other generic nymphs, particularly Gold-Ribbed Hare's Ears and Pheasant Tails, work well also. Don't limit nymphing to mayflies—caddis larva and pupa are also effective. At the other end of the mayfly life cycle, a rusty spinner in appropriate size will effectively imitate most mayfly spinner falls. For streamer fishing, Black-Nosed Dace live here and the classic buck-tail imitation is effective.

Moving downstream from the first catch and release section, the area between it and the second catch and release section is about 2.5 miles with some decent pools and pocket water, though nothing to rival the upper stretch. The second catch and release segment begins where Russell Brook enters the Beaverkill and contains some very good fishing; it is also generally less crowded than the upper catch and release. The last five miles of the Beaverkill, after the second catch and release area, is probably the least popular section of the river. However, the area where Trout Brook comes in near the village of Peakville and the last stretch just before the river joins the East Branch, known as the "Jaws," offer good fishing. The Jaws is particularly well populated with Hendricksons and caddis.

The fish in the Beaverkill are predominantly stocked brown trout. The state puts in nearly 18,000 fish each spring. There is only modest natural reproduction. Browns stocked here generally have clipped adipose fins (the small fin on the back in front of the tail) so anglers can quickly tell if a fish is wild or not. However, because of the amount of food available, the stocked fish grow well and are reputed to become very picky within a few months. In addition to the browns, recent infor-mal surveys have found scattered wild rainbows all the way up to Horse Brook. These fish undoubtedly come in from the Delaware, and they are mostly 10 inches or less in size.

One difficulty with the Beaverkill is warmer water in summer. The fishing slows down considerably after June. In addition to warm water, wild fish face the obsta-cle of degraded tributaries that make spawning difficult. The lower end of a num-ber of the feeders have been damaged by recent storms, including the devastating flood of 1996. In conjunction with Delaware County, Trout Unlimited is trying to restore several of the most important tributaries. On Horse Brook, restoration work has made the channel narrower and deeper—allowing water entering the Beaverkill to remain cool—and created a series of classic plunge pools enabling spawning fish to ascend the stream. Similar work is planned for Horton and Russell brooks as well. (Despite the good fishing at tributaries, anglers should refrain from fishing at the mouths whenever the trout stack up here in summer. When the surrounding water is 70 degrees or more, fish taken from a cold water refuge and then released will generally not survive).

In addition to looking for tributaries, anglers are well advised to fish the shady part of the river. The Beaverkill generally runs east to west, so the shade is typically on the south side of the river. Since the river is wide and the access points are generally on the north bank, a fast-action 9-foot, 5-weight rod is useful, as is the ability to reach cast and mend line.

Regulations governing the Beaverkill vary by section. On the Upper Beaverkill, including the Covered Bridge Campground, the normal trout season applies: April 1 to October 15, with five fish a day of any size permitted. On the rest of stream, beginning where County Route 7/State 206 crosses the Upper Beaverkill (in Delaware County, about 3 miles above Junction Pool), there is an extended trout season running from April 1 to November 30, with 5 fish over 9 inches allowed to be taken. Within this portion of the river are the two catch and release sections. The first begins at Fordon's Pool, about 1 mile below Junction Pool, and runs 2.5 miles downstream to roughly what is called the Mountain Pool. The second catch and release section runs 2.6 miles, approximately from Butternut Grove Pool to Chiloway Pool, just below where Whirling Eddy Brook enters the river.

This is a small crowd for Cairn's Pool.

Stream Facts: Beaverkill

Seasons
- From first crossing of County Route/State 206 , upstream—April 1 to October 15; downstream of Route 206 crossing—April 1 to November 30. All year in the two catch and release sections (see below).

Special Regulations
- Catch and release only in two special fishing areas. Sullivan/Delaware County line 2.5 miles downstream; Butternut Grove 2.6 miles to Chiloway Pool.

Fish
- Mostly brown trout; some wild rainbows from the Delaware River, a few wild brookies.

River Characteristics
- Freestone stream, runs riffles and pools; 30-60 feet wide in main stretch, narrower in upper river. Easy wading at most pools, can be rocky elsewhere.

River Flows
- Best in spring and fall; somewhat lower and considerably warmer most summers.

Beaverkill—Major Hatches

INSECT	J	F	M	A	M	J	J	A	S	O	N	D	FLIES
Black\Brown Stone 12													Elk Hair Caddis, Stonefly Nymphs
Blue Winged Olives 16-24													Comparadun, Parachute, CDC Emerger, Compara-Emerger. Pheasant Tail Nymph
Little Black Caddis (Chimarra) 16-18													Elk Hair Caddis, Goddard Caddis, Bead-Head Pupa
Light & Dark Hendrickson 12-14													Light and Dark Hendrickson, Comparadun or Parachute, dark brown Hendrickson Nymph
Light & Dard Grannom (Shad Fly) 12-14													Elk Hair Caddis, Lafontaine Deep Pupa and Emergent Sparkle Pupa, Bead-Head Nymphs, Soft Hackle Wets
Caddis Green, Gray, Tan 12-18													Elk Hair Caddis, Lafontaine Deep Pupa and Emergent Sparkle Pupa, Bead-Head Nymphs, Soft Hackle Wets
Sulphurs 14-20													Comparadun, Parachute, CDC Emerger, Compara-Emerger, Pheasant Tail Nymph, Hare's Ear Nymph
March Brown 10-12													Comparadun, Extended Body Dry Flies, Hare's Ear Nymph
Gray Fox 12-14													Comparadun, Extended Body Dry Flies,
Green Drake 10-12													Coffin Fly Spinner, Comparadun, Extended Body Dry Flies, Zug Bug
Light Cahill/Potomanthus 10-16													Cream Variants, Comparaduns, Cahill Wet Fly, Light Hare's Ear Nymph
Slate Drake (Isonychia) 12													Comparadun, Extended Body Dry Flies, Leadwing Coachman, Zug Bug
Trico 22-26													Trico Spinner, Griffith's Gnat
Ants Hoppers/Crickets Beetles													Dubbed Ants, Sinking Ants, Letort Hoppers\Crickets, Foam Beetles

WILLOWEMOC CREEK

Willowemoc Creek is in some ways a smaller version of the Beaverkill it joins. A freestone stream that starts out small and grows on its way to Junction Pool, the Willow is an excellent place to fish, especially if you want to avoid the dense crowds at the more famous pools on the Beaverkill.

The Willowemoc gets its start in the mountains of Sullivan County, near the village of the same name. Here it is a small, rocky stream with a decent population of wild brook trout. Like the Upper Beaverkill, much of the land in this section of the Willowemoc is private. There is some public access just above and below the village of Willowemoc, along Route 82, and parking at Conklin Hill Road. Also, Fir Brook, which merges with the headwaters of the Willowemoc, has public access off Willowemoc Road. It is also a brook trout fishery, but receives a stocking of about 350 browns each year.

Above the town of Livingston Manor and for the rest of its 15-mile trip to the Beaverkill, the Willowemoc becomes a larger, deeper river from 20 to 40 feet across. The fish population changes, too, with more of the stocked and occasional wild browns and fewer brook trout. Starting below the village of Parkston, there is public access on most of the stream from Debruce Road. The Willowemoc is particularly accessible to disabled anglers. Project Access, founded by the late Joan Stoliar, built and maintains four "Easy Access" sites on the Willow: at the Covered Bridge in Livingston Manor (the inaugural site), two at the Catskill Fly Fishing Center and another at Hazel Bridge Pool. The ramps accommodate everything from wheelchairs to anglers with bad knees.

An important difference between the Willowemoc and the Beaverkill is the insect life. There are good mayfly hatches here, but they are not as dense or as varied as those on the Beaverkill. (For mayflies, the Green Drake in particular is not important here.) And, on the Willowemoc, caddis predominate, especially below Livingston Manor. In spring, the small black caddis that is common throughout the Catskills can be found here. The light and dark Shad Flies also appear in mid-May. After that, a green caddis, around size 16, hatches off and on through June. Tan and spotted varieties are around in mid-summer, and the large ginger caddis hatches sporadically in late summer.

For the caddis, fishing dry flies can be difficult. A Lafontaine Deep Sparkle Pupa in correct color and size is excellent as a caddis emergence is beginning. As more fish feed near the surface, the Emergent Sparkle Pupa—essentially the same fly with a trailing shuck and a small deer hair wing—will often work better than a dry fly. One trick often used is dropping an adult caddis imitation in the middle of a rise form. Caddis leave the water so fast the trout often miss them, and they will aggressively hit another fly in the same spot.

Terrestrials like ants and beetles are valuable on a smaller stream like the Willowemoc in the dead of summer (or anytime nothing is hatching). A Black-

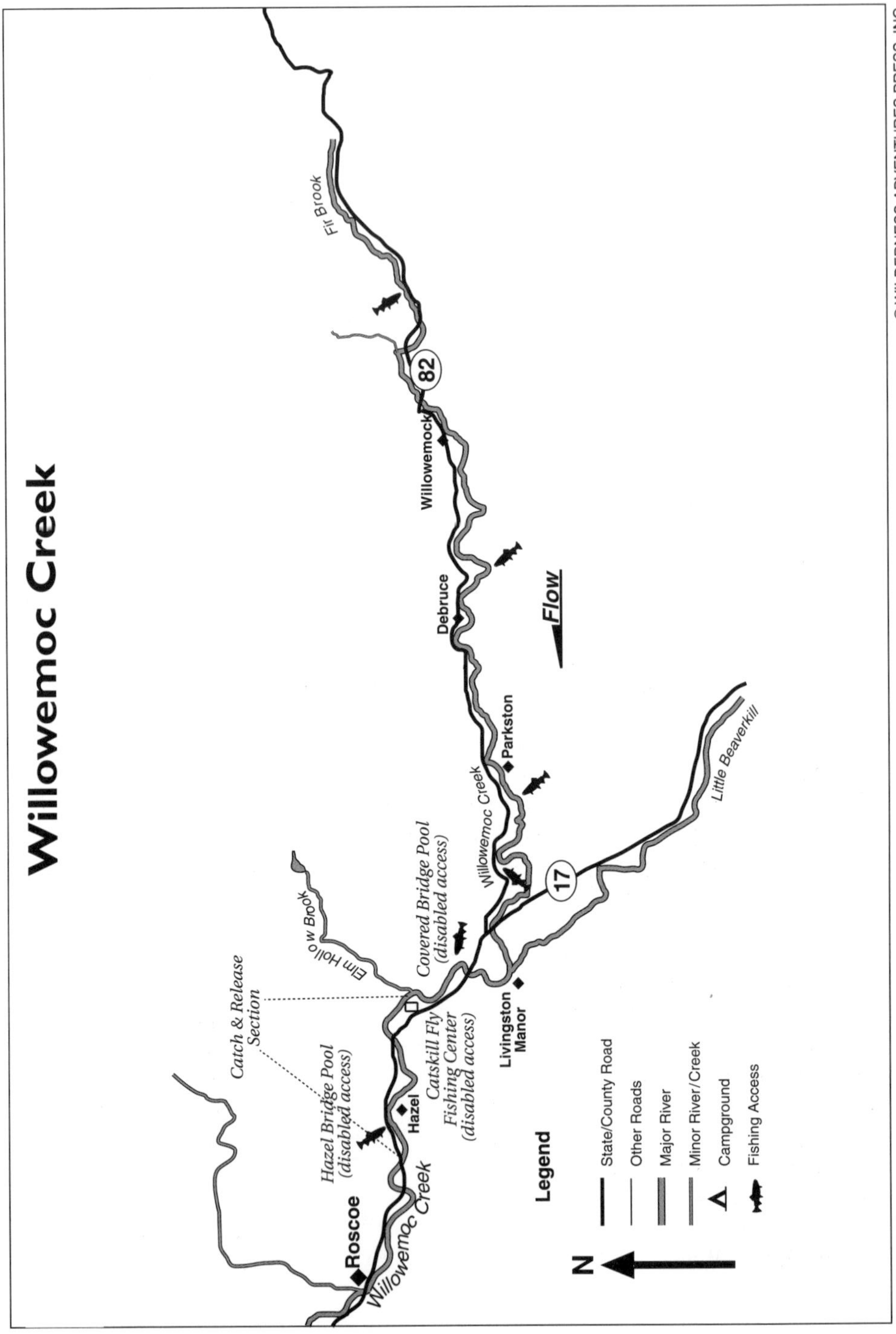

Willowemoc Creek

© WILDERNESS ADVENTURES PRESS, INC.

Fir Brook

82

Willowemock

Debruce

Flow

Parkston

Willowemoc Creek

Little Beaverkill

17

Elm Hollow Brook

Covered Bridge Pool
(disabled access)

Catch & Release
Section

Hazel Bridge Pool
(disabled access)

Catskill Fly
Fishing Center
(disabled access)

Livingston
Manor

Hazel

Roscoe

Willowemoc Creek

Legend

	State/County Road
	Other Roads
	Major River
	Minor River/Creek
▲	Campground
	Fishing Access

N

Nosed Dace is also worth a try. Whatever the fly, a 4-weight is generally heavy enough on the Willowemoc.

Not to be outdone by its more famous neighbor, the Willowemoc has its own catch and release section which runs about 3.2 miles from the entrance of Elm Hollow Brook (a spot sometimes called Decker's Eddy) to the second crossing of the stream by the Route 17 Quickway. This section has excellent runs and pools. Probably the most famous among them—the Willowemoc's version of Cairn's Pool—is the Hazel Bridge Pool. It is found where Hazel Brook enters the stream, about a half-mile before the lower end of the catch and release section. The Catskill Fly Fishing Center and Museum also offers a good stretch both above and below its bridge.

The Willowemoc is heavily stocked with brown trout—it receives more than 16,000 fish each year. Though there is little natural reproduction here, the fish do holdover well, and fish up to 14 inches are not uncommon. The Willowemoc can suffer from excess warming in summer. By the end of June, temperatures routinely reach 70 degrees or more. Thus, it is best fished in spring and again in fall.

As noted above, the catch and release section is 3.2 miles long and is open year round. The Willowemoc outside the catch and release area, up to the iron bridge in the village of Parkston (several miles above Livingston Manor) is open from April 1 to November 30. Above that point it closes October 15.

The Willowemoc at the Catskill Fly Fishing Center Bridge.

Stream Facts: Willowemoc Creek

Seasons
- From Iron Bridge at Parkston upstream—April 1 to October 15; downstream from the Iron Bridge—April 1 to November 30. All year in "special fishing area" (catch and release) section.

Special Regulations
- Catch and release only "special fishing area," from mouth of Elm Hollow Brook 3.2 miles downstream to second Route 17 Quickway crossing east of Roscoe, NY.

Fish
- Mostly stocked brown trout; more wild brookies upstream.

River Characteristics
- Medium-sized freestone stream, runs, riffles and pools; 20-40 feet wide.

River Flows
- Best in spring and fall; lower and warmer most summers.

Willowemoc Creek—Major Hatches

INSECT	J	F	M	A	M	J	J	A	S	O	N	D	FLIES
Blue Winged Olives 16-24			X	X	X	X	X	X	X				Comparadun, Parachute, CDC Emerger, Compara-Emerger, Pheasant Tail Nymph
Little Black Caddis (Chimarra) 16-18				X									Elk Hair Caddis, Goddard Caddis, Bead-Head Pupa
Light & Dark Hendrickson 12-14				X									Light and Dark Hendrickson, Comparadun or Parachute, dark brown Hendrickson Nymph
Light & Dark Grannom (Shad Fly) 12-14					X								Elk Hair Caddis, Lafontaine Deep Pupa and Emergent Sparkle Pupa, Bead-Head Nymphs, Soft Hackle Wets
Caddis Green, Gray, Tan 12-18					X	X							Elk Hair Caddis, Lafontaine Deep Pupa and Emergent Sparkle Pupa, Bead-Head Nymphs, Soft Hackle Wets
Sulphurs 14-20					X	X							Comparadun, Parachute, CDC Emerger, Compara-Emerger, Pheasant Tail Nymph, Hare's Ear Nymph
Light Cahill/Potomanthus 10-16						X	X						Cream Variants, Comparaduns, Cahill Wet Fly, Light Hare's Ear Nymph
Slate Drake (Isonychia) 12						X			X				Comparadun, Extended-Body Dry Flies, Leadwing Coachman, Zug Bug
Trico 22-26								X	X				Trico Spinner, Griffith's Gnat
Ants Hoppers/Crickets Beetles					X	X	X	X	X	X			Dubbed Ants, Sinking Ants, Letort Hoppers/Crickets, Foam Beetles

Catskill Fly Fishing Center

Fishing the Catskill waters offers a taste of tradition all by itself. But for true immersion in the history of flyfishing, pay a visit to the Catskill Fly Fishing Center and Museum in Livingston Manor.

The museum, and its extensive collection of tackle and memorabilia, is dedicated to the long history of flyfishing in the Catskills. In fact, the museum's collection—including classic rods, reels and flies—is so broad that only about ten percent can be exhibited at one time. Executive Director Paul Dahlie, who has headed the museum since 1999, is eager to take advantage of the rich and diverse collection by rotating the displays.

Like the Catskills region itself, the museum has a particular focus on fly tying. The tying room of the renowned Darby family, whose shop was only a mile up the road, has been recreated in the museum. Also on permanent exhibit are the flies of eight legendary local tiers, including Theodore Gordon, Art Flick, the Darbys and the Dettes. Though Paul Dahlie is reluctant to put price tags on the collection, he notes that the six original Theodore Gordon flies on display would probably fetch $5,000 each on the open market.

Despite the history visible everywhere here, the museum is also about the present. "I would like to see this be not only a museum," Dahlie says, "I really think our future lies in education." That mission is reflected in programs ranging from the display of memorabilia in local libraries to more ambitious projects such as a bank-side tree planting program for third graders students and an extensive ecology course for children 8 to 14 conducted at the museum over 4 summer weekends.

For the casual visitor, the museum offers a series of lectures, including demonstrations throughout the fishing season by some of the world's best fly tiers and rod makers. And, if looking at all the flies and tackle gives you the urge to fish, the CFFC&M also has a mile of shore line on the Willowemoc, entirely open to the public.

The Catskill Fly Fishing Center and Museum is located at 5447 Old Route 17, Livingston Manor, New York. It is open every day 10 a.m. - 4 p.m. from April through October; Tuesday through Friday 10 a.m. - 1 p.m. from November through March. Suggested Admission Donations: Adults $3.00; Children (under 12) $1.00; Seniors $1.00. For additional information call 914 439-4810 or visit their web site at www.cffcm.org.

Inside the Catskill Fly Fishing Museum.
(Photo by Eric Bessette, courtesy of CFFC&M)

SMALL CATSKILL STREAMS

There are more than a hundred small streams in the Catskills. Although these streams inevitably take a back seat to the big, famous rivers, they should not be ignored. They can provide a haven for anglers looking to get away from the most crowded waters in the region. And they provide a chance to practice a simpler kind of fishing when you've grown weary of long casts, precise imitations and picky fish.

The fishing in these streams is pretty similar from one to another. They are usually no more than 15 feet across—often half that—and generally rocky and steep. The fish hold wherever they can. Anglers should be alert to any slightly deeper or more sheltered water. Bankside cuts, spots in front and back of boulders and small pools at the end of riffles are the usual targets in small stream fishing. Not all of these streams have bridges across them, but when they do the pools there should not be missed.

The fish in the small Catskill streams are primarily wild brook trout. These beautiful, native fish generally do not get very large; anything more than 10 inches is a trophy. The brookies are more gullible than browns or rainbows, especially in these small waters where they must feed opportunistically to survive. If something is hatching, by all means imitate it, but generic patterns will simplify your fishing. A traditionally tied Adams is an ideal dry fly for mountain brook trout. The fish will also rise to gaudier patterns; it is great fun to catch a small wild fish on an old-fash-

Brook trout like these can be found in many small Catskill streams.

ioned Royal Coachman (wet or dry). Humpies are effective, and their buoyancy makes them good for faster stretches. Almost any small stream has overhanging foliage so terrestrials are a good portion of the brookies diet. Small black ant patterns are good, and beetles even better as they're a bigger meal, float well and when tied with foam are virtually indestructible.

Although wild mountain brook trout feed hungrily, they are not necessarily easy to catch. These fish live in shallow water and are extremely wary of overhead predators. Anglers must stalk carefully, a misstep or a bad cast and you can skip ahead to the next pool. Approaching the fish from below whenever possible will help avoid spooking them.

In addition to the challenge of wary fish, getting off a good cast in narrow, brushy waters is easier said than done. Often, you'll be dapping as much as casting. That leaves the angler with a choice of equipment: a short rod—7 feet or even less—to aid casting or a longer rod—up to 9 feet—to make dapping easier. Remember that you can always hold the longer rod above the grip to shorten the casting arc in tight spots.

Generally, small freestone waters are best fished in spring and again at the end of the season. In summer they will run lower and warmer. Look for the better shaded streams in July and August, or head toward the source for cooler water.

Along with the population of wild brookies, small streams will contain browns (or rainbows) where they enter larger waters that hold those fish. By all means try your luck with them; they are generally found at the lower reaches of streams. However, some anglers prefer to avoid spawning tributaries in fall (spring for rainbows) to allow fish to reproduce. At a minimum, try to stay out of the streambeds during spawning season to avoid trampling on the redds.

Below is a partial list of small Catskill streams with at least some public access, listed by the rivers they feed (heading downstream).

West Branch Delaware
- Lake Brook: Access at lower end off Route 10 near Hobart.
- Betty Brook: Access off Betty Brook Road and Route 10, below South Kortright.
- Little Delaware River: Off Route 28 outside Delhi. Small stocking of brown trout.
- Mountain Brook (tributary of Little Delaware): Reached on Route 6 and Crescent Valley Road in Bovina.
- East Brook: Access off Route 10 in Walton and farther upstream, south of Mundale.
- Sands Creek: Access off Route 67, about halfway between Cannonsville Reservoir and Hancock.

East Branch Delaware
- Bush Kill: Access off Route 49 between Margaretville and Arkville. Closes September 30.

- Huckleberry Brook: Access from Route 28 and Route 3 above Dunraven. Closes September 30.
- Mill Brook (tributary to Pepacton Reservoir): Access from Jim Alton Road. Closes September 30.
- Fall Clove (tributary to Pepacton Reservoir): Fall Clove Road. Closes September 30.
- Trout Brook: Access from Route 30 or East Branch Delaware in Shinhopple.
- Baxter Brook: Access from Route 30 in Harvard.
- Morrison Brook: Access from Route 30 below Harvard.
- Read Creek: Access from Old 17 below Earlys Flat. Open 1st Saturday after April 11 to September 30.
- Larkin Brook: Access outside Peas Eddy. Open 1st Saturday after April 11 to September 30.

Beaverkill
- Horse Brook: Access from Old Route 17.
- Russell Brook: Access from Russell Brook Road.
- Trout Brook: Access at junction and along Burnwood Road and Methol Road.

Willowemoc
- Fir Brook: Access from Willowemoc Road/Round Pond Road above village of Willowemoc. Small stocking of brown trout.
- Sprague Brook: Access from Route 82/Debruce Road.
- Stewart Brook: Access from Old Route 17 and Route 123.
- Mongaup Creek: Access from Mongaup Road.

Neversink
- Wolf Brook: Access throughout "Unique Area." catch and release.
- Eden Brook/Little Eden Brook: Access throughout "Unique Area." catch and release.

Esopus
- Bushnellsville Creek: Access from Stream and Route 47.
- Broadstreet Hollow: Access from stream.
- Chichester Creek/Stony Clove: Access from 214.
- Woodland Valley Creek: Access from Woodland Valley Road. Small brown trout stocking.

Schoharie
- Little West Kill: Access from Falke Road.

On small Catskill streams, you'll often have to cast from the banks.

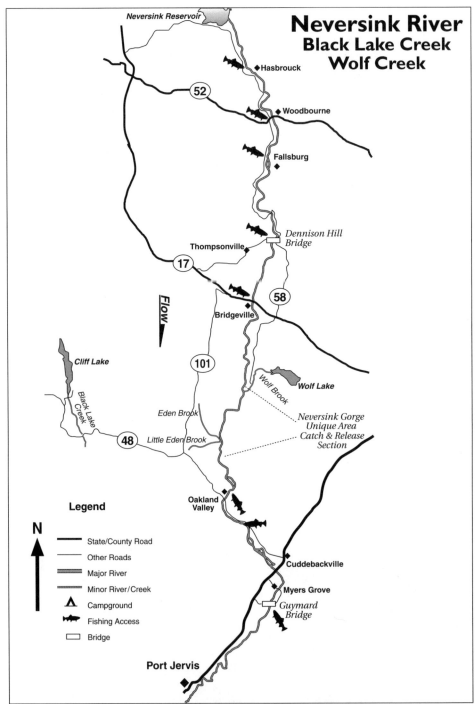

Neversink River
Black Lake Creek
Wolf Creek

Neversink Reservoir

Hasbrouck

52

Woodbourne

Fallsburg

Dennison Hill
Bridge

Thompsonville

17

58

Flow

Bridgeville

Cliff Lake

101

Wolf Brook

Wolf Lake

Black Lake Creek

Eden Brook

Neversink Gorge
Unique Area
Catch & Release
Section

48

Little Eden Brook

Oakland
Valley

Legend

N

——— State/County Road
——— Other Roads
▭▭▭ Major River
——— Minor River/Creek
▲ Campground
🐟 Fishing Access
▭ Bridge

Cuddebackville

Myers Grove

Guymard
Bridge

Port Jervis

NEVERSINK RIVER

The Neversink River runs a close second to the Beaverkill in flyfishing history. It was here that Theodore Gordon, adapting British techniques, fathered American dry fly fishing. Fly angling pioneers George Labranche and Edward Ringwood Hewitt also fished these waters early in the last century. While the intervening hundred years have not always been kind to the Neversink, including the construction of a dam and reservoir in the 1930s, this is still an excellent trout fishery with a good mix of brown trout, primarily stocked, and wild brookies. As a bonus, the Neversink offers a rare opportunity to catch landlocked salmon in a stream setting. Smallmouth bass and shad can also be taken on flies at the Neversink's lower end.

The Neversink begins as two small streams, the east and west branches, which rise in the hills of Ulster County and run approximately 8 miles to their junction in Claryville in Sullivan County. Anglers can skip the East Branch—its waters are beautifully clear but nearly sterile due to high acidity. The West Branch offers good fishing for wild brook trout and a few browns in a small stream setting. The brook trout are plentiful, but on the small side.

The land on the West Branch is almost entirely private. However, it is possible to fish the West Branch on the property of the Frost Valley YMCA by staying at their cabins or by purchasing a seasonal fishing pass, currently $125. The YMCA property also gives access to Pigeon and High Falls brooks and Biscuit Creek, tributaries to the West Branch of the Neversink which all hold wild brookies. The Frost Valley YMCA can be contacted at 914-985-2291.

The Neversink's main stem begins at Claryville and here the fishing for a mix of browns and brookies gets more sophisticated. The river from Claryville down to the reservoir is also where landlocked salmon run up from the reservoir and provide a unique opportunity for Catskill anglers. The landlocks were first planted in the Neversink Reservoir in the late 1970s at the urging of DEC official Bill Kelly and others. They have taken hold quite well, feeding on the reservoir's abundant smelt. In addition to some natural reproduction, about 6,000 landlocked salmon fingerlings are stocked in the reservoir and the extreme lower end of the river each year.

The fishing for landlockeds usually involves targeting fall spawning fish just above the reservoir. A bucktail streamer, especially a Black Ghost, is the fly of choice. Though the spawners are not easy to hook, the effort is worth it: the landlocked salmon here are strong, beautiful fish that run up to 18 inches.

Unfortunately, access to the main stem of the Neversink above the reservoir is scarce. Below Claryville, the only public access is the DEP's property around the reservoir that encompasses the extreme lower end of the river. A DEP watershed permit is required.

Below the reservoir, the primary trout water of the Neversink begins. The river runs about 40 miles to Port Jervis where it empties into the Delaware River, but it is the first 30 miles or so, roughly to Cuddebackville, which are trout waters holding a mix of wild brookies and stocked browns. About 10,000 browns are stocked in the river each year. There are also naturally reproducing browns in the Neversink; probably the greatest concentration is in the 7 miles from the dam to Fallsburg, according to the DEC's Bob Angle.

The first portion of the river, between the reservoir outlet and Route 17 in Bridgeville, flows smoothly over a sandy and weedy bottom and resembles a spring creek, although there are a few riffles. Fish will hold along banks and at the occasional big boulders. There are decent minimum releases from the reservoir (though anglers would like more), so the section above Route 17 stays reasonably cool throughout the season. Still, the fishing usually gets better even closer to the dam in summer. The most consistently cool water will be found within 8-10 miles of the dam.

Access along the entire river below the reservoir is quite good, though parking is difficult in a few places. Where Route 52 crosses the river, about 6 miles from the dam, there is a very deep and rocky pool below the bridge. A big wet fly swung through this pool can take some large fish. Be aware that the strike may occasionally turn out to be a sunfish. Downstream of Route 52 but before Route 17, the area around Dennison Hill Bridge, off Ranch Hill Road, affords some of the best fishing on the river. There are rocky ledges offering good holding structure, underwater springs and a wealth of hatches. Sulphurs and Blue Winged Olives are especially prolific here. Bob Ewald, an instructor and rod maker who lives in the area, finds that emerger patterns often work better here than duns.

Good hatches throughout the lower Neversink include Hendricksons, Sulphurs, Light Cahills and *Isonychia*. The *Isonychia* nymph makes a good search-

The Neversink Gorge offers good fishing in virtual solitude.

ing fly, as does a beadhead caddis pupa in cream or green. If the trout fishing isn't enough, it is also possible to catch a landlocked salmon here. Ewald reports that a few landlockeds do get through the dam into the lower river.

South of Route 17, the Bridgeville Road DEC access represents the upper end of the Neversink Gorge. Here the water becomes fast and rocky, with plenty of good pockets. To fish the gorge in earnest, though, head farther downstream to the aptly named Neversink River Unique Area. This nearly 5,000-acre preserve, privately held until the early 1990s, is both outstanding and underused. The nearly six miles of water within the Unique Area is generally fast and rocky and the fish here are mostly wild browns and brookies; no fish are stocked in the gorge. The best trout fishing is in spring and fall.

The access here is public but deliberately limited which helps keep the fishing, and the entire experience, special. There are only two entry points: at the upper end off Katrina Falls Road and at the lower end from Bushkill Road/County Route 101. In both cases you must park and walk to the stream along cleared and well marked, but sometimes rocky, paths through the woods. In the upper access, at Katrina Falls Road, the walk is about one mile, while from Bushkill Road it is nearly twice as long. At either entrance, it is best to bring a backpack and carry your waders to the streamside, though breathable waders paired with sturdy wading boots will also work. In either case, travel as light as possible. Do bring some water and a snack, though.

In addition to the Neversink fishing in the Unique Area, the upper access path reaches the river right near Wolf Brook, a good spot for small wild brook trout. Similarly, the lower entry provides access to Eden Brook and Little Eden Brook, which also hold brookies.

The pocket water in the gorge also contains smallmouth bass that come into their own in summer. These are all wild fish, averaging around 10 inches, but running as big as 15 inches. Guide Ray Otullich considers Neversink smallmouth the ideal target for beginning anglers and anyone looking for a natural fishing experience. He finds that a small Turk's Tarantula, usually with a tan body, is a very effective dry fly for these fish. For streamers, he recommends a rabbit strip, tied matuka style—black, rust or olive in clear water, chartreuse when the river is murky.

The Neversink and all tributaries in the Unique Area are catch and release only. The area is open from a half-hour before sunrise to a half-hour after sunset. Be sure to bring a flashlight if you plan to fish until closing.

Below the gorge, the Neversink enters Oakland Valley Flats, another good fishing section that is at its best in spring. As the name implies, the river is less steep here. The mayfly hatches are good, and there are abundant cased green caddis in a size 14. The adult caddis are usually tan in the same size. The water is similar down to the Hoag Road Access where a museum to the old Delaware and Hudson (D&H) Canal is located. (A ramp for the disabled is planned for the Hoag Road Access.)

Anglers in the Hoag Road area are likely to pick up as many smallmouth as trout in mid-summer. Below this point, the lower Neversink becomes pretty good smallmouth water. As in the gorge, look for deep pockets and pools.

Shad

Shad from the Delaware make their way into the lower Neversink in large enough numbers to make fishing worthwhile. The best time is early May, and they will be available here a bit earlier than in the Delaware above Port Jervis. They can go as far as the cement barrier near Cuddybackville, but the biggest concentration of shad is reportedly near Guymard Bridge where Hunter Road crosses the river in the village of Guymard. As with shad everywhere, this is more a spin fisher's game, but they can be caught on the fly. Any of the bright shad flies will work. Swing your fly down through a pod of fish, then strip back, alert for the shad's soft take.

Stream Facts: Neversink River

Season
- Trout and landlocked salmon: April 1 to October 15.
- Shad: all year.
- Smallmouth: third saturday in June to November 30.

Special Regulations
- Downstream of Neversink Reservoir trout taken must be 9 inches or more.
- Throughout Neversink Unique Area (Neversink Gorge), from Mercer Brook downstream to Orange/Sullivan County Line, the river and its tributaries are catch and release, artificial lures only. Landlocked salmon are subject to a 3 fish per day, 15-inch limit.

Fish
- Mostly brown trout, some wild brookies, especially above reservoir. Landlocked salmon spawn in main river above reservoir. Smallmouth in lower reaches. Shad in May, up to barrier at Cuddybackville.

River Characteristics
- Freestone stream above Neversink Reservoir, smaller above Claryville, wider after west and east branches merge. Tailwater below reservoir, warming seasonally below Route 17.

River Flows
- Freestone portion best in spring and fall, low and warm most summers. Some coldwater releases through season, better within 10 miles of the reservoir in summer.

Neversink River—Major Hatches

INSECT	J	F	M	A	M	J	J	A	S	O	N	D	FLIES
Little Black\Brown Stone 12-14			▬										Black Elk Hair Caddis, Dark Hare's Ear Nymph
Lt. And Dark Hendrickson 12-14				▬									Comparaduns, Down Wing Deer Hair Emergers, Rusty Spinners, Hendrickson Nymphs
Caddis Green, Gray, Tan 14-20					▬▬▬▬▬								Elk Hair Caddis, Bead-Head Cream or Green Pupa, Soft Hackle Wets
Blue Winged Olives 16-20					▬▬▬▬								Comparaduns, CDC Emergers, Pheasant Tail Nymphs
March Brown 10					▬								Extended-Body Mayfly or Comparadun
Sulphurs 12-16						▬							Comparaduns, CDC Emergers, Snowshoe Rabbit Emergers, Pheasant Tail Nymphs
Gray Fox 12-14						▬							Gray Fox Variant
Light Cahill/Potomanthus 12-16						▬▬							Cream Variants, Comparaduns, Light Hare's Ear Nymphs
Slate Drake (Isonychia) 12						▬		▬					Extended-Body Mayfly or Comparadun, Zug Bug
Ants Hoppers/Crickets Beetles				▬▬▬▬▬▬									Dubbed Ants, Letort Crickets\Hoppers, Foam Beetles
Streamers	▬▬▬▬▬▬▬▬▬▬▬▬												Gray Ghost, Black-Nosed Dace, Zonker

Rondout Creek

Rondout Creek runs from the Catskill Mountain Forest Preserve through Sullivan and Ulster counties into Rondout Reservoir, then out the other end. The two sections are both fishable for trout, but distinct.

The upper Rondout Creek runs about nine miles from its headwaters to the reservoir. In this section it is a good wild brook trout stream—one of the better ones in the region according to biologist Mike Flaherty of the DEC. It is also one of the few places brook trout are stocked, with about 3,000 small fish put in each year. Most of this upper stretch falls within a state forest preserve, so access is readily available. The stream can be reached from Route 46, and closer to the reservoir from Route 153.

The lower section of the Rondout primarily holds warmwater fish. However, small but steady cold water releases from the dam make the first mile or so a decent tailwater stream. There is a mix of wild brook trout and brown trout here, with more browns as you move downstream. The wild browns are supplemented by about 2,500 stocked fish per year. About 3,000 small rainbows are stocked as well. The hatches here would be typical of the area. Access to this lower portion is from Route 55, where much of the land is unposted.

Vernoy Kill

The Vernoy Kill (sometimes spelled Vernooy) is a small mountain stream in Ulster County that merges with the lower portion of Rondout Creek. The Vernoy holds a good population of wild brown and brook trout. It is stocked with about 400 small browns a year. There is state forest land at its headwaters and recently a couple of private groups acquired a large parcel of land along the Vernoy, which they plan to give to the state. Once a management plan is put in place, there will be ready access to good fishing along virtually the entire segment of the Vernoy above Route 209 (along Lundy Road).

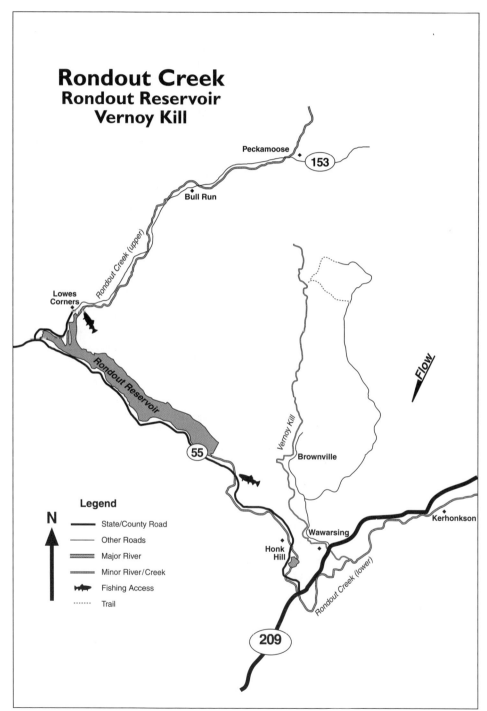

Rondout Creek
Rondout Reservoir
Vernoy Kill

Peckamoose
153

Bull Run

Rondout Creek (upper)

Lowes
Corners

Rondout Reservoir

Flow

55

Vernoy Kill

Brownville

Kerhonkson

Legend

N

— State/County Road
— Other Roads
▓▓ Major River
═ Minor River/Creek
🐟 Fishing Access
······ Trail

Wawarsing

Honk
Hill

Rondout Creek (lower)

209

MONGAUP RIVER

The Mongaup River flows some 20 miles through Sullivan and Orange counties on its way to the Delaware River. There are three reservoirs along the lower Mongaup, and it is the 4-mile stretch from the last of these, Rio Reservoir, to the Delaware that is most desirable as trout water.

The Rio Reservoir generates electricity so there are periodic released of water into the lower Mongaup. This tailwater is rocky and the banks are steep. Access to this gorge is from the top near the dam, from a couple of dead-end streets off of Route 31 on the west side of the river, and from just above Route 97 near the river's mouth. A steep hike is required; cleated wading boots and a staff are recommended.

The reward for this effort is some good pocket water fishing for browns and some occasional brookies and rainbows. This section is not stocked, so the fish are generally wild and can grow to 15 inches. Because the flows are erratic, the Mongaup is best avoided in summer. Fish it in spring and again in fall. A big nymph would be ideal for picking the pockets. The mouth of the Mongaup will also attract Delaware trout when a decent amount of water is coming through.

The Mongaup below Rio Reservoir is subject to the general trout season of April 1 to October 15, but only 3 fish of 12 inches or better may be kept.

BLACK LAKE CREEK

The lower section of this small creek flows out of Cliff Lake, a dammed impoundment, and runs a little over a mile into the Mongaup River above Rio Reservoir (below Swinging Bridge Reservoir). Minimum releases from the dam sustain a good population of wild brookies. This section falls within the Mongaup Wildlife Management Area and access is a hike in from Chapin Road.

ESOPUS CREEK

The Esopus is a classic Catskill stream filled with runs, riffles and pools that carve out a semi-circle through the mountains before emptying into Ashokan Reservoir. Despite its appearance, though, the Esopus has two faces, starting as a freestone stream, then effectively becoming a tailwater where it receives water by underground tunnel from the Schoharie Reservoir (an infusion which may hurt, as well as help, the fishing).

The Esopus begins on Slide Mountain as a small mountain creek. For nearly 10 miles, until just above the village of Big Indian, it is narrow and steep with a rocky bottom. This upper portion of the creek is at its best in spring and fall. The fish here are mostly brown trout, with a few rainbows that make their way upstream along with a few small brookies. This section of the creek is best fished with a 7-foot rod; nothing heavier than a 4-weight is needed. Most of the land in this stretch is pri-

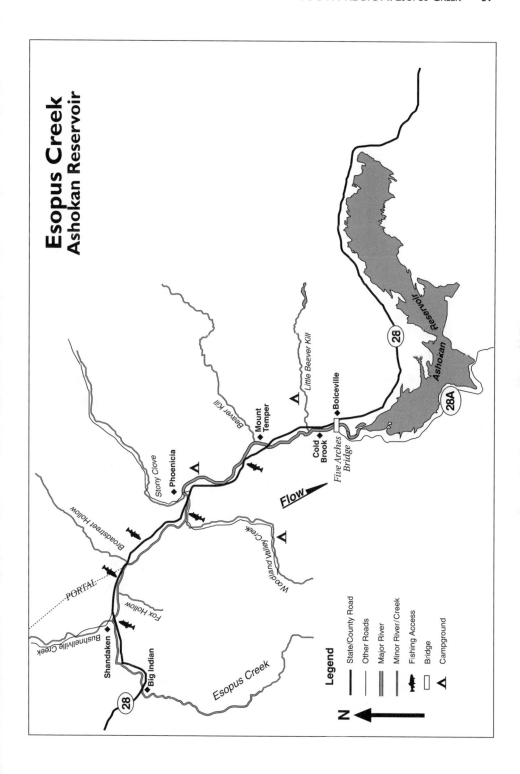

vate, but along Route 47/Oliverea Road, which parallels the stream, there are a few parcels owned by the state and not posted.

Above Big Indian, three tributaries enter and the Esopus becomes wider. For the next 3 miles to the village of Shandaken, it is a medium-sized freestone stream. The fish here are a mix of stocked and some naturally reproducing browns plus naturally reproducing rainbows. Both types of fish can grow quite large, especially the wild rainbows that come out of the lower river or the Ashokan Reservoir to spawn. The rainbows spawn in March, before trout season begins, but can be caught in April as they make their way back downstream.

To catch early season fish, local guide Hank Rope recommends a Gold-Ribbed Hare's Ear Nymph tied with a bead head or an olive Woolly Bugger. The Esopus has traditionally been considered a wet fly stream, and these are still highly recommended. Winged wet flies with Hare's Ear or Cahill bodies work, but the local favorite is a Leadwing Coachman. This imitates the *Isonychia* that is prevalent in the Esopus. The wet flies are fished singly or in groups of two or even three (admittedly a nightmare to cast) and swung downstream through pools and riffles. For dry flies, traditional Catskill ties, supplemented by the Adams, and for faster water the Ausable Wulff, do work. For slower water switch to comparaduns, parachutes or CDC patterns.

The controversial Portal going full blast.

In general, the mayfly hatches follow Art Flick's schedule pretty closely (in fact, Flick studied hatches here early in his career, before moving on to the Schoharie). Along with the *Isonychia*, the Hendricksons of spring and Light Cahills in July are prolific hatches. There are also Blue Winged Olives that hatch throughout summer, getting smaller as the season progresses, and some sporadic caddis. Unlike the Schoharie, though, the Green Drakes are not important on the Esopus.

From Shandaken down to the Ashokan Reservoir the character of the creek is altered dramatically by the inflow of water from the Schoharie Reservoir. The Shandaken Tunnel brings this water 18 miles under the Catskill Mountains and deposits it in the Esopus at the "Portal." This cold reservoir flow traditionally made the last third of the Esopus a virtual tailwater with steady hatches and a very dense population of self-sustaining rainbow trout. Although the rainbows were generally small, guide and instructor Bert Darrow notes that even novice anglers could catch dozens of fish on wet flies here.

However, in recent years many local anglers have said the Portal has actually hurt the fishing. Particularly since the devastating floods of 1996, they have claimed to see a steady decline in the number and size of wild rainbows below the Portal. They also argue that hatches below the Portal have become much sparser. These observers say the Portal releases are not consistently cool enough, and more important, too turbid with silt from the Schoharie Reservoir. By contrast, the DEC says it has not detected a decline in the rainbow population.

Whatever the precise state of the rainbow population, most agree that the fishing for wild rainbows is not as good as it once was in the last dozen miles of the stream. The visiting angler has a few solutions. One is to fish the prime lower section during times of moderate Portal releases. In addition, fish the last stretch at Five Arches Bridge in Boiceville (note that the inlet area right at the reservoir requires a DEP Watershed Permit). Depending on the volume of water being released, the water may be clearer by that point. Turbid water or not, this is an excellent, wide section of the stream, which offers an opportunity to fish Woolly Buggers and Black-Nosed Dace to large fish, along with dries and wets. Another obvious solution is simply to fish above the Portal. In spring and fall, this section fishes well. Except in wet summers, the period from mid-July to mid-September can bring low and warm water here.

Many of the creek's tributaries hold fish and can attract spawning rainbows in spring. Guides Rope and Darrow identify the following as productive feeder streams (heading downstream): Bushnellville Creek, Fox Hollow, Broadstreet Hollow, Woodland Valley Creek (which receives its own small stocking of brown trout in its last mile), Stony Clove/Chichester Creek, the Beaver Kill (no connection to the more famous river) and Cold Brook.

A permanent solution to the problems attributed to the Portal may still be years off. Extended negotiations among New York State, New York City (which operates the Portal) and various conservation groups failed to yield any agreement about the Portal releases. In spring of 2000, several groups, including the Catskill

Mountains Chapter of Trout Unlimited and Theodore Gordon Flyfishers, commenced a lawsuit against New York City, claiming its Portal releases violate the Clean Water Act. The suit asks both that future releases comply with the Act and that alleged past damage be repaired.

In addition to this serious conservation issue, a more temporary but sometimes irksome problem for Esopus anglers is the large number of tubers who float down the creek in summer. A steady flow of the "rubber hatch" can put down the trout and ruin an otherwise perfect day. Fortunately, tubers are mostly out in July and August during midday—a time of year when anglers are well advised to fish in early morning and just before dark on any stream. Also, floating usually happens between Cemetery Pool (just below the Broadstreet Hollow tributary) and the village of Mt. Tremper where the Beaver Kill comes in. If you avoid that stretch during the summer, you'll miss most of the tubers.

Depending on water temperatures, anglers may encounter smallmouth bass from the reservoir in the last mile of the Esopus. The Ashokan has hefty smallmouth—up to 19 inches—which can be fished for in summer.

Stream Facts: Esopus Creek

Season
- April 1 to November 30.

Special Regulations
- None.

Fish
- A mix of wild rainbows (possibly fewer rainbows than in past years) and stocked browns.

River Characteristics
- Freestone stream above Shandaken Tunnel (the Portal). Below Shandaken effectively a tailwater.

River Flows
- Freestone portion best in spring and fall, low most summers, tributaries can provide cooler water. Below Shandaken, Portal releases uneven in height and duration. Releases can be turbid.

Esopus Creek—Major Hatches

INSECT	J	F	M	A	M	J	J	A	S	O	N	D	FLIES
Black\Brown Stone 12-18			▬										Elk Hair Caddis, Stonefly Nymphs
Quill Gordon 12-14				▬									Quill Gordon Dry, Quill Gordon Wet
Blue Quill 16-18				▬									Blue Quill Dry, Pheasant Tail Nymph
Light & Dark Hendrickson 12-14				▬									Light and Dark Hendrickson, Comparadun or Parachute, dark brown Hendrickson Nymph
Blue Winged Olives 16-24					▬▬▬▬▬▬								Comparadun, Parachute, CDC Emerger, Compara-Emerger, Pheasant Tail Nymph
Sulphurs 14-20					▬▬▬								Comparadun, Parachute, CDC Emerger, Compara-Emerger, Pheasant Tail Nymph, Hare's Ear Nymph
March Brown 10-12					▬▬								Comparadun, Extended-Body Dry Flies, Hare's Ear Nymph
Gray Fox 12-14					▬								Comparadun, Extended-Body Dry Flies
Light Cahill/Potomanthus 12-16						▬▬							Cream Variants, Comparaduns, Cahill Wet Fly, Light Hare's Ear Nymph
Slate Drake (Isonychia) 12						▬		▬					Comparadun, Extended-Body Dry Flies, Leadwing Coachman, Zug Bug
Caddis Green, Gray, Tan 14-18						▬▬▬▬▬							Elk Hair Caddis, Lafontaine Deep Pupa and Emergent Sparkle Pupa, Bead-Head Nymphs, Soft Hackle Wets
Trico 22-26						▬▬▬							Trico Spinner, Griffith's Gnat
Ants Hoppers/Crickets Beetles			▬▬▬▬▬▬▬▬										Dubbed Ants, Sinking Ants, Letort Hoppers\Crickets, Foam Beetles
Streamers	▬▬▬▬▬▬▬▬▬▬▬▬												Black-Nosed Dace, Wooly Bugger

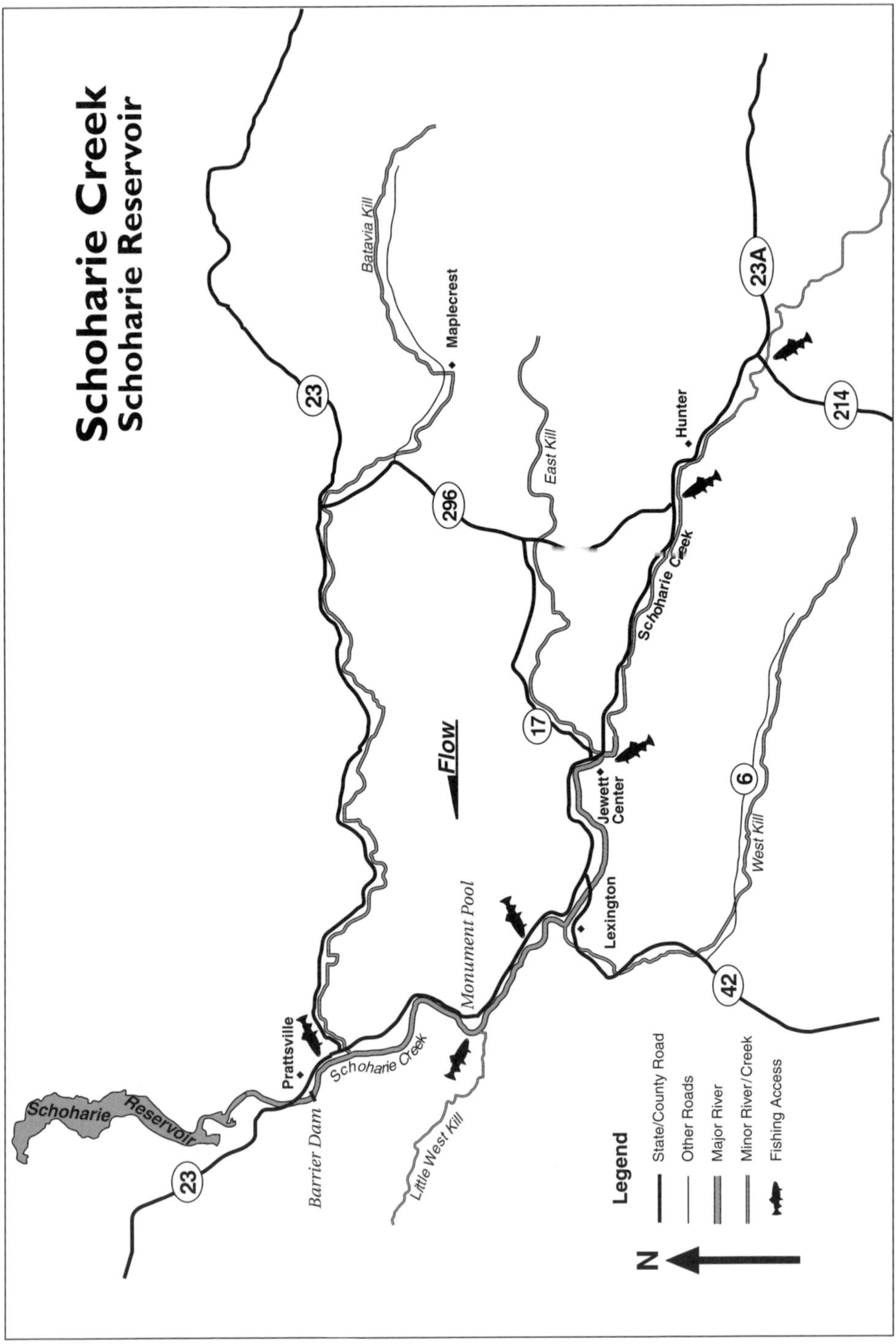

Schoharie Creek
Schoharie Reservoir

© WILDERNESS ADVENTURES PRESS, INC.

Batavia Kill

• Maplecrest

23

296

East Kill

23A

• Hunter

214

Schoharie Creek

Flow

17

Jewett
Center ◆

West Kill

6

Lexington ◆

Monument Pool

42

Prattsville
◆

Schoharie Creek

Schoharie Reservoir

23

Barrier Dam

Little West Kill

Legend

—— State/County Road
—— Other Roads
—— Major River
—— Minor River/Creek
🐟 Fishing Access

N ←

SCHOHARIE CREEK

Much of what we know about hatches comes from Schoharie Creek. Here, in the 1940s, Art Flick closely studied the lifecycle and hatching behavior of mayflies, ultimately setting out the accumulated wisdom in his *Streamside Guide*. The hatches Flick described have held up well on the Schoharie, although the fishing sometimes suffers from low flows. Nevertheless, this is still a good brown trout stream that is less heavily fished than other well-known Catskill rivers.

The Schoharie (pronounced "Skoharee") gathers on the northern slope of Hunter Mountain, the Catskills' second highest peak. It begins its 25-mile trip to Schoharie Reservoir as a steep mountain stream, dropping 500 feet in its first mile. The uppermost section of the stream harbors a small population of wild trout, mostly browns with a handful of rainbows and brookies. The best section for these fish is upstream of the intersection of Route 214 and Route 23A (roughly where Gooseberry Creek enters).

The prime brown trout water in the Schoharie is farther downstream, running roughly 15 miles in Greene County from the village of Hunter to the village of Prattsville just above the reservoir. There are runs and riffles, along with some very deep pools, including those that form where the tributaries enter. The creek runs parallel to Route 23A and there is ample public access and parking on this main stretch.

In particular, the pool where Demming Road/Wright Road crosses the stream downstream (northwest) of Hunter is a good place to start. Farther downstream, the pools below the Maplewood Cemetery provide good holding water, even when the water is low. The mouth of the East Kill tributary is also productive.

Several miles downstream in the village of Lexington, the West Kill enters (near the site of the old West Kill Tavern run by Art Flick) and the river widens. The next 2 or 3 miles offer some of the best fishing on the Schoharie. The pool formed by the West Kill is deep and productive. About two miles down, near where the Little West Kill enters, there is a sharp bend in the creek near a stone tablet dedicated to Art Flick. Known as Monument Pool, the slow moving water here is 3-6 feet deep. Because of the sandy bottom, it is a breeding ground for Green Drakes in late May. These very large flies bring up big fish. The white-bodied spinner stage of the Green Drake, the Coffin Fly, is the imitation to use in this stretch when the flies return to the water to lay their eggs. (One occasional problem with the Schoharie from this point on down is the presence of clay in the water, stemming from erosion on the West Kill.)

The sandy bottom at Monument Pool is an exception on the Schoharie, which is generally quite rocky. This makes felt bottoms essential (with cleats if you have them). A wading staff is a good idea, too. As for tactics, the fish often hold behind the large boulders. A short, careful cast upstream to these holding spots with a high floating fly like a Wulff is known to be effective. Downstream presentations will be trickier, requiring longer casts and careful mending.

*Pools at tributaries like the Little West Kill are good
spots to fish the Schoharie.*

In Prattsville, the Batavia Kill (a decent trout stream in its own right) enters the Schoharie. Just below there is a barrier dam erected in the 1930s at Flick's prompting to keep smallmouth bass from the Schoharie Reservoir out of the upper stream. As a result, the fishery from the dam down to the reservoir is mixed bass and trout. The pool just below the dam is a good one, but heavily pounded with spinning gear.

The trout in the Schoharie are almost exclusively browns. The state puts in more than 15,000 fish each year, including about 1,500 two-year-olds. There is some holdover thanks to the cool water tributaries, and the number of fish that survive doubtless improves during cooler summers,

Given the wealth of mayfly hatches on the Schoharie, it is a good place to match what is hatching, with the appropriate nymph, emerger or dry fly. The stocked fish here are generally not as selective as some of the wild fish elsewhere in the Catskills, and the traditional dry fly patterns—many described by Flick himself—still work. Classic winged wet flies, like Quill Gordons, Hendricksons and Cahills work well when those flies are hatching. Edward Bartholomew, a tier and cane rod maker who has fished the Schoharie for 50 years, rigs three flies: a nymph at the point, a winged wet part way up and a dry fly with palmered hackle to simulate a drowned emerger. He says tangles will be reduced if you tie on the two upper flies with stiff material half hitched at right angles to the main leader. It is not unheard of to get "a double" (two fish on at once) using this setup.

For prospecting, try a Pheasant Tail Nymph. Keep in mind that many of the best hatches here are large in size—make the nymph a 14 or even a 12. Casting conditions are good through most of the Schoharie, because of its width and a relative lack of bankside vegetation. A longer rod, 8 ½ to 9 feet in a 5-weight will work fine.

The upper Schoharie ends at the Schoharie Reservoir, operated by New York City—actually the first of two on the stream. A few miles below is the Blenheim-Gilboa Reservoir, run by the New York State Power Authority. Unfortunately, there are no regular releases from the Schoharie Reservoir into the 2- to 3-mile stretch of the creek between the two reservoirs. However when water comes over the top of the dam in spring, the rainbow trout from Blenheim-Gilboa will run up the temporary flow. Following the devastating floods of 1996, this area was set aside as a preserve. There is some hope that in the future there will be coldwater releases into this portion of the creek, which could become an excellent rainbow fishery.

Below the Blenheim-Gilboa Reservoir the Schoharie heads to its junction with the Mohawk River and is primarily a warmwater fishery. However, the Blenheim-Gilboa does release some water into the lower Schoharie and there are some rainbows here. They are generally found in the first few miles of this lower section, thanks to the releases and a couple of feeder streams. Hatches are similar to the upstream section, with March Browns reported to be particularly dense. This lower section of the Schoharie also holds a good population of hellgrammites.

In addition, there are smallmouth here and walleye in the deep pools that can exceed 20 inches. For the walleye, Bartholomew likes to use an old fashioned Nine-Three streamer, which imitates the local fall fish. A Black-Nosed Dace imitation should also work. The streamer should be retrieved slowly through deep water. Access to this section can be had at Max Schaul State Park, which straddles the stream, and at Boucks Island just downstream of the park.

There are no special regulations for trout on the Schoharie, which means the season ends October 15. Walleye fishing is also subject to the standard season, the first Saturday in May to March 15. For smallmouth (and largemouth) the normal season is applicable: from the third Saturday in June to November 30.

Stream Facts: Schoharie Creek

Season
- Trout: april 1 to October 15.
- Smallmouth: first Saturday in June to November 30.

Special Regulations
- None.

Fish
- Brown trout plus occational rainbows between Schoharie and Blenheim-Gilboa reservoirs. A few rainbows, along with smallmouth and walleye below Blenheim-Gilboa Reservoir.

River Characteristics
- Freestone stream, wide and rocky.

River Flows
- Best in spring and fall, low and warmer most summers.

Schoharie Creek—Major Hatches

INSECT	J	F	M	A	M	J	J	A	S	O	N	D	FLIES
Black\Brown Stone 12-14													Elk Hair Caddis, Stonefly Nymphs
Little Black Caddis (Chimarra) 16-18													Elk Hair Caddis, Goddard Caddis
Quill Gordon 12-14													Quill Gordon Dry, Quill Gordon Wet
Blue Quill													Blue Quill Dry, Pheasant Tail Nymph
Lt. And Dark Hendrickson 12-14													Light and Dark Hendrickson, comparadun or parachute, dark brown Hendrickson Nymph
Blue Winged Olives 16-20													Comparadun, Parachute, CDC Emerger, Compara-Emerger, Pheasant Tail Nymph
Sulphurs 14-20													Comparadun, Parachute, CDC Emerger, Compara-Emerger, Pheasant Tail Nymph
March Brown 10-12													Comparadun, Extended-Body Dry Flies
Gray Fox 12-14													Comparadun, Extended-Body Dry Flies,
Green Drake 10-12													Coffin Fly Spinner, Comparadun, Extended-Body Dry Flies,
Light Cahill/Potomanthus 12-16													Cream Variants, Comparaduns, Cahill Wet Fly Light Hare's Ear Nymph
Slate Drake (Isonychia) 12													Comparadun, Extended-Body Dry Flies, Leadwing Coachman, Zug Bug
Caddis Green, Gray, Tan 14-18													Elk Hair Caddis, Lafontaine Deep Pupa and Emergent Sparkle Pupa, Bead-Head Nymphs, Soft Hackle Wets
Trico 22-26													Trico Spinner, Griffith's Gnat
Ants Hoppers/Crickets Beetles													Dubbed Ants, Sinking Ants, Letort Hoppers\Crickets, Foam Beetles
Streamers													Nine-Three, Black-Nosed Dace

SCHOHARIE CREEK TRIBUTARIES

In addition to providing good pools on the Schoharie, these feeders offer trout fishing of their own. These Schoharie tributaries are all open April 1 to October 15, with 5 fish per day permitted.

East Kill

An important tributary of the Schoharie, the East Kill is also a pretty good trout stream. It flows from Colgate Lake and empties into the Schoharie, all in the town of Jewett. From the mouth of the stream to roughly Beaches Corner the stream is stocked with about 2,400 browns. Above Beaches Corner the stream holds a good population of wild brown trout. Access to this upper stretch is available from occasional unposted sections along Route 22C and Route 78 near the source. Near the mouth, the East Kill can be reached from Route 17.

Batavia Kill

Batavia Kill is another tributary of the Schoharie that has stocked fish in its lower half and some wild fish in the upper reaches. The stream rises in the town of Windham and winds along the border of several towns before meeting the Schoharie just upstream of Plattesville. The first 11 miles above the Schoharie are stocked with about 6,000 browns. Above the village of Maplewood, where Routes 40 and 56 intersect, the stream has a decent population of naturally reproducing trout, about half browns and half brookies.

West Kill

Though known in the past for good brown trout fishing, the West Kill suffers badly from silt and turbidity caused by eroding clay banks. The situation was made worse during the flood of 1996 and is believed by some to be a main culprit for turbidity in Schoharie Creek, the reservoir and ultimately the Portal releases into the Esopus.

The stream is stocked with 700 small browns each year. Route 42 runs parallel to the lower section. Informal access can be found on Route 6 along the upper portion, probably a better bet to avoid the silt.

United States Geological Survey Web Site

Is the river running high this weekend? Is the water warm enough for mayflies to hatch or too hot to fish for trout? Thanks to the United States Geological Survey and the Internet, anglers no longer need to be streamside to get answers to these questions. Real-time flows, and some temperature information, is available for many New York streams on the USGS Web site.

The USGS maintains nearly a thousand monitoring stations on moving waters in New York. While most of these record data for occasional collection in the field by USGS technicians, more than 100 of the sites transmit the information directly to the USGS for posting at the Web site. The Web site is revised throughout the day, with updates every few hours.

The flow information is recorded as "stage" or water height, which is then converted to flow volume, given as cubic feet per second, using a formula derived from the topography of each river bed. Temperature information is provided only for about 15 of the monitoring sites. However, this short list includes major rivers like the Delaware (all three branches), the Beaverkill, the Esopus, the Neversink and the Hudson.

The Web site presents graphs, as well as the numerical data, indicating current flow and temperatures for a seven-day period. More importantly, a historical average of flows for the same week in prior years is marked on the graphs. The historical information is valuable, but the current data is even more useful if you know the river a bit. On many rivers, local tackle shops, lodges or guides will be able to tell you how a river fishes at a given flow.

The USGS has recently revised the format and options for retrieving flow and temperature data. The old page (less flexible but a bit more user friendly) is at the following lengthy web address:

www.dnyalb.er.usgs.gov/rt-cgi/gen_tbl_pg.

(There is also a link to the old format page at the new page.)

The new page, which allows users to screen by county, river system and desired information (among other criteria) is found at www.water.usgs.gov/ny/nwis/rt. Follow the link to "Statewide Streamflow Table." This new page also allows lists of search criteria to be downloaded to a computer for future retrieval.

CATSKILL RESERVOIRS

The Catskill reservoirs are home to very large trout, as well as smallmouth bass, and in some cases walleye. Most of the trout in the reservoirs are browns, though Ashokan Reservoir has a good population of rainbows. The trout run from large to truly enormous—fish of 10 to 15 pounds are not uncommon and trout of 20 pounds are occasionally caught. Cannonsville and Pepacton reservoirs in particular are best known for big, wild browns. However, the trophy fish are generally caught on bait or lures fished deep from boats equipped with portable fish finding equipment.

Flyfishers, by contrast, would be hard pressed to catch the largest reservoir fish. Access is one problem. The size of these lakes, from 1,000 to 8,000 acres, usually necessitates a boat, and a special New York City permit (in addition to the required access permit) is needed to take a boat on a reservoir. The permits are specific to each reservoir and require that the boat be inspected and steam cleaned, then left at the shore between uses. In other words, no canoes, cartop boats or float tubes allowed. (These rules are designed to keep foreign organisms out of the reservoirs.) If you know someone with a boat, by all means bring your fly gear along, but keep in mind that DEP rules currently prohibit professional guiding on the reservoirs, including the use of a guide's boat.

These restrictions make it difficult—but not impossible—for fly anglers to catch fish on the reservoirs. In spring, and briefly again in fall, large trout will cruise in the shallows of the reservoirs. April is generally the best month. Though these are generally not the largest of the reservoir residents, fish in the 4- to 6-pound range are a possibility. At these times, a floating or sink tip line with a streamer pattern to match the resident alewives can take fish. The cruising fish will surface feed on occasion, but that is a hit or miss proposition.

The old saw about 90 percent of the fish being in 10 percent of the water is never more true than in these large lakes. Look for trout in coves and around tributaries, as some small streams run directly into the reservoirs. Be alert, as well, for signs of feeding trout, including the splash of fleeing baitfish.

All the reservoirs are subject to special New York City regulations. The Cannonsville and Pepacton reservoirs are subject to early closings and special catch limits. Cannonsville closes to trout fishing on October 15, and 3 fish of 12 inches or more can be kept. Pepacton closes earlier, on September 30, and catches are limited to 2 fish of 15 inches or more (only one over twentyone inches).

Smallmouth are best fished early or late in the day in summer and early fall. Shallow coves and points are the best spots. Use either poppers and sliders or streamers to imitate the dominant baitfish.

A New York City Reservoir permit is required. The same offices handle the boat permits.

A few of the reservoirs offer some unique opportunities:

Schoharie Reservoir

The Schoharie Reservoir is shallower than most of the others and is therefore primarily a warmwater fishery with good populations of smallmouth and walleye. Local anglers report that when the water is drawn down, submerged walls are exposed, which a careful angler can walk on to get out into the water. There are some trout here—about 2,000 browns are stocked each year—and the fishing for them is open year round.

Neversink Reservoir

The same landlocked salmon discussed in the Neversink section are resident in the reservoir and can be caught here. Generally, smelt patterns imitating the local baitfish would be the way to go. Obviously, a boat will greatly improve your chances. Reports are that a floating ant, even the somewhat unrealistic Chernobyl Ant, will take trout and landlockeds when they are at the surface. Of course, leaving a fly to float in place for minutes on end is not every fly angler's idea of fun. There is also a good smallmouth population here. Trout and landlocked salmon fishing on the Neversink closes October 15; three fish of 12 inches or more may be kept.

Rondout Reservoir

Rondout has a good brown trout population, and an even better lake trout population. Like the browns, the lakers can be found in the shallows early in the season. After that, however, they are deep-running fish, and out of reach of fly gear. Both lake trout and browns can be targeted here from April 1 to November 30. Three fish of each type can be taken, the lakers must be 18 inches, the browns (or other trout) 12 inches.

Ashokan Reservoir

As with its main tributary, the Esopus, the primary trout here are rainbows. Browns are stocked as well, and there are very good populations of walleye and smallmouth. The Ashokan is the largest reservoir, covering more than 8,000 acres, which makes flyfishing from shore here a serious challenge.

Note: As a security precaution, in September 2001 the DEP barred all access to its property in the Catskill watershed (as well as in the Croton System) until further notice. As a result, fishing in the six Catskill reservoirs is prohibited until the ban is lifted. Fishing on all area streams, except those portions on city property adjacent to reservoirs, remains unaffected. For up-to-date information, contact the DEP at 888-337-6921 or visit their website, www.nyc.gov/dep.

Catskills Hub Cities

Deposit

ACCOMODATIONS PRICE KEY
$ Up to 60 dollars per night
$$ 61 to 99 dollars per night
$$$ 100 to 150 per night
$$$$ 51 and up per night

HOTELS/MOTELS
Chestnut Inn At Oquaga Lake, 498 Oquaga Lake Rd, Deposit, NY 13754 /
607-467-2500 / $$-$$$

Deposit Motel, Route 17 Exit 84, Deposit, NY 13754 / 607-467-2998 / $

West Branch Angler and Sportsman's Resort, Route 17, Deposit, NY, 13754 /
607-467-5525 / 3 and 4 person cabins available / Fly shop, guides, boats,
shooting; pool; restaurant / $$-$$$

CAMPGROUNDS/RVs
Forest Hill Park, Ostrander Rd, Windsor, NY 13865 / 607-655-1444
Kellystone Park Campsite, 51 Hawkins Rd, Nineveh, NY 13813 / 607-639-1000

RESTAURANTS
Crane's Restaurant, 68 Second Street, Deposit NY, 13754 / 607-467 2406 / Home
cooked food in 1930s setting

Corner Deli, 9 Pine St, Deposit, NY 13754 / 607-467-3300

Katie's Kafe, 121 Front St, Deposit, NY 13754 / 607-467-3206

FLY SHOPS
West Branch Angler, Route 17, Deposit, NY 13754, 607-467-5525
/ www.westbranchangler.com

Hornbeck's Sport Shop, 8 Pine St, Deposit, NY 13754 / 607-467-4680

AUTO REPAIR
S&S, 148 Second St., Deposit, NY 13754, 607 467-2929

AIRPORT
Sidney Municipal Airport, Lower River St, Sidney, NY 13838 / 607-561-2346

Sullivan County Intl Airport, County Road 183A, White Lake, NY 12786 / 914-
583-6600

HOSPITAL/CLINIC
Barnes-Kasson County Hospital, 400 Turnpike St, Susquehanna, PA 18847 / 570-
853-3135

Sidney Hospital, 43 Pearl St W, Sidney, NY 13838-1300 / 607-561-2100

Hancock NY/Starlight PA

HOTELS/MOTELS

Delaware River Club, Rt 191, Starlight PA, 800-662-9359 / www.mayfly.com /
One and two bedroom suites, pool, playground 2 mile of private frontage on
West Branch / Fly shop / $$

Glenmorangie Lodge, State Road 4033, Box 86, Starlight, PA 18461 / 570-798-
2350 / 100 Single 125 Double / $$

Timberline Motel, Route 17, Hancock, NY / 607-467-2042 / Singles from 35 / $

Wild Rainbow Lodge, Route 97, Hancock NY 13783 / 717-635-5983 / On Main
Stem of Delaware / $$-$$$

CAMPGROUNDS/RVs

Delaware River Club (see address and phone above)

Soaring Eagle Camp Ground, RR 1, Equinunk, PA 18417 / 570-224-4666

RESTAURANTS

La Salette Restaurant, Golf Course Road, Hancock, NY 13783 / 607-637-2505

Country Bake Shoppe & Deli, 38½ E Front Street, Hancock, NY 13783 /
607-637-5200

Circle E Diner, 97 E Front Street, Hancock, NY 13783 / 607-637-9905

FLY SHOPS

Delaware River Club, HC1 Box 1290, Starlight PA 18461 / 800-662-9359 /
www.mayfly.com / Flyfishing school and guiding.

Joe McFadden's Fly & Tackle Shop, Route 97, Box 188, Hankins, NY 12741
/ 845-887-6000

River Essentials, HC1 Box 1025, Starlight, PA 18461 / 570-635-5900 (branches in
Honesdale & Steamtown PA) / www.riveressentials.com / Flyfishing school
and guiding.

Wild Rainbow Outfitters, Route 191, Starlight PA 18461 / 717-635-5983 /
Includes guiding

AUTO REPAIR

Andys Body Shop, Route 97, Hancock, NY 13783 / 607-637-5786

AIRPORT

Sullivan County Intl Airport, County Road 183A, White Lake, NY 12786-9645
/ 845-583-6600

HOSPITAL/CLINIC

Barnes-Kasson County Hospital, 400 Turnpike St, Susquehanna, PA 18847-1638
/ 570-853-3135

Community General Hospital, 5065 State Route 97, Callicoon, NY 12723-5033
/ 845-887-5530

Liberty/Monticello

HOTELS/MOTELS

Best Western Motel, 21 Raceway Road, Monticello, NY   12701 / 845-796-4000 / $$

Days Inn, 25 Sullivan Avenue, Liberty NY 12754 / 914-292-7600 / $$

Mountainview Inn, 913 Shandalee Road, Liberty NY   12758 / 845-439-5070 / restaurant: lunch and dinner / $-$$

CAMPGROUNDS/RVs

All Seasons Campsite, Kiamesha, NY, 12751, 845-794-0133,

Hunter Lake Campground, 177 Hunter Lake Driver, Parksville, NY, 12768 / 845-292-3629

RESTAURANTS

Mountainview Inn, (see above) 9-16

Trout and Bear Restaurant, near exit 96 of Route 17, Liberty, NY 12754 / 845-439-3999

FLY SHOPS

Joe McFadden's Fly Shop, Route 97, Hankins NY / 845-887-6000

AUTO REPAIR

Sam's Service Station, 2 Sullivan Avenue, Liberty , NY / 845-292-7720

Marty's Service Center, 4083 Route 42, Monticello, NY / 845-794-5025

Airport

Sullivan County Intl Airport, County Road 183A, White Lake, NY 12786 / 845-583-6600

HOSPITAL/CLINIC

Community General Hospital, Bushville Road, Harris, NY 12742 / 845-794-3300

Roscoe/Livingston Manor

HOTELS/MOTELS

Rockland House, Rockland Road, Roscoe NY 12776 / 607-498-4240 /
Restaurant for lunch and dinner / $

East Branch Motel and Cabin, Old Route 17, East Branch / 607-363 2959 / $

Downsville Motel, Downsville, NY / 607-363-7575 / $

The Beaverkill Valley Inn, Lew Beach, New York 12753 / 914-439-4844 /
www.beaverkillvalley.com / $$$$

CAMPGROUNDS/RVs

Covered Bridge Campsite, Conklin Hill Road, Livingston Manor, NY 12758 /
914-439-5093

Beaverkill State Campground, Livingston Manor, N.Y., 12758 /845-439-4281 /
800-456-CAMP

Ox-Bow Campsites, East Branch NY / 113 Sites, 80 with water and electricity /
May 1 to October 15 / 607 852-7620

RESTAURANTS

Rockland House, Rockland Road, Roscoe NY 12776 / 607-498-4240

Riverside Cafe, 3882 Old Route 17, Roscoe, NY 12776 / 607-498-5305

The Old Schoolhouse Inn, Upper Main Street, Downsville, NY 13755 /
607-363 7814 / Restored turn of the century schoolhouse

FLY SHOPS

The Beaverkill Angler, Stewart Ave., Roscoe, NY, 12776 / 607-498 5194 /
www.beaverkillangler.com

Catskill Flies, Stewart Ave, Roscoe NY 12776 / 607-498-6146 /
www.catskillflies.com

Fur, Fin and Feather Sport Shop, DeBruce Road, Livingston Manor, NY 12758 /
845-439-4476

Al's Wild Trout, HC 89, Shinhopple NY, 13755, 607-363-7135 /
www.catskill.net/alstrout / On banks of East Branch

TACKLE SHOPS

Al's Sport Shop, Downsville, NY / 607-363-7740 / next to Pepacton Reservoir

AUTO REPAIR

Kirchner Chevrolet, Broad Street and Route 17, Roscoe, NY, 12776 /
845-439-4360

AIRPORT

Sullivan County Intl Airport, County Road 183A, White Lake, NY 12786-9645 /
845-583-6600

HOSPITAL/CLINIC

Community General Hospital, 5065 State Route 97, Callicoon, NY 12763 /
845-887-5530

Margaretville Memorial Hospital Route 28, Margaretville, NY 12455 /
845-586-2631

Phoenicia/Boiceville

HOTELS/MOTELS

Cobblestone Motel, 80 Rte 214, Phoenicia NY 12464 / 845-688-7871 / Near Esopus/Chichester Creek / $

Lodge at Catskill Corners, 5368 Route 28, Mt. Tremper, NY 12457-5318 / 914-688-2828 / $$$$

Phoenicia Hotel, 57 Main Street, Phoenicia NY 12464 / 845-688-7500 / $

CAMPGROUNDS/RVs

Wilson Campground, County Route 40 / 845-679-7020 / Tenting Only

Woodland Valley Campground, Route 28 / 914-688-7647 / Tenting Only

RESTAURANTS

Al's Restaurant, 10 Main St, Phoenicia, NY 12464 / 845-688-5880

Boiceville Inn, Route 28, Boiceville, NY 12412 / 845-657-8500

Brio's, Main Street, Phoenicia NY 12464 / 845-688-5370

FLY SHOPS

Catskill Flies, 309 Mt Cliff Road, Hurley, NY 12747 / 845-434-268

Ampro Sports, 743 Route 28, Kingston, NY 12401 / 845-331-9440 / Flyfishing section

Morne Imports, Main Street, Phoenicia, NY 12464 / 845-688-7738 / Flyfishing section

AUTO REPAIR

Big Indian Service Center, Route 28 (near Route 47), Big Indian, NY 12464 / 845-254-4000

AIRPORT

Kingston-Ulster Airport, Flatbush Rd. Kingston, NY 12401 /845 914-336-8400

HOSPITAL/CLINIC

Margaretville Memorial Hospital, Route 28, Margaretville, NY 12455 / 845-586-2631

Hunter/Prattsville/Windham

HOTELS/MOTELS

Echo Valley Motel, Route 23A, Lexington, NY 12452 /518-989-6511 / $-$$
Four Seasons Inn, 1486 Rte 23, Prattsville NY /518-299-3248 / $-$$
Hideaway Hotel, Huntersfield Rd, Prattsville, NY 12468 /518-299-3616 / $$
Hotel Vienna, Rte 296, Windham, NY   12496 /518-734-5300 / $$
Wedgewood Inn Bed & Breakfast, 353 Main Street, Schoharie, NY 12157 /
    518-295-7663 / $-$$

CAMPGROUNDS/RVS

Wilson Campground, County Route 40 / 845-679-7020 /Tenting Only, / No
    hookups
Woodland Valley Campground, Route 28 / 845-688-7647 /Tenting Only / No
    hookups

RESTAURANTS

Hideaway Hotel Restaurant (see address/phone above) German-American food
Brandywine, Route 23, Windham NY 12496 / 518-734-3838 / Continental cuisine
Prattsville Tavern, Main St, Prattsville, NY 12468 / 518-299-8579

FLY SHOPS

Blue River Anglers, Route 30 Middleburgh, NY / 518-295-8280 /
    www.northeastflyfishing.com

AUTO REPAIR

Hunter Peters Auto Repair, Main Street, Hunter, NY 12442 / 518-263-4713
Jerrys Service Station, Main Street, Hunter, NY 12442 / 518-263-4259

AIRPORT

Kingston-Ulster Airport, Flatbush Rd. Kingston, NY 12401 / 845-336-8400

HOSPITAL/CLINIC

Margaretville Memorial Hospital, Route 28,   Margaretville, NY 12455-3739 /
    845-586-2631

Middletown/Port Jervis

HOTELS/MOTELS
Hampton Inn, 20 Crystal Run Rd, Middletown, NY 10941 / 845-344-3400$$
Super 8 Motel, 563 Rte 211 East, Middletown, NY 10940 / 845-692-5828$$-$$$

CAMPGROUNDS/RVs
Korn's Shawangunk Kill Campground, 60 Meyer Road, Middletown NY 10940 /
   845-386-3433
Oakland Valley Campground, County Route 7, Cuddybackville, NY 12729 /
   845-754-8732
American Valley Campground, Guymard Tpk, Godeffroy NY, 12729 /
   845-754-8388

RESTAURANTS
Casa Mia, Rte 211 East, Middletown, NY 10940 / 845-692-2323
Flo-Jean Restaurant, 2 Pike Street, Port Jervis, NY 12771 / 845-856-6600

TACKLE SHOPS/SPORTING GOODS
Bait Bucket, 313 Route 211 West, Middletown, NY 10940 / 845-344-4774
Curt's Sporting Good, 390 Route 97, Sparrow Bush, NY 12780 / 845-856-5024
O&H Bait Shop, 24 Main Street, Chester, NY 10918 / 845-469-2566
Sam & Mabel's, 138 W Main St., Port Jervis, NY 12771

AUTO REPAIR
Toms Auto Repair, 73 Fowler Street, Port Jervis, NY 12771 / 845-858-2755
Gloster Service Center, 54 Tower Drive, Middletown, NY 10941 / 845-692-5454

AIRPORT
Orange County Airport, 500 Dunn Road, Montgomery, NY 12549 /
   845-457-4925

HOSPITAL/CLINIC
Horton Medical Center, 110 Crystal Run Road, Middletown, NY 10941 /
   845-692-0066
Mercy Community Hospital, 160 E Main Street, Port Jervis, NY 12771 /
   845-856-5351

CATSKILL GUIDES

Each of these guides covers most Catskill streams. They generally offer both wading and float trips. Many offer instruction as well.

Big Indian Guide Service
Hank Rope
P.O. Box 150
Big Indian, NY 12410
845-254-5904

Delaware River Club/Al Caucci Fly Fishing
HC Box 1290
Starlight, PA 18461
570-635-5880; 800-6 MAYFLY
e-mail: aucfbn@1acc.com
www.mayfly.com

Ed's Fly Fishing & Guide Services
Shokan, NY 12481
845-657-6393

Fly Fishing with Bert & Karen
Bert Darrow
1070 Creek Locks Road
Rosendale, NY 12472
845-658-9784

Glenmorangie Lodge
Patrick Schuler
Box 86
Starlight, PA 18461
570-798-2350

Rick Miller Fly Fishing
P.O. Box 277
Roscoe, NY 12776
e-mail: milflyfish@aol.com
845-439-5050

Ray Ottulich
P.O. Box 264
Stone Ridge, NY 12484
e-mail: mgtbltp@aol.com
845-687-0869
members.aol.com/mgwildfish

Outdoor Adventures
Jim Costolnick
HC 1 Box 1835
Starlight, PA 18461
570-635-5935
e-mail: jimmycoz@goplay.com
www.outdooradv-coz.com

Reel Em In Guide Service
Kevin Riley
13 Fall Street
Port Jervis, NY 12771
845-856-3009
e-mail: reelemin@citlink.net
www.geocities.com/Yosemite/Geyser/1822

Gone Fishing Guide Service
Anthony Ritter
P.O. Box 230
Narrowsburg, NY 12764
845-252-3657
www.gonefishing-gs.com

River Essentials
HC1 Box 1025, Starlight, PA 18461
(branches in Honesdale & Steamtown PA)
570-635-5900
www.riveressentials.com

Judd S. Weisberg
Rt 42, Box 177
Lexington, NY 12452
518-989-6583
e-mail: aware@mhonline.net

West Branch Angler & Fishing Resort/Wild Rainbow Outfitters
P. O. Box 102
Deposit, NY 13754

West Branch Angler
607-467-5525
Wild Rainbow Outfitters: 570-635-5983
e-mail: wbangler@tds.net
www.westbranchangler.com

FLYFISHING INSTRUCTION

Esopus School of Fly Fishing
Bob Ewald
261 Van Keuren Ave
Pine Bush, NY 12566
845-361-5069

East of the Catskills

These streams are too far east to truly be considered part of the Catskills, and most anglers skip these waters in favor of the major Catskill streams. Though not up to the level of the best Catskill waters, they are still worth exploring. They can provide some enjoyable fishing—primarily for stocked trout—and a chance to fish without the crowds of more famous rivers.

The Rockland County and eastern Orange County streams are primarily put and take, in part because of their lower elevation. The eastern halves of Ulster and Greene counties do not offer fishing to rival the Esopus or the Schoharie (or their tributaries) in the western portions. However, there are some decent streams here, and in addition to stocking, the upper sections of these waters have some naturally reproducing fish.

ROCKLAND COUNTY AND
EASTERN ORANGE COUNTY

RAMAPO RIVER

The Ramapo River begins with the confluence of several small streams near Schunnemunk Mountain in Orange County. The river heads south through lower Orange County and Rockland County before crossing into New Jersey.

The Ramapo receives a large stocking of nearly 5,000 trout each year. The stocking is done from Arden Valley Road in Orange County down to Sloatsburg in Rockland County, a distance of about 7 miles. The lack of holdover or spawning— due largely to warm water in summer—make this primarily a put and take trout stream, best fished in the spring. Although the Ramapo is open to trout fishing year round, there is currently no fall stocking so winter fishing will not yield many trout. Instead, the open season is designed to allow fishing in mid-March just after the first stocking.

When the trout fishing declines in summer, the warmwater fishing improves on the Ramapo. The Ramapo contains some smallmouth bass, along with rock bass and good-sized panfish. The smallmouth run in the 6- to 11-inch range. They will hit surface dry flies or poppers and sliders. A 5- or 6-weight rod is ideal.

The Ramapo runs along local Route 17 (not the Quickway), for much of its distance (the railroad and Interstate 87/New York Throughway also border the stream). There are a number of informal parking and access spots, some clearly marked as fishing permitted. In some of these spots, you'll need to carefully cross the single lane railroad tracks to get to the stream. There is dedicated DEC access with parking on East Village Road off Route 17 in Tuxedo directly opposite the large gated entrance to Tuxedo Park. There is a deep pool right at the access point that

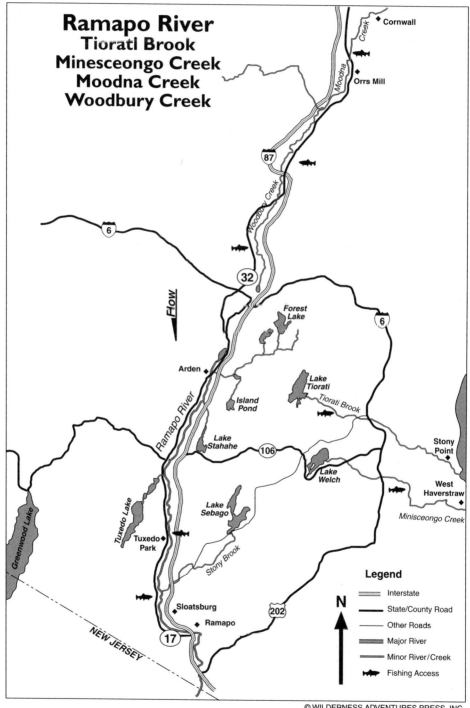

Ramapo River
Tiorati Brook
Minesceongo Creek
Moodna Creek
Woodbury Creek

Cornwall

Orrs Mill

Moodna Creek

87

Woodbury Creek

6

32

Flow

Forest Lake

6

Arden

Lake Tiorati

Tiorati Brook

Island Pond

Stony Point

Lake Stahahe

106

Lake Welch

West Haverstraw

Ramapo River

Tuxedo Lake

Lake Sebago

Minisceongo Creek

Greenwood Lake

Tuxedo Park

Stony Brook

Sloatsburg

202

Ramapo

17

NEW JERSEY

Legend

N

═══	Interstate
▬▬	State/County Road
──	Other Roads
▓▓	Major River
═══	Minor River/Creek
🐟	Fishing Access

© WILDERNESS ADVENTURES PRESS, INC.

holds a good mix of local warmwater fish. A bit further downstream, the Seven Lakes Drive crossing offers access and another good pool.

Just below the Orange/Rockland border, the Stony Brook enters the Ramapo. The first mile or so from the mouth of this tributary receives its own stocking of about 500 small brown trout.

The Ramapo, as noted, is open to trout fishing year round. The standard smallmouth season, from the third Saturday in June through November 30, applies.

TIORATI BROOK

Tiorati Brook, in its lower reaches also called Cedar Pond Brook, is a small gem in Rockland County. Flowing out of Lake Tiorati, near the Appalachian Trail, the stream runs about 7 miles to its confluence with the Hudson River. Except for its upper end at the lake, it is contained entirely within the town of Stony Point.

What makes Tiorati special is that its waters stay colder than many other local streams, thanks in part to a series of underwater springs. This means good holdover of the roughly 500 small brown trout stocked here each year downstream of the Palisades Parkway. More important, Tiorati supports a healthy population of naturally reproducing browns along much of its length. Leslie Supornant, a biologist with the DEC in Region 3, says the wild fish run 9-12 inches, but that fish up to 18 inches can be found here, with the larger fish typically in the lower half of the stream.

The lake itself, and the upper half of the brook, are within Harriman State Park, which has ample parking and trails to the brook. Central Drive runs along the stream for much of its length, providing informal access.

MINESCEONGO CREEK

This creek runs nearly parallel to Tiorati in Rockland County, emerging from a lake in Harriman Park—Lake Welch—and running to the Hudson. It receives a larger stocking of about 1,400 browns each year. However, this stream only has a handful of wild browns—most of the angling is for stocked fish. The stocked portion begins just upstream of the Palisades Parkway and continues for about 1.5 miles below. Access is available from Route 106.

MOODNA CREEK

Moodna Creek runs about five miles from its origins in the town of Cornwall to its mouth at the Hudson River. The stream is heavily stocked, with nearly 2,000 small rainbow trout and about 600 browns, including nearly 300 two-year-olds. Like most other area streams that are at low elevations, there is little reproduction or holdover here, so it is essentially a put and take trout fishery. The stocked waters run about 2.5 miles from the Route 32 Bridge to the junction with Woodbury Creek. Access can be had from Route 32.

Woodbury Creek

Woodbury Creek, which meets Moodna Creek in the town of Cornwall, does have some natural reproduction of brown trout. Woodbury also receives a relatively modest stocking of about 1,100 brown trout over a five-mile stretch from Pine Hill Road to the confluence with Moodna Creek. Informal access is available from Route 32, which parallels the stream for much of its run.

Shawungunk Kill

Located along the northwestern border of Orange County, this stream is primarily a put-and-take trout stream. It is heavily stocked with rainbows—nearly 5,000 per year—along with a few hundred brown trout. Stocking is done primarily in a roughly 18-mile stretch where the stream forms the border first with Sullivan County and then Ulster County. Access is from a series of roads crossing Route 7, which runs roughly parallel to the stream.

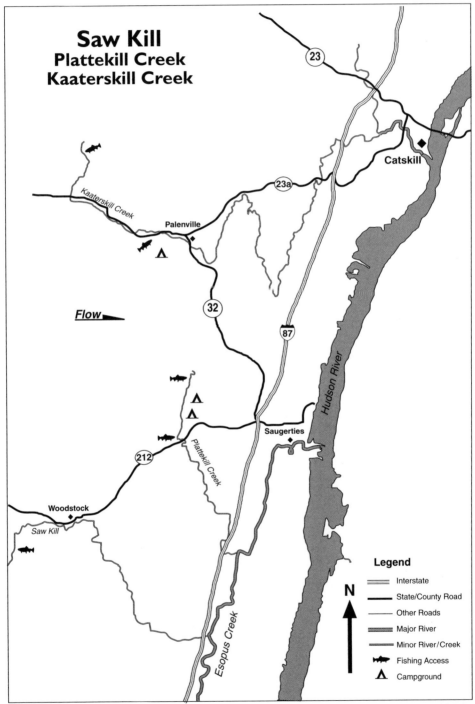

Saw Kill
Plattekill Creek
Kaaterskill Creek

Kaaterskill Creek

Palenville

Catskill

Flow

Palenville

23

23a

32

87

Hudson River

212

Plattekill Creek

Saugerties

Woodstock

Saw Kill

Esopus Creek

Legend

≡	Interstate
▬	State/County Road
—	Other Roads
▓	Major River
▬	Minor River/Creek
🐟	Fishing Access
Λ	Campground

N

© WILDERNESS ADVENTURES PRESS, INC.

EASTERN ULSTER AND GREENE COUNTIES

SAW KILL

This stream in Ulster County has steep rocky headwaters that come down from the Catskills. This upper portion holds stocked and naturally reproducing brown trout and wild brook trout. The stocking is entirely of browns—about 2,000 each year—and the stocked stretch runs about 8 miles from Route 212 to the Woodstock town line. As with the nearby Plattekill, the stream is most easily accessed at road crossings.

PLATTEKILL CREEK

The Plattekill is in northern Ulster County. It runs about 6 miles in the town of Saugerties, where it joins the lower end of the Esopus. The stream is heavily stocked with brown trout, about 3,300 in all. Roughly an 8-mile stretch is stocked from where Route 212 crosses to the end of the town of Woodstock. The upper stretch of the stream is cold enough for fish to holdover, and there is some natural reproduction of browns and some rainbows, too. This rocky and steep upper section is the best portion to fish. Below, as the stream approaches the lower Esopus near the Hudson, some trout are stocked by local clubs with DEC approval, but it is strictly put and take.

ROCKLAND LAKE

This 250-acre lake in the town of Clarkstown is stocked with small tiger muskellunge by the state. Though tiger muskie stocking in this part of the state has not always been successful, this lake has proved to be one of the exceptions. Tiger muskie fishing with a fly would involve a heavy weight outfit and some big streamer flies like Deceivers and Dahlberg Divers. A bite tippet is essential. The lake can be reached from Rockland Lake State Park. Tiger muskellunge can be targeted from the first Saturday in May through March 15.

GREENWOOD LAKE

Greenwood Lake, a large body of water that straddles the New York-New Jersey border, is also stocked with tiger muskellunge by the state. These fish, which do not reproduce, have held over reasonably well here. In addition, non-hybrid muskellunge are privately stocked here with the state's approval and have taken well. Either is a trophy for the flyrodder. Given the lake's size of about 1,000 acres, it is best fished from a boat. There are several private liveries on the lake.

As a border water, Greenwood Lake is subject to special regulations. Both muskellunge and tiger muskellunge are open to fishing here all year, with a limit of one fish a day of 36 inches or more. A New York license is valid on the New Jersey half of the lake, but only when fishing from a boat.

KAATERSKILL CREEK

This creek runs about 18 miles, from North Mountain in Ulster County into Greene County. The Greene County section of the stream, in the town of Catskill, gets a stocking of about 2,200 small brown trout. This section has marginal temperatures and is primarily put and take. Upstream of Palenville, roughly where Routes 32A and 23A intersect, there is a healthy wild trout population, with more rainbows than browns. This roughly five-mile section from the source to Palenville is the place to seek out, and can be reached from Route 23A, which it parallels. The normal trout season of April 1 to October 15 applies.

East of the Catskills—Major Hatches

INSECT	J	F	M	A	M	J	J	A	S	O	N	D	FLIES
Black\Brown Stone 12-14				■									Black Elk Hair Caddis, Dark Hare's Ear Nymph
Lt. And Dark Hendrickson 12-14				■	■								Comparadun, Down Wing Deer Hair Emergers, Rusty Spinners
Caddis Green, Gray, Tan 14-20				■	■	■	■	■					Elk Hair Caddis, Bead-Head Cream or Green Pupa
Blue Winged Olives 16-20				■	■					■			Comparaduns, CDC Emergers, Pheasant Tail Nymph
March Brown 10					■								Extended-Body Mayfly or Camparadun
Sulphurs 12-16					■	■							Comparadun, CDC Emerger, Pheasant Tail Nymph, Hare's Ear Nymphs
Light Cahill\ Potomanthus 12-16						■	■						Cream Variant, Comparaduns, Light Hare's Ear Nymph
Trico 22-26						■	■	■	■				Tricc Spinner, Griffith's Gnat
Slate Drake (Isonychia) 12						■		■	■				Extended-Body Mayfly or Camparadun, Zug Bug
Ants, Hoppers\Crickets, Beetles							■	■	■	■			Dubbed Ants, Letort Crickets\Hoppers, Foam Beetles

East of Catskills Hub Cities

Newburgh/New Paltz/Kingston/Sloatsburg

HOTELS/MOTELS

Holiday Inn, 90 State Rte 17-K, Newburgh NY   12550 / 845-564-9020 /
Restaurant 6:30a.m. to 10p.m. / $$

Days Inn 601 Main Street, New Paltz, NY   12561 / 845-883-7373 / $

Mohonk Moutain House, 1000 Mountain Rest Road, New Paltz 12561 /
845-255-1000 / S200-475, D 315-500 / Full resort including lake fishing /
Restaurant 8a.m.-8p.mm / $$$$

Holiday Inn, 503 Washington Street, Kingston, NY   12401 / 845-338-0400 / Pool
/ Restaurant open 6am-10pm / $$$

Super 8 Motel, 487 Washington Street, Kingston, NY   12401 / 845-338-3078 / 24
hour restaurant adjacent / $

CAMPGROUNDS/RVS

Hidden Valley Lake Campground, County Route 26, Kingston, NY /
845-338-4616

Yogi Bear Resort, Albany Post Road, off US 44, Gardiner NY, 12525 /
845-255-5193

KOA Newburgh, Freetown Highway, off Highway 32, Newburgh NY 12550 /
845-564-2836

RESTAURANTS

Banta's Steak and Stein, 935 Union Ave., Newburgh, NY 12553 / 845-564-7678
$8-24

Locust Tree Inn, 215 Huegenot St., New Paltz, NY   12561 / 914-255-0120 / $8-18

Anna's Luncheonette, 491 Broadway, Newburgh, NY 12550 / 845-562-1220

FLY SHOPS/TACKLE SHOPS

Fishermans Corner, 183 Foxhall Avenue, Kingston, NY 12401 / 845-340-1358

Ampro Sports, 743 State Route 28, Kingston, NY 12401 / 845-331-9440 /
Flyfishing section

River Basin Sport Shop, 66 W Bridge St, Catskill, NY 12414 / 518-943-2111 /
Flyfishing section)

Davis Sport Shop, Route 17, Sloatsburg, NY 10974 / 845-753-2198 /
www.davissport.com

AUTO REPAIR

J&H Service Center, 138 Cornell St., Kingston, NY / 845-339-5435

AIRPORT

Orange County Airport, 500 Dunn Road, Montgomery, NY   12549 /
845-457-4925

Kingston-Ulster Airport,1161 Flatbush Rd, Kingston, NY 1240 / 845-336-8402

HOSPITAL/CLINIC

Kingston Hospital, 396 Broadway,   Kingston, NY 12401 / 845-331-3131

Greater Hudson Valley Health, 600 Stony Brook Ct, Newburgh, NY 12550 /
845-568-6050

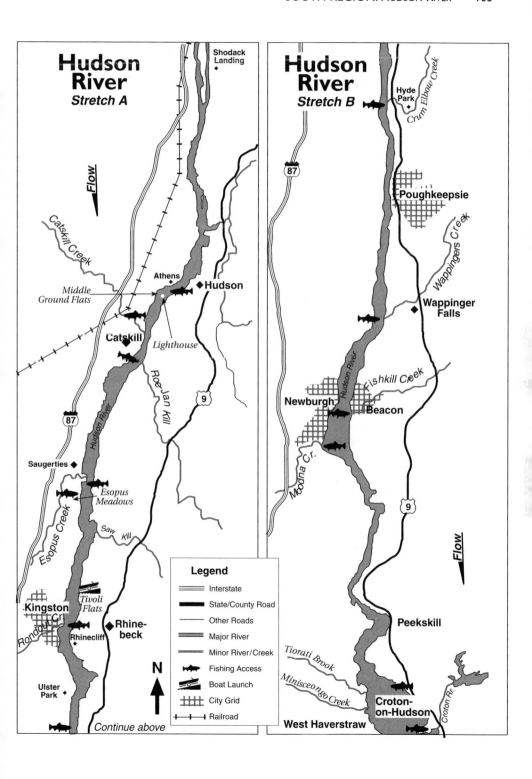

LOWER HUDSON RIVER

The lower Hudson River is not a river at all, but an estuary. Throughout this section of the state, the Hudson's freshwater mixes with sea water and the river's flow and height are affected by the tides.

Not unlike the big reservoirs, the Hudson River offers excellent fishing that is largely impractical for fly anglers. The river holds resident largemouth and smallmouth bass. More significantly, both spawning and smaller resident stripers are found in the river.

Stripers

The most sought after fish here are large stripers—with females up to 50 pounds—that migrate into the river to spawn. Indeed, the improved health of the Hudson is a major factor in the larger population of stripers on the East Coast. Estimates are that roughly half of all East Coast stripers spawn here or in the Chesapeake. Stripers spawn in the Hudson from April to June, but the middle of May is generally the peak time to fish for spawners.

Although large stripers are routinely taken on the fly in marine waters, it is difficult to catch the largest stripers on flies in the Hudson. The enormous size of the river—up to three miles wide in some places—makes a boat nearly essential. Spawning stripers generally suspend in deep water and are difficult to reach and entice with fly gear. Though many fishing boats ply these waters, you'll see few if any fly anglers on them. Instead, most of the big stripers are taken on baits like chunks of bunker or live eels, or on trolled lures.

A flyfisher's best chance of catching stripers in the Hudson is targeting smaller fish in or near the tributaries. Small, feeding stripers will chase baitfish, usually herring, up these creeks. The lower end of these streams and the flats right at the mouths are the places to go. Spring is a good time, but the feeding of the small, resident stripers is not dependant on spawning and continues into the summer.

The period just after high tide is generally considered the best time to fish outside feeder creeks. It pays to check a tide chart for the river, which you'll find in some of the local fishing publications. A tide chart is also available online at www.boatingonthehudson.com/tides.htm. As the high tide recedes, stripers will often wait for baitfish being flushed out of the stream mouths. Fishkill Creek, Wappinger Creek, the Roe-Jan Kill, the Esopus, Moodna Creek, Rondout Creek and Catskill Creek are all reputed to offer good opportunities to catch small stripers. The area outside the Croton River in Westchester County offers ready access from Croton Point County Park.

On occasion, the feeding stripers will go directly into the tidal sections at the mouth of the streams; this usually happens at high tide. The tidal sections of the feeder streams are up to the first dam or until the stream bed rises to an elevation a few feet above the sea level of the Hudson itself. For stripers in the stream, try the railroad trestle at the bottom of Catskill Creek at the village of Catskill in Greene County, or any of the other streams listed above.

In addition to the streams, there are a number of marshy backwaters on the Hudson, and the same striper feeding takes place at the mouth of these inlets when the water rushes back into the main river as the tide recedes. These exit points are commonly referred to as "blow holes."

Whether at a stream or blow hole, a transition line between the outgoing waters and the main river water, the "mud line," is often visible and is an important holding area. Locals recommend stripping a streamer through these seams—typically a Deceiver or Clouser to imitate the large herring population. Nick Rash, who lives near the river and fishes for stripers by boat and on foot uses three different flies. One is a simple, unweighted baitfish imitation tied with Puglisi Sea Fibers, with a white underwing and chartreuse, yellow or blue on top. A Clouser Minnow in chartreuse and white and a black Deceiver round out his recommendations. For a bit more action on the Clousers, Tim Brune and his colleagues at Orvis New York recommend using white marabou for the underwing.

Small stripers can be caught in the Hudson on fly gear.

You will not catch the largest Hudson stripers at streams and "blow holes," but fish of 15 to 18 inches are still fun. You don't need the heaviest saltwater gear, either; an 8- or 9-weight outfit will work fine. Don't rely on trout reels, though, a larger reel with plenty of backing and a good drag is important. One of the long sink tips in 200- or 300-grain weight will help cast and get the fly down.

Even though the biggest spawning females are extremely difficult to catch with fly gear, some larger males can be caught in the main river. These fish—up to 12 pounds or more—are found in the shallow water, generally facing into the current on falling or rising tides. Again, a streamer imitation should be stripped along seams of moving water. Use larger flies, 5-6 inches in length. The fly rod should be larger as well; Rash goes as big as a 12-weight and a 400-grain sinking tip. Good shallow flats on the Hudson include the Esopus Meadows, about 3 miles below the mouth of the Esopus along the western shore, Tivoli Flats north of Rhinebeck on the eastern shore (which has a public boat ramp nearby) and the Middle Ground Flats near the Hudson Athens Lighthouse at Catskill, New York.

The open season for striped bass in the Hudson and its tributaries is March 16 to November 30. One fish per day of 18 inches or longer may be kept.

Smallmouth

There is a fairly good smallmouth population in the Lower Hudson, but again they are not easy to reach with fly gear. Generally, smallmouth (and largemouth) territory is north of Cornwall, across from the Putnam County-Dutchess County border. Ideally, a fly angler should be in a boat, looking for the kind of structure that smallmouth like: points of land, piers, bridge abutments and rocks. Streamers imitating small baitfish or poppers and sliders on the surface in lower light and early or late in the season should work.

Lower Hudson River Hub Cities

See the following hub cities in the indicated regions:

Westchester-Putnam Region: White Plains
Dutchess-Columbia Region: Poughkeepsie, Hudson
Rockland-Orange-Ulster Region: Newburgh/New Paltz/Kingston

NEW YORK CITY FLY SHOPS

Even though there is no trout fishing in New York City, there are a couple of excellent fly shops that offer a full selection of rods, reels and lines, waders and outerwear, tying materials and flies. They can also give advice on flyfishing throughout New York State and around the world.

Orvis New York, 522 Fifth Avenue (corner of 44th Street), New York, NY 10036 / 212-697-3133 / National Orvis Web site: www.orvis.com / Full service flyfishing and tying, guiding and instruction available

Urban Angler, 118 East 25th Street (3rd Floor), New York, NY 10010 / 212-979-7600 / e-mail: urbang@panix.com / www.urban-angler.com / Full service flyfishing and tying, guiding and instruction available

The following tackle and sporting goods shops have flyfishing equipment and related products:

Angler's World, 16 East 53rd Street, New York, NY 10022; 212-755-3400

Capitol Fishing Tackle, 218 West 23rd Street (7-8th Avenues), New York, NY 10011; 212-929-6132; e-mail: capcony@aol.com; www.captialfishing.com; flyfishing section

Paragon Sports, 867 Broadway (18th Street), New York, NY 10003; 212 255-8036; www.paragonsports.com; flyfishing section

Shooters and Anglers Sports Shop, 61-05 Grand Avenue, Maspeth (Queens), NY; 718-894-6122; flyfishing section

T. J. Huntsmon & Co., 36 West 44th Street, New York, NY 10036; 212-302-2463

Westchester and Putnam Counties

These two counties north of New York City contain some remarkably good fishing, primarily in the tailwaters of the Croton Reservoir System. The impoundments here were the original upstate reservoir system for New York City, to which they still provide water (though now dwarfed in volume by the Catskill reservoirs). Fishing in any of the connecting streams (and the reservoirs) requires a New York City Watershed Permit. The fishing is worth the trouble, and the permit is free. The two counties also offer some freestone streams, which are not up to the best tailwater fishing, but can be fun in spring and fall.

WEST BRANCH CROTON RIVER

The West Branch of the Croton River, or just the "West Branch" to local anglers, is really three separate rivers. The first is a .5-mile long section running from Boyd's Corner Reservoir to the West Branch Reservoir in the town of Kent in Putnam County. The second is considerably longer, a 2.5-mile section that runs from West Branch Reservoir to Croton Falls Reservoir and contains only wild brown trout. The final section, probably the premier flyfishing water in the Croton Watershed, runs about a mile from the Croton Falls Reservoir into the East Branch of the Croton River.

Boyd's Corner Reservoir to West Branch Reservoir

This upper section of the West Branch is just half a mile long and receives less angling pressure than the other portions. In the past, problems with fish survival, perhaps due to low oxygen or high temperature, reduced the quality of this fishery. Recent surveys, though, reveal a much improved fish population.

About 750 brown trout are stocked here each year, including 100 two-year-old fish. Because this section, unlike the next two, is open until October 15, anglers may encounter spawning browns from the West Branch Reservoir in the last few weeks of the season. Access is available at pulloffs along Route 301/Kent Cliffs Road in the town of Kent. As with all the connecting rivers in the Croton System, a New York City Watershed Permit is required.

West Branch Reservoir to Croton Falls Reservoir

It is astonishing to find an entirely wild trout population this close to New York City, but this section of the West Branch boasts just that. Brown trout thrive in this 2.5-mile section of the river without any stocking, thanks to cool, clear water and plentiful insect life.

The water here is rarely more than 25 feet wide and well canopied by trees. A mostly rocky bottom with a few silty sections provides structure for the trout and

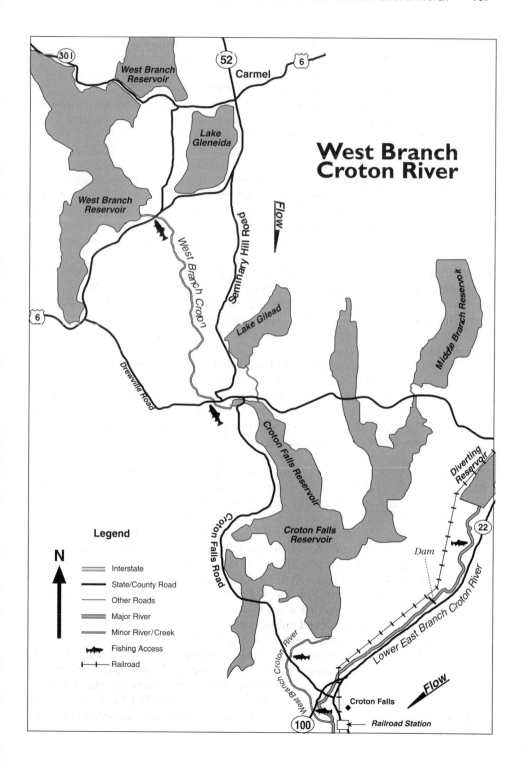

insects. The abundance of overhead cover and the cold water source from the West Branch Reservoir ensure that the West Branch runs cold and clear. The releases from the reservoir are fairly steady and the stream runs at a moderate pace, although its does pick up speed at its lower end near Croton Falls.

Because of its good water and structure, the West Branch provides a wealth of hatches. In fact virtually the entire spectrum of mayflies are represented here, including Blue Winged Olives, large Light Cahills and prolific Sulphur hatches. Caddis are also plentiful in this section, particularly near the source, probably because in their aquatic form, they eat plankton from the reservoir water.

It pays to match the hatch here. If fish are rising but reluctant to take your dry fly offering, they may be feeding just under the surface. If so, pick a nymph or emerger form of the fly you see hatching. For more generic fishing, try a Pheasant Tail or Hare's Ear Nymph, with a bead head if you are in one of the deep pools. An Elk Hair Caddis, fished both dead drift and skittered, is reported to be a good dry fly searching pattern here as well.

Seining reveals a healthy number of scuds, particularly at the upper end of the river, which is not surprising in a tailwater. The scuds run about size 14, in a very light tan, almost white. Many anglers neglect this opportunity, but if nothing is hatching, a scud pattern would be a good choice for a searching pattern. The abundant vegetation also means a steady diet of ants and beetles, along with a few crickets and hoppers.

The wild browns are plentiful but tend to run small, about 6 to 10 inches, although fish up to 12-15 inches are caught. The Croton Falls Reservoir probably has the best brown trout population of the Croton reservoirs and some of these fish ascend this section of the West Branch each fall to spawn. But, like spawners everywhere, they are difficult to catch. In addition, the opportunity to catch spawning fish here is limited by the earlier closing date of September 30.

Even though they run small, the resident fish in this river can humble anglers. They can be extremely skittish, darting away as you get close enough to cast. Stealth is at a premium here; be patient and wade slowly and carefully along the rocky bottom. Keep to the edges of the stream or up on the banks wherever possible. Stay low when approaching the pocket-sized pools and small cuts where the fish hold. You may need to cast to several pools up or downstream to have a chance. The wariness of the fish and the smallness of the stream make the occasional deep pools especially valuable. In particular, there are several large and deep pools in the last 0.3 miles of the river, upstream of the Drewville Road crossing. On a good day, you can take a number of fish from each of these pools. Use a smaller rod, nothing more than a 7- or 7½-foot, 4- to 5-weight.

There are only two unmarked public access points to the river. But with a little hiking, an angler can cover the entire river and have virtual solitude. The upper access is where Route 6 crosses the stream, within sight of the West Branch Reservoir outlet. The downstream access is at Drewville Road where it intersects Cherry Hill and Seminary Hill roads in the town of Carmel. As noted, the fishing in this section of the river closes two weeks early, on September 30. If they insist, anglers can keep 5 fish of 9 inches or better. A New York City Reservoir Permit is required.

Croton Falls Reservoir to Croton River East Branch

This southernmost stretch of the West Branch is the most popular with fly anglers, and for good reason: it is probably the best trout stream in the area. Although only one mile long, it is home to a healthy mix of stocked and wild brown trout.

This section of the West Branch runs deep and cool from the Croton Falls Reservoir and ends where it joins the lower section of the East Branch of the Croton River. The best section of the river is roughly the first half-mile between the reservoir outlet and Route 100, at the village of Croton Falls in the Westchester County town of Somers. There are a number of pools (as deep as 10 feet) interrupted by faster flats that still hold trout among large rocks. Below Route 100 the stream is straight with less structure, but will still produce fish.

The insect life here is abundant and has the full run of mayflies, including a prolific Sulphur hatch, various caddis and a few stoneflies. There are also plenty of midges, in light and dark adult colors, anywhere from size 20-26. If you see them around, you can try your luck with a small dry, or for something more visible a midge cluster such as a Griffith's Gnat. Even if no midges are hatching, a tiny pupa imitation would make a useful searching pattern here, alone or as a dropper.

Thought this stretch is wider and a bit less overgrown than other area streams, terrestrials can still work, too. The deeper pools and runs here make a beadhead nymph with a soft hackle collar an effective searching fly. As with the middle section of the West Branch, tan scuds, as well as some in light olive, are plentiful here, so don't limit yourself to nymph and pupa imitations when fishing deep. Because of its greater width, a longer rod can be used here—up to 8 ½ feet in a 4- or 5-weight.

If you fish on a weekday and approach the stream on Route 100/202, you'll see dozens of cars parked on the road. Don't be discouraged; most of these are overflow parking from the Croton Falls railroad station nearby. On the other hand, some of them will almost certainly be fishing as the quality fishing in this stream is no secret. You can expect company, especially on weekends and during the evenings. Fish off-hours whenever possible. The proximity of the Croton Falls railroad station makes this area accessible to anglers without cars.

The fish here are browns and the state stocks nearly 1,400 nine-inch fish each year, half in the spring and the other half in the fall. There is both substantial natural reproduction and good holdover. The biggest of the fish here, up to 20 inches, are wild.

The increased population of stream-born fish here is a good example of how a wise management policy can make a good stream even better. The DEC limited this segment of the West Branch to catch and release, artificials only, in late 1994. Among their goals was to increase the number of large fish and the percentage of wild fish. Studies done in 1996 and again in 1998 indicate the plan is working. The percentage of trout over 12 inches has gone from about 3 percent before the catch and release policy to about 15 percent. Equally significant, by 1998 wild fish represented more than half the total trout by weight, from less than one-third before the special regulations. This stream closes on September 30. As already mentioned, it is catch and release only. The NYC Watershed Permit is required.

An angler on the Croton Falls Outlet, near Route 100.

Stream Facts: West Branch Croton River

Seasons
- Boyd's Corner Reservoir Outlet: April 1 to October 15.
- West Branch Reservoir Outlet (West Branch Reservoir to Croton Falls Reservoir) and Croton Falls Outlet section (from Croton Falls Reservoir to confluence with Croton River East Branch) April 1- September 30.

Special Regulations
- Boyd's Corner Reservoir Outlet: None.
- West Branch Reservoir Outlet: Trout taken must exceed 9 inches.
- Croton Falls Reservoir Outlet: Catch and release only.
- NYC Reservoir Permit required in all sections.

Fish
- Mostly brown trout.
- Boyd's Corner Reservoir Outlet: Mostly stocked fish.
- West Branch Reservoir Outlet: Predominantly wild fish.
- Croton Falls Reservoir Outlet: Mostly stocked fish, substantial percentage of wild fish.

River Characteristics
- All three sections are tailwaters, Croton Falls outlet deeper, other two shallower and rockier.

River Flows
- Relatively steady all year.

West Branch Croton—Major Hatches

INSECT	J	F	M	A	M	J	J	A	S	O	N	D	FLIES
Little Black Caddis (Chimarra) 16-18				■									Elk Hair Caddis, Goddard Caddis, BeadHead Pupa
Blue Winged Olives 16-20				■									Comparadun, Parachute, CDC Emerger, Compara-Emerger, Pheasant Tail Nymph
Light & Dark Hendrickson 12-14					■								Light and Dark Hendrickson, Comparadun or Parachute, dark brown Hendrickson Nymph, Rusty Spinner
Sulphurs 14-20					■								Comparadun, Parachute, CDC Emerger, Compara-Emerger, Pheasant Tail Nymph, Hare's Ear Nymph
Caddis Green, Gray, Tan 14-18						■		■					Elk Hair Caddis, Lafontaine Deep Pupa and Emergent Sparkle Pupa, Bead-Head Nymph, Soft Hackle Wet
Light Cahill 14-16						■							Cream Variant, Comparadun, Cahill Wet Fly, Light Hare's Ear Nymph
Trico 22-26								■					Trico Spinner, Griffith's Gnat, Trico Nymph
Ants Hoppers/Crickets Beetles										■			Dubbed Ant, Sinking Ant, Letort Hopper\Cricket, Foam Beetle
Midges	■												Brassie, Midge Pupa, Midge Dry, Griffith's Gnat
Scuds, Tan & Olive 12-14	■												Scud Pattern

New York City Water Supply Fishing Permit

A free New York City fishing permit (in addition to a valid New York State fishing license) is required to fish the streams connecting one reservoir with another in the Croton Watershed (including the Amawalk Outlet of the Muscoot, both sections of the East Branch Croton and the three sections of the West Branch Croton). The same permit is required for all 14 reservoirs of the Croton System (Amawalk, Bog Brook, Cross River, Croton Falls, Diverting, East Branch, Lake Gilead, Lake Gleneida, Kensico, Middle Branch, Muscoot, New Croton, Titicus and West Branch). This permit also allows fishing in the New York City reservoirs in the Catskills (Schoharie, Rondout, Ashokan, Pepacton, Cannonsville and Neversink), though it is not required for the watershed streams in the Catskills.

To obtain a watershed fishing permit, you must bring a current New York State fishing license to any of the following offices of the New York City Department of Environmental Protection:

New York City
- 1250 Broadway, 8th Floor, Manhattan; 212-643-2172

Croton Watershed Area
- 1 Belden Road, Carmel NY 10512; 845-232-1309

Catskill Area
- Route 42 (off Rte 55), Grahamsville, NY 12740; 845-985-2524
- Route 30, Downsville, NY 13755; 607-363-7009 (near Pepacton Reservoir)
- Three miles from Route 28 (at Ashokan Reservoir), Shokan, NY 12481; 845-657-2663

Permits are issued from March 15 to October 15. Hours for the New York City office are 9 a.m. to 4 p.m., Monday to Friday. The four upstate offices are open 8:30 a.m. to 4 p.m. Tuesday to Saturday. It is worth calling ahead to check the dates and office hours, current license requirements and office locations (the New York City office has moved at least once in recent years).

The permit must be carried with you while fishing in the applicable waters. Permits currently issued are good for five years. Older permits issued without expiration dates, marked "Valid Until Revoked," remain in effect.

Boat Permits

Boat permits are available only for individual reservoirs. To protect the water supply, the boat in question must be inspected, steam cleaned and left at the shore of the reservoir in question between uses. (This means if you want permits for three reservoirs, you'll need three different boats.) Only rowboats between 11 and 14 feet long are allowed. Boats brought to and from the water, including cartop boats, canoes and float tubes, are prohibited. For information about obtaining a boat permit, contact any of the offices listed above.

Note: As a security precaution, in September 2001 the DEP closed all public access to its property in the Croton Watershed (as well as in the Catskills) until further notice. As a result, fishing in the 14 Croton System reservoirs, and in those streams which connect one reservoir to another, is prohibited until the ban is lifted.

Croton System streams now off-limits include all three sections of the Croton West Branch, both sections of the Croton East Branch, the lower Muscoot River (Amawalk Outlet), the Cross River Outlet and the Titicus Outlet. Area streams not on city property remain open, including the Cross River (Inlet), the last segment of the Croton River (below New Croton Reservoir), Stone Hill River\Beaver Dam Brook and the Mianus River.

At the time publication, the DEP has not announced when, or if, the waters will be reopened—though it is considered unlikely to occur before spring of 2002. For up-to-date information, contact the DEP at 888-337-6921 or visit their website, www.nyc.gov/dep.

The East Branch, looking upstream from Brady's Bend.

EAST BRANCH CROTON RIVER

The East Branch of the Croton River comes in two parts, the well known and heavily fished upper section running from East Branch Reservoir to Diverting Reservoir and the less popular lower portion which flows from Diverting Reservoir to its junction with the Croton Falls Outlet section of the West Branch (which shortly thereafter enter Muscoot Reservoir).

The Upper East Branch Croton River
(East Branch Reservoir to Diverting Reservoir)

This 2.5-mile stretch, which falls entirely within the Putnam County town of Carmel, is by far the more productive and popular of the two sections. Along with the Croton Falls Outlet section of the West Branch and the Amawalk Outlet of the Muscoot River, it is part of triumvirate of top local trout streams.

The upper East Branch has good water and a series of pools, flats and riffles along its length. However, deep pools are more prevalent here than in other area streams. The steady flows, along with good insect life, provide excellent holdover for the trout. The fish are a mix of browns and rainbows, with about 1,400 and 600 respectively stocked each year.

Although there is only modest natural reproduction, the holdover trout grow to impressive size; a 15- to 18-inch trout is not uncommon. Every local angler seems to know that this section of the East Branch yielded a 10-pound trout back in 1983. That trophy fish was caught on a streamer, which work here even though the stream, like most of these tailwaters, doesn't hold many baitfish. And, unlike some of the smaller streams in the region, the large, deep pools of the East Branch make this a good place to fish a minnow imitation. Traditional bucktail patterns like a Black-Nosed Dace or Grey Ghost will work. With the depth of the pools, a Clouser Minnow would also be a good choice. There are some crayfish here, so a brown and orange Woolly Bugger or a more precise crayfish imitation should also take fish.

The East Branch's best pools include the bend pool near Route 22 known as Brady's Bend and the Trestle Pool behind Brewster Town Hall. These, and most of the best water, are in the upper two-thirds of the section; most of the anglers are here, too. Good fishing can also be found in the lower third of the stream, below Route 6/Main Street in Brewster. This section is mostly a deep, wide run that is capable of holding good fish and can be easily accessed from a wooded area along it northern bank.

Wading is generally easy due to the mud and gravel bottom, although some rocks, downed trees and overhanging brush are found in a few of the narrower sections. Because of its width, you can use a somewhat longer rod here than on many other area streams, but anything more than 8 to 8½ feet is probably unnecessary and may create problems in a few of the tighter sections.

The Upper East Branch supports a wide variety of insect life. Among mayflies, the Hendricksons, Sulphurs and Blue Winged Olives are most plentiful. The rela-

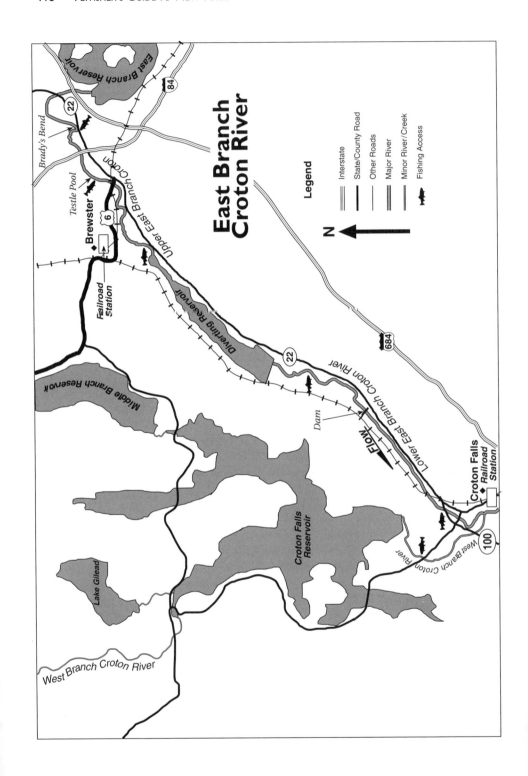

tively slow flow in the best pools puts a premium on drag free floats and accurate imitations. As elsewhere in demanding conditions, low-riding duns and emergers (or floating nymphs) are more likely to draw strikes than traditional, heavily hackled dry flies.

Caddis are also abundant here. Look for the small black caddis—size 16 or so with a charcoal body and white wings—early in the season. Later, olive and tan caddis in 14 and 16 are prevalent. As with mayfly hatches, consider switching from dries to a caddis emerger, such as the simple X-Caddis or the more elaborate Lafontaine Emergent Sparkle Pupa. A Lafontaine Sparkle Pupa fished deep will also take fish when caddis start to emerge.

Although the East Branch is a bit wider than some other area streams, bankside brush and trees provide a steady diet of ants and beetles to the fish. Don't be afraid to try a beetle during a hatch; they are a big enough meal to draw attention. Also, remember that terrestrials often sink below the surface so try a drowned ant fished alone or as a trailer.

Plentiful midges anywhere from size 22 on down, in both light and dark colors, are also an important food source here. When nothing is happening, a small larva imitation with a crystal flash or thread body and small dubbed head tied in colors to match the natural can be used alone or as a dropper.

The midges are particularly important here because it is one of the very few area streams that is open year round. While wading in cold weather can be rough, you are more likely, but by no means certain, to have a piece of the stream to yourself. Slowly drifted nymphs, either large ones to attract fish or very small ones to imitate the midge larva in the stream, may get these slow moving winter trout to bite. On a bright, warm winter day, a midge hatch may bring trout to the surface. If so, try to match the size and color of the hatch (usually cream, gray or black). Anglers report that a Griffith's Gnat or other midge cluster imitation is very effective during the winter hatches, and much easier to see on the water.

Access for cars is plentiful along Route 22. Even better, the East Branch Croton offers New York City residents the rare opportunity to fish by train.

This section of the East Branch is limited to one fish of 14 inches or better. As already noted, there is no closed season. A NYC Watershed Permit is required.

Lower East Branch Croton River (Diverting Reservoir to West Branch)

The lower section of the East Branch runs about 2.5 miles from Diverting Reservoir to its junction with the West Branch. From there it is only another half-mile to the Muscoot Reservoir. The stream here straddles Westchester and Putnam counties and has a dam about halfway to the junction. Some of the sections, particularly below the dam, are gorge-like and very fast with big rocks. Upstream flows can be slow and somewhat swampy.

The section is accessible from various pullovers on Route 22. Though not nearly as popular as the upper section, it is heavily stocked. Roughly 1,000 small brown trout and 2,000 small rainbows are put in each year, along with 500 two-year-old trout that average around 14 inches. Holdover here is generally good, and in 2000 a DEC survey found fingerling brown trout in the lower East Branch, confirming that there is some natural reproduction here as well.

Insect life is similar to the upper section of the East Branch. The Watershed Permit is required and the standard trout season regulations apply: April 1 to October 15, five fish per day permitted.

This East Branch brown took a beetle imitation.

Stream Facts: East Branch Croton River

Seasons
- East Branch Reservoir Outlet: Year round.
- Diverting Reservoir Outlet: April 1 to October 15.

Special Regulations
- East Branch Outlet: One trout per day, 14 inches or more.
- Diverting Reservoir Outlet: None.

Fish
- Mix of stocked brown and rainbow trout; some natural reproduction of browns.

River Characteristics
- Tailwater; EastBranch Outlet is slower with more deep pools. Diverting Reservoir Outlet is slow in upper half above dam, faster and rockier in lower portion.

River Flows
- Generally even; Diverting Reservoir Outlet occasionally subject to high water.

East Branch Croton—Major Hatches

INSECT	J	F	M	A	M	J	J	A	S	O	N	D	FLIES
Little Black Caddis (Chimarra) 16-18													Elk Hair Caddis, Goddard Caddis, Bead-Head Pupa
Blue Winged Olives 16-20													Comparadun, Parachute, CDC Emerger, Compara-Emerger, Pheasant Tail Nymph
Light & Dark Hendrickson 12-14													Light and Dark Hendrickson, Comparadun or Parachute, dark brown Hendrickson Nymph, Rusty Spinner
Sulphurs 14-20													Comparadun, Parachute, CDC Emerger, Compara-Emerger, Pheasant Tail Nymph, Hare's Ear Nymph
Caddis Green, Gray, Tan 14-18													Elk Hair Caddis, Lafontaine Deep Pupa and Emergent Sparkle Pupa, Bead-Head Nymph, Soft Hackle Wet
Light Cahill 14-16													Cream Variant, Comparadun, Cahill Wet Fly, Light Hare's Ear Nymph
Trico 22-26													Trico Spinner, Griffith's Gnat, Trico Nymph
Ants Hoppers/Crickets Beetles													Dubbed Ant, Sinking Ant, Letort Hopper\Cricket, Foam Beetle
Midges													Brassie, Midge Pupa, Midge Dry, Griffith's Gnat
Scuds, Tan & Olive 12-14													Scud Pattern

Fishing by Train

New York City anglers without cars shouldn't be discouraged—two of the best Croton streams can be reached by train. Metro North Railroad can take you from Grand Central Terminal to within walking distance of the Croton Falls Outlet of the West Branch and the East Branch Reservoir Outlet of the East Branch.

For the West Branch, take the Metro North Harlem Line to Croton Falls Station. The trip from Grand Central is a little over an hour and costs around ten dollars one way during peak hours (about eight dollars off-peak). From the station, it is about .25 miles to the Route 100 Access, about another .5 miles to the Croton Falls Road Access, which is worth the extra walk.

The next stop on the same train is Brewster Station, which lets you out close to the East Branch of the Croton River. Figure an extra five minutes travel time; the cost is the same. From the Brewster Station (not Brewster North station), it's about a .5-mile walk down hill to the Trestle Pool (which is behind the town hall on your left) and a long flat stretch just across the road. You can also walk upstream along Route 22, watching out for passing cars, to Brady's Bend about a mile farther (past the used car dealership). In fact, with careful attention to the schedules and one extra fare, it is possible to fish both the East and West branches of the Croton in a single trip.

Plan to travel light when fishing by train. Bring a shoulder bag or backpack to carry your gear to the stream and to carry clothes, shoes, food and water from one place to another on the water. Although these areas are generally safe, it's best to keep your bag nearby while wading. Bring some food and water with you to the stream; both stations have restaurants and delis nearby.

Train schedule and fare information for the Metro North Railroad is available at 212-532-4900 or online at www.mta.nyc.ny.us/mnr/.

CROTON RIVER

Below the New Croton Reservoir the mingled waters of the East and West branches emerge as the Croton River and run three miles to the Hudson. Though not nearly as good fishing as the two branches, there are some trout here.

Though access is tight, roughly the first half-mile of this section is accessible from Croton Gorge County Park just after the reservoir. Because the reservoir water is saved for New York City, the releases fluctuate considerably; plan to fish the Croton primarily in spring. About 900 rainbow trout and 200 browns are stocked in the first mile or so of the Croton River.

As discussed in the section on the Hudson River, small resident striped bass can be caught in or just outside of the mouth of the Croton, and smallmouth can be found at the lower end as well. Though the mouth is difficult to reach on foot, the area just outside it can be fished from Croton Point Park.

No Watershed Permit is required for this last segment of the Croton, which is open for trout from April 1 to October 15.

RESERVOIRS OF THE CROTON WATERSHED

These reservoirs provide some excellent fishing, but are not very conducive to angling with a fly rod. Very large trout swim in most of the Croton reservoirs, along with smallmouth and panfish. In addition, two of the lakes have lake trout and one has recently been stocked with tiger muskellunge.

The Croton reservoirs were built around the turn of the century to provide water to New York City. There are 14 impoundments in all. They are considerably smaller than the reservoirs upstate; most of these reservoirs have a surface area under 1,000 acres, while the upstate reservoirs are as much as 8 times that size. However, shore fishing—especially with a fly rod—is still difficult. It is best done in spring, and again in fall, when trout are most likely to cruise the shallows.

As with the Catskill reservoirs, most of the angling is done by spin fishermen. The best chance of taking fish here is from a boat, which gives ready access to all areas of the shoreline and the deep water as well. However, the same restrictions on boating apply here as upstate: a special permit good only for a single reservoir is required and the designated boat must remain at the shore of the reservoir when not being used. Unfortunately, float tubes are not permitted.

In addition to fishing at the right times of year, it is important to pick the right spots. Points of land, drop-offs and inlets are obvious choices, as are coves where trout may chase baitfish. Bear in mind that reservoir trout will cruise, not hold in place. This means the angler will also have to move and stay alert for signs of feeding fish.

Mayfly hatches are generally not important to reservoir anglers, but caddis larva and pupa can be effective. As with the upstate reservoirs, alewives are plentiful in the Croton impoundments, so a streamer with a light belly and grayish

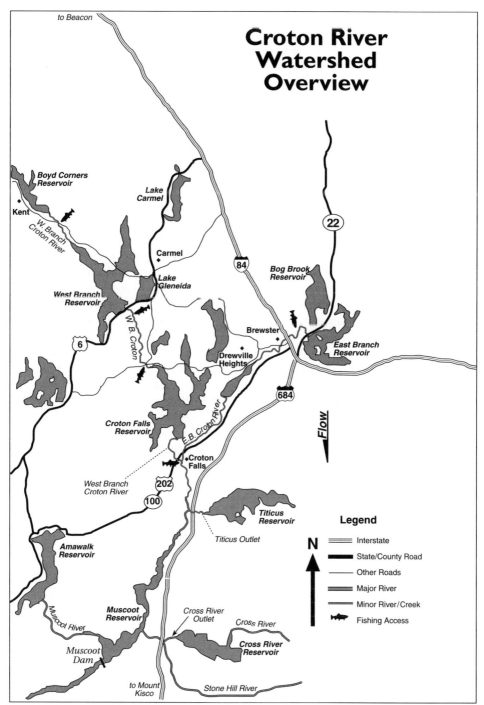

Croton River
Watershed
Overview

© WILDERNESS ADVENTURES PRESS, INC.

blue/black back would be an effective imitation. For a more generic imitation, try a black Zonker with a silver underside (be sure to use the traditional curved belly on the fly to imitate the alewife's wide profile).

The trout are almost exclusively browns, though Gilead, Gleneida and West Branch have modest populations of rainbows. The best brown trout population is considered to be in Croton Falls Reservoir. The trout fisheries said to be least worth visiting are Diverting, East Branch, Muscoot and New Croton reservoirs. All of the New York City reservoirs in Westchester and Putnam counties are open to trout fishing year round. Generally, three trout of 12 inches or better may be taken, although Croton Falls Reservoir is limited to a single fish of 18 inches or more.

Smallmouth bass are found in most of the waters; Bog Brook and Cross River reservoirs have the best smallmouth populatioins. The smallmouth are not subject to special regulations in the reservoirs, which means the season is the third Saturday in June to November 30. Five smallmouth of 12 inches or better are allowed.

In addition to the trout, two reservoirs have lake trout. Kensico has been stocked with lake trout off and on since the late 1980s, and Gleneida has had lake trout stocked for more than 10 years. There is probably some natural reproduction in both, but Kensico is thought to have the better lake trout fishery.

Like other trout, lakers can be taken in the shallows early in the season. If there are any doubts that large lakers can be voracious shoreline feeders, a catch in Kensico a few years ago should put it to rest. An angler who kept a 24-inch lake trout from the reservoir cleaned the fish and discovered bones inside that did not appear to be from a fish; a state biologist confirmed the bones came from a red squirrel. Like other trout, lakers may be fished for in the reservoirs all year, but the limit is three fish of at least 21 inches.

Alone among the Croton reservoirs, New Croton Reservoir is stocked with small tiger muskellunge, a program begun in 1998. While these hybrid fish are sterile, they are expected to grow, and should begin reaching legal size of 30 inches in the next few years. Legal season for tiger muskies is from the first Saturday in May through the following March 15.

CROSS RIVER OUTLET

Running from the large Cross River Reservoir about .4-miles to Muscoot Reservoir in the town of Bedford, this outlet is sometimes considered a continuation of the Cross River. However, unlike that freestone section, this tailwater has a cool steady flow and good holdover potential.

The Cross River Outlet is rarely more than 30 feet wide, but it is fairly deep in some spots. The flow is slow and steady, providing good holding water for stocked browns and rainbows, which include about 100 two-year-old browns. When the Muscoot Reservoir is full, as it often is, the mouth of the river at Route 22 is wide, slow and weedy. However, the water here remains cool and fishable. Although a spawning trout in fall is still a possibility here, the Muscoot Reservoir does not have as large a trout population as some other area reservoirs, so the odds are especially slim.

Access to the Cross River Outlet is primarily from Route 35, which runs the length of the stream. There is informal parking along the road, but you'll need to hike through some tall grass to get to the river. Although it has less easy access than some other area rivers, the stream is heavily fished, especially in spring.

Improved holdover makes the stream worth a try throughout the season. Ronald Pierce, Senior Aquatic Biologist for the DEC Region 3 notes that in the past, this water's shortage of dissolved oxygen hampered the ability of trout to holdover. However, an aerating pipe has now been installed at the dam outlet, and stocked trout should live and grow year round.

Hatches are consistent with other tailwaters in the area. There are no special regulations on the Cross River Outlet, which closes October 15, but a NYC Watershed Permit is mandatory.

CROSS RIVER INLET

In a region rich with tailwaters, the Cross River flows into, not out of, a reservoir. As a result, it is a more typical small stream, with some pleasant fishing but with a risk of low flows and warm water in the middle of summer.

The Cross River runs about three miles to the Cross River Reservoir. (The Cross River is sometimes referred to as the Waccabuc.) Virtually all of that length falls within the town of Pound Ridge in Ward Pound Ridge Reservation, a county park, which provides a protected environment for the river. The river can be reached along its entire length within the park. There are two main parking spots, one about halfway up, the other directly beside the stream at Kimberly Bridge not far from the source. This is a good spot to fish, with a deep bridge pool, but anglers can expect to compete with each other and with people using the nearby picnic grounds. The water just below the bridge is shallower with many rocks, apparently added for structure, providing good holding lies. The river is only about 10-15 feet wide, except in a few places where it widens and slows down. From a sign about 50 yards

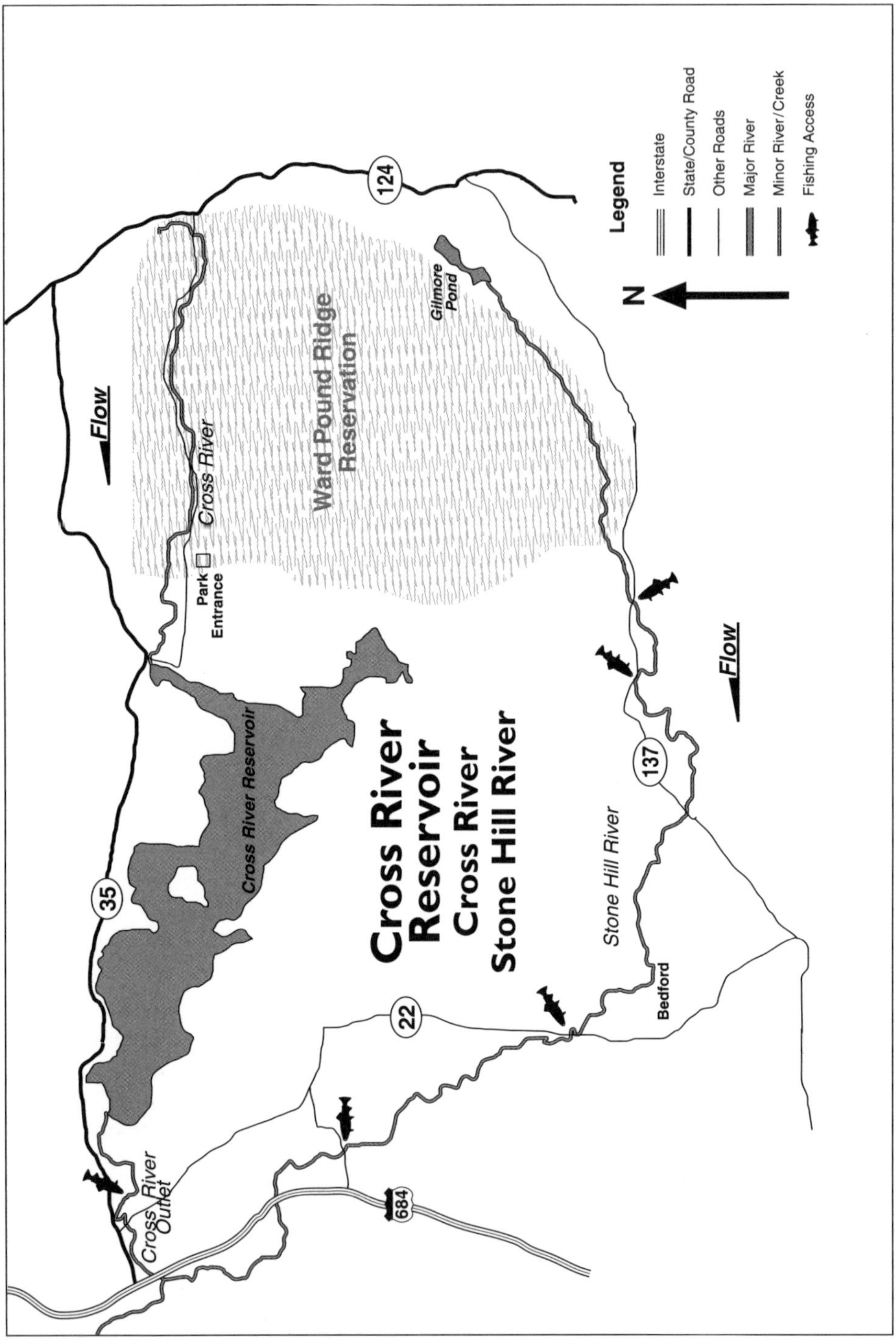

Cross River
Reservoir
Cross River
Stone Hill River

Ward Pound Ridge
Reservation

Cross River

Cross River Reservoir

Stone Hill River

Gilmore
Pond

Park
Entrance

Cross River
Outlet

Bedford

Flow

Flow

N

124

35

22

137

684

Legend

Interstate
State/County Road
Other Roads
Major River
Minor River/Creek
Fishing Access

© WILDERNESS ADVENTURES PRESS, INC.

below Kimberly Bridge to well into the lower end of the river, this is catch and release only.

About 500 browns are stocked annually. There are wild brookies occasionally caught, particularly near the headwaters. There is probably some natural reproduction of browns as well. The hatches here are similar to other local streams, from the early season mayflies to Blue Winged Olives in the fall. Because it is not a tailwater, the hatches will be earlier and can be seriously affected by rainfall or drought. Typically, the Hendricksons hatch here is a good one. The river is also full of crayfish; some locals come here just to catch them. Although the tight conditions and relatively shallow water make streamer fishing difficult, a crayfish imitation crawled along the rocky portions should attract fish.

Trout are not the only fish in these waters; there are panfish, including sunfish, here as well. This can make prospecting for trout difficult, especially with a nymph: you set the hook only to discover a small sunny on the line. The mixed species put a premium on sight fishing, which is often possible in this small water. You may also see an occasional smallmouth bass holding in one of the pools. These fish come up from the Cross River Reservoir, which contains a healthy smallmouth population. If you do spot a smallmouth, try tempting it with a large nymph or a crayfish imitation. (Remember that you cannot legally target black bass—smallmouths or largemouths—until the third Saturday in June.)

As already mentioned, this water can run extremely low in summer, with only a trickle in the riffles and low water even in the best pools. This will cause the remaining fish to pod up in the small pools or at springs. While the abundance of trout may be tempting, they really should be left alone at this time.

The normal trout regulations are in effect on the Cross River. Because it does not originate in a New York City reservoir, anglers here do not need a watershed permit (except right at the reservoir, which is marked accordingly). Ward Pound Ridge Reservation is open year round with a per-car fee of $3.50 for county residents, and $7 for non-residents. There are also tent sites and cabins available in the park (see White Plains in the Hub Cities for more information).

TITICUS OUTLET

A small stream running only a half-mile from Titicus Reservoir to New Croton Reservoir in the town of North Salem, Titicus Outlet nevertheless provides some good fishing for stocked browns and rainbows.

The state stocks about 150 nine-inch brown trout and 400 rainbows of the same size each year. There is good holdover of both types of stocked trout. Rainbows are not known to reproduce in this stream (or other area streams), but there is probably a bit of natural reproduction of browns.

The hatches are similar to those for the other streams in the Croton system. The large, size 14 Sulphur that hatches in afternoon and evening in early to mid-June is especially dense. During such heavy hatches the Route 22 Bridge Pool will be full of rising fish, and even the recently stocked fish can become picky. Dry flies will often be ignored in such conditions; instead try emergers, which the fish seem to key on, or a Sparkle Dun (a comparadun tied with an antron shuck instead of split tails). In addition to the standard mayflies and caddis, scuds are present here and the overhanging brush on such a small stream should provide a steady diet of terrestrials to the trout.

The primary entrance is where Route 22 crosses the stream at Titicus River Road near the stream's mouth at Muscoot Reservoir. You can also try to get in farther up on Titicus Road, but the stream is so short, you can wade the entire length from the lower end. The river is no more than 15 feet wide, except where it widens toward its mouth; a small rod is essential. Much of it is rocky, providing good lies for the fish but requiring careful wading. The Titicus Outlet closes on the standard October 15 date and there is a five fish limit. A NYC Watershed Permit is required.

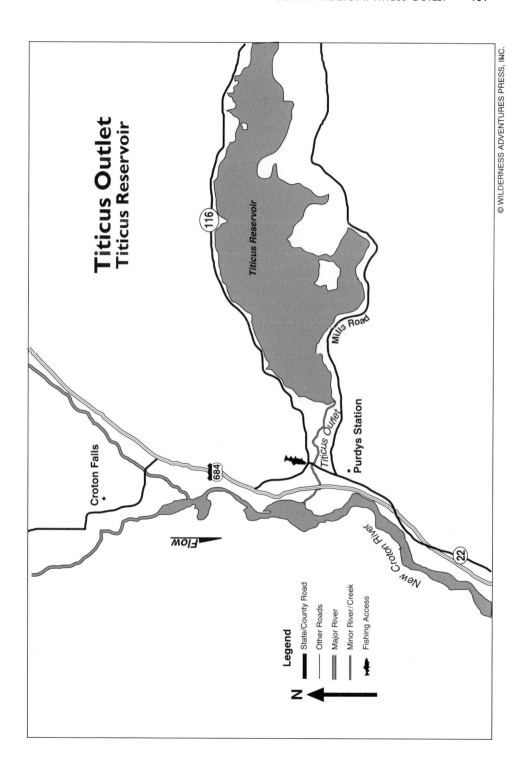

Titicus Outlet
Titicus Reservoir

MUSCOOT RIVER

Amawalk Inlet and Amawalk Outlet

The Muscoot River is composed of two different segments, a freestone stream that runs into the Amawalk Reservoir, sometimes called the Amawalk Inlet, and the far more renowned tailwater that runs from the Amawalk Reservoir to the Muscoot Reservoir, generally known as the Amawalk Outlet (or just the Amawalk).

Amawalk Inlet

This section rises in the Putnam County town of Carmel by the confluence of outlets from Secor Lake and Kirk Lake. From that junction it runs approximately 2.8 miles until it joins the Amawalk Reservoir across the border in Westchester County. This stream is fairly narrow and brushy, and because it is a freestone stream it is subject to low water in summer. Still, the DEC stocks nearly 1,000 small brown trout here each year.

Access is available at the extreme lower end right next to the reservoir on Route 202, roughly in the middle at Route 6 near Mahopac Avenue, or farther up at Route 6N. There are no special regulations for this stream, and a Watershed Permit is not required.

Amawalk Outlet

This is the far more popular section of the Muscoot River. Good holdover of stocked browns in the upper third of the stream and good natural reproduction in the lower two-thirds makes this one of the best trout streams in the Croton Watershed. (In May of 2001, a chlorine spill killed mosst of the trout in the Amawalk Outlet. It does not appeat the habitat was permanently damaged. Additional trout have been stocked and the population should recover over time.)

This tailwater runs about 2.75 miles from the Amawalk Reservoir to the Muscoot Reservoir. About three-quarters of a mile downstream a pond forms at an old dam. This upper section gets about 1,000 small trout each year. The dam is generally impassable to fish, at least heading upstream, although a few of the stocked fish may make it downstream. This upper section is small and rocky until Mohansic Creek enters about .3 miles down from the dam. From here to the pond, the river becomes deeper and slower.

The trout population below the dam is almost exclusively wild. The population is healthy, with fish of 12 inches available and 20 inches not unknown. The rare, but wonderful small wild brook trout is occasionally taken in the lower section as well. This lower end of the stream is mostly rocky with riffles and decent-sized pools. Stealth is important. Take your time and don't expect to wade the entire stream in one visit.

Hatches are healthy, with Hendricksons in late April and early May and Sulphurs two or three weeks later. As is true everywhere, and especially with wild fish, low floating imitations like parachutes, comparaduns and thorax ties work

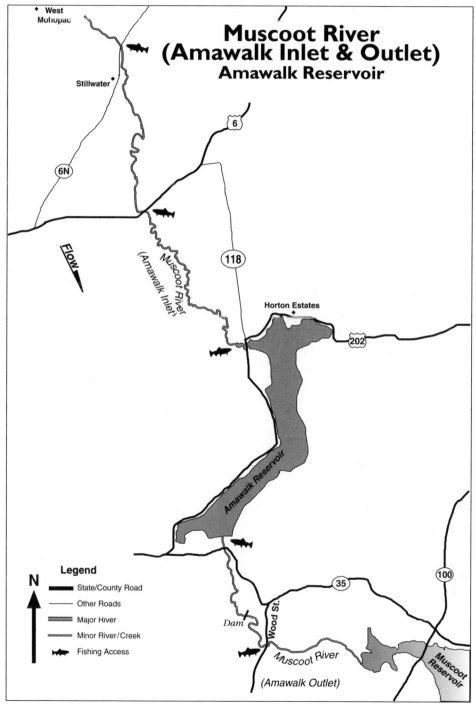

Muscoot River
(Amawalk Inlet & Outlet)
Amawalk Reservoir

West Mohopac

Stillwater

Horton Estates

Flow

Muscoot River
(Amawalk Inlet)

Amawalk Reservoir

Dam

Wood St.

Muscoot River

(Amawalk Outlet)

Muscoot Reservoir

Legend

N

State/County Road
Other Roads
Major River
Minor River/Creek
Fishing Access

© WILDERNESS ADVENTURES PRESS, INC.

better than old-fashioned Catskill dries. Similarly, the vulnerable emerger stage of a hatch is often more attractive to trout than a dry.

There are two access points on the Amawalk Outlet: from Route 35 at its source and about 1.5 miles downstream at Wood Street. This means that to cover the stream, you should plan to wade or walk along the bank. Generally, New York City owns the banks of all the streams that connect the various reservoirs.

The entire Amawalk Outlet, both above and below the dam, is limited to artificial lures and three trout of 12 inches or more. The stream closes early, on September 30. As with other reservoir connections, a NYC Watershed Permit is required.

The rocky waters of the Amawalk Outlet.

Stream Facts: Muscoot River

Seasons
- Amawalk Inlet: April 1 to October 15.
- Amawalk Outlet: April 1 to September 30.

Special Regulations
- Amawalk Inlet: None.
- Amawalk Outlet: Artificial lures only, 3 fish, 12 inches or better.

Fish
- Amawalk Inlet: Stocked brown trout.
- Amawalk Outlet: Stocked browns above dam, mostly wild browns below.

River Characteristics
- Inlet: Freestone stream, runs, riffles and pools.
- Outlet: Tailwater, rocky with riffles and pools.

River Flows
- Inlet: Best in spring and fall; somewhat lower and considerably warmer most summers.
- Outlet: Steady flows from reservoir.

Muscoot River/Amawalk Outlet—Major Hatches

INSECT	J	F	M	A	M	J	J	A	S	O	N	D	FLIES
Little Black Caddis 16-18													Elk Hair Caddis, Goddard Caddis, Bead-Head Pupa
Blue Winged Olives 16-20													Comparadun, Parachute, CDC Emerger, Compara-Emerger, Pheasant Tail Nymph
Light & Dark Hendrickson 12-14													Light and Dark Hendrickson, Comparadun or Parachute, dark brown Hendrickson Nymph, Rusty Spinner
Sulphurs 14-20													Comparadun, Parachute, CDC Emerger, Compara-Emerger, Pheasant Tail Nymph, Hare's Ear Nymph
Caddis Green, Gray, Tan 14-18													Elk Hair Caddis, Lafontaine Deep Pupa and Emergent Sparkle Pupa, Bead-Head Nymph, Soft Hackle Wet
Light Cahill 14-16													Cream Variant, Comparadun, Cahill Wet Fly, Light Hare's Ear Nymph
Trico 22-26													Trico Spinner, Griffith's Gnat, Trico Nymph
Ants Hoppers/Crickets Beetles													Dubbed Ant, Sinking Ant, Letort Hopper\Cricket, Foam Beetle
Midges													Brassie, Midge Pupa, Midge Dry, Griffith's Gnat
Scuds, Tan & Olive 12-14													Scud Pattern

STONE HILL RIVER/BEAVER DAM BROOK

This freestone stream, which carries these two names in its upper and lower parts respectively, rises in the southern end of Ward Pound Ridge Reservation and ends at Muscoot Reservoir, near Cross River Outlet. In all, it runs about five miles.

The stream holds brown trout; about 900 are stocked by the state each year. There is decent holdover here and perhaps some natural reproduction as well. In addition there are reports of occasional wild brookies in this stream. The fish run small here, in the 10- to 12-inch range.

There are three primary places to gain access to the river. The headwaters and first portion of the stream are reachable within the reservation, but unlike neighboring Cross River, they are far from the park's main road, so plan on a substantial hike. Outside the park, there are a number of street crossings along the stream's length in Bedford. Finally, near its end, the stream passes through Beaver Dam Sanctuary Park.

This is not a part of the New York City water supply system, so except for the mouth at the reservoir, which is marked, no watershed permit is required. Also, normal state trout season and regulations apply.

MIANUS RIVER

The Mianus River is better known as a Connecticut stream, but there is some decent fishing in its headwaters in Westchester. This freestone stream, which runs in Bedford and Pound Ridge, is stocked with about 800 small brown trout each year. These fish holdover and there is some natural reproduction as well. In addition, some of the tiny tributaries hold wild brook trout. Access to the Mianus can be had from several road crossings, from Bedford Village Memorial Park and, just before the Connecticut border, from Mianus River Gorge Preserve. The river is subject to the normal trout season of April 1 to October 15.

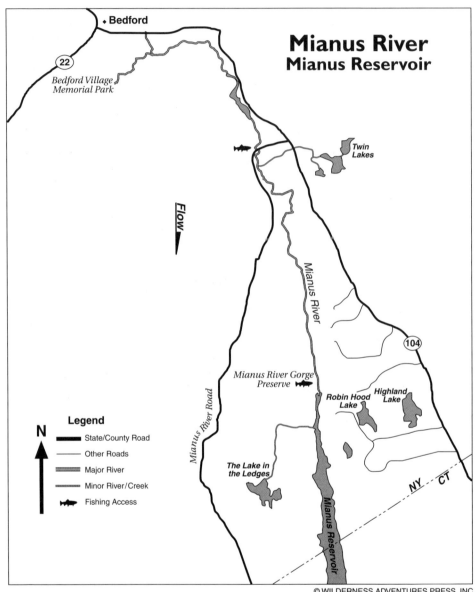

© WILDERNESS ADVENTURES PRESS, INC.

Westchester/Putnam Counties Freestone Streams—Major Hatches

INSECT	J	F	M	A	M	J	J	A	S	O	N	D	FLIES
Blue Winged Olives 16-20													Comparadun, Parachute, CDC Emerger, Compara-Emerger, Pheasant Tail Nymph
Light & Dark Hendrickson 12-14													Light and Dark Herdrickson, Comparadun or Parachute, dark brown Hendrickson Nymph, Rusty Spinner
Sulphurs 14-20													Comparadun, Parachute, CDC Emerger, Compara-Emerger, Pheasant Tail Nymph, Hare's Ear Nymph
Caddis Green, Gray, Tan 14-18													Elk Hair Caddis, Lefontaine Deep Pupa and Emergent Sparkle Pupa, Bead-Head Nymph, Soft Hackle Wet
Light Cahill 14-16													Cream Variant, Comparadun, Cahill Wet Fly, Light Hare's Ear Nymph
Trico 22-26													Trico Spinner, Griffith's Gnat, Trico Nymph
Ants Hoppers/Crickets Beetles													Dubbed Ant, Sinking Ant, Letort Hopper\Cricket, Foam Beetle

Westchester / Putnam Hub Cities

White Plains/Bedford

HOTELS/MOTELS

Ramada Inn, 94 Business Park Drive, White Plains, NY   1050 /
845-273-9090 / Restaurant 7am to 10pm / $$$
Renaissance Westchester Hotel, 80 West Red Oak Lane, White Plains, NY 10604 /
845-694-5616 / Restaurant 6:30 a.m. to 10 p.m. / $$$$

CAMPGROUNDS/RVS

Ward Pound Ridge Reservation, Route 121, Pound Ridge, NY / 845-63-3493 /
Cabins and tent sites
Croton Point Park, Croton Point Ave., Croton-on-Hudson, NY / 845-271-3293
Fahnestock State Park, Fahnestock Corners, Pillipstown, NY / 845-225-7507

RESTAURANTS

Muscoot Inn, 105 Somerstown Rd, Katonah, NY   10536 / 845-232-9877
Bistro 22 Restaurant, Route 22, Bedford, NY   10506 / 845-234-7333
Red Rooster Drive In, 1566 Route 22, Brewster, NY 10509 / 845-279-8046

FLY SHOPS

Bedford Sportsman Inc, 25 Adams St, Bedford Hills, NY 10507 / 845-666-8091 /
www.bedfordsportsman.com
CONNECTICUT
Orvis, 432 Boston Post Road, Darien CT, 06820 / 203-662-0844
Orvis, 71 Ethan Allen Highway, Route 7, Ridgefield, CT / 203-544-7700
The Compleat Angler, 987 Post Road, Darien, CT   06820 / 203-655-9400
Fairfield Fly Shop, 917 Post Road, Fairfield CT   06430 / 203-255-2896
Sportsman Den of Greenwich, 33 River Rd., Cos Cob, CT 06867 / 203-869-3234
Valley Angler, 56 Padanarum Road, Danbury, CT   06811 / 203-792-8324

AUTO REPAIR

R.J.T. Motorist Services, 101 Westmoreland Ave., White Plains, NY 10601 /
845 948-1100

AIRPORT

Westchester County Airport, 240 Airport Rd # 202, White Plains, NY 10604 /
845 285-4860

HOSPITAL/CLINIC

Westchester County Medical Center, 95 Grasslands Road, Valhalla, NY   10595 /
845-285-7000
White Plains Hospital Center, 41 E Post Road, White Plains, NY   10601 /
845-681-0600

Dutchess and Columbia Counties

Dutchess and Columbia lack the prime tailwaters of the Croton Watershed; however, the freestone streams here flow from higher elevations and a number of them are capable of supporting holdover and natural reproduction, especially in their upper reaches. The rolling hills in the eastern half of this area, and the Hudson Valley to the west, both offer beautiful scenery.

WAPPINGER CREEK

Wappinger Creek is the longest trout stream in Dutchess County. It runs about 25 miles from the town of Stanford where several small streams meet at its headwaters, through Washington, Pleasantville and Poughkeepsie before draining into the Hudson. The water encompasses small stream fishing in its upper reaches, larger

Bill Newcomb fishing the upper reaches of Wappinger Creek.

freestone character for much of its length and a slower shallow section best known for warmwater fishing near its mouth.

For nearly its entire length, Wappinger is heavily stocked. About 11,000 brown trout are put in each year, with about 1,000 of them larger two-year-old fish. In addition, about 2,000 rainbow trout are stocked in the lower reaches of the stream.

There are a number of dedicated public access points along the length of the creek, along with unofficial bridge access. The bridges are where much of the stocking takes place. Local spin and bait anglers hit these bridge pools heavily right after the stocking truck comes through, and some of the stocked trout don't spend a night in the stream. This is a good argument for float stocking of the creek (which is done in some sections), and for wading up and down from the access points.

The Stanford Recreation Park is a good place to fish the stream's headwaters. Here, Wappinger is a classic small stream, about 10-15 feet wide. It is very rocky in this section and a wading staff or big stick would be helpful. Although stocked browns are the staple, you might pick up an occasional brook trout this far up in the stream. Farther downstream Wappinger becomes wider and less steep and there is lengthy bankside access where Jameson Hill Road crosses the stream. This section can be waded extensively and there is a deep pool at the bridge (where a beadhead nymph has been known to take fish). According to Ron Pierce of DEC, the portion of Wappinger Creek northeast of the Taconic Parkway has some natural reproduction of browns. In general, that upper half of the stream stays relatively cool in the summer, although it is still advisable to fish late in the day in July and August.

Access on the lower half of the stream can also be had in the town center of Pleasant Valley at Bower Park and at the recreation park near the town hall. In Pleasant Valley there is a dam on Wappinger Creek. This point marks the beginning of the lower 12 miles, in which fishing is permitted year round. At its lower end, in Poughkeepsie, Wappinger is primarily a warmwater fishery, and the trout fishing here is put and take. At its mouth, the creek can also hold stripers from the Hudson in late spring and early summer.

Hatches here, and in most of the streams in Dutchess and Columbia, include some larger early season mayflies, particularly the Hendricksons and summer Cahills, along with and Sulphurs and Olives in much of the season, supplemented by caddis. Ants, beetles and less common crickets and hoppers round out the trout's diet. As most of the fish are stocked, a basic selection of light and dark mayflies, some Pheasant Tail and Hare's Ear Nymphs, along with a green caddis larva, and some terrestrials will be enough to match most insects. Add a Black-Nosed Dace and perhaps a Clouser or two for deep sections and your box will be properly filled.

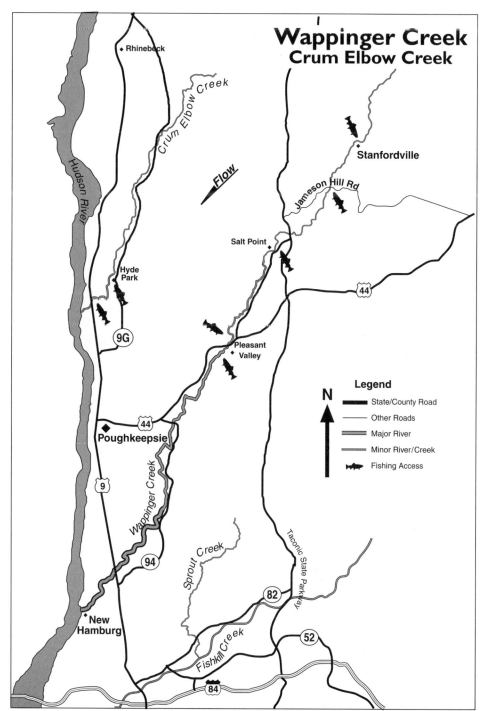

Wappinger Creek
Crum Elbow Creek

Rhinebeck

Crum Elbow Creek

Flow

Hudson River

Stanfordville

Jameson Hill Rd

Salt Point

Hyde
Park

44

9G

Pleasant
Valley

Legend

N

State/County Road
Other Roads
Major River
Minor River/Creek
Fishing Access

44

Poughkeepsie

9

Wappinger Creek

94

Sprout Creek

Taconic State Parkway

82

New
Hamburg

52

Fishkill Creek

84

© WILDERNESS ADVENTURES PRESS, INC.

Dutchess/Columbia Counties—Major Hatches

INSECT	J	F	M	A	M	J	J	A	S	O	N	D	FLIES
Little Black\Brown Stone 12-14													Black Elk Hair Caddis, Dark Hare's Ear Nymph
Caddis Green, Gray, Tan 14-20													Elk Hair Caddis, Bead-Head Cream or Green Pupa
Blue Winged Olives 16-20													Comparadun, CDC Emerger, Pheasant Tail Nymph
March Brown 10													Extended-Body Mayfly or Comparadun
Light & Dark Hendrickson 12-14													Comparaduns, Down Wing Deer Hair Emergers, Rusty Spinners, Hendrickson Nymphs
Sulphurs 12-16													Comparadun, CDC Emerger, Pheasant Tail Nymph
Gray Fox 12-14													Gray Fox Variant
Light Cahill/ Potomanthus 12-18													Cream Variants, Comparadun, Light Hare's Ear Nymph
Trico 22-26													Trico Spinner, Griffith's Gnat, Trico Nymph
Ants Hoppers/Crickets Beetles													Dubbed Ant, Sinking Ant, Letort Hopper\Cricket, Foam Beetle
Streamers													Black-Nosed Dace, Clouser Minnows

ROELIFF-JANSEN KILL

The Roeliff-Jansen Kill, generally called the Roe-Jan, is one of the longer streams in this section of the state. It runs primarily through Columbia County, dipping into Dutchess and ending at the Hudson River in Germantown—about 30 miles in all.

It is the upper portion of the stream, upstream from Route 9, that offers the best public trout fishing. This section is heavily stocked with brown trout; over 13,000 fish in all, about 1,200 of these two-year-olds. There is some natural reproduction here and fish up to 16 inches can be found in the deeper holes.

Although there is a lot of posted land on the Roe-Jan, the main trout section has some well spaced accesses. There is bridge access just south of the village of Hillsdale, on Black Grocery Road just off Route 22, and another where Wiltsie Bridge Road crosses the stream in the Columbia County town of Ancram.

Closer to Taconic Parkway, there is a good stretch of public water on the northern bank where Dutchess County Route 50/Cors Road and Dutchess Route 56/Turkey Hill Road intersect. The trip to this section of the stream is a nice drive that takes you through rolling farmlands lined by stone fences in upper Dutchess and lower Columbia counties.

The Roe-Jan's deep water is ideal for streamers.

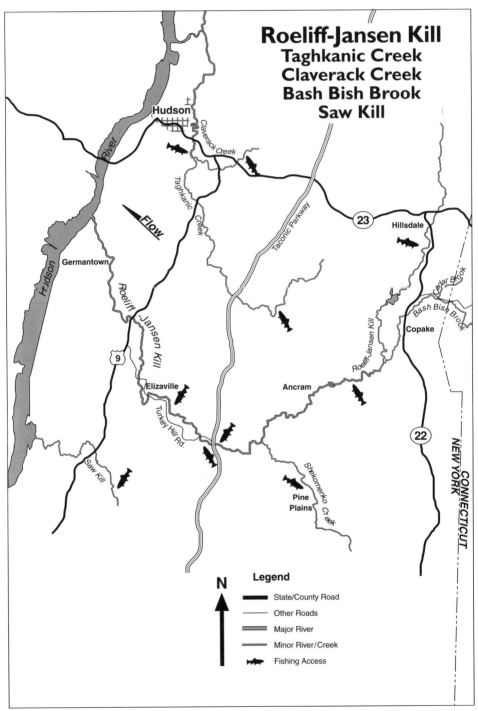

Roeliff-Jansen Kill
Taghkanic Creek
Claverack Creek
Bash Bish Brook
Saw Kill

Hudson

Claverack Creek

Taghkanic Creek

Flow

Hudson River

Germantown

Roeliff-Jansen Kill

Taconic Parkway

23

Hillsdale

Cedar Brook

Bash Bish Brook

Copake

9

Elizaville

Turkey Hill Rd.

Ancram

Roeliff-Jansen Kill

22

Saw Kill

Shekomenko Creek

Pine
Plains

NEW YORK

CONNECTICUT

N

Legend

State/County Road

Other Roads

Major River

Minor River/Creek

Fishing Access

© WILDERNESS ADVENTURES PRESS, INC.

Good riffles at the Turkey Hill Road Access end in a very deep bridge pool that cries out for a big weighted nymph or streamer. In fact, there is deep, fast water along much of the Roe-Jan. According to Don Traver of Don's Tackle in nearby Red Hook, the Roe-Jan is primarily streamer water, and he recommends Muddler Minnows, Black-Nosed Dace and Grey and Black Ghosts to imitate the plentiful baitfish. A sink tip is useful in high water, but a floating line will work most of the time. This stretch of the stream is fairly wide— from 30 to 50 feet—so a longer rod is not a problem.

While baitfish are plentiful, hatches are sparser on the Roe-Jan than some other streams in the area and lean more heavily to caddis. An Adams and a cream or yellow dry fly size 14-20 along with a couple of generic nymphs, say Hare's Ear and Pheasant Tail (with beadheads for faster water), should be sufficient for mayflies. Add some Elk Hair Caddis and a green nymph for the larva and pupa and you'll be well covered.

Although the rolling Berkshire Hills do provide cooler water, plan to fish the Roe-Jan in May and June and again in September. High, discolored water, apparently due to the farms along its banks, can be a problem on the stream after heavy rains. As noted in the Hudson section, striped bass can be taken in the mouth of the Roe-Jan or just outside it.

There are no special regulations on the Roe-Jan, which follows the standard trout season of April 1 to October 15.

BASH BISH CREEK

Bash Bish Creek runs cold from Massachusetts, across the border and down into the Roe-Jan in the town of Copake. Its mountainous source keeps it cool for its entire trip. The stream is not stocked, but holds brown trout that reproduce naturally. The creek's steep, rocky upper section can be reached within Taconic State Park. Cedar Brook, a small wild stream that enters Bash Bish within the park, is also worth fishing. (Taconic State Park is extensive; the area to seek is near the intersection of Route 22 and Route 344 in Copake Falls.) Because of the ready access, this portion is heavily fished. Big fish have been found on the lower half, west of Route 22. Look for access in this section where Route 7A/Old Route 22 crosses the stream.

SHEKOMEKO CREEK

This small creek crosses from northern Dutchess County into Columbia County where it joins the Roe-Jan. Shekomeko is stocked with about 500 brown trout each year. Access has been a problem here in recent years, but there is some available along Silvernails Road in the town of Pine Plains.

CRUM ELBOW CREEK

Crum Elbow Creek rises in the town of Rhinebeck and flows about ten miles into the Hudson River at Hyde Park. (Don't be put off by the creek's name, reportedly a reference to the Crum family that owned land on the bank). The creek possesses a variety of water types, from slow moving to steep, fast gorge water.

Public access on Crum Elbow is limited, but can be found in the town of Hyde Park. The National Park Service allows fishing on the grounds of the Vanderbilt Mansion near the stream's end. They prefer that you park in the rear lot, off West Market Street, which is much closer to the stream. The water is steep and fast, but just upstream on the mansion grounds there is a slow moving impoundment. There is also access to some smoother water upstream at Hacket Hill Town Park at the intersection of Route 9G and East Market Street.

Crum Elbow Creek is stocked with about 1,000 small brown trout each year and, unusual for this area, about the same number of rainbow trout as well. Like most of the streams at lower altitudes in this region, it is mostly put and take and fishes better in spring. There are no special regulations and the trout season closes October 15.

FISHKILL CREEK

This stream runs through the southeast corner of Dutchess County. It begins in the town of Union Vale near the center of the county and runs southwest to the Hudson near Beacon. It is primarily put and take, but receives a heavy stocking of more than 5,500 browns. Access can be found along Route 82, which parallels the stream for much of its length.

Sprout Creek and Jackson Creek

This is a tributary of the Fishkill and receives its own substantial stocking of 4,600 brown trout. Access is at various road crossings in the towns of Wappinger and Fishkill.

Sprout Creek has its own tributary, Jackson Creek, which enters the stream near the Taconic Parkway. Jackson Creek gets a small stocking of about 700 browns.

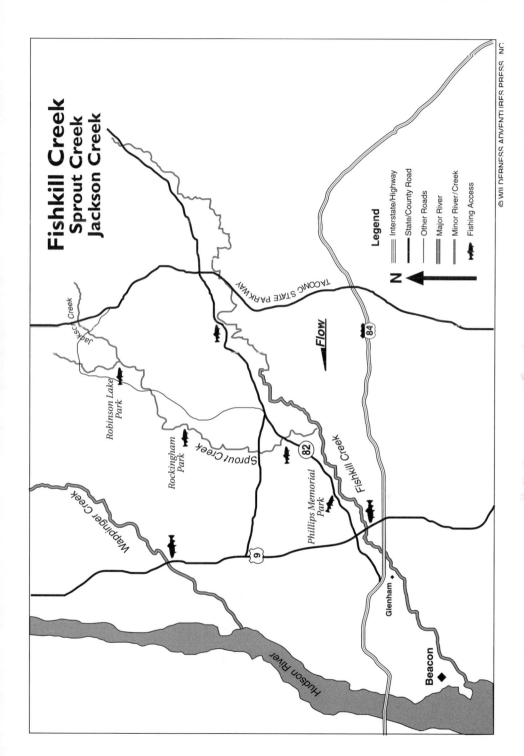

Fishkill Creek
Sprout Creek
Jackson Creek

Legend
Interstate/Highway
State/County Road
Other Roads
Major River
Minor River/Creek
Fishing Access

N

Jackson Creek

Robinson Lake Park

Rockingham Park

Sprout Creek

Phillips Memorial Park

TACONIC STATE PARKWAY

Flow

84

82

Fishkill Creek

Wappinger Creek

9

Glenham

Beacon

Hudson River

© WILDERNESS ADVENTURES PRESS, INC.

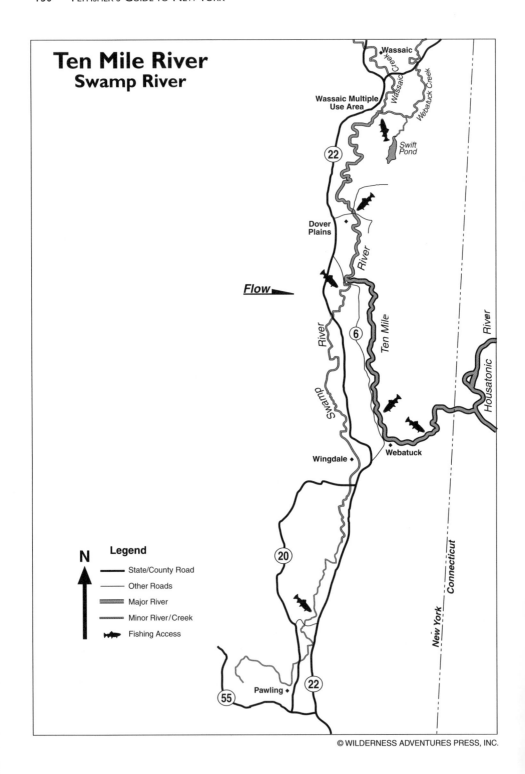

© WILDERNESS ADVENTURES PRESS, INC.

TEN MILE RIVER

Along with Wappinger Creek and the Roe-Jan, the Ten Mile River is one of the area's large trout streams, although it heads in the opposite direction. The river rises at the confluence of Wassaic and Webatuck creeks in Amenia, is fed by the Swamp River in Dover and exits the state at the Connecticut border before its short remaining trip to the Housatonic.

This is fairly big water, up to 50 feet across, with a steady flow in spring and some good hatches. Spring brings small black stoneflies and occasional tan caddis in size 14. Small Sulphurs in 16-18 are also heavy around the end of May. It's certainly worth trying to match the hatch, but this is not technical fishing. A generic dry fly like an Adams or equivalent light bodied fly, traditional or parachute, should work for surface-feeding fish. Bill Newcomb, first president of the Ten Mile River chapter of Trout Unlimited, likes to fish the Usual in small sizes, first on top as a dry, then stripped back at the end of the drift. This often yields hard strikes. You can fish this in the generic version or change dubbing to match the color of flies coming off.

Access is limited on the Ten Mile River. There is public access in the town of Dover Plains, at the American Legion Post near the intersection of Mill Street and Maple Lane. (The Ten Mile River Chapter is also seeking public access from the Metro North Railroad that crosses the stream nearby.) There are also some bridge accesses along Route 22.

Near the Craft Village on the Ten Mile River.

Closer to the Connecticut border, the Webatuck Craft Village on Route 55 in Wingdale is not dedicated public access but generally allows fishing. There may be a sign expressly permitting fishing; if not, ask at Hunt Country Furniture or one of the shops on the stream. The water at this lower end picks up speed, especially in spring, and has some very deep cuts and ledge pools along the rocky bottom. A small feeder stream enters a few hundred yards above the bridge. You can wade well up and down from the bridge, but be careful of fast water and deep holes.

A weighted streamer would be a good way to search this wide portion of the river. David Duff, an avid fly angler and craftsman who works on the river's banks, recommends swinging a soft hackle wet fly into the pools in a size to match hatching activity. He suggests you skip the traditional silk bodies, though, and use a dubbed version like the Hare's Ear and Partridge.

The Ten Mile is heavily stocked in three short sections near the access points. About 11,000 brown trout are put in each year. The trout season is April 1 to October 15 on the Ten Mile River and no special regulations apply.

WASSAIC CREEK

The Wassaic is a tributary of the Ten Mile River and in some ways is a miniature version of it. Its nine-mile run from the town of Northeast to the Ten Mile River near the border of Amenia and Dover has deep runs and pools along with wide shallower runs and a maximum width of 30 to 40 feet.

The Department of Environmental Conservation maintains a multiple-use site on the lower end of the Wassaic that offers a long stretch of public access. There are some very deep holes in this section.

No fish are stocked directly in the Wassaic (though some stocked trout probably come in from the Webatuck) and there is known to be good wild reproduction of brown trout here, with fish up to 16 inches taken. The Wassaic closes on October 15.

WEBATUCK CREEK

The Webatuck joins with the Wassaic Creek to form the Ten Mile River. It receives a heavy stocking of brown trout, almost 3,000 each year, including more than 300 two-year-olds. There is decent holdover and the stream may see some natural reproduction as well. There is no formal access on the Webatuck, but you can get into the stream from local Route 3. It is also possible to wade upstream from the Wassaic Multiple Use Area into the Webatuck. Hatches and fishing are typical of the local smaller streams, and standard regulations apply.

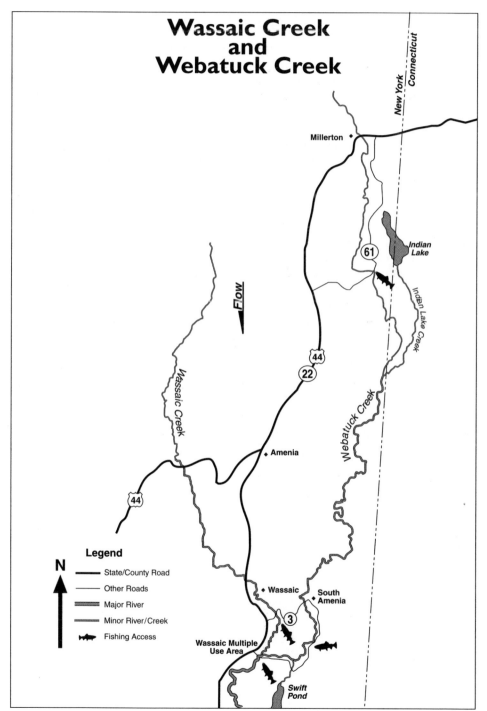

Wassaic Creek and Webatuck Creek

New York
Connecticut

Millerton

Indian Lake

61

Indian Lake Creek

Flow

44
22

Wassaic Creek

Webatuck Creek

Amenia

44

Legend

N

State/County Road
Other Roads
Major River
Minor River/Creek
Fishing Access

Wassaic

South Amenia

3

Wassaic Multiple Use Area

Swift Pond

© WILDERNESS ADVENTURES PRESS, INC.

SWAMP RIVER

Draining from a large wetland in the town of Pawling, the Swamp River runs north about seven miles until it empties into the Ten Mile River in the neighboring town of Dover. Though swamps are mucky places, they act as natural water filters and this effect is evident on the Swamp River, which runs very clear for its entire length.

Because of its short run and posted land there are essentially only two public access points. One is located at River Road in Pawling. Downstream, you can reach the stream at the bridge crossing in Dover on Dutchess County Route 6 (Old Post Road). The water is not terribly deep and no more than 15 feet across, so you can wade as far as your energy will take you.

The Swamp is better fished in spring; it runs low in summer. Because of its small size and unusually clear water, stealth is important here. Insect life is typical of local waters. The Swamp is a narrow stream with overhanging vegetation, so an ant or small beetle pattern should work well here when no hatches are evident.

DEC stocks the water with about 750 small brown trout and about 400 small brookies near the headwaters in Pawling. The Swamp is open for trout fishing only from April 1 to September 30, with no special regulations.

SAW KILL

A small stream that runs about four miles to the Hudson, the Saw Kill is stocked for a total of about three miles in the town of Red Hook. It receives a modest stocking of brown trout, and some brookies as well. Access is limited to the bridges and the recreational park in the town of Red Hook at the northern end of Dutchess County. The stream can be fished until October 15.

The Kinderhook in Valatie.

Kinderhook Creek

Kinderhook Creek, a long stream in Columbia County, begins near the Massachusetts border in neighboring Renssellaer County and winds its way about 25 miles to the Hudson. There is some big, rocky water and some slower flow along the way.

The upper half of the stream, roughly above Interstate 90, is best. This section can be fished in the town of New Lebanon where Adams Crossing Road intersects Route 20. In Chatham, there is access at the intersection of Route 66 and Bachus Road and again at Pitt Road and where Route 32 crosses in the village of Malden Bridge. The first access is near where Green Brook enters, this brook can bring occasional wild rainbows into the stream and is worth fishing as well.

Farther downstream, there are a couple of convenient access points in the village of Valatie and in the town of Kinderhook. Jason Nastke, the village's young outdoorsman mayor is eager to develop local fishing, and new access has been opened at the Pachaquack Preserve on Elm Street near Route 203. Fishing is also permitted below the falls in the center of town. The very deep pool here demands a heavily weighted streamer or nymph. Although the stocking currently ends just upstream of this area, some fish do drop down. Stocking is expected to expand to cover the new access.

Kinderhook Creek receives a large stocking: about 17,000 brown trout each year. Downstream from the Adams Crossing Road Access in New Lebanon the trout season is April 1 to November 30, above that the season ends October 15.

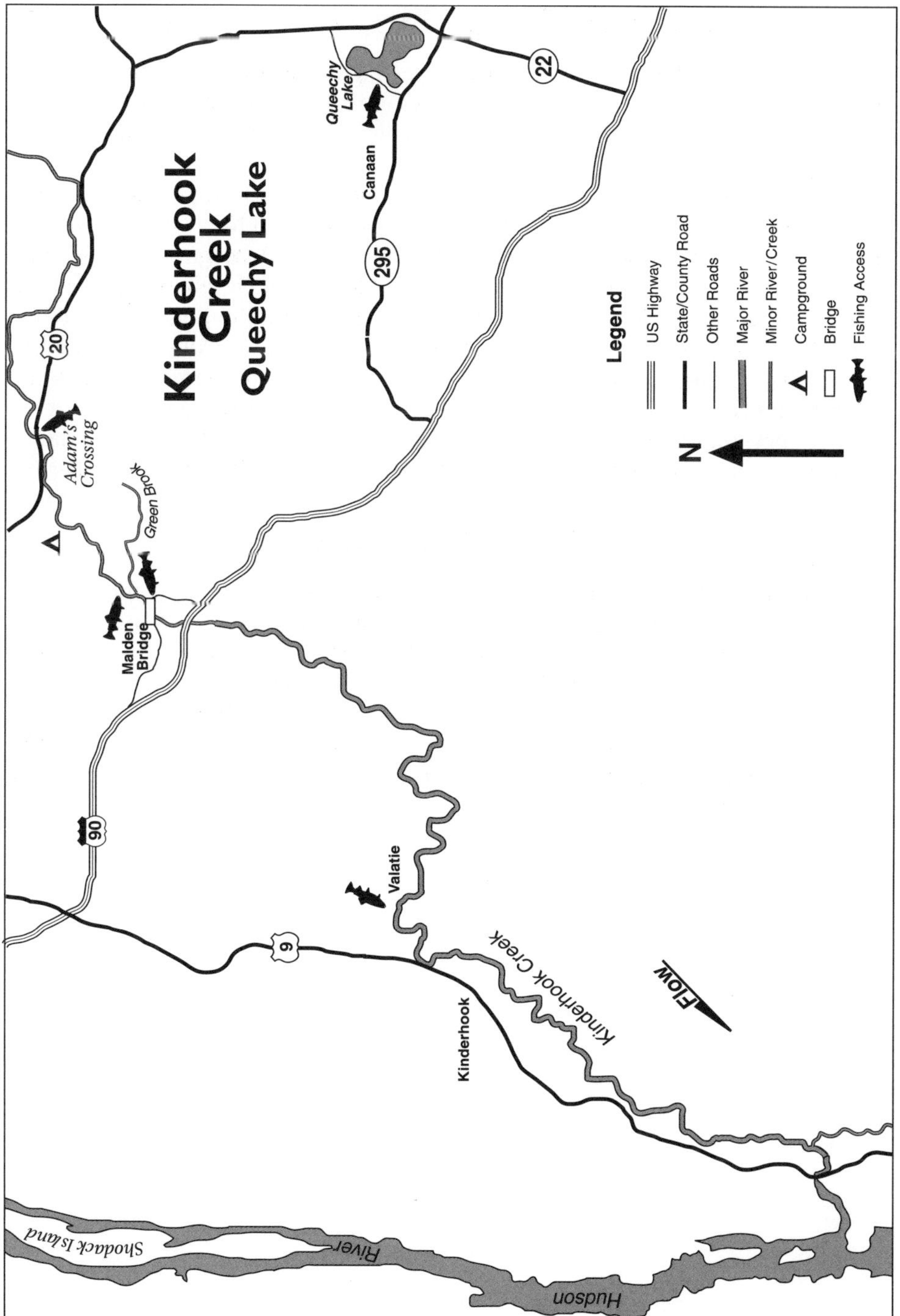

Kinderhook
Creek
Queechy Lake

Legend

US Highway
State/County Road
Other Roads
Major River
Minor River/Creek
Campground
Bridge
Fishing Access

N

Queechy
Lake

Canaan

22

295

Adam's
Crossing

Green Brook

Malden
Bridge

90

20

Valatie

9

Kinderhook

Kinderhook Creek

Flow

Shodack Island

River

Hudson

© WILDERNESS ADVENTURES PRESS, INC.

CLAVERACK CREEK/TAGHKANIC CREEK

Claverack Creek is a tributary of the larger Taghkanic, which combine and run to Kinderhook Creek just before it empties into the Hudson in the village of Columbiaville. Together the two streams receive about 5,500 small brown trout each year.

Access to Taghkanic is somewhat limited. In addition to bridges, there is access at the New Forge State Forest in the Town of Taghkanic on New Forge Road II off Route 82. (Not nearby Lake Taghkanic State Park, which offers warmwater fishing.)

Claverack Creek is a bit more accessible, with several closely set spots in the towns of Claverack and Greenport. Above the village of Philmont, Route 9 offers some bridge access. This upper section holds some wild brookies in addition to stocked fish. Claverack can also be fished where Roxbury Road crosses, near Route 17 and where Route 23 crosses in the village of Red Mills. Farther downstream, there are two spots on Route 29: at the intersection with Webb Road and just upstream.

No special regulations apply to these two streams, which both close October 15.

QUEECHY LAKE

This medium-sized lake is near the Massachusetts border in the town of Canaan. It is stocked with roughly equal numbers of small brown and rainbow trout, about 3,600 in all. The lake is up to 40 feet deep and the rainbows in particular are reported to holdover well and grow up to 18 inches.

There is public parking and access off Route 30. The parking area is a substantial walk from the lake, but a small canoe or float tube could be carried in. The lake is open to trout fishing year round (and is often ice fished), three fish per day may be kept, 12 inches or longer.

Dutchess and Columbia Counties Hub Cities

Poughkeepsie

HOTELS/MOTELS

Econo Lodge, 426 Sout road, Poughkeepsie, NY 12601 / 845-452-6600 / 24 hour restaurant / $$$

The Inn at the Falls, 50 Red Oaks Mills Road, Poughkeepsie, NY 12603 / 845-462-5770 / $$$

Village Inn, 6 Route 9S, Rhinebeck, NY, 12572 / 845-876-7000 / $-$$

CAMPGROUNDS/RVs

Interlake RV Park, 45 Lake Drive, Rhinebeck, NY, 12572 / 845-266-5387

Mills-Norrie State Park, Old Post Road, Staatsburg, NY 12580 / 845-889-4646

Snow Valley Campground, Route 9, Fishkill, NY 12524 / 845-897-5700

RESTAURANTS

Palace Diner, 194 Washington Street, Poughkeepsie, 12601 / 845-473-1576

River Station Steak and Seafood, 1 Water Street, Poughkeepsie, 12601 / 845-452-9207 / Open till midnight / 2a.m. Friday-Saturday

Hudson's Ribs and Fish, 2014 US Rte 9, Fishkill, 12524 / 845-297-5002

La Parmagiana, 37 Montgomery Street, Rhinebeck, NY 12572 / 845-876-3228,

FLY SHOPS

Don's Tackle, 69 S Broadway, Red Hook, NY 12571 / 845-758-9203

Orvis Sandanona, Route 44A, Millbrook, NY 12545 / 845-677-9701, small shop, flyfishing school

CONNECTICUT

Housatonic Meadows Fly Shop, 13 Route 7, Cornwall Bridge, CT 06754 / 860-672-6064

Housatonic River Outfitters, 7 Railroad St, West Cornwall, CT 06796 / 860-672-1010

AUTO REPAIR

Rube & Sons Auto Shops, 505 South Road, Poughkeepsie, NY / 845-462-5100

AIRPORT

Stewart NY International Airport, Newburgh, NY 12550 / 845-564-2100

Dutchess County Airport, New Hackensack Road, Wappingers Falls, NY 12590 / 845-463-2000

HOSPITAL/CLINIC

St. Francis Hospital, 35 North Road, Poughkeepsie, NY 12601 / 845-471-2000

Vassar Brothers Hospital, 45 Reade Place, Poughkeepsie, NY 12601 / 845-454-8500

Northern Dutchess Hospital, 10 Spring Brook Ave, Rhinebeck, NY 12572 / 845-876-3001

Hudson

HOTELS/MOTELS
Joslen Motor Lodge, 320 Joslen Blvd, Hudson, NY 12534 / 518-828-7046 / $$
St. Charles Hotel, 1618 Park Place, Hudson, NY 12543 / 518-822-9900 /
  Restaurant / $$

CAMPGROUNDS/RVS
Lake Taghkanic State Park, 11 miles south of Hudson on Highway 82 /
  518-851-3631

RESTAURANTS
Rebeccas, 1618 Park Place (at St. Charles Hotel), Hudson, NY 12543 /
  518-822-9900
Blue Plate, 1 Kinderhook Street, Chatham, NY 12037 / 518-392-7711
Columbia Diner, 717 Warren St., Hudson, NY 12534 / 518-822-1830

TACKLE SHOPS
River Basin Sport Shop, 66 W Bridge St, Catskill, NY 12414 / 518-943-2111

AUTO RENTAL/REPAIR
Tillson's Auto Repair, 15 Varick St, Hudson, NY 12534 / 518-828-3913

AIRPORT
Stewart NY International Airport, Newburgh, NY 12550 / 845-564-2100
Dutchess County Airport, New Hackensack Road, Wappingers Falls, NY 12590 /
  845-463-2000

HOSPITAL/CLINIC
Columbia Memorial Hospital, 71 Prospect Ave, Hudson, NY 12534 /
  518-828-7601

Hillsdale

HOTELS/MOTELS
Linden Valley Inn, Route 23 two miles east on NY 23, NY / 518-325-7100 / $$$
Simmon's Way Village Inn, 33 Main Street, 12546 / 518-789-6235 / $$$$
Swiss Hutte, Route 23 / 413-528-6200 / $$$

CAMPGROUNDS/RVs
Lake Taghkanic State Park, 11 miles south of Hudson on Highway 82 /
518-851-3631

RESTAURANTS
Aubergine, Junction Rtes 22 & 23 / 518-325-3412 / Dinner only
Dutch Treat, Route 23, Craryville, NY 12521 / 518-325-5107
Swiss Hutte, Route 23 / 413-528-6200
Canaan Market, Route 295/Queechy Lake, Canaan, NY 12029 / 518-781-4163
Crossroads Diner, Route 22 & Route 23, Hillsdale, NY 12529 / 518-325-3129

FLY SHOPS
River Run Orvis Dealer, 271 Main St, Great Barrington, MA 01230 /
413-528-9600

AUTO REPAIR
Roe Jan Auto Ctr., 9010 Route 22, Hillsdale, NY 12529 / 518-325-5302

AIRPORT
Stewart NY International Airport, Newburgh, NY 12550 / 845-564-2100
Dutchess County Airport, New Hackensack Road, Wappingers Falls, NY 12590 /
845-463-2000

HOSPITAL/CLINIC
Fairview Hospital, 29 Lewis Ave, Great Barrington, MA 01230 / 413-528-0790

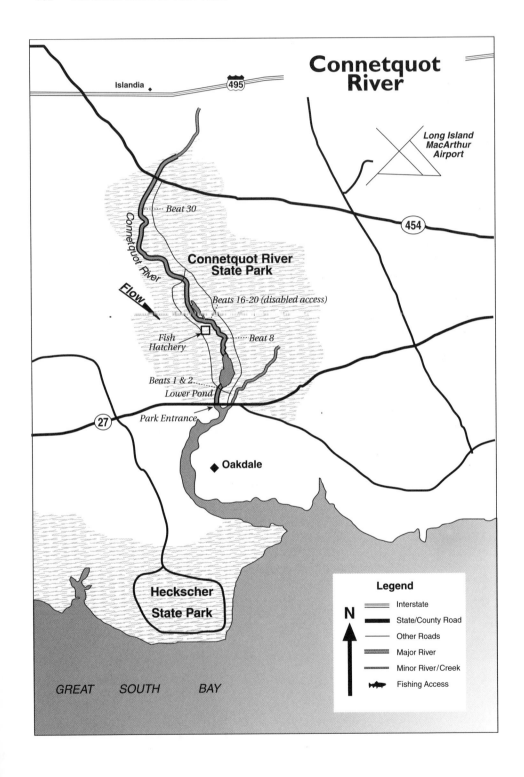

Connetquot River

Islandia

495

Long Island
MacArthur
Airport

454

Beat 30

Connetquot River

Flow

**Connetquot River
State Park**

Beats 16-20 (disabled access)

Fish
Hatchery

Beat 8

Beats 1 & 2
Lower Pond

Park Entrance

27

◆ **Oakdale**

Heckscher

State Park

Legend

N

≡ Interstate
━ State/County Road
─ Other Roads
▦ Major River
≡ Minor River/Creek
🐟 Fishing Access

GREAT   SOUTH   BAY

Long Island

Long Island is well known among anglers for saltwater fish like stripers, blues and flounder—and even tuna and marlin. But there is fine freshwater flyfishing here, too. The best fishing for trout in a trio of spring creeks in Suffolk County: the Connetquot, the Nissequoque and the Carmans. A few smaller streams also have trout, as do a number of stocked ponds.

CONNETQUOT RIVER

The Connetquot River offers anglers a chance to catch huge stocked trout in a clubby, wooded setting. This spring-fed river runs approximately 8.5 miles from its source near the Long Island Expressway in the village of Islandia to its wide, brackish mouth in Great South Bay, above Fire Island. The majority of the river's length, and its renowned fishing for very large trout, falls within Connetquot State Park. The 3,500-acre park is on the former site of the South Side Club, a private fishing preserve which opened as a state park in 1973.

The hatchery adjoining the stream provides a dense mix of very large brown, rainbow and brook trout to Connetquot anglers. Fish in the 15- to 20-inch range are common here, and to use a much overworked phrase, the trout here can truly be measured in pounds, not inches. Up to 30,000 trout are stocked each year. Park Supervisor Gil Bergen says that the largest stocking is of brook trout, followed by the browns and the rainbows. In addition to the three basic trout species, a few tiger trout, a cross between brown and brook trout, end up in the Connetquot. There are also a handful of searun fish, predominantly brown trout, that migrate in from the ocean each fall. Fish do hold over, and there may be some natural reproduction—but it is difficult to tell when they are mixed in with the large number of stocked fish. Also, many of the fry would surely become food for the hungry stocked fish before they get very large.

The Connetquot's spring waters maintain a smooth, steady flow and reliable temperatures in the mid-50s to mid-60s. However, unlike some other spring creeks, the river does not boast a wealth of hatches. More importantly, the large stocked fish are generally not selective. Steve Metzler, a fishing guide and instructor who fishes the river frequently, has observed that fish that have spent more time in the river begin to key on hatches, particularly in the evening. When they do, he notes, the fish can become selective. At those times, accurate imitations of Blue Winged Olives, Light Cahills and Hendricksons among mayflies, as well as various caddis, may become important.

Most of the fishing here, though, is done with generic attractor flies. Metzler recommends a Royal Wulff as a good choice when dry fly fishing. Basic subsurface flies used include Hare's Ear Nymphs, scuds and various colors of both dark and bright Woolly Buggers. Deceivers and Muddler Minnows fished along the banks work well for the browns.

A standard trout stream rod of 7½ to 8½ feet in a 4- or 5-weight will work well on the stream. Only unweighted flies and lines are permitted on the stream within the park. For streamer fishing in the ponds, where deep-running fish up to 30 inches are found, go up to a 6- or 7-weight, with a sink tip or even a full sinking line. A large Deceiver or Mickey Finn streamer is a good choice on the pond.

Befitting its origins as a private club, the Connetquot works on a "beat" system. A reservation for a 4-hour session is made up to a week in advance by telephone. Then the 30 beats—seven on the two ponds, the remainder on the stream—are assigned on a first come, first served basis at the start of each session. In the beats above the hatchery anglers are required to cast from platforms or shore, rather than wading in the stream. Different anglers have their favorite beats, but beats 8-12 on the lower end of the river and beats in the high 20s seem to be preferred. Beats 16-20 are reserved for disabled anglers and those over 60.

As pleasant as the reserved sessions and beat system is, it can work to the angler's disadvantage when the fish in your beat just aren't biting. One obvious solution is to go with a friend and switch beats halfway through the session. Even better, a number of local fishing organizations, including the New York City, Long Island and Art Flick chapters of Trout Unlimited run group outings to the river, some of which are open to non-members. Anglers on these trips have a chance to fish all the water in the park for an entire day. Check with the organizations for dates and openings. (Contact information for Trout Unlimited and many of its chapters can be found at the end of this book.)

Connetquot Park fishing is open from February through September. In February and March there are two sessions per day, in morning and afternoon. During those months fishing is strictly catch and release. From April through the end of the season an evening session is added and anglers may keep two fish. The fee for each session is $15. For reservations and information call 631-581-1005.

The Tidal Section of the Connetquot

The mouth of the Connetquot below Route 27/Sunrise Highway is tidal and brackish. A small section of this water is available at the Bubble Falls DEC Access off the eastbound side of Route27A/Montauk Highway. In the tidal Connetquot anglers can find perch, pickerel and occasional resident trout. In addition, small bluefish and migrating stripers can sometimes be caught here. While mostly plied by spin fishermen, an intrepid flyfisher with a streamer might hook a blue or striper here.

Searun trout are also a possibility at the lower end of the Connetquot. These strong silvery fish are seen in the lower river each fall, but they are not present in large numbers. Like all spawning trout, they are difficult to catch. Searun fish may also come upstream into Rattlesnake Creek, which connects to the Connetquot at its lower end within the park. There is access to a small portion of Rattlesnake Creek along Route 27A/Montauk Highway. The tidal sections of all streams are open year round.

A gentleman with a Montague cane rod and a large Connetquot rainbow.

Stream Facts: Connetquot River

Season
• Within Connetquot State Park, February through September (reservations required).
• Outside state park, April 1 to November 30; Tidal Section (below Route 17/Sunrise Highway) open all year.

Special Regulations
• Within Connetquot Park: flyfishing only, barbless hooks (flattened barbs permitted), no lead weight or weighted lines in stream. Two fish per session April to September, catch and release only February and March.

Fish
• Large stocked brook, brown and rainbow trout in park. Stocked and occasional searun browns in tidal section.

River Characteristics
• Park section is smooth, even flowing spring creek. Tidal section wide and brackish. Upper portions of park section can be weedy.

River Flows
• Steady and cool.

Connetquot River—Major Hatches

INSECT	J	F	M	A	M	J	J	A	S	O	N	D	FLIES
Black\Brown Stone 12-16													Elk Hair Caddis, Stonefly Nymphs
Little Black Caddis (Chimarra) 16-18													Elk Hair Caddis, Goddard Caddis, Bead-Head Pupa
Caddis Green, Gray, Tan 14-18													Elk Hair Caddis, Lafontaine Deep Pupa and Emergent Sparkle Pupa, Bead-Head Nymph, Soft Hackle Wet
Blue Winged Olives 16-22													Comparadun, Parachute, CDC Emerger, Compara-Emerger, Pheasant Tail Nymph
Light & Dark Hendrickson 12-14													Light and Dark Hendrickson, Comparadun or Parachute, dark brown Hendrickson Nymph, Rusty Spinner
Sulphurs 14-18													Comparadun, Parachute, CDC Emerger, Compara-Emerger, Pheasant Tail Nymph, Hare's Ear Nymph
Light Cahill 14-16													Cream Variant, Comparadun, Cahill Wet Fy, Light Hare's Ear Nymph, Cream Spinner
Trico 22-26													Trico Spinner, Griffith's Gnat, Trico Nymph
Midges-White,Gray, Black, 20-28													Brassie, Midge Pupa, Midge Dry, Griffiths Gnat
Scuds Tan,Olive Pink 12-14													Scud Pattern
Streamers													Wooly Buggers, Zonkers

NISSEQUOQUE RIVER

The Nissequoque River, another of Long Island's three major spring creeks, runs north about seven miles from its origins in Smithtown to its mouth on Long Island Sound. As with the Connetquot, much of the flyfishing on the Nissequoque is done on a reserved beat system within a state park. The Nissequoque also offers several miles of public access fishing downstream from the park, and a long tidal section with the potential for large fish.

The upper end of the Nissequoque falls within Caleb Smith State Park, once the site of the Wyandanch Club. Brookies, browns and rainbows raised in the Connetquot hatchery are stocked in the Nissequoque, but the stocking is not as dense here, and the fish may run a bit smaller. DEC biologists say there is also natural reproduction of both brook trout and brown trout here. Many fingerlings probably end up as forage for the stocked fish, but the numerous back channels in the Nissequoque give the wild fish a fighting chance.

While the fish population is smaller here than in the Connetquot, the insect population is generally larger. Hatches run the gamut from spring emergences of Quill Gordons, Hendricksons and March Browns to later hatches of Cahills, Sulphurs and Blue Winged Olives. Even more prevalent than the mayflies are the substantial populations of caddis, along with the midges, scuds and cress bugs you would expect to find in a spring creek.

Early in the season, a Woolly Bugger works well—brookies seem to prefer it in yellow. Fred Thorner, who teaches in the flyfishing school here, likes to attach a small nymph to the bend of a Woolly Bugger. He finds he gets as many hits on the trailer as the streamer. Thorner often uses a bead-chain nymph, a simple fly with an antron and Hare's Ear dubbed body and bead-chain eyes.

Later in the season, nymphs and dry flies will work better than the attractors. Although the stocked fish are not usually selective, it is important to pay attention to what they are eating. In particular, notice where in the water column the fish are feeding and which stage of a hatching insect they are focused on. For a general searching dry fly, an Elk Hair Caddis is probably a better bet than a mayfly. In fact, the Elk Hair can become more effective when it's waterlogged. The Nissequoque's small width and brushy banks make it a good place for ants and beetles. Foam versions will float better, especially since many sections of the stream make it difficult to dry your fly with false casting.

The Nissequoque's width mandates a short rod, 7 feet or less. Also, underwater weeds can make nymph fishing tricky later in the season. Even with a small rod, it can be difficult to approach the fish in narrower sections without spooking them. Careful wading along with a willingness to pay out line downstream, rather than actually cast, will yield more fish in the tightest spots.

There are a total of 13 beats in Caleb Smith Park. Beats 2-9 are on the stream (there is no beat 1), with the remaining 5 beats on the two nearby ponds. Fishing in the ponds is done from platforms along the shore. Beat 14 has the small back pond all to itself. In the ponds, a Woolly Bugger, the bead-chain nymph or a marabou damselfly nymph will work. The larger pond is especially weedy, but channels are cut through to make subsurface fishing easier. At dusk, toward closing, pond fish will often rise to hatching Callibaetis or other flies and an emerger dubbed with Hare's Ear will work well.

The stream beats here are longer than those in the Connetquot, which compensates in part for their narrowness, and all the beats permit wading. In fact, anglers who fish the stream often prefer the narrow, upper stream beats, 2 through 4. With only 8 rods on the stream at a time, the atmosphere tends to be informal. Anglers on the Nissequoque are often willing to share a productive beat, if asked politely.

Fishing in Caleb Smith is done only during the trout season, April 1 to October 15. There are two fishing sessions each day, four hours per session, although a third evening session is added on weekends and holidays from April through September. Reservations are taken up to two weeks in advance, and beats are selected 30 minutes before each session. Fishing is with barbless flies only; no weight is permitted on leaders. Anglers can keep 2 trout per session of 9 inches or better.

Caleb Smith Park is also host to the Nissequoque River Fly Fishing School, which offers 4-hour classes for beginning or advanced students and private instruction by the hour. To make fishing reservations or for information on the school, call 631-265-1054.

An angler at Beat 7 on the Nissequoque.

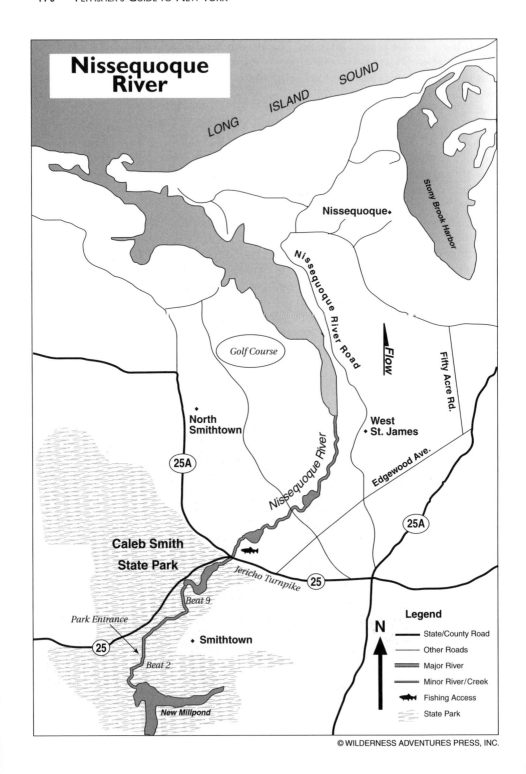

Downstream of Caleb Smith State Park

The Nissequoque continues downstream for about three miles from the boundary of Caleb Smith Park, becoming tidal and brackish in its last one to two miles. The state stocks about 500 brown trout—half of these two-year-old fish—and about 750 rainbows in these public waters. Just outside the park, an area known as White's Pool is accessible at the intersection of Route 25 and 25A. This section has stocked fish, especially in spring. A few hundred yards downstream there is a small local park where Landing Avenue crosses the river, and the stream here has a good caddis population.

Farther downstream, the water widens out and becomes tidal. It is possible to fish from shore, but a canoe or boat is a better bet. The best time is probably at low tide when the stream channel is visible. Fishing here would take some persistence with a streamer, but it might prove worth the effort; browns up to 8 pounds have been caught in the tidal section. Most of these large fish are believed to be stocked fish from the park that drop down into the lower river. There are probably some searun fish as well.

The section between Caleb Smith State Park and the tidal portion of the Nissequoque is open April 1 to November 30, with five fish per day permitted. The tidal section, roughly from the municipal golf course on down, is open all year.

Don't ignore the Nissequoque's lower reaches.

Stream Facts: Nissequoque River

Season
- Within Caleb Smith State Park, April 1 to October 15 (reservations required).
- Outside state park, April 1 to November 30; Tidal section (below municipal golf course) open all year.

Special Regulations
- Within Caleb Smith Park: flyfishing only, barbless hooks (flattened barbs permitted), no weight on leaders. Two trout per session, nine inches or longer.

Fish
- Large stocked brook trout, browns and rainbows in park. Stocked trout and occasional searun browns in tidal section.

River Characteristics
- Park section is smooth, even flowing spring creek, narrow in upper beats. Much of the park section, and park ponds are weedy. Long tidal section wide and brackish, stream channel visible at low tide.

River Flows
- Steady and cool.

Nissequoque River—Major Hatches

Nissequoque--Major Hatches

INSECT	J	F	M	A	M	J	J	A	S	O	N	D	FLIES
Black\Brown Stone 12-16													Elk Hair Caddis, Stonefly Nymphs
Little Black Caddis (Chimarra) 16-18													Elk Hair Caddis, Goddard Caddis, Bead-Head Pupa
Caddis Green, Gray, Tan 14-18													Elk Hair Caddis, Lafontaine Deep Pupa and Emergent Sparkle Pupa, Bead-Head Nymph, Soft Hackle Wet
Blue Winged Olives 16-22													Comparadun, Parachute, CDC Emerger, Compara-Emerger Pheasant Tail Nymph
Light & Dark Hendrickson 12-14													Light and Dark Hendrickson, Comparadun or Parachute, dark brown Hendrickson Nymph, Rusty Spinner
Sulphurs 14-18													Comparadun, Parachute, CDC Emerger, Compara-Emerger Pheasant Tail Nymph, Hare's Ear Nymph
Light Cahill 14-16													Cream Variant, Comparadun, Cahill Wet Fly, Light Hare's Ear Nymph, Cream Spinner
Trico 22-26													Trico Spinner, Griffith's Gnat, Trico Nymph
Midges-White,Gray, Black, 20-28													Brassie, Midge Pupa, Midge Dry, Griffith's Gnat
Scuds, Pink & Gray 12-14													Scud Pattern
Terrestrials													Foam ants and beetles
Streamers													Woolly Buggers

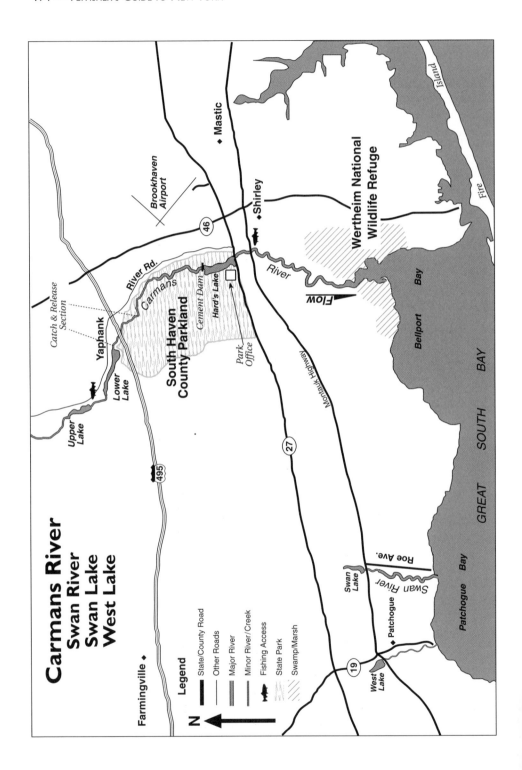

Carmans River

Legend has it that statesman Daniel Webster landed a 14-pound brook trout on the Carmans River in the 1800s, a scene Currier & Ives commemorated in a well-known print. While you won't find a fish that large in this stream today, there is still a healthy population of wild brook trout in this river. Rainbows and browns are stocked here as well, and the lower, tidal section offers a chance at sea run fish.

Like the other two major trout streams on Long Island, the Carmans rises from natural springs. Beginning in the village of Middle Island, it flows south 9 miles to the Great South Bay. The first fishable stretch of the Carmans is the .75-mile long section in the town of Yaphank, between two ponds on the stream: Upper Lake and Lower Lake. This section is stocked each year, and the adjoining lakes are also stocked. Small and weedy, this section is tricky to fish, and the tactics will often resemble dapping rather than casting. Access is also limited, but there is a small park where Upper Lake feeds into the Carmans. An eager angler could also put a canoe in here.

The bulk of the river, and its best fishing, are contained within South Haven County Park. Like the main stretches of the Connetquot and Nissequoque, this part of the Carmans was once private water—the Suffolk Club, later the Suffolk Lodge—before it was acquired by Suffolk County. Unlike the other two spring creeks, the Carmans does not have an assigned beat system. Anglers present their current fishing licenses and pay a fee at the park entrance—currently $2 per day or $30 for the season—and are permitted to fish all the waters within the park. (The park can be contacted at 631-854-1414.) When you drive on the unpaved road that runs along the river, you will see section numbers that correspond to platforms on the river. These are for autumn duck hunting, not fishing. The numbers are useful, though, if you are planning to meet friends on the stream or simply wish to find the spot you liked last time.

There are plenty of spots worth returning to here. The primary flyfishing territory—in fact, limited to flyfishing—is the section upstream from the Cement Dam, usually called the "C Dam." The dam creates a wide impoundment where the stocked rainbows and browns often congregate. The dam is not high, so it is possible to wade across the impoundment. A streamer stripped through here, or a nymph or scud slowly drifted, will give you a shot at these fish; however, this section is heavily fished.

As you head upstream from the impoundment, the river remains wide for several hundred yards. A couple of wing diverters along the way provide some structure and are good places to find fish. So too are the occasional bends in the river. Since anglers enter and exit from the road on the east side of the river, the western bank, often under trees, becomes a common holding spot for the trout.

A much larger set of diverters, about five feet high, is found just before a set of power lines that cross the river. This diverter creates a popular deep pool that usually holds fish. The river narrows noticeably above this point, making casting and stalking tricky. As you move up the river from the Cement Dam, the percentage of

Eric Thorner with a Carmans River brown trout.

brookies increases. This population is entirely wild and is thought to be descended from the original native population. An 11-inch brookie is on the large side, but wild fish in the 16-inch range are caught. The section above the power lines is strictly catch and release (and like everything above the Cement Dam, flyfishing only).

Below the Cement Dam the river is wide and slow moving, and is open to spin fishing. The park segment of the river ends with the impoundment at Hard's Lake. Here a boat for fishing can be rented by the hour. Hard's Lake receives a separate stocking of roughly 1,800 small rainbows and 1,300 browns, about 200 of which are two-year-olds.

The Carmans has a wealth of hatches, and there are frequently more than one type coming off at once. This can make fishing complicated, but the brookies are not as picky as wild browns. Mayflies cover the spectrum here, with Sulphurs and Olives among the most prevalent. That said, the mayfly hatches are not as dense as the best Catskill hatches and are outnumbered by the caddis and midges that abound here. A green caddis pupa pattern or small midge pupa is a good searching pattern when there is no hatch on the Carmans. An Elk Hair Caddis in tan, rather than a generic mayfly, should be the first resort for dry fly prospecting. Scuds, in pink or a bluish gray, are often neglected by anglers, but not by the fish.

Underwater weeds and bankside vegetation grow in during late spring and early summer and make approaching and casting to fish tricky. This is compounded by the smooth water and even flows. Dave Thompson, president of the local Art Flick chapter of Trout Unlimited and a long-time Carmans angler, often fishes a long distance straight downstream to avoid spooking fish. Whatever the angle of your cast, a drag-free presentation is essential. For nymphing, a dead drift is also important, although raising the rod at the end of the drift—the Leisenring Lift—seems to induce strikes.

In addition to wild brook trout, the Carmans is stocked with about 1,500 rainbows each year, along with roughly 1,000 browns. In response to anglers concerned about the effects on the wild brook trout, stocking of two-year-old browns has been eliminated in the upper portion of the river. Visiting anglers can do their part toward protecting the native fish by ignoring the three fish limit and returning all brookies to the water unharmed. In fact, the DEC recommends just that (and is considering making all brook trout fishing in Suffolk County catch and release).

Tidal Section of Carman's River

The tidal section begins south of Route 27/Sunrise Highway, then enters Wertheim National Wildlife Refuge. Access is available on the upper end, and a canoe can be carried in (although it is a long walk). There is also a boat rental on Montauk Highway (see Yaphank/Middle Island Hub City at the end of this section). The lower Carmans is stocked with about 1,000 brown trout each year, including 300 large fish.

There are sporadic searun fish here, but not really enough to target. There are plans to build a fish ladder to get fish past the small falls near Route 27, which could promote a larger searun population.

Stream Facts: Carmans River

Season
- South Haven County Park (Yaphank Avenue downstream to Hard's Lake Dam) April 1 to September 30.
- Above park (Yaphank Avenue): April 1 to November 30.
- Tidal Section open all year.

Special Regulations
- Above South Haven County Park: None.
- Within Southhaven Park, above Cement Dam, flyfishing only. Above electric power (LILCO) lines flyfishing and catch and release only.

Fish
- Wild brook trout, more common in upper river; stocked brown and rainbow trout. A few searun fish in tidal section.

River Characteristics
- Park section is smooth, even-flowing spring creek. Becomes very wide in lower park section. Tidal section wide and brackish.

River Flows
- Steady and cool, very slow in portion just above Cement Dam.

Carmans River—Major Hatches

INSECT	J	F	M	A	M	J	J	A	S	O	N	D	FLIES
Black\Brown Stone 12-16													Elk Hair Caddis, Stonefly Nymphs
Little Black Caddis (Chimarra) 16-18													Elk Hair Caddis, Goddard Caddis, Bead-Head Pupa
Caddis Green, Gray, Tan 14-18													Elk Hair Caddis, Lafontaine Deep Pupa and Emergent Sparkle Pupa, Bead-Head Nymph, Soft Hackle Wet
Blue Winged Olives 16-22													Comparadun, Parachute, CDC Emerger, Compara-Emerger, Pheasant Tail Nymph
Light & Dark Hendrickson 12-14													Light and Dark Hendrickson, Comparadun or Parachute, Hendrickson Nymph, Rusty Spinner
Sulphurs 14-18													Comparadun, Parachute, CDC Emerger, Compara-Emerger, Pheasant Tail Nymph, Hare's Ear Nymph
Light Cahill 14-16													Cream Variant, Comparadun, Cahill Wet Fly, Light Hare's Ear Nymph, Cream Spinner
Trico 22-26													Trico Spinner, Griffith's Gnat, Trico Nymph
Ants Hoppers/Crickets Beetles													Dubbed Ant, Sinking Ant, Letort Hopper\Cricket, Foam Beetle
Midges-White,Gray, Black, 20-28													Brassia, Midge Pupa (dubbed, thread or crystal flash body), Midge Dry, Griffith's Gnat

SWAN RIVER/EAST SWAN LAKE

This small river runs about three miles in the town of Brookhaven. About half of it is above East Lake (confusingly, also known as Swan Lake and East Swan Lake), the remaining tidal portion runs from the lake to Patchogue Bay on the south shore.

The portion of the river below the lake receives a stocking of 500 yearling brown trout, while 400 browns and 400 rainbows are stocked in the lake each year. There is also a naturally reproducing population of small brook trout in the lake. Like all brook trout on Long Island, this population is fragile; although fish over 10 inches can legally be taken, it is far better to release them. Largemouth bass are also resident in the lake. The tidal portion of the river—as with other tidal rivers—is open to fishing year round. The lake and the freshwater portion of the stream are open for trout from April 1 to November 30. Access to the stream portions is from a few dead-end roads that abut the stream. The lake can be reached at the intersection of Main Street and Lake Drive.

CARLL'S RIVER

Belmont Lake, Southard's Pond, Argylle Lake

The Carll's River, sometimes called Carll's Creek, connects these three lakes, flowing about four miles from its source at Belmont Lake to its mouth on the south shore of Long Island. Its entire length is contained within a green belt composed of Belmont Lake State Park and a couple of local parks.

The longer upper section of the river runs between Belmont Lake and Southard's Pond, a distance of about 1.5 miles. This stretch should hold fish nearly year round, although probably not in the dead of summer. Conditions are quite tight in this portion of the river and dapping rather than casting is in order. That means a long rod may actually work better here. There is a deep pool just south of Sunrise Highway/Route 27 and above Southard's Pond that should hold some of the bigger fish in this stretch of the river.

The second section of the river runs only about three-quarters of a mile from Southard's Pond to Argylle Lake. This stretch is much shorter than the upper portion, but it is also wider, allowing some actual casting. While trout won't hold over through the dog-days of most years, in cooler, wetter summers like 1996 and 2000 they can still be spotted here in August. In these years the stocked trout should have enough time to get to impressive size by fall, not to mention the following spring. Don't look for much in the way of hatches here, especially mayflies; however, there should be some caddis in this stream and a larva or pupa imitation is a good bet for subsurface fishing.

The state stocks roughly a thousand fish in each stretch of the river, half rainbows and half browns. In addition, about 650 rainbows and 150 browns are stocked in Argylle Lake. These fish are unlikely to hold over in the shallow lake, but they may work their way into the stream. Also, Southard's Pond gets an annual stocking of about 600 fish, all rainbows. Belmont Lake receives a small stocking of about 350 fish, mostly rainbows. This lake, unlike the other two, is used for multiple recreation—including rented paddleboats—that would hamper flyfishing.

Like most waters in Suffolk County, the stream and the lakes are open to trout fishing for an extended season that runs from April 1 to November 30. Five trout per day may be kept.

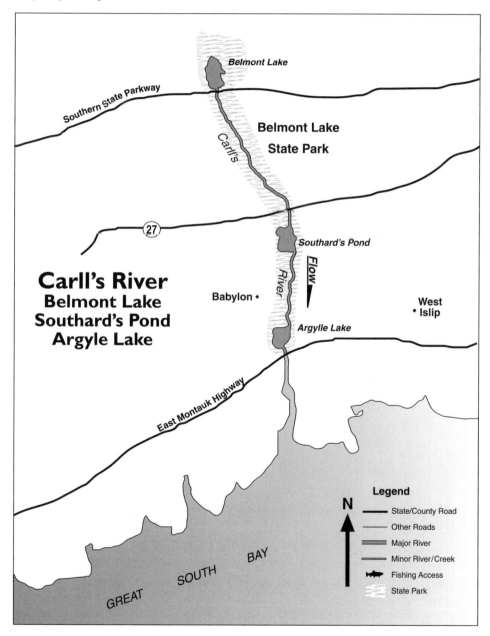

Carll's River
Belmont Lake
Southard's Pond
Argyle Lake

PECONIC RIVER

The Peconic is primarily known as a stream for warmwater fish, but its upper section also holds trout. The stream receives about 200 small browns and 80 two-year-olds. The presence of a few springs and generally cool temperatures make conditions good for holdover, but there is no hard information on the population. Stocking is done downstream from Connecticut Avenue, between the villages of Manorville and Calverton. The section stocked with trout runs roughly one mile to the railroad tracks where the river widens into a small pond. This stretch is wadeable, but you can also put in a small canoe here.

The DEC has three access points on this stretch of the river where a canoe can be launched. You must have a free DEC permit to use these sites. The upper canoe launch area is a small site near the village of Calverton, where Connecticut Avenue crosses the river. The second area is also in Calverton, about a quarter-mile downstream from Connecticut Avenue along River Road. The third point is where Edwards Avenue crosses the river at the lower end of the impoundment which marks the end of the trout stocking section. The last two sites provide a few parking spots.

Caddis, and warmwater staples such as damselflies and dragonflies, are the most likely hatches on the Peconic. A streamer is also a good bet.

Farther down, the Peconic is a warmwater fishery. It also widens out and becomes more conducive to canoeing, although there are a few places where wading remains possible. This section holds largemouths and some good-sized pickerel. There is no need to get fancy when targeting these fish, just try a popping bug, but add a small bite tippet for the pickerel's sharp teeth.

DEC Managed Lands Access Permit

The DEC manages several parcels on Long Island that are only accessible by permit. These include four sites on the upper Peconic River (and part-time access to Deep Pond).

The free permit is obtained by submitting an application to the DEC Region 1 Office. When you receive an application you'll be asked to indicate the areas you wish to use (for freshwater fishing, check off the Otis Pike and Peconic areas and the Deep Pond Cooperative). Applications must be accompanied by a copy of your fishing license and a self addressed, stamped envelope. Permits are valid for three years.

The permit application can be obtained by contacting DEC Region 1 at DEC-Sporting License Office, SUNY Building 40, Stony Brook, NY 11790; 631-444-0273.

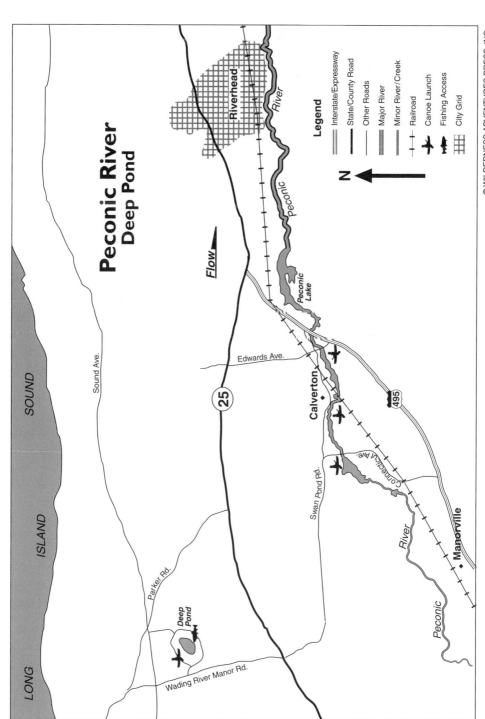

Peconic River
Deep Pond

Legend

Interstate/Expressway
State/County Road
Other Roads
Major River
Minor River/Creek
Railroad
Canoe Launch
Fishing Access
City Grid

N

Flow

Riverhead

Peconic River

Peconic

Peconic Lake

Edwards Ave.

Calverton

495

Swan Pond Rd.

Connecticut Ave.

Manorville

Peconic River

Peconic River

25

Parker Rd.

Deep Pond

Wading River Manor Rd.

Sound Ave.

LONG

ISLAND

SOUND

MASSAPEQUA CREEK

Massapequa Creek is the best trout stream in Nassau County, but it does not compare to the three major streams in Suffolk. There is a long, narrow portion of the creek above Massapequa Reservoir, but it is the short, wide stretch that runs a bit over a half-mile between the reservoir and the separate Massapequa Lake that is of most interest to fly anglers. Both stillwaters and the stream fall within Massapequa Park and Massapequa Preserve.

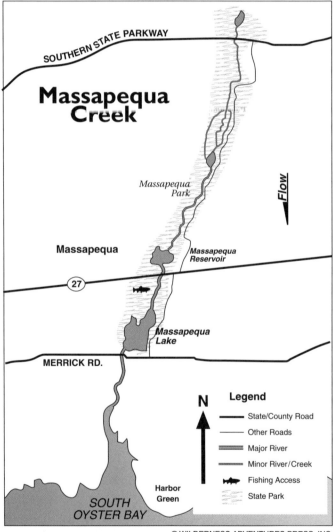

© WILDERNESS ADVENTURES PRESS, INC.

Like other streams in the area, hatches are not frequent, although a caddis pupa or larva would be a good bet. The creek does hold a large population of killi-fish, and the larger browns undoubtedly feed on these. The killifish are brownish-olive on top with a tan belly and black vertical stripes. A two-inch minnow imitation in roughly these colors, such as a freshwater Deceiver with dyed brown or tan grizzly hackle, would make an effective imitation.

The state stocks this small stretch of the creek with about 450 rainbows each year and 200 two-year-old brown trout. Like all Nassau County waters, there is no closed season. That, combined with the stocking of some fish in fall, makes this a good place to go on those sunny February and March days when you just can't wait for spring.

Massapequa Reservoir is stocked annually with over 2,500 fish, about 1,500 rainbows and the rest browns. Few of the trout hold over.

Long Island Ponds

NASSAU COUNTY

In addition to Massapequa Reservoir, the following ponds in Nassau County are stocked with trout. All permit fishing year round.

Oyster Bay Mill Pond

This 20-acre pond is located on the north shore of Long Island in Nassau County, near the village of Oyster Bay. More than 1,100 trout are stocked here each year, including a fall stocking. About 600 of the stocked fish are rainbows, the remainder are browns, including 400 two-year-olds. Largemouth bass and white perch hold here naturally.

Shoreline access is somewhat limited but a National Fish and Wildlife property on the southern shore will permit access. Portable boats and float tubes are also allowed.

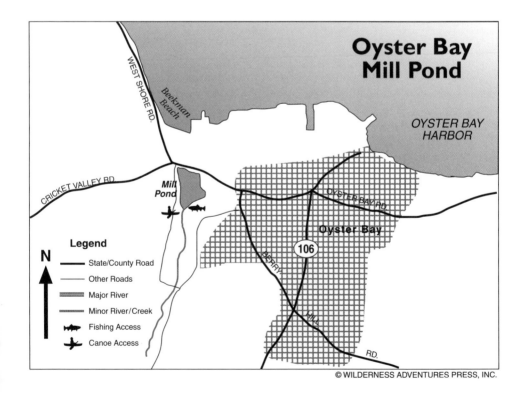

Upper Twin Pond

This small pond between Wantagh and Bellmore in Nassau County (sometimes called Newbridge Pond and not to be confused with Twin Pond in Suffolk County), is stocked annually with about 1,100 brown trout, mostly two-year-olds, and about 1,200 rainbows. The pond, along with neighboring Lower Twin Pond and Wantagh Mill Pond—both of which have largemouths but no trout—is located in Mill Pond County Park at the intersection of Wantagh Parkway and Sunrise Highway/27.

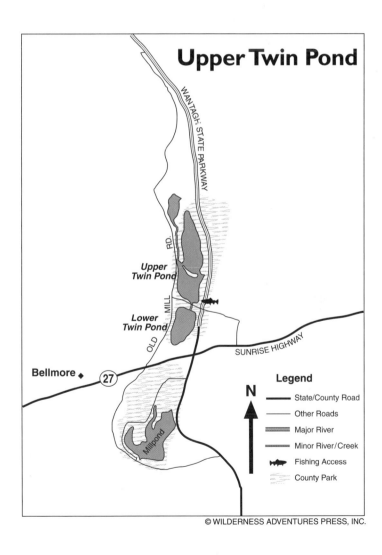

South Pond/McDonald's Pond

These two ponds are located in Hempstead State Park. Each October they are stocked with a mix of brookies, browns and rainbows from the Connetquot hatchery for a family fishing event held near the end of the month. South Pond receives about 700 fish, while tiny McDonald's Pond gets 400. Although many of these fish are caught and kept during the event, another 500 and 400 fish respectively are put in the two ponds about a month later. Both waters are subject to a three fish per day limit.

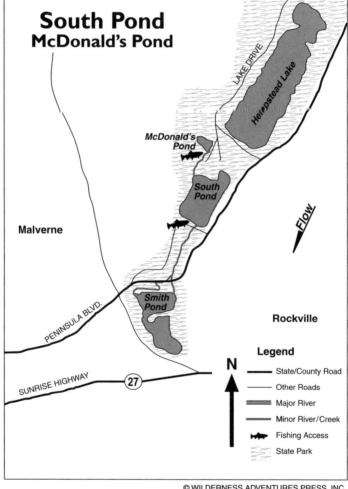

© WILDERNESS ADVENTURES PRESS, INC.

SUFFOLK COUNTY

The following lakes and ponds offer better than average fishing or special fishing opportunities.

Laurel Lake

This is a 30-acre lake on eastern Suffolk's North Fork in the town of Southold. The state stocks about 600 small trout here each year, half browns and half rainbows. The smaller stocking reflects the good holdover this lake offers. DEC Region 1 biologist Greg Koslowski considers this one of the best places outside the rivers to catch a large trout on Long Island. The 8-inch fish stocked in spring quickly grow to 14 inches by fall.

These fish feed readily on the killifish that are plentiful in the lake. There are Callibaetis and a few other hatches here on late summer and fall evenings that make the water boil with fish. In addition to the trout, there are largemouth bass and pickerel here.

Unlike some other stocked ponds in the east end of Long Island, there are no restrictions for non-residents on parking or access. There is good access from a state park and conservation area on the southern shore of the lake. There is no boat launch, but cartoppers can be carried and a float tube is possible, too. Trout fishing is permitted year round on Laurel Lake.

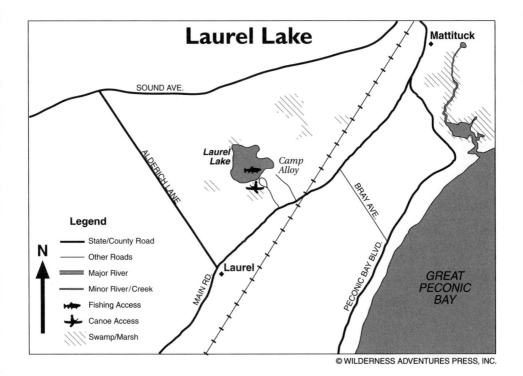

© WILDERNESS ADVENTURES PRESS, INC.

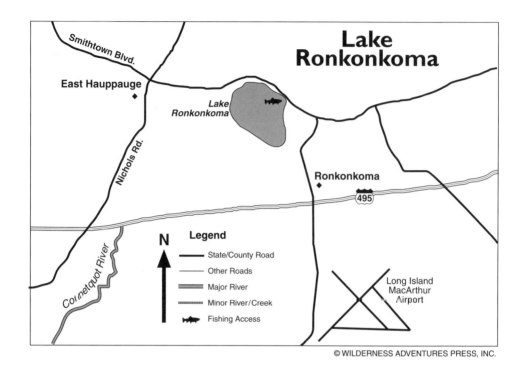

© WILDERNESS ADVENTURES PRESS, INC.

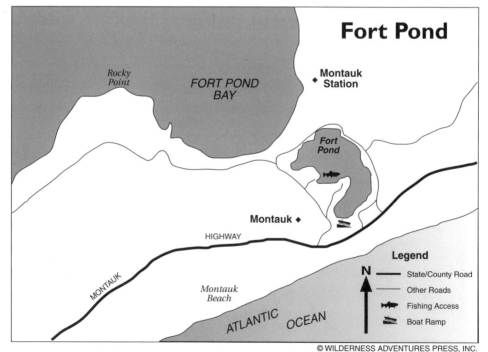

© WILDERNESS ADVENTURES PRESS, INC.

Lake Ronkonkoma

Lake Ronkonkoma is a deep-water lake near the village of the same name, a few miles from Connetquot State Park. Covering over 240 acres, it is one of Long Island's largest lakes.

This is not a trout fishery, but walleye have been stocked here for several years. The primary motivation was to control the white perch population, but there were also hopes of creating a walleye fishery. Reports seem to justify this optimism. In formal surveys, walleye have been found in the 15-inch range, up from only 8 to 9 inches when stocked, and anglers report seeing fish up to 20 inches. This is primarily bait and spin fishing, but since the walleye are known to hit live minnows, there is every reason to think a persistent fly angler with a sink tip line and a minnow imitation should be able to take walleye here, too. Lake Ronkonkoma also has a small naturally reproducing population of smallmouth bass.

Ronkonkoma is one of the more accessible stillwaters on Long Island. There is access for disabled anglers and a boat launch available. The walleye in Lake Ronkonkoma may be targeted from May 1 through March 15 (in other words, only about 6 weeks are closed). Smallmouth may be fished during an extended season from the first Saturday in June through March 15, but the portion of the season from December 1 to March 15 is strictly catch and release.

Fort Pond

Fort Pond is in Montauk near the end of Long Island's South Fork. Like Lake Ronkonkoma, it is a large, deep-water pond of nearly 200 acres. The fish population is also similar to Lake Ronkonkoma; there are no trout, but walleye are stocked in addition to a wild smallmouth population.

There is less hard information available on the success of the walleye stocking here, but the conditions make it likely that they will grow as well as they do in Lake Ronkonkoma. About 8,000 fingerling walleye are stocked each year. The smallmouth population here is larger than in Ronkonkoma. Fort Pond has steep sides and fishing for both species will require sink tip or full sinking lines and persistence.

There is DEC access, and a boat launch is provided. Fort Pond has the same seasonal restrictions as Lake Ronkonkoma. Walleye season runs from May 1 through March 15. Smallmouth may be fished from the first Saturday in June through March 15, but from December 1 to March 15 all smallmouth must be released.

West Lake

This small 20-acre lake near Patchogue in the town of Brookhaven along the south shore of Long Island is stocked with trout. About 1,000 rainbows are stocked each year, along with 800 brown trout. There is informal access at West Main Street that affords an opportunity to hand carry a canoe or other light craft.

Mill Pond (Sayville)

A 6-acre stillwater in the village of Sayville, Mill Pond is stocked with about 500 small rainbows each year. Access is at Montauk Highway on the south shore of the pond.

Deep Pond

Located in the town of Riverhead, this 32-acre pond is on land owned by the Boy Scouts. However, through an agreement with the state, anglers with the special, free DEC access permit can fish here, subject to restrictions. Specifically, permit holders may fish on weekdays from September 15 to June 15. With the general trout season in Suffolk County running from April 1 to November 30, this means permit holders may fish for trout here from April 1 to June 15 on weekdays, and again from September 15 to the end of November.

Deep Pond receives a modest stocking each year, about 400 small brown trout and an equal number of small rainbows. The lake's depth, reflected in its name, allows holdover of the stocked fish. There is also a good population of pickerel. Hand-carried boats, using paddles or electric motors, are permitted during the angling periods for permit holders.

Long Island Hub Cities

Central Islip/Brentwood

HOTELS/MOTELS

Bayshore Motor Inn, 300 Bay Shore Rd., Bay Shore, NY 11706 / 631-666-7275 /
$$

Bay Shore Hotel, 1 Park Plz, Bay Shore, NY 11706 / 631-665-9872 / $$

CAMPGROUNDS/RVS

Hecksher State Park, East Islip / 631-581-2100

RESTAURANTS

Bayberry Cafe, 526 Main St., Islip, NY 11751 / 631-224-4967

Tangs, 712 Main St., Islip, NY 11751 / 631-277-2828

FLY SHOPS

See Long Island Fly Shops at end of this section

TACKLE SHOPS

Beckmann's Fishing Tackle, 803 Sunrise Hwy, Lynbrook, NY 11563 /
516-593-7288

Franks Hunting and Fishing, 91 Carleton Ave, Islip Terrace, NY 11752 /
631-277-8266

Lakeside Outdoor Center, 335 Smithtown Boulevard, Ronkonkoma, NY 11779 /
631-585-0756

AUTO REPAIR

Richie's Towing, 92 Carleton Ave., Islip Terrace, NY 11752 / 631-581-4664

AIRPORT

Long Island Macarthur Airport, 100 Arrival Ave., Ronkonkoma, NY 11779 /
631-467-3210

Town of Brookhaven Airport, Dawn Drive, Shirley, NY 11967 / 631-281-5100

HOSPITAL/CLINIC

Brookhaven Memorial Hospital, Patchogue, NY 11772 / 631-654-7100

University Hospital & Medical Center, Stonybrook, NY 11790 / 631-444-1010

Smithtown/Hauppauge/Centerreach

HOTELS/MOTELS

Towne House Motor Inn, 880 W Jericho Tpke, Smithtown, NY 11787 /
631-543-4040 / $

Sheraton, 110 Vanderbilt Motor Pkwy, Hauppauge, NY 11788 /
631-231-1100 / $$$

CAMPGROUNDS/RVS

Hecksher State Park, East Islip / 631-581-2100

RESTAURANTS

Nickels Cafe, 482 Route 111, Smithtown, NY 11787 / 631-348-0808

Casa Rustica, 175 W Main St, Smithtown, NY 11787 / 631-265-9265

FLY SHOPS

See Long Island Fly Shops at end of this section

AUTO REPAIR

Rayco, 1884 Middle Country Road, Centereach, NY / 631-585-3800

Smithwest Service Center, 303 Maple Ave, Smithtown, NY / 631-265-9885

AIRPORT

Long Island Macarthur Airport, 100 Arrival Ave., Ronkonkoma, NY 11779 /
631-467-3210

Town of Brookhaven Airport, Dawn Drive, Shirley, NY 11967 / 631-281-5100

HOSPITAL/CLINIC

Brookhaven Memorial Hospital, Patchogue, NY 11772 / 631-654-7100

University Hospital & Medical Center, Stonybrook, NY 11790 / 631-444-1010

Yaphank/Middle Island

HOTELS/MOTELS
Inn at Medford, 2695 Route 112, Medford, NY 11763 / 631-654-3000 / $$$
Best Western Inn, 1730 N Ocean Ave, Holtsville, NY 11742 / 631-758-2900 / $$$$

CAMPGROUNDS/RVs
Riverside Campgrounds, 7 Saint Regis Street, Brookhaven, NY 11719 /
315-389-4771
Wildwood State Park, Wading River, NY / 631-929-4314

RESTAURANTS
Carmans River Inn, 450 Main St, Yaphank, NY 11980 / 631-345-3302
Country Diner, 837 Middle Country Rd, Middle Island, NY 11953 / 631-924-2885

FLY SHOPS
See Long Island Fly Shops at end of this section

TACKLE SHOPS
Smith Point Bait and Tackle and Marine Supply, 396 William Floyd Parkway,
Shirley, NY 11967 / 631-281-3766
Mastic Bait and Tackle, 1586 Montauk Highway, Mastic, NY 11950 /
631-281-9360
B&B Tackle and Sports, 320 Main Center, Moriches, NY 11955 / 631-878-9280
Dicks Bait and Tackle, 286 Neighborhood Rd, Mastic Beach, NY 11951 /
631-281-9070
J&J Bait and Tackle, 265 West Main Street, Patchogue, NY 11772 / 631-654-2311

BOAT RENTAL
Carmans River Canoe, 2979 Montauk Highway, Brookhaven, New York 11719 /
631-286-1966

AUTO REPAIR
Alson Car Care, 805 Route 25, Middle Island, NY / 631-924-6115
M.D. Auto Repair, 46 Division Street, Patchogue, NY / 631-758-7171

AIRPORT
Long Island Macarthur Airport, 100 Arrival Ave., Ronkonkoma, NY 11779 /
631-467-3210
Town of Brookhaven Airport, Dawn Drive, Shirley, NY 11967 / 631-281-5100

HOSPITAL/CLINIC
Brookhaven Memorial Hospital, Patchogue, NY 11772 / 631-654-7100
University Hospital & Medical Center, Stonybrook, NY 11790 / 631-444-1010

Riverhead

HOTELS/MOTELS

Budget Host Inn, 30 East Moriches Road, NY 11901 / 631-727-6200 / $$
Ramada East End, 1830 Rt 25, East Moriches, NY 11901 / 631-369-2200 / Restaurant / $$$
Wading River Motel, 5890 Middle Country Road, Wading River, NY 11792 / 631-727-8000 / $$

CAMPGROUNDS/RVs

Riverside Campgrounds, 7 Saint Regis Street, Brookhaven, NY 11719 / 315-389-4771
Dorothy P Flint 4-H Camp, Sound Avenue, Riverhead, NY 11901 / 631-727-7513

RESTAURANTS

Meeting House Creek Inn, Meeting House Creek Road / 631-722-4220

FLY SHOPS

See Long Island Fly Shops at end of this section

TACKLE SHOPS

Stalker Outfitters, 381 Riverhead Road, Suite 8, Westhampton Beach, NY 11978 / 631-288-3844
Jamesport Bait & Tackle, Main Road, Jamesport, NY 11947 / 631-722-3219
Atlenkirch Precision Tackle, Shinecock Canal, Hampton Bays, NY 11946 / 631-728-4110

AUTO REPAIR

Phil's Auto & Truck Repair, 508 Northville Turnpike, Riverhead, NY / 631-727-2666

AIRPORT

Suffolk County Airport, Westhampton Beach, NY 11978 / 631-288-5410

HOSPITAL/CLINIC

Central Suffolk Hospital, 1300 Roanoke Ave., Rivehead, NY 11901 / 631-548-6000

Long Island Fly Shops

The fly shops on Long Island are not necessarily near the hub cities that serve the major rivers, so they are listed together here. All offer a full range of rods, reels, flies and accessories.

NASSAU COUNTY
Orvis, 50 Glen Cove Road, Greenvale, NY 11548 / 516-484-1860

SUFFOLK COUNTY
Camp-Site Sports, 1877 New York Ave., Huntington, NY / 631-271-4969 /
www.campsite.net

Cold Spring Outfitters, 37 Main Street, Cold Spring Harbor, NY 11724 /
631-673-8937

The Fly Fishing Store, 4105 Sunrise Highway (Route 27), Bohemia, NY 11716 /
631-563-1323 / www.flyfishingstore.com / Bohemia store is near Connetquot
Park

Long Island Guides

These guides cover Long Island streams and ponds, offering instruction as well as guiding.

MARK MALENOVSKY
10 Sterling Place
Sayville, NY 11782
631-589-0065

STEVE METZLER
631-928-0503
e-mail: stevemetz@worldnet.att.net

New York - Central Region

Central Region

This thin slice of the state falls between the Catskills to the South and the Adirondacks to the North, and is divided by the Hudson River. In the eastern portion, excellent trout fishing is found in the Battenkill and some nearby streams. West of the Hudson, several Mohawk Valley streams offer trout, with West Canada Creek the premier water.

EAST OF THE HUDSON RIVER
Renssellaer and
Washington Counties

BATTENKILL RIVER

Though widely known as a Vermont stream, the Battenkill actually runs for about 18 miles in New York, from the state line to the Hudson River. Along the way its clear, cool, smooth-flowing waters offer very challenging fishing for wild browns and brookies, and for (somewhat) easier stocked browns.

The Battenkill crosses the Vermont/New York border in the Washington County town of Salem. From the border to just above the village of Shushan—roughly six miles in all—the stream is not stocked. Most of this stretch, from the border to the covered bridge at Eagleville, is subject to special regulations: year round fishing permitted, three fish per day of 10 inches or more.

The wild trout section of the Battenkill holds browns and some brookies (which are more common as you head upstream) and catching these fish is a challenge even for skilled anglers. Finding the trout can be tricky. With the river's lack of structure they often hold in deep or covered water and move into pools and shallows only to feed. There are a variety of hatches, but they are not as dense here as

Battenkill River
& Hudson River

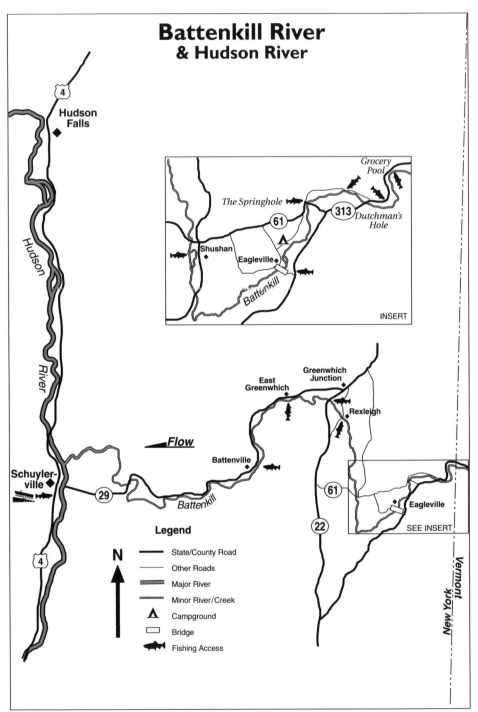

INSERT

Legend

N

— State/County Road
— Other Roads
— Major River
— Minor River/Creek
Λ Campground
▭ Bridge
🐟 Fishing Access

in some other top streams, and the fish do not often rise freely to the natural duns, much less their imitations. As a result, emergers in or below the film and spinner imitations during or after a hatch are much more commonly used here. Parachute patterns are a staple of knowledgeable anglers, serving to mimic both the adult and spinner forms of mayflies (and, when tied on curved hooks, resembling emergers as well). For traditional spinners, hackle tip wings or hackle wrapped and clipped are said to work better than poly wings, and quill rather than dubbed bodies are also recommended.

If no rises are seen—a common occurrence on the Battenkill—try a soft hackle wet fly. Fished down and across on a tight line, these are useful searching patterns. The wets should be gray or brown in early season (roughly through June), cream or pale yellow to imitate Sulphurs and Cahills in summer, and dark in the fall. If you can avoid tangles, try two wets at a time. Riffled water, especially where it flows into a calmer pool, is the prime target for wet fly fishing. Nymph imitations are sometimes used, but they aren't always effective, perhaps due to the very clear water.

Even though duns are not the best weapon here, it pays to know the hatches for emergers and spinners. Hendricksons are good in early to mid-May, along with Blue Quills. There are reliable hatches of small yellow stoneflies, imitated by Yellow Sallies, and sporadic caddis (best imitated with various emerger patterns). Late spring into summer brings Sulphurs and Cahills. The Tricos of late summer and fall are plentiful, and fishing to trout—especially wild ones—with these small flies is very challenging. Plan on long leaders, careful stalking and a dose of patience.

The Battenkill's clear water makes stealth essential.

An angler fishing the Battenkill's special regulations section. (Photo by Greg Cuda)

There are also baitfish in the Battenkill, and even a couple of well-known local streamers: the Battenkill Shiner and the Shushan Postmaster. Tyer and netmaker Mark Francatto likes to use a Bugger with a silver beadhead, brown body, black tail and mixed brown and black hackle. He finds it works particularly well drifted where fast water heads into slower flows. There are many olive brown sculpins in the stream, so an imitation of these—such as a woolhead Muddler Minnow—would be a good choice. In addition, the Battenkill holds crayfish, which are reasonably imitated by Woolly Buggers. As in most waters, streamers here are lures for fewer, bigger fish and best used at (or before) dawn, or when the water is cloudy.

Even without streamers, big wild browns are taken in the Battenkill, perhaps more commonly as the overall population of stream-bred fish has declined. After years of whispering, the falling number of wild fish on both sides of the border is now openly discussed and the two states are actively studying the problem, though the precise cause has not been identified. A recent shocking survey on the New York side did find a larger population of wild fingerling and yearling browns than expected, so the wild population might be on the upswing.

In addition to the decline in wild fish, another concern for Battenkill anglers is the proliferation of kayaks and canoes. The best way to avoid boaters is to fish early and late (before 10 a.m. and after 5 p.m.) and perhaps skip July and August weekends entirely. Despite all the recreational boating, float fishing is rare on the Battenkill. The trout are spooked by the boats and almost all fish can be reached by wading.

After the first six miles, the New York water below Shushan is actively stocked; about 23,000 browns in all are put in. These fish rise freely immediately after they are put in, but they soon become acclimated to the water and exhibit many of the same habits as wild fish. They also hold over well, thanks to frequent underwater springs.

In both the wild and stocked sections, most of the Battenkill is open to the public through fishing easements. For the wild stretch of stream, there is a good pool where Route 313 crosses and another several hundred yards upstream; these are known for especially dense Trico hatches in late summer and fall. Farther down is the pool named for Lee Wulff and nearby, where Route 61 crosses, is the Springhole—reportedly another Wulff favorite. At the Springhole, fish will sometimes rise both in the main current and in back eddies. Careful casting and mending are required, though, to deal with tricky currents. In addition, the Eagleville Bridge on Eagleville Road has dedicated parking and stream access to good pools below and above the large midstream island.

In the stocked section good spots include the covered bridge in Rexleigh (an especially picturesque site) off Skellie Road and Route 61 in the village of Battenville and the Route 29 crossing in East Greenwich (pronounced "Green Witch"). Trout fishing continues to the village of Greenwich, but it is not as good as the water upstream. Toward the end of its run, the Battenkill water warms and some tiger muskies are stocked at the extreme lower end.

Stream Facts: Battenkill River

Seasons
- April 1 to October 15; roughly three-mile special regulations section from Vermont border to Eagleville Covered Bridge open all year.

Special Regulations
- Special regulations section three fish per day, 10 inches or more.
- Rest of stream, five fish any size, plus five brook trout under eight inches.

Fish
- Wild browns and some brookies in first six miles, stocked and holdover browns along with some wild fish below.

River Characteristics
- Medium width, generally slow moving, cobbled bottom, relatively easy wading.

River Flows
- Generally steady, smooth surface; water remains cool due to underground springs.

The Eagleville Bridge on the Battenkill's catch-and-release section

Battenkill River—Major Hatches

INSECT	J	F	M	A	M	J	J	A	S	O	N	D	FLIES
Black\Brown\Yellow Stone 14-18				▮									Stonefly Nymphs, Yellow Sallies, Dries
Blue Quill			▮	▮									Blue Quill Dry, Spinner, Soft Hackles
Lt. And Dark Hendrickson 12-14				▮	▮								Light and Dark Hendrickson Parachutes, Emergers, Spinners
Caddis Green, Grey, Tan 14-18				▮	▮	▮	▮	▮					Lafontaine Deep Pupa and Emergent Sparkle Pupa Soft Hackle Wets, Bead-Head Nymphs
Blue Winged Olives 16-22				▮	▮								Parachute, Emergers, Spinners
Sulphurs 14-20					▮	▮							Comparadun, Parachute, CDC Emerger, Compara-Emerger, Pheasant Tail Nymph, Hare's Ear Nymph
Light Cahill 12-14					▮	▮	▮						Cream Variant, Comparadun, Cahill Wet Fly, Light Hare's Ear Nymph,
Trico 20-24							▮	▮					Trico Spinner, Griffith's Gnat
Streamers	▮	▮	▮	▮	▮	▮	▮	▮	▮	▮	▮	▮	Battenkill Shiner, Shushan Postmaster, Bucktail Patterns, Woolly Buggers (including crayfish colors)

LITTLE HOOSIC RIVER

The Little Hoosic runs north in Renssellaer County from near the village of Center Berlin to its confluence with the Hoosic River at Petersburgh Junction—about 10 miles in all. This small stream isn't stocked and is home to a population of small wild browns and rainbows.

Upstream the "river" is very small, no more than five feet across. Downstream (north) of Berlin, the stream is slightly bigger, although it is rarely more than 8-10 feet across. As with most small streams, wade carefully and don't ignore any structure or slightly deeper spots. In addition to caddis and mayflies, terrestrials are a good choice, especially in the brushy upper half.

Formal access is available off Rout 22 at Brimmer Farm Road in Berlin and where Route 346 crosses the stream near its mouth in Petersburg Junction. At the latter access, the stream is a bit wider and easier to fish and anglers can wade downstream to the confluence with the Hoosic. There are also informal access points along Route 22, which parallels the river.

The stream is open for the normal trout season, April 1 to October 15. Five fish may be taken, but they must be nine inches or more. A better option for this small, wild stream is to put back all the fish you catch.

The Little Hoosic has a good population of wild fish.

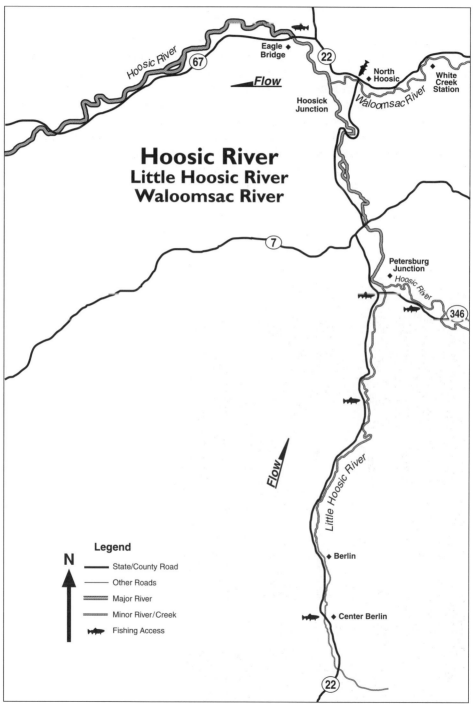

Hoosic River
Little Hoosic River
Waloomsac River

Hoosic River

Eagle Bridge

North Hoosic

White Creek Station

Hoosick Junction

Waloomsac River

Flow

Petersburg Junction

Hoosic River

Flow

Little Hoosic River

Berlin

Center Berlin

Legend

N

———— State/County Road

———— Other Roads

▨▨▨ Major River

▨▨ Minor River/Creek

🐟 Fishing Access

© WILDERNESS ADVENTURES PRESS, INC.

WALLOOMSAC RIVER

The Walloomsac crosses the Vermont border near the village of White Creek Station and flows south about 8 miles to the Hoosic River at Hoosick Junction (with the added "k"). The stream is heavily stocked with about 6,000 browns each year.

The entire stream tends to warm in summer, and after the village of North Hoosic—about 5 miles from the Vermont border—the trout fishing falls off. (However, you may encounter large trout from the Hoosic at the mouth of the Walloomsac.) The river is known locally for quickly returning to normal after rain and runoff, so it's a good stream to fish when others in the area are still running high. The Walloomsac gets a standard array of mayfly and caddis hatches and has a good Trico hatch in August and September.

Access can be found along Route 22 just north of the Route 7 crossing, and where Cottrell Road crosses upstream of North Hoosic. Parts of the stream can be rocky, particularly in the steep gorge in the town of Walloomsac, where Route 22/67 crosses the river. No special regulations or seasons apply to the river.

The rocky gorge on the Walloomsac.

Some big trout can be found in the Hoosic's slow current.

HOOSIC RIVER

This stream, which runs west out of Vermont near Petersburg Junction and on to the Hudson, is a bit of a sleeper. Once largely devoid of fish due to tanneries along its banks, today it does hold trout. While no longer stocked, it has some wild browns and rainbows that make up in size what they lack in numbers. (It remains to be seen if a toxic spill in 2001 has further reduced trout density.)

The Hoosic is wide and has slow moving sections along with some faster, riffled water. The better trout water is upstream of the village of Eagle Bridge. (Downstream of Eagle Bridge anglers may encounter smallmouth bass.) Summer temperatures are a limiting factor in the trout section, and it is much better fished early in the season. The mouths of feeders such as the Walloomsac and Little Hoosic are said to be good places to hit. There are some mayflies, including the White Fly, Sulphurs and Cahills, along with caddis, particularly in tan and cream colors.

Because the streambed is wide and poorly shaded, dry fly fishing is mostly reserved for evenings. For earlier hours, deeply-fished nymphs, Woolly Buggers and leech patterns are more productive. Access can be tricky on the Hoosic, but there are some pulloffs at Route 346 along the railroad tracks (take care when walking across the single lane track). Asking permission from landowners is also worth a try.

Like the Little Hoosic, the Hoosic is subject to the normal season but only fish of nine inches or more may be kept. Again, better to put them back.

METTAWEE RIVER

An excellent small wild fishery in Vermont, this stream becomes wide on the New York side, offering fishing for stocked rainbows and browns, and a few wild fish. Local anglers note that some fish kills in the past decade have reduced the Mettawee's productivity, but it is still worth fishing.

The Mettawee crosses the border at Granville and flows about 14 miles before emptying into the barge canal near Whitehall. About 8,000 trout are stocked, a bit more than half are rainbows. Anglers near the state line may encounter some of the wild rainbows and browns from the other side of the border.

Primarily a caddis river in New York, there are also some Cahills, Gray Foxes, and Olives in the stream. It is more popular with bait fisherman, but fly anglers can and do fish it. The width, up to 100 feet across, makes it a good place for streamers like Woolly Buggers. The New York portion, particularly at the lower end, is subject to high summer temperatures, and it is best fished in spring and fall. Caution should be used in wading as the shale bottom is often slippery with algae.

Access on the Mettawee is found along Routes 22 and 22A, and there is parking along 22A west of the village of Granville. The normal trout season and regulations apply to the river.

POULTNEY RIVER

Part of this river lies in Vermont, but about 12 miles of the lower section becomes the border between the two states before it empties into the lower end of Lake Champlain (known as East Bay). About 900 small trout are stocked by the state in the Poultney each year, a bit more than half are rainbows. The stocking is in the upper half of the New York run, in the Washington County town of Hampton. The Poultney is more popular with local spin and bait anglers than with flyfishers.

No special regulations apply to the Poultney, but anglers without a Vermont license should remain on the New York side of the stream, as there is no reciprocal license arrangement here.

HUDSON RIVER

This middle section of the Hudson is well downstream of the Adirondack trout section and upstream of barriers impassable to migrating stripers and shad. Instead, the fishing here is for a variety of warmwater species, with smallmouth bass the most popular target for fly anglers. (PCB pollution kept this section off-limits to anglers for many years, but catch and release fishing was made legal in 1995.)

Smallmouth up to five pounds can be taken, although 12 inches is a typical size. The water is large and a boat is helpful, but wading is possible, especially when water is diverted to the Champlain Boat Canal.

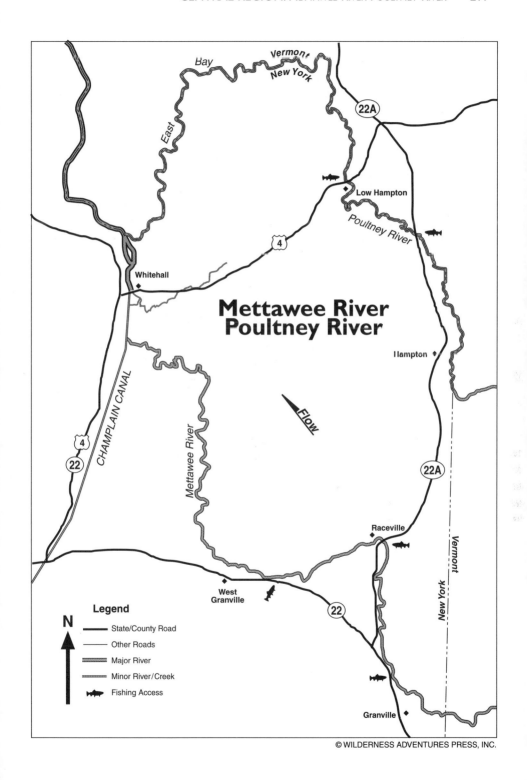

Legend

N

State/County Road
Other Roads
Major River
Minor River/Creek
Fishing Access

Locals recommend the section around Shuyerville on the western bank as a good place to fish. There is a public launch for those with boats, and wading access can be had here. Look for fish holding at ledges and boulders. In fall, smallmouth congregate around feeder creeks, so the mouths of the Battenkill, the Hoosic and the Mohawk are worth checking.

A mix of floating and sinking tip lines in 6- to 8-weight will work. For subsurface fishing, crayfish and Woolly Buggers are useful, and Peter Brown of the Lower River Fly Shop likes a large Hare's Ear Nymph (size 6). There are some summer hatches of caddis that can bring smallmouths to the surface.

The standard black bass season, from the third Saturday in June to November 30, applies to Hudson smallmouth. As noted above, the Hudson (and all its tributaries to their first barriers) is catch and release only from Bakers Falls in the village of Hudson Falls to the Federal Dam at Albany.

American Museum of Fly Fishing

In addition to offering trout fishing on the Battenkill and nearby Mettawee, Manchester Vermont is home to the American Museum of Fly Fishing. The museum is a worthwhile side trip for anyone interested in the lore and history of the sport; with exhibits of fishing art and antique tackle and flies.

The museum is located at the intersection of Route 7A and Seminary Avenue near the center of town. It is open daily except holidays from 10 a.m. to 4 p.m. For additional information call 802-362-3300, or visit their Web site at www.amff.com.

Renssellaer and Washington Counties Hub Cities

Cambridge/Greenwich/Whitehall

ACCOMODATIONS PRICE KEY
$ Up to 60 dollars per night
$$ 61 to 99 dollars per night
$$$ 100 to 150 per night
$$$$ 151 and up per night

HOTELS/MOTELS
Cambridge Inn Bed & Breakfast, 16 West Main Street, Cambridge, NY 12816, /518-677-5741 / $-$$
Cambridge Hotel, 4 West Main Street, Cambridge, NY 12816 / 518-677-5626 / $$
Sunshine Inn, 2624 State Route 40, Greenwich, NY 12834 / 518-692-2997 / $-$$

CAMPGROUNDS/RVS
Battenkill River Sports & Campground, 937 State Route 313, Cambridge, NY 12816 / 518-677-8868

RESTAURANTS
Cambridge Hotel Restaurant, 4 West Main Street, Cambridge, NY 12816 / 518-677-5626
Cambridge Diner,
   9 East Main Street, Cambridge, NY 12816 / 518-677-3546 (B/L)
   111 Main Street, Greenwich, NY 12834 / 518-692-8016
Burger Den Restaurant, 2869 Route 22, Cambridge, NY 12816 / 518-677-5781

FLY SHOPS
The Lower River, 4337 Route 22, Salem NY 12865 / 518-854-3138
VERMONT
Orvis, Historic Route 7A, Manchester, VT 05254 / 802-362-3622

GUIDES
Peter Davidson, P.O. Box 336, Salem, NY   12865 / 518-854-3370

AUTO REPAIR
Bain's Service Center, 182 South Main Street, Salem, NY 12865 / 518-854-3000

AIRPORT
Saratoga County Airport, 410 Greenfield Avenue, Ballston Spa, NY / 12020 /518-885-5354

HOSPITAL/CLINIC
Mary Mc Clellan Hospital, 1 Myrtle Avenue, Cambridge, NY 12816 / 518-677-2611
Southwestern Vermont Medical, 100 Hospital Drive, Bennington, VT 05201 / 802-442-6361

MOHAWK VALLEY AND VICINITY

The Mohawk Valley is caught between the southernmost Adirondacks and the northeastern tip of the Catskills. The trout fishing is primarily in the Mohawk's tributaries rather than the river itself, thought it does have some trout in its upper portion. West Canada creek is the best stream in the area, and is one of the better trout streams in the state.

WEST CANADA CREEK

This wide tailwater—more a river than a creek—flows more than 40 miles from the southern foothills of the Adirondacks to the Mohawk River near Herkimer. Extensive access for most of its length and good holdover for stocked brown trout make this the premier trout stream in the Mohawk Valley region. It also offers a good opportunity to fish from canoes and kayaks.

The headwaters of West Canada Creek flow from a series of small lakes in lower Hamilton County, known collectively as the West Canada Lakes. This upper section runs about 15 miles to Hinckley Reservoir, which is created by the first of four dams on the stream. Above Hinckley, West Canada is a typical mountain trout stream with wild brook trout. Below the reservoir, the stream widens greatly and the main trout fishing begins. Browns are heavily stocked in the four miles from Hinckley to the dam at Trenton Falls, and some brook trout are stocked as well.

A catch and release section extends below Trenton Falls Dam for a distance of about 2.5 miles and is open to fishing year round. The combination of the catch and release rule and good habitat yield some big fish in this area; browns in the 20- to 24-inch range are not unknown. Anglers can park at the dam and work their way down. In addition, there are several parking lots and informal pulloffs along Route 28 and on Trenton Falls Road, which runs along the western shore. Partridge Hill Road on the eastern bank also allows access and is unpaved as it runs past the DEC access on Putnam Road.

Below Trenton Falls the creek widens considerably and is a good place to bring a canoe or float tube. In fact, the water below Trenton Falls has become popular with non-fishing kayakers and canoeists. Kayaks and canoes can be put in just below the dam. They can also be launched at several points along Partridge Hill Road, but launching at the steep banks is easier with lightweight craft. Take-out points are available at the Putnam Road DEC Access or either of the two DEC accesses downstream, about two and four miles respectively from Putnam Road. Fishing continues to Newport, then falls off a bit for the rest of the run down to the dam in Herkimer and the last short leg to the Mohawk.

West Canada was long known more for caddis than for mayflies, although recent water quality improvements have begun to reverse their order of importance. Still, caddis in all colors hatch all season long and local anglers recommend carrying various imitations of all three stages. When fishing in the fall, be prepared

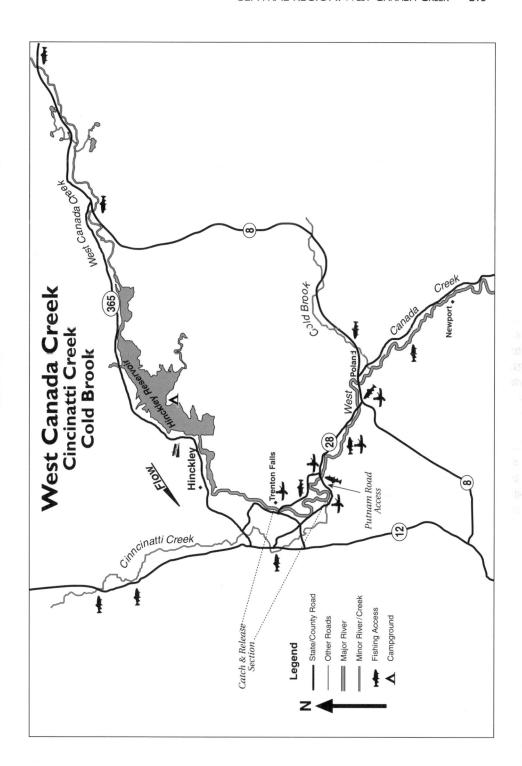

West Canada Creek
Cincinatti Creek
Cold Brook

Legend

State/County Road
Other Roads
Major River
Minor River/Creek
Fishing Access
Campground

N

Catch & Release
Section

Putnam Road
Access

Hinckley Reservoir

Hinckley

FLOW

Trenton Falls

Cinncinatti Creek

West Canada Creek

Cold Brook

West
Poland

Canada Creek

Newport

for the large orange Pumpkin Caddis that emerges in late September and October. For caddis fishing on top, local angler Ken Ziobro recommends supplementing the typical Elk Hair pattern with the X-Caddis—an emerger imitation with an elk hair wing and a trailing shuck. The improving mayfly hatches include Hendricksons, sporadic Sulphurs, a good-sized summer Cahill (hatching late into the evening) and Green Drakes. The Coffin Fly—the big, white spinner stage of the Green Drake hatch—is reported to be particularly effective. In late August and early September, large White Flies hatch on West Canada. A white comparadun in size 12-14, is a good imitation and some local anglers trail a CDC emerger off the end. A bit later, Tricos hatch well here. For nymphing, beadheads including Prince and Hare's Ear versions are useful throughout the season.

As might be expected in a stream with four dams, flows are a concern on West Canada. Orion Power has recently acquired these hydroelectric facilities and is reported to be cooperating with anglers to improve flows. Still, there will be fluctuations and low water can produce difficult conditions. For the water below Trenton Falls, flow projections for the upcoming 24 hours can be obtained by calling the Waterline at 800-452-1742 and entering the six-digit code for West Canada Creek, which is 365124.

As already noted, fishing in the catch and release section below Trenton Falls is open year round. From the end of that section to the mouth, fishing is open for an extended season to November 30. Upstream of the catch and release section, the normal trout season applies.

CINCINATTI CREEK

This small stream, which marks the lower end of the catch and release section on West Canada, is a brown trout fishery that receives a stocking of about 2,500 small fish each year. In addition, there is believed to be some natural reproduction of browns here. Access is available from crossings at Route 12/28 and smaller local streets and from Plank Road, which parallels the creek.

COLD BROOK

Another tributary of West Canada Creek, Cold Brook enters about five miles south of the catch and release section, near the village of Poland. The stream is only about four miles long and holds a population of wild brook trout. The brook parallels Route 8, which offers informal access.

No special regulations apply to either Cincinatti Creek or Cold Brook.

West Canada Creek in the catch and release
section downstream of Trenton Falls.

Stream Facts: West Canada Creek

Seasons/Regulations
- Above Trenton Falls catch and release area: April 1 to October 15 no special regulations.
- Trenton Falls Bridge to mouth of Cincinatti Creek (about 2.5 miles): trout fishing open all year, catch and release only.
- Cincinatti Creek downstream: April 1 to November 30, no special regulations.

Fish
- Wild brookies upstream of Hinckley Reservoir, stocked and holdover browns along with some wild fish below.

River Characteristics
- Small above Hinckley Reservoir, medium to very wide below.

River Flows
- Varies with flows from four dams.

West Canada Creek.

West Canada Creek—Major Hatches

CENTRAL REGION: West Cananda Creek — 219

INSECT	J	F	M	A	M	J	J	A	S	O	N	D	FLIES
Lt. And Dark Hendrickson 12-14					■								Light and Dark Hendrickson Parachute, Emergers, Spinners
Caddis Green, Gray, Tan, Orange 12-18					█	█	█	█	█	█			Bead-Head Caddis Larva, Lafontaine Deep Pupa and Emergert Sparkle Pupa, X-Caddis Emerger, Elk Hair Caddis
Blue Winged Olives 16-22					█	█	█	█	█	█			Parachute, Emergers, Spinners
Sulphurs 14-20						█	█						Comparadun, Parachute, CDC Emerger, Compara-Emerger, Pheasant Tail Nymph
Green Drake 10-12						█							Nymph, Coffin Fly Spinner, Extended-Body Patterns
White Fly 12-14								█	█				Comparaduns, CDC Emerger, Soft Hackle Wet Fly, Light Hares Ear Nymph

ORISKANY CREEK
and Chenango Canal

This 20-mile long stream flows north from near Oriskany Falls until it reaches the Erie Canal/Mohawk River near the city of Utica. It is primarily a brown trout fishery.

Near its beginning, Oriskany is actually part of the Chenango Canal. This was reportedly a better portion years ago before channelization and the removal of structure. Still, the section downstream of Route 20 has apparently held up well. The canal receives a small stocking each year, and there is some natural reproduction. Local anglers report taking fish up to 20 inches here on occasion. Due to its small size and overgrowth, the canal is lightly fished, but an intrepid bushwhacker with a short rod would have a shot at these sizeable browns. The canal water is cooled by underground springs and small flies are common, including a good Trico hatch in late summer and fall. Stealth is essential in the slow moving canal water; one or two casts is all you'll get.

Downstream, as the creek crosses north into Oneida County, it becomes a free flowing trout stream. The upper half of the stream, roughly to the village of Clinton, stays reasonably cool through the summer thanks to underwater springs. Large numbers of brown trout, about 15,000 in all, are put in by the state and there are some places for them to holdover.

A healthy brown from Oriskany Creek.

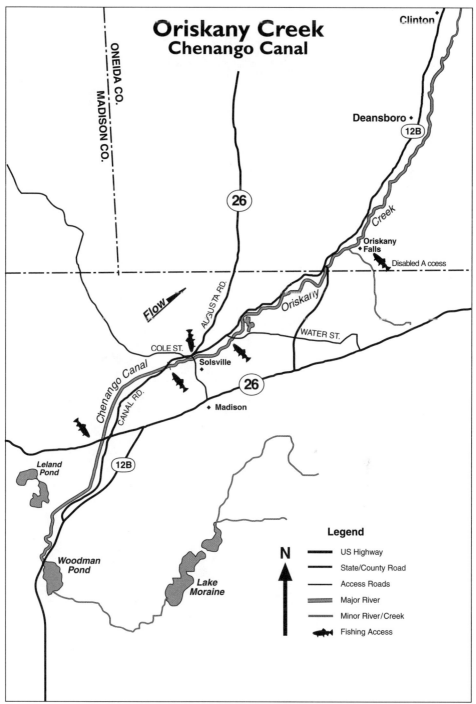

Oriskany Creek
Chenango Canal

Clinton

ONEIDA CO.
MADISON CO.

26

Deansboro

12B

Creek

Oriskany
Falls

Disabled Access

Flow

AUGUSTA RD.

Oriskany

WATER ST.

COLE ST.

Solsville

26

CANAL RD.

Chenango Canal

Madison

Leland
Pond

12B

Woodman
Pond

Lake
Moraine

Legend

N

US Highway

State/County Road

Access Roads

Major River

Minor River/Creek

Fishing Access

Oriskany Creek downstream of the canal section.

As it approaches the Mohawk it warms up and the trout fishing falls off. The fish are well fed here; the Oriskany has a full complement of mayfly hatches and good caddis populations. Blue Quills and Hendricksons are common in spring, followed by Sulphurs and some large Green Drakes. Caddis in various colors are around in summer and fall, including the large Pumpkin Caddis. Midges are also common here, and anyone fishing in summer should have tiny dries and pupa imitations to match.

Canal Road abuts the canal portion of the Oriskany and Route 12B follows the creek for most of its free flowing trout section. There is access at Cooper Street in Oriskany Falls, including a ramp for the disabled. Upstream where Water Street crosses just below Solsville, there are public fishing rights and a coffer dam that provides good holding water. In this section the stream is not more than 15 feet wide, but there are some surprisingly deep pools. Just above Solsville there is an access to the lower end of the canal, above and below a small waterfall, but the paths are heavily overgrown, as is the sign, so you'll need to watch carefully for the pulloff.

The Oriskany is subject to varying regulations on its trip to the Mohawk. On the canal section, from Route 46 to the beginning of the flowing stream (roughly at the small village of Solsville), trout fishing is permitted all year, with 5 trout of 12 inches or better allowed. On the flowing portion, normal trout season and regulations apply until the bridge at Deansboro (in Oneida County). Below Deansboro to the mouth, trout fishing is permitted all year, but is catch and release only from October 15 to March 31. At other times in this section, 5 trout of any size may be taken.

KAYADEROSSERAS CREEK

This creek, usually called the "Kaydeross" by local anglers, loops through Saratoga County on its way to Saratoga Lake and offers fishing for stocked and some holdover brown trout. It tends to warm up a bit sooner than other streams in the vicinity so it is a good bet for late March and early April. Early season fishing is possible, as most of the trout section of the stream is open for fishing year round.

The trout section on the Kayaderosseras runs from the headwaters northwest of the village of South Corinth to roughly Route 50 in the village of Ballston Spa. Brown trout exclusively are stocked on the creek—more than 11,000 each year including about 1,000 two-year-olds. Spring and fall are the best times to fish the stream as the water warms too much in summer. Some fish do hold over.

Anglers will find a few mayfly hatches, including some March Browns, but more generic dry fly and nymph patterns will usually work. Try Hare's Ear Nymphs, particularly along the steep banks found in many parts of the stream. Soft hackles in hare's ear and other light and dark body colors will also work. Green caddis larva and green and tan Elk Hair Caddis imitations are particularly valuable as the stream holds many of the naturals. The Kayderosseras is generally slow moving and casting conditions can be tight in places.

Access is good along most of the stream, with extensive easements from the source all the way to Ballston Spa. In addition to informal pulloffs, there is dedicated parking at the Holmes Road crossing off Route 9N in South Corinth, where Spier Falls Road/Route 19 cross in North Greenfield. Farther downstream, there is angler parking at Bockes Road near the village of Porter Corners, where Route 29 crosses (the Hatch Bridge) in Rock City Falls and at Galway Road/Route 45 in Factory Village.

The year round trout fishing on the Kayaderosseras runs down to the last railroad crossing. The last few miles, below the trout water, are completely closed to fishing from March 16 to the first Saturday in May to protect spawning walleye.

Glowegee Creek, a small fishable stream that joins Kayoderosseras at the village of Milton Center, receives its own small stocking of brown trout. It can be reached from the Route 49 or Lewis Road crossings or from its mouth.

The "Kaydeross" is a good place to go in the early season.

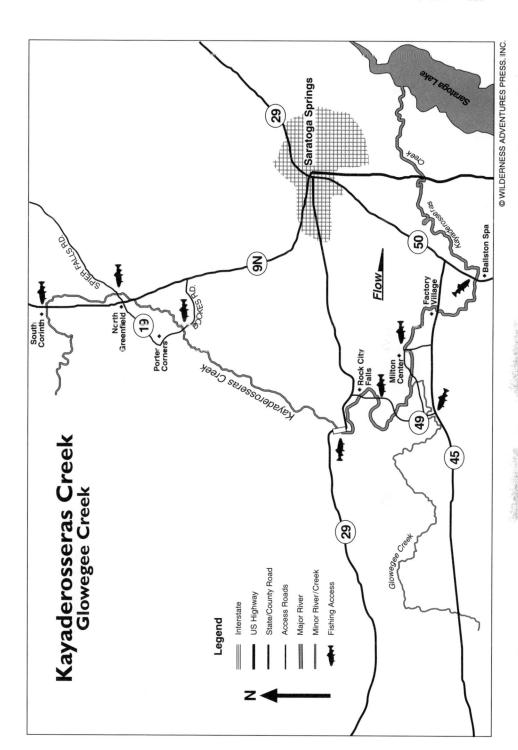

Kayaderosseras Creek
Glowegee Creek

Legend

Interstate
US Highway
State/County Road
Access Roads
Major River
Minor River/Creek
Fishing Access

N

Saratoga Springs

29

Saratoga Lake

Creek

50

Kayaderosseras

Ballston Spa

9N

Flow

Factory
Village

SPIER FALLS RD.

19

South
Corinth

North
Greenfield

Porter
Corners

BOCKES RD.

Kayaderosseras Creek

Rock City
Falls

Milton
Center

49

45

29

Glowegee Creek

MOHAWK RIVER

The Mohawk holds primarily warmwater species; however, a roughly 10-mile stretch in Oneida County offers fishing for stocked browns and a few rainbows.

Most people know the Mohawk as a wide, slow moving, eastern flowing stream. But in its trout section the river is a smaller stream running south into the Delta Lake impoundment and out the other side. About eight miles above the impoundment, the stream splits into west and east branches. This upper portion of the stream is especially small and has native brookies in addition to stocked browns and some rainbows. About 4,500 stocked fish are put in, primarily in the town of Ava, above Delta. In addition, the East Branch, small water that runs from near the small village of West Leyden to meet the West Branch near the village of that same name, receives a small stocking of browns.

The last portion of the main river above Delta Lake, about four miles from the Westernville Bridge upstream to the confluence with the Lansing Kill, is open for an extended season of April 1 to November 30, with five trout of any size permitted. Upstream of the Lansing Kill, the normal trout season and regulations apply. (The Lansing Kill is fishable as well, and receives a stocking of about 3,000 small browns each year.)

The lower portion of the Mohawk, from the dam to the point in the city of Rome where it crosses the Erie Canal and turns east, is wider and slower than the upper portion. This section is heavily stocked with browns, about 9,000 in all including 1,500 two-year-old fish. The lower Mohawk is governed by the standard trout season and regulations.

SAQUOIT CREEK

This stream, sometimes spelled Sauquoit, begins in the southeast corner of Oneida County and runs north into the city of Utica where it joins the Mohawk. The stream is stocked with brown trout, about 4,600 including a few hundred two-year-old fish. Most of the stocking is done in New Hartford, just outside of Utica. Access can be had along Route 8, which parallels the Sauquoit.

The lower (northern) portion of the stream, from Pinnacle Road in the village of Sauquoit to the confluence with the Mohawk, is open for trout fishing until November 30, with five fish of any size permitted. Upstream, the creek is subject to the ordinary trout season and limit.

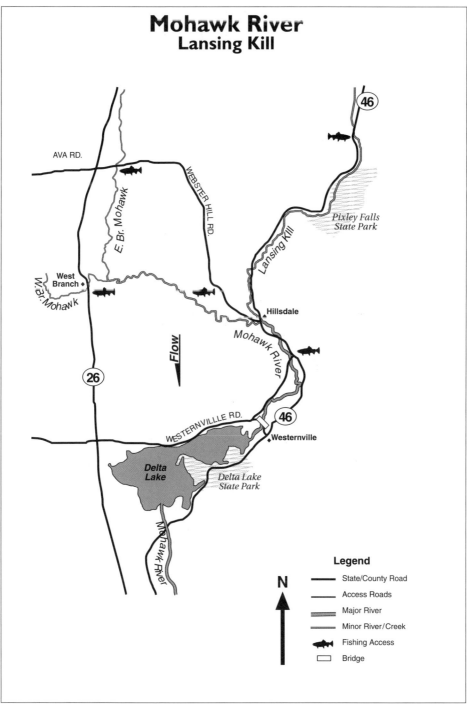

Mohawk River
Lansing Kill

AVA RD.

E. Br. Mohawk

WEBSTER HILL RD.

West
Branch

W. Br. Mohawk

Lansing Kill

Pixley Falls
State Park

Hillsdale

Mohawk River

Flow

26

WESTERNVILLLE RD.

46

Westernville

Delta
Lake

Delta Lake
State Park

Mohawk River

N

Legend

State/County Road
Access Roads
Major River
Minor River/Creek
Fishing Access
Bridge

46

© WILDERNESS ADVENTURES PRESS, INC.

Mohawk River—Major Hatches

INSECT	J	F	M	A	M	J	J	A	S	O	N	D	FLIES
Blue Quills 16-18													Blue Dun Parachute, Spinners, Pheasant Tail Nymphs
Lt. And Dark Hendrickson 12-14				▮									Light and Dark Hendrickson Parachute, Emergers, Spinners
Caddis Green, Gray, Tan 14-18					▮								Bead-Head Caddis Larva, Lafontaine Deep Pupa and Emergent Sparkle Pupa, X-Caddis Emerger, Elk Hair Caddis
Blue Winged Olives 16-22					▮				▮				Parachute, Emergers, Spinners
Sulphurs/Cahills 14-20						▮							Comparadun, Parachute, Emergers, Hare's Ear and Pheasant Tail Nymphs
Green Drake 10-12						▮							Nymph, Coffin Fly Spinner, Extended-Body Patterns
White Fly 12-14								▮					Comparaduns, CDC Emerger, Soft Hackle Wet Fly, Light Hare's Ear Nymph

Sauquoit Creek

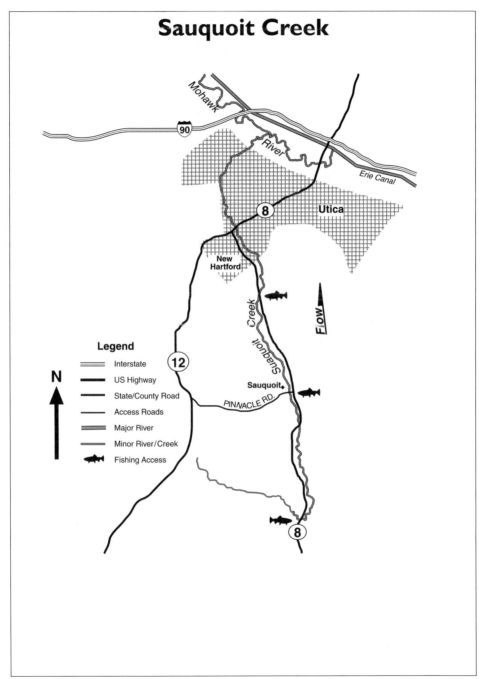

90

Mohawk

River

Erie Canal

8

Utica

New Hartford

Creek

Sauquoit

FLOW

Legend

	Interstate
	US Highway
	State/County Road
	Access Roads
	Major River
	Minor River/Creek
	Fishing Access

N

12

Sauquoit

PINNACLE RD.

8

Mohawk Valley Hub Cities

Saratoga Springs/Glen Falls

ACCOMODATIONS PRICE KEY

$ Up to 60 dollars per night
$$ 61 to 99 dollars per night
$$$ 100 to 150 per night
$$$$ 151 and up per night

HOTELS/MOTELS

Inn at Saratoga, 231 Broadway, Saratoga Springs, NY 12866 / 518-583-1890 / $$$
Springs Motel, 189 Broadway, Saratoga Springs, NY 12866 / 518-584-6336 / $-$$
Roosevelt Motel, 2961 State Rte 9, Saratoga Springs, NY 13476 / 518-581-8472 /
    $$
Super 8 Motel, 191 Corinth Road, Glen Falls, NY 12804 / 518-761-9780 / $
Queensbury Hotel, 88 Ridge Street, Glen Falls, NY 12801 / 518-792-1121 / $$$-
    $$$$
(Note: Accomodations are scarce in August due to the horse racing season)

CAMPGROUNDS/RVS

Moreau Lake State Park, US 9, Glen Falls NY / 518 793-0511, 148 Sites / No
    hookups / Lake fishing and swimming
Whispering Pines Campsites, 550 Sand Hill Road, Greenfield Center, NY 12833 /
    518-893-0416 / 70 sites, 13 hookups, 30 water/electric, stream fishing

RESTAURANTS

Old Firehouse Restaurant, 543 Broadway, Saratoga Springs, NY 12866 /
    518-587-0047 / Steaks and seafood, converted firehouse
Chez Pierre Restaurant, 340 US 9, Saratoga Springs, 12831 / 518-793-3350 /
    French
Country Corner Cafe, 25 Church Street, Saratoga Springs, 12831 / 518-587-7889

FLY SHOPS

Angler Essentials, 7 Glenwood Drive, Saratoga Springs, NY 12866 / 518-581-0859
Walton's Sport Shop, 59 Lake Avenue, Saratoga Springs, NY 12800 /
    518-584-7151

AUTO REPAIR

Marion Avenue Mobil, 58 Marion Ave., Saratoga Springs, NY 12866 /
    518-584-8313

AIRPORT

Saratoga County Airport, 410 Greenfield Ave., Ballston Spa, NY 12020 /
    518-885-5354
Albany County Airport, 737 Albany Shaker Road, Albany, 12211 / 518-242-2200

HOSPITAL/CLINIC

Saratoga Hospital, 211 Church Street, Saratoga Springs, 12866 / 518-587-3222

Amsterdam/Gloversville/Johnstown/Schenectady

Hotels/Motels

Holiday Inn, 308 North Comrie Avenue, Johnstown, NY 12095 / 518-762-4686 / $$

Days Inn, 167 Nott Terrace, Schenectady, NY 12308 / 518-370-3297 / $$

Glen Sanders Mansion, 1 Glen Avenue, Schenectady, NY 12302 / 518-374-7262 / Restaurant / $$$

Super 8 Motel, Rte 30 South, Amsterdam, NY 12010 / 518-843-5888 / $-$$

Campgrounds/RVs /

Arrowhead Marina & RV Park, 2 Van Buren Lane, Schenectady, NY 12302 / 68 sites / 34 full hookups / On Mohawk River

Royal Mountain Campsite, 4948 Route 29, Johnstown, NY 12095 / 518-762-1946 / 65 sites, water/electric

Restaurants

Raindancer Steak Parlour, 4582 Route 30, Amsterdam, NY 12010 / 518-842-2606 / Steaks and chops

Union Hall Inn, 2 Union Place, Johnstown, NY 12095 / 518-762-3210 / Seafood and vegetarian

Glen Sanders Mansion, 1 Glen Avenue, Schenectady, NY 12302 / 518-374-7262

Fly Shops

Goldstocks Sporting Goods, Scotia

Galaxy Sports, 4 Freemans Bridge Road, Scotia, NY 12302 / 518-382-2037

Nick's Field & Stream, 1511 Broadway, Schenectady, NY 12306 / 518-382-7908

Taylor and Vadney, 3071 Broadway, Schenectady, NY 12306, 518-374-3030 / www.taylorandvadney.com

Auto Repair

Family Tire and Auto, 712 State Street, Schenectady, NY 12307, 518-374-3326

Airport

Albany County Airport, 737 Albany Shaker Road, Albany, NY 12211 / 518-242-2200

Schenectady County Airport, 21 Airport Road, Scotia, NY 12302 / 518-399-0111

Hospital/Clinic

Amsterdam Memorial Hospital, 4988 State Highway 30, Amsterdam, NY 12010 / 518-842-3100

Conifer Park-Mediplex Regional Hospital, 79 Glenridge Road, Scotia, NY 12302 / 518-399-6446

Utica/Rome/Oneida/Herkimer

HOTELS/MOTELS

Radisson Hotel, 200 Genesee Street, Utica, NY 13502 / 315-797-8010 / $$$
Red Roof Inn, 20 Weaver Street, Utica, NY 13502 / 315-724-7128 / $-$$
Quality Inn, 200 South James Street, Rome, NY 13440 / 315-336-4300 / $$
Super 8 Motel, 215 Genesee Street, Oneida, NY 13421 / 315-363-5168 / $
Herkimer Motel, 100 Marginal Road, Herkimer, NY 13350 / 315-866-0490 / $-$$

CAMPGROUNDS/RVS

Verona Beach State Park, Highway 13, Oneida, NY 13421 / 315-762-4463 / 45 sites / No hookups, lake fishing and swimming
Elmtree Campsites, Highway 5, Herkimer, NY 13350 / 315-724-6678 / 36 sites / 12 full, 17 w/e
Delta Lake State Park, Highway 46, Rome, NY 13440 / 315-337-4670 / 101 sites / No hookups / Lake fishing and swimming

RESTAURANTS

Baby Boomer's Cookery & Lounge, 527 East Albany Street, Herkimer, NY 13350 / 315-866-3183
Babe's Macaroni Grill & Bar, 80 North Genesee Stree, Utica NY 13501 / 315-735-0777
Hook, Line and Sinker, 8471 Seneca Turnpike, Utica, NY 13413 / 315-732-3636 / Seafood and steak
Kitlas Restaurant, 2242 Broad Street, Rome, NY 13440 / 315-732-9616 / Seafood and ribs

FLY SHOPS

(These fly shops serve anglers in the Central Region of New York and in the Southern Adirondacks)
Mad River Sports, 207 Clark Street, Canastota, NY 13032 / 800-231-9314
Rising Trout Outfitter, 587 Main Street, New York Mills, NY 13417 / 315-736-0353 / www.risingtroutoutfitter.com, near Utica, guide and float plane trips, school

AUTO REPAIR

Maugeri's Auto Repair, 501 Albany Street, Utica, NY 13501 / 315-733-5033
Oneida Service Center, 68 Lenox Avenue, Oneida, NY 13421 / 315-363-0008

AIRPORT

Oneida County Airport, 5900 Airport Road, Oriskany, NY 13424 / 315-736- 4171

HOSPITAL/CLINIC

St. Elizabeth Medical Center, 2209 Genesee Street, Utica, NY 13501 /
Faxton Hospital, 1676 Sunset Avenue, Utica, NY 13502 / 315-738-6200

New York - North Region

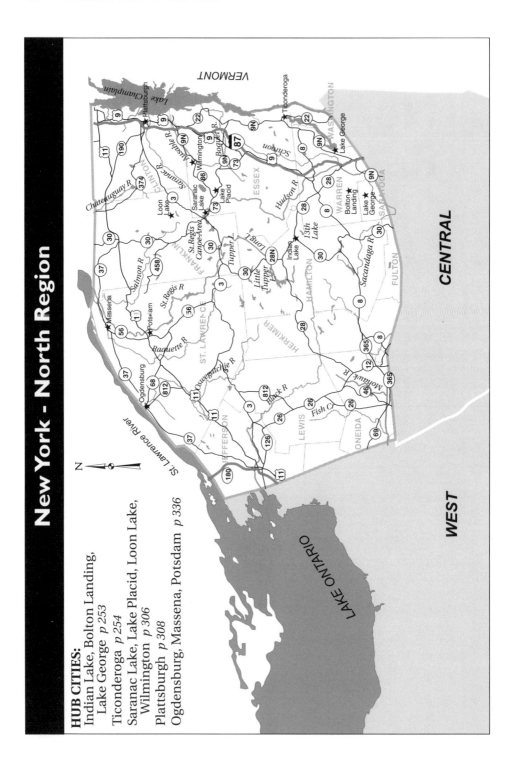

HUB CITIES:
Indian Lake, Bolton Landing,
    Lake George *p 253*
Ticonderoga *p 254*
Saranac Lake, Lake Placid, Loon Lake,
    Wilmington *p 306*
Plattsburgh *p 308*
Ogdensburg, Massena, Potsdam *p 336*

North Region

This section of New York is composed mostly of the Adirondack Mountains—typified by classic mountain fishing on fast pocket waters, including the Ausable and Saranac rivers. Still, there is more smooth water here than its reputation might indicate. In addition to the trout, several of the streams that empty into Lake Champlain get runs of landlocked salmon. And while the best-known waters run east, there are some excellent rivers that drain north into the St. Lawrence that deserve to be fished more often. The southern Adirondacks, though not as remote as the northern portion, offer some good fishing, including in the Hudson Gorge.

It's usually the big, famous streams like the Ausable and the Saranac that draw anglers north (or south from Canada), but small stream angling is a wonderful part of fishing in the Adirondacks. Wild brook trout are plentiful in hundreds of small waters here. In fact, in many of these streams, five additional brookies of under eight inches may be kept, and even dedicated catch and release anglers will occasionally take a small brook trout during camping trips.

Camping and fishing go together naturally here. The heart of this area falls within the Adirondack Park. The park, created in 1892, covers over five million acres. Extensive portions are privately owned and whole villages fall within its boundaries; only about 40 percent of the land is owned by the state. Still, there is more wilderness than any one person could explore in a lifetime, and plenty of space for hikers and campers—with or without fly rods—to get away from any hint of civilization.

For getting away, stillwater fishing is ideal. Unlike in other parts of New York, ponds and lakes are a major part of flyfishing for trout and salmon in the Adirondacks. While some of this can be done from shore, it is in canoes and kayaks that flyfishing Adirondack ponds comes into its own. The seclusion of a camping and canoe trip is a unique feature of the "North Country" fishing experience.

Southern Adirondacks

Fishing in this portion of the Adirondacks, roughly south of Port Henry on Lake Champlain, usually takes a back seat to angling in the better-known waters to the north. Still, it includes major streams like the Sacandaga, the Schroon and the Upper Hudson and its tributaries, and floating is popular on these last two streams. The southern Adirondacks are a bit more populated than the upper portion of the mountains and probably see more tourists, as well, but they still have a great deal of secluded territory.

Hudson Headwaters

Anyone familiar with the wide, estuary portion of the lower Hudson will be surprised to see it as a small, rocky mountain stream in the Adirondacks. Emerging from tiny Lake Tear of the Clouds on Mount Marcy (the state's highest peak), and fed by the Opalescent River near its source, the river winds its way east and south through Essex and Warren counties. It is fishable from a few access points, by hiking in and by overnight float trips through the remote gorge area.

Although trout may be found all the way down to the entrance of Glen Creek near the town of Warrensburg, the prime trout water is from the headwaters down to the town of North Creek. The river is primarily small pocket water in its first 12-mile segment from roughly the village of Newcomb to the confluence with the Indian River.

Below the junction with the Indian River, the fishing reaches its peak. Here, a mix of rainbows and browns are stocked which, along with the occasional brookie, can be found in heavy pocket water and a mixture of runs, riffles and pools. (This portion includes the stretch generally thought of as the Hudson Gorge, although some maps mark the gorge well upstream.) The gorge section itself is remote from roads. For the ambitious angler the Blue Ledges Trail near Minerva will provide a healthy hike to the stream (with access to the Boreas River as well). Downstream, at the village of North River, the river runs adjacent to Route 28 and can be easily reached.

To fish all of the gorge water, however, overnight float trips are the way to go. These usually start near the confluence with the Indian River, which is used to put water in the Hudson precisely for floating. Inflatables rather than drift boats are typically employed and anglers spend a night or two camping. The fishing is a mix of wade and boat fishing and the trips generally end at North River about 15 miles downstream. The best time to fish the Hudson Gorge, by boat or on foot, is from late May to the end of June and again from late August through September.

The browns and rainbows in the gorge run 12-14 inches, though 18-inchers are taken. The river here offers good hatches of March Browns and Blue Winged Olives, along with Hendricksons which are reportedly better some years than others. A good *Isonychia* hatch usually turns up in late August and September. Caddis are

Hudson River Headwaters
and Tributaries

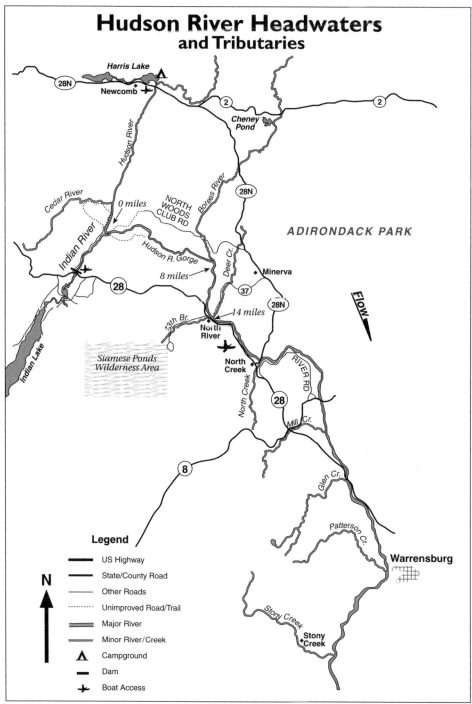

ADIRONDACK PARK

FLOW

Legend

▬▬	US Highway
▬	State/County Road
—	Other Roads
⋯⋯	Unimproved Road/Trail
▬	Major River
—	Minor River/Creek
◬	Campground
▬	Dam
✛	Boat Access

N

predominant, however, usually in green or olive with light wings in size 12 and 14. This makes the standard Elk Hair Caddis an ideal dry fly for the river. For heavier water Peter Hunkins of Beaver Brook Outfitters recommends an Irresistible Caddis, with spun deer hair for flotation. Various emergers or pupas are also important; Hunkins says a simple green pupa with a black head and a bead (tungsten if possible) is a reliable deep-water nymph.

In addition to matching mayflies and caddis, stonefly nymphs and streamers are useful. The streamers should have action and often need weight to get down in the deeper and faster sections. Coneheaded Marabou Muddlers in various colors and weighted black and olive Buggers are good bets.

Below North River, Route 28 parallels the stream for about five miles down to the village of North Creek. This is a good, often neglected stretch to trout fish on foot. The river is generally wadeable here, but it is wide—more than 100 yards in places—and rocky. Access is available from Route 28 and River Road in the upper portion below North River and from the Route 8 crossing, Harrington Road and Route 28 again as you approach Glen Creek. As noted below, many of the feeders receive their own stockings and the mouths of these tributaries are a good place to target as you head downstream. Below North Creek, the river warms and increasingly becomes a smallmouth fishery. From the headwaters to below Warrensburg the Upper Hudson is open to fishing all year, with the standard five fish per day permitted.

Stream Facts: Hudson Headwaters

Seasons
- In Essex, Hamilton and Warren counties; headwaters to below Warrensburg: All year.

Regulations
- Five fish, any size.

Fish
- Mixed stocked and holdover browns and rainbows, occasional brook trout.

River Characteristics
- Mostly pocket water, riffles and pools mixed in. Widens after Indian River enters.

River Flows
- Generally, higher in spring, lower in summer and fall, short bursts of extra water from Indian River for recreational purposes.

The headwaters of the Hudson River are rocky and steep—very different from the estuary portion in southern New York.

Hudson Tributaries

A number of tributaries in the Hudson headwaters offer good fishing. Most receive stocked fish and hold some wild brookies as well. They are worth seeking out, especially when the Hudson is running high and fast.

These streams fall within Essex, Hamilton and Warren counties. Unless otherwise noted, the standard trout season applies, and all allow an extra five brook trout under eight inches to be kept. The most important fisheries are listed below, starting upstream.

Cedar River

This short, fairly large stream, (not to be confused with the Cedar River Flow to the southwest) enters about three miles above the Hudson's sharp left turn at the Indian River. It offers riffles and long sections of flat water and is generally underfished. Hatches are similar to the upper Hudson, with Red Quills and Adams patterns said to be particularly effective. Small streamers like Grey Ghosts, Mickey Finns and Black-Nosed Dace also work well.

Indian River

The Indian River, which marks the starting point for Hudson River Gorge trips, is also a trout fishery in its own right. Most of the fishing is done in the first mile below the dam, which is open to the public (above the land of a private fishing club). The stream is stocked with about 2,500 browns a year, including 300 two-year-olds.

Flows can fluctuate with dam releases on the Indian River.

The river is mostly pocket water and can be heavy with runoff at times. In addition, the dam is used to provide recreational releases to the Hudson and anglers should be aware of potential high water from dam releases. While these schedules can change, the releases are reported to take place from 10 a.m. to noon every day until the third week in June. Thereafter, they are at the same time on Tuesdays, Thursdays and weekends. Trout fishing on the Indian River is open all year.

Deer Creek

This small flow, sometimes called Fourteenth Brook, enters the Hudson's eastern shore in the village of North River. In addition to native brook trout, it receives a small stocking of browns from the state, and some two-year-olds from Essex County. Access to the lower half is found along Fourteenth Road/Route 37. North Woods Club Road and Route 28N cross the creek in its upper reaches.

Thirteenth Brook

Entering the Hudson almost directly opposite Deer Creek, Thirteenth Brook runs about three miles from Thirteenth Lake to the river. No fish are stocked directly in the stream, but browns and rainbows are put in the lake and some undoubtedly make it to the brook. It may also hold some wild brook trout.

Thirteenth Lake Road runs along the brook, which is open for an extended season to November 30.

North Creek

North Creek runs about four miles, joining the Hudson in the town of the same name. The county puts in about 2,300 brook trout each year and the state adds about 1,200 browns and an equal number of rainbows, along with a few hundred brookies. In addition, the county puts in a couple of hundred small rainbows in North Creek Recreation Pond, a small impoundment near the stream's mouth. There are public fishing rights for about one mile upstream of Sodom Road (south toward Route 8) and a bit more upstream from where Roaring Brook enters near Holcombville.

Mill Creek

This small, pretty stream runs from Garnet Lake in the town of Johnsburg in Warren County about 8 miles to the Hudson. Rarely more than 25 feet across, it offers fishing for brook trout put in by Warren County and supplemented by some natural reproduction. The state puts in 5,000 browns and half as many brookies. Don't expect big fish in Mill Creek: the average is 7-10 inches.

Garnet Lake Road parallels the upper half of the stream, while Route 8 tracks the lower portion. There are public fishing rights covering segments of Mill Creek from the headwaters near Garnet Lake to the area near the mouth. The lower section, from where Heath Road crosses on down, is said to be a good stretch—especially the pool at the mouth. The normal trout season applies, and like most Warren County waters, five fish plus five brook trout under eight inches may be kept.

Boreas River

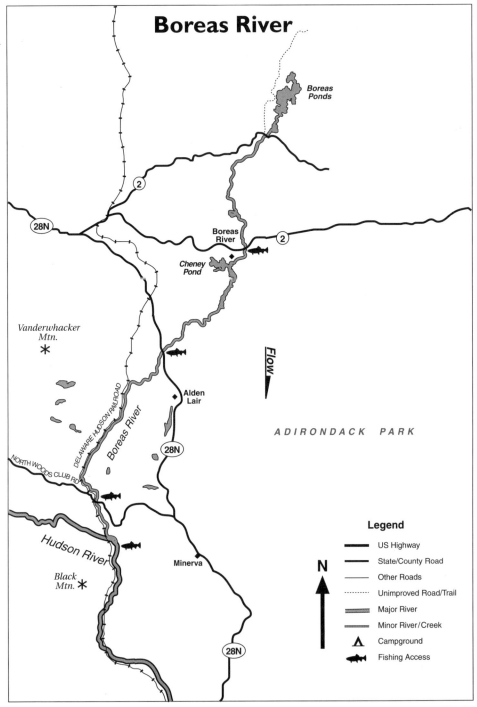

Boreas River

This substantial river meets the Hudson near the Essex County town of Minerva. As noted in the description of the Hudson, it can be reached from the Blue Ledges Trail that goes into the Hudson Gorge area. A few miles upstream it is crossed by North Woods Club Road. Well upstream, Route 28N crosses and there is formal access.

The stream can also be fished near its headwaters, above Cheney Pond where Route 2 crosses. In this section, in the town of North Hudson, the state stocks about 1,300 fish, mostly brook trout, and Essex County adds about 800 fish, again mostly brookies. Downstream, in Minerva, about 4,500 fish are put in by the DEC and Essex County. These are a mix of mostly browns and rainbows with a few brook trout. There are no special regulations on the Boreas River.

The Boreas is primarily an early season river that suffers from low flows in summer. Some of the good early hatches here include March Browns, Hendricksons and small black caddis.

This is high, early season water on the Boreas. The river can run low in summer.

GLEN CREEK

Flowing about nine miles east into the Hudson, this stream has brook trout in its upper reaches and brown trout in the lower half. The brookies are apparently all wild; about 800 browns are stocked by the state each year. Although best fished in spring, the large pool at the mouth may offer good fishing in summer to evening hatches.

PATTERSON BROOK AND STONY CREEK

These two small streams are in the southern half of Warren County, well below the prime trout water on the Hudson. Still, they are worth fishing and anglers should also try the outlets of the streams in the Hudson itself.

Patterson Brook, the northernmost stream of the two, runs about five miles and enters the Hudson in the village of Warrensburg. It receives about 3,000 brook trout from the county and state. Patterson is subject to low water and is best fished in spring and fall.

Stony enters near the southern border of Warren County and gets a few hundred brookies from the county, a few hundred more from the state and about 1,400 browns

SCHROON RIVER

The Schroon River (pronounced "Skroon") begins in the town of North Hudson in Essex County and flows nearly due south about 10 miles into Schroon Lake in Warren County. After the lake it emerges as a larger flow and continues 15 miles until emptying into the Hudson at Warrensburg.

Upper Schroon

This portion of the river, above the lake, is relatively small mountain water for most of its run. This upper half is stocked with brookies and browns by both the state and Essex County. In all, about 2,500 brookies and browns (including about 1,800 two-year-olds) are put in, along with a few hundred rainbows.

In addition, a large number of landlocked salmon are stocked in the river's mouth, as well as in the lake. Some of these fish do ascend the river in the fall. They can be taken on streamers near the mouth and can occasionally be found in the lower half of the river. (They also sometimes show up in the Branch River, a tributary that enters at the village of North Hudson.) Alder Meadow Road crosses the stream and gives access to the last mile or so (which is otherwise a long hike from Route 9). Fishing is open all year for both trout and salmon in the section below Alder Meadow Road. Route 9 parallels the entire Upper Schroon, providing access points along the way.

Lower Schroon

After emerging from Schroon Lake, the river passes through some swampland before resuming its 15-mile trip to the Hudson. It is roughly the first 10 miles of this stretch, from the lake downstream to the village of Riverbank, that is trout water. All

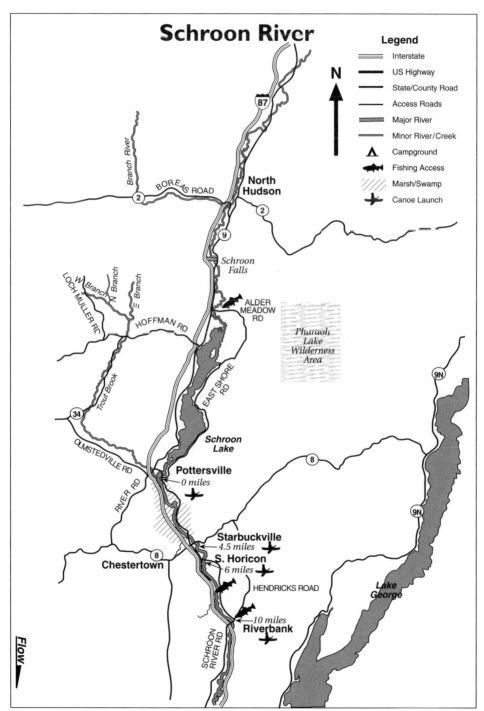

Schroon River

Legend

≡≡≡	Interstate
▬▬	US Highway
──	State/County Road
──	Access Roads
▬▬	Major River
──	Minor River/Creek
▲	Campground
➤	Fishing Access
///	Marsh/Swamp
✈	Canoe Launch

North Hudson

Branch River

BOREAS ROAD

Schroon Falls

LOCH MULLER RD

W Branch
N Branch
E Branch

HOFFMAN RD

ALDER MEADOW RD

Pharaoh Lake Wilderness Area

Trout Brook

EAST SHORE RD

Schroon Lake

OLMSTEDVILLE RD

RIVER RD

Pottersville
— 0 miles

Starbuckville
— 4.5 miles
S. Horicon
— 6 miles

Chestertown

HENDRICKS ROAD

Lake George

— 10 miles
Riverbank

SCHROON RIVER RD

Flow

© WILDERNESS ADVENTURES PRESS, INC.

three species are stocked in this section by the state and Warren County, but rainbow trout predominate. About 17,000 of these are put in, including about 5,000 12- to 14-inch fish, in addition to 4,000 browns and 2,300 brookies. A few landlocks from Schroon Lake—and possibly some lakers too—find their way into the lower river.

The lower river has more than a mile of fishing rights at Schroon River Road at the Chester town line and a bit more, along with dedicated parking, upstream of Hendricks Road in Riverbank. Fishing here is not limited to wading; the Lower Schroon is a good place to fish from a canoe or kayak. There are two primary floats, the first from below the lake in Pottersville to the dam in Starbuckville, a distance of about five miles. This upper float has some good structure in the form of weeds and sunken timber that should be a focus for fishing, especially below the surface. (This is equally true for wading anglers in this section.)

The second main float, and the better trout fishing, is from below the dam at Starbuckville to Riverbank, a distance of about six miles. It is also possible to fish the upper two miles of this section down to the canoe access at South Horicon, or from South Horicon about four miles to Riverbank.

For wading anglers, the roughly three mile section from Starbuckville to Chestertown is the prime fishing. The river is rocky and like most Adirondack rivers must be waded carefully. For anglers on foot there are occasional access points along Schroon River Road, which parallels most of the Lower Schroon. There is also about a mile of access near the village of Tumblehead Falls, beginning about a mile upstream of Riverbank.

Whether by boat or on foot, the Lower Schroon fishes best in May and June and again in the fall. Summer flyfishers should plan to fish at the end of the day. The occasional small landlocks that make their way over the dam are usually taken by fly anglers on streamers or dries in mid-June. Below Riverbank, trout fishing tails off, but there is good angling for smallmouth and northern pike—although Warren County does stock about 1,000 rainbows near the confluence with the Hudson.

There can be good mayfly hatches on the Schroon, but they are known to be a bit unpredictable; much better in some years than others. Various Wulff patterns along with some Adams and some light flies to imitate Cahills and Sulphurs should suffice for mayfly dries. Caddis larva, pupa and dries will be at least as important. There are also stoneflies here and retired Conservation Officer Ron Robert who lives nearby often uses a black stonefly nymph in the pocket water.

As already noted the Upper Schroon from Alder Meadow Road to the lake is open year round, with five trout of any size and two landlocks of 18 inches or more permitted. The rest of the Upper Schroon is subject to normal trout season and regulations.

The entire Lower Schroon can be fished all year, and five trout of any size may be kept. However, the first half of the lower river, from the lake to the dam in Starbuckville, is subject to a limit of two lake trout of 18 inches or more and three landlocks of at least 15 inches.

The Schroon River near its junction with the Hudson.

Trout Brook

This small but lengthy stream runs south on the western side of Schroon Lake before joining the lower river just below the swampy lake outlet. It primarily holds stocked brook trout put in by the state and at its lower end by Warren County (about 3,500 total fish are stocked). There are some wild brookies in the upper reaches, which divides into three branches: north, east and west. But the stream here is quite narrow.

In the upper stretch the west branch is accessible from Lock Muller Road, but the other two branches would require a substantial hike. Just below the junction of the three branches, Hoffman Road crosses and Route 34 runs parallel to the stream until the river turns east for its trip to the Schroon. In the last portion of the stream, there is access off Olmsteadville Road and Route 9. No special regulations apply to Trout Brook.

Stream Facts: Schroon River

Seasons/Regulations
- Upper Schroon (above the lake), regular season and limit for trout, two land-lockeds of 18 inches or better; last portion from Alder Meadow Road to the lake open year round.
- Lower Schroon (below the lake), open all year, but first part, from lake to Starbuckville, limit is two lake trout of 18 inches and three landlocked salmon of 15 inches.

Fish
- Stocked and holdover rainbows, browns and brookies, occasional landlockeds and lakers from Schroon Lake.

River Characteristics
- Upper Schroon small rocky water; Lower Schroon wider, smoother. Can be weedy below the lake.

The Adirondacks by Train

Early in the last century, long before the Thruway and Northway were opened, vacationers came to the Adirondacks on trains. Anglers in southern or western New York State who don't have cars—or simply don't want to make the long drive—can still reach the area by rail. Amtrak has service from the cities of Buffalo, Rochester, Syracuse, and points in between to Schenectady (Albany), where connection can be made to trains north. Service from New York City and points north will take passengers directly to the mountains.

The primary stops for anglers would be Whitehall or Saratoga in the southern Adirondacks, and Westport and Plattsburgh farther north. All are along the eastern edge of the Adirondacks. Unless you're being met, you will need to rent a car on arrival. Whitehall and Saratoga have rental agencies in town, as does Plattsburgh in the north. Westport, which is near Lake Placid, will require a cab ride or a drop-off arrangement to get a vehicle.

From the south, travel is from Penn Station on Amtrak's Adirondack Line, with additional stops at Yonkers, Croton, Poughkeepsie and Albany. Schedules can change, but there is currently one train per day, leaving between 8 a.m. and 9 a.m. (except for an additional afternoon train to Saratoga Springs). Travel time is about 3 hours and 30 minutes to Saratoga Springs and 4 hours 20 minutes to Whitehall (current fares $40-$47). For the northern Adirondacks, travel times are 5 hours 30 minutes to Westport and about an hour longer to Plattsburgh (fares $49-$53).

Passengers from the west will need to travel east to Schenectady (Albany) and wait a couple of hours for a connecting train heading north. From Buffalo, travel time is about 4 hours 40 minutes. To make the 11:30 to noon departure at Shenectady, it is necessary to take one of two early trains from Buffalo at 5 a.m. or 6 a.m. (leaving Rochester about an hour later, and Syracuse about an hour after that). Total one-way fares to Plattsburgh for both legs are Buffalo $59, Rochester $52 and Syracuse $38, proportionally less for southern destinations.

Amtrak can be reached at 800-USA-RAIL (872-7245) or www.amtrak.com.

In addition to the national rental chains—Hertz, Avis, National and Enterprise—the following local car rental agencies are near the center of the indicated destinations:

- **Whitehall:** A1 Xpress Rent A Car, 45 Poultney Street, Whitehall, NY 12887; 518-499-0575.
- **Westport:** Closest rentals are about 10-20 miles outside town.
- **Plattsburgh:** Auto Exchange, 762 Route 3; 518-562-8462; Price Less Car Rentals, 762 State Route 3 # 4; 518-562-9070.
- **Saratoga:** A US Choice Auto Rental, 360 Maple Avenue; 518-583-4448; Saratoga Car Rental, 360 Maple Avenue; 518-583-4448; Saratoga Chrysler Plymouth, 35 Lake Avenue; 518-584-1821.

Sacandaga River & Mill Creek

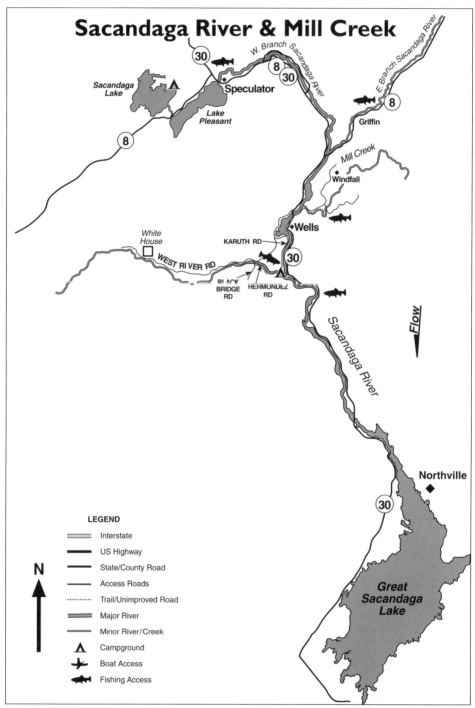

LEGEND

═══ Interstate

▬▬ US Highway

── State/County Road

── Access Roads

·········· Trail/Unimproved Road

▬▬ Major River

══ Minor River/Creek

⛺ Campground

✈ Boat Access

🐟 Fishing Access

N

© WILDERNESS ADVENTURES PRESS, INC.

SACANDAGA RIVER

This river in Hamilton County is formed from two branches that merge and flow into Great Sacandaga Lake. Sometimes called Sacandaga Reservoir, Great Sacandaga Lake is an impoundment and not to be confused with the smaller Sacandaga Lake to the northwest.

Of the two branches, the seven-mile West Branch offers the better angling. It is a brown trout fishery, heavily stocked by the state (about 4,500 fish per year), and some wild brookies may be found in the upper reaches. There is good access to the West Branch from its headwaters near the village of Speculator to the beginning of the main river near Windfall; Route 30/Route 8 parallels the stream for most of this run. Despite the access, it is not heavily fished.

In case the two lakes named Sacandaga aren't confusing enough, there is a tributary to the main Sacandaga River which is also called the West Branch of the Sacandaga on some maps. This second "West Branch" enters the river near the village of Wells, about three miles downstream of the original junction. Apparently, this feeder is not stocked, but might be worth trying for wild brookies, and perhaps some browns that come in from the Sacandaga. It can be reached from the adjacent West River and Hermondez Roads.

The brown trout fishery continues onto the main river, and is at its best to the village of Wells about four miles downstream. The main Sacandaga runs along Route 30, which provides access. There is a small impoundment on the river at the village of Wells, after which it emerges and runs along Caruth Road as well as Route 30. Trout stocking ends as the river flows into the town of Hope, and the stream becomes a warmwater fishery.

Sacandaga fishing requires a bit of persistence; the river has sections of good looking water that actually hold few if any trout. The usual mix of Wulffs, Adams and light mayflies along with various caddis stages and stonefly nymphs will cover most fishing on the river. Black-Nosed Dace and Muddler Minnows will also take fish. It's definitely a spring and fall stream and vulnerable to high temperatures.

The East Branch of the Sacandaga is neglected, but worth a look. This stream is not stocked, but can be fished for native brookies. It runs along Route 30 at the eastern edge of the Siamese Pond Wilderness Area.

MILL CREEK

This small feeder joins the main portion of the Sacandaga from the eastern side just above the small impoundment at Wells. It receives about 500 small browns a year, and its mouth is a good place to hit when fishing the creek or the main river. Mill Creek's lower half can be reached from Windfall and Dorr roads.

Both branches of the Sacandaga, as well as Mill Creek, are subject to the standard trout season and regulations, except that 5 additional brookies under 8 inches may be taken. The last couple of miles of the main river are completely closed to fishing from March 16 to the first Saturday in May to protect the reservoir's spawning walleye. However, this is well downstream of the main trout fishing.

Southern Adirondacks—Major Hatches

INSECT	J	F	M	A	M	J	J	A	S	O	N	D	FLIES
Blue Winged Olives 14-20													Pheasant Tail Nymphs, Comparaduns, Standard Dries
Caddis Green, Gray, Tan, Orange 12-18													Bead-Head Caddis Larva, Elk Hair Caddis, Irresistable Caddis
Stoneflies 8-14													Light and Dark Nymphs (sporadic hatches)
Lt. And Dark Hendrickson 12-14													Light and Dark Hendrickson Parachute, Emergers, Spinners
Sulphurs 14-20													Comparaduns, Standard Dries, Pheasant Tail Nymph
Light Cahills 14													Comparadun, Standard Dries, Light Hare's Ear Nymph
Small Yellow Stonefly 12-14													Elk Hair Caddis, Small Yellow Stimulator
Slate Drake (Isonychia)													Zug Bug, Slate Drake Dry, Wulffs
Trico 20-24													Trico Duns, Griffith's Gnats
Streamers													Woolly Buggers, Muddlers and Marabou Muddlers, all with and without cone heads

Southern Adirondacks Hub Cities

Indian Lake/Bolton Landing/Lake George

ACCOMODATIONS PRICE KEY

$	Up to 60 dollars per night
$$	61 to 99 dollars per night
$$$	100 to 150 per night
$$$$	151 and up per night

HOTELS/MOTELS

Victorian Village Resort Motel, 4818 Lake Shore Drive, Bolton Landing, NY 12814 / 518-644-9401 / $$

The Sagamore, 110 Sagamore Road, Bolton Landing, NY 12814 / 518-644-2626 / $$$$

Knights Inn and Mohawk Motel, 435 Canada Street, Lake George Village 12845 /518-668-2143 / $$-$$$

Admiral Motel, 401 Canada Street, Lake George, NY 12845 / 518-668-2097 / $-$$

CAMPGROUNDS/RVS

Mohawk Camping, 3144 Lake Shore Drive, Lake George, NY 12845 / 518-668-2760, 75 sites17 full / 58 water/electric, on lake

Lewey Lake Campground (Adirondack State Forest), Highway 30, Indian Lake, NY 12842 / 518-648-5266, no-hookups, lake fishing / (Lewey Lake Campground is just one of many state owned campgrounds in the Adirondacks / Call 800-456-CAMP for additional sites and reservations.)

RESTAURANTS

Trillium, 110 Sagamore Road, Bolton Landing, NY 12814 / 518-644-262, at Sagamore Resort

The Log Jam, 1484 Route 9, Lake George, NY 12845 / 518-798-1155

Villa Napoli, 46-10 Lakeshore Drive, Bolton Landing, NY 12814 /518-644-9047 / Opens 8 a.m.

FLY SHOPS

North Country Sports, Thirteenth Lake Road, North River, NY 12856 / 518-251-4299 / Guiding available / Near Siamese ponds

Peace Pipe Fishing Outfitters, 4375 Lake Shore Dr., Diamond Point, NY / 518-668-9203 / www.fish307.com

Beaver Brook Outfitters, Route 28 & Route 8, Wevertown, NY 12886 / 888-454-8433, www.beaverbrook.net / Orvis Dealer / Float Trips

AUTO REPAIR

Family Tire and Auto, 712 State Street, Schenectady, NY 12307 / 518-374-3326

AIRPORT
Floyd Bennett Memorial Airport,   443 Queensbury Avenue, Queensbury, NY 12804 / 518-792-5995

Saratoga County Airport, 410 Greenfield Avenue, Ballston Spa, NY 12020 / 518-885-5354

HOSPITAL/CLINIC
Glens Falls Hospital, 100 Park Street, Glens Falls, NY 12801 / 518-792-3151

Ticonderoga

HOTELS/MOTELS
$ Circle Court Motel, 440 Montcalm Street West, Ticonderoga, NY 12883 / 518-585-7660, SD 50-60

CAMPGROUNDS/RVS
Paradox Lake Campground, Adirondack State Forest, Highway 74, Ticonderoga, NY 13754 / 532-7451 / No hookups

RESTAURANTS
Hot Biscuit Diner, 428 Montcalm Street, Ticonderoga, NY 12883 / 518-585-3483 / Open 6 a.m.

FLY SHOPS
Vermont Field Sports, 1458 Route 7 South, Middlebury, Vermont   05753 / 802-388-3572

AUTO REPAIR
Lakeshore Garage, Lake Shore Drive, Hague, NY 12836 / 518-543-6556

AIRPORT
Ticonderoga Municipal Airport, Old Chilson Road, Ticonderoga, NY 12883 / 518-585-7317

Adirondack Regional Airport, Lake Clear Road, Saranac Lake, NY 12983 / 518-891-4600

HOSPITAL/CLINIC
Moses Ludington Hospital, 2 Wicker Street, Ticonderoga, NY 12883 / 518-585-2831

Northeastern Adirondacks

This portion of the Adirondacks, whose waters drain east into Lake Champlain, hosts several of the state's most famous trout waters. An enormous body of water that is only exceeded by the five Great Lakes, Lake Champlain itself does see some flyfishing. More important, it provides runs of landlocked salmon to several of its tributaries. This area also offers excellent fishing for small wild brook trout, often in tributaries to the larger streams and rivers.

AUSABLE RIVER

The Ausable, with its classic pocket water, good hatches and cool summer temperatures is one of the state's premier trout waters. Like some of the best Catskill streams, the Ausable also offers a lot of history: Ray Bergman fished these waters and developed the Gray Wulff here; the Usual and the Ausable Wulff were also first tied and fished on this stream.

The Ausable begins in Essex County as two separate parts, the east and west branches, which meet at Ausable Forks. All three segments of the river offer trout fishing, but the West Branch is easily the best water.

Not all of the Ausable's West Branch is pocket water.
This smoother flow runs along River Road.

West Branch Ausable River

The fast, boulder-strewn waters of the West Branch look—and fish—like ideal pocket water. Stocked and some wild brown trout, along with some stocked rainbows, hide among the big rocks in the West Branch. Wild brook trout can also be found in its upper reaches. As its name reflects (French for "River of Sand") the Ausable also has slower waters with typical riffles, runs and pools. The hatches are very good on the Ausable: classic Art Flick mayfly hatches, pushed back by a few weeks, supplemented by stoneflies, caddis and baitfish.

The West Branch begins near the town of Lake Placid and flows roughly 20 miles to the beginning of the main river in Ausable Forks. Good fishing begins near Route 73 near the village of North Elba. Here the water is relatively small and wild brookies are the staple, with a small supplemental brook trout stocking by Essex County. Shortly downstream, the Ausable veers away from Route 73 and runs parallel to River Road (or Riverside Drive) until the road and the river both hit Route 86.

This four-mile stretch has smoother water—riffles and runs and a number of very attractive bend pools—along with some more typical rocky sections. Some land here is posted, but there is enough strategically placed access to make much of it reachable to the wading angler. Don Jones of Jones Outfitters in Lake Placid advises that this section is particularly good for Hendricksons in May and Tricos in August, with Tricos especially heavy above the one lane bridge that crosses the stream. Sulphurs, Cahills and Olives round out the hatches on River Road. The

The West Branch at Shadow Rock has rougher water.

slowest sections here often require small flies, including tiny Tricos and Olives, and the fish are notably pickier than in the fast water. This section also contains the beginning of a 2.2-mile "catch and release" section where fishing is permitted year round. The section begins at the outlet of Holcomb Pond, about two-thirds of the way along River Road, and ends at Monument Falls on Route 86.

By the time the river reaches Monument Falls, and for most of its remaining run to the village of Wilmington, the West Branch becomes the boulder filled, rapid flow for which it is famous. Here, short-line nymphing and big, bushy flies are the norm. The West Branch stays cool through most summers, although in July and August fishing mornings and evenings will be most productive, with spinner falls common at night. The mouths of cool tributaries are also worth seeking out in mid-summer. There are various pulloffs along Route 86.

The area from the dam in Wilmington down to Ausable Forks, where the main stem of the river begins, has lots of good pocket water that is not as heavily fished as upstream spots. The same applies to the water just upstream of the dam junction, called the Bush Country by locals.

Here, and anywhere in the region with fast water, anglers should observe basic precautions. Felt soles are essential and some people recommend cleats, but others think they make things worse on the smooth, rounded boulders. Also, a wading staff can be indispensable in fast water. Slow, careful wading is called for around big rocks. Don't go in too deep in fast water and avoid the heaviest rapids entirely. Plan to fish with a friend; if you're going alone, let someone know where you will be (a cell phone is not a bad idea either—for emergencies only, please.)

As for rods and reels, an 8- to 9-foot rod of 5- or 6-weight is ideal for early season and faster water. In the slower portions, you can drop down to a 4- or even 3-weight for smaller flies, but you'll obviously sacrifice some versatility.

Fly selection on the West Branch is dictated partly by hatches and partly by the kind of water being fished. Early in the season when water is high, big stonefly nymphs and streamers such as Woolly Buggers, leeches and white or black Zonkers are the order of the day. There are some early season Olive hatches, but fishing small imitations in high water is rarely productive.

As the water comes down in May, dry flies and smaller nymphs and wets come into their own. On the smoother water—like that along River Road—you'll want parachutes and comparaduns to match the hatches, along with CDC or other emerger patterns. But these will quickly sink in faster water. Instead, the Ausable's pocket water demands heavily hackled traditional patterns, including the Wulff series for fishing among the big Ausable boulders. Elk Hair Caddis and the Yellow Sally stonefly are also buoyant searching flies that draw strikes on the West Branch.

The Green Drake hatch is brief (as it is everywhere) but can cause voracious feeding, especially to the Coffin Fly spinners. The drake hatch moves upstream over a two-week period, so anglers need to be at the right section at the right time. The mulititude of mid-stream boulders makes *Isonychia* dry flies more productive here than most streams, as many adults fall into the stream after hatching on

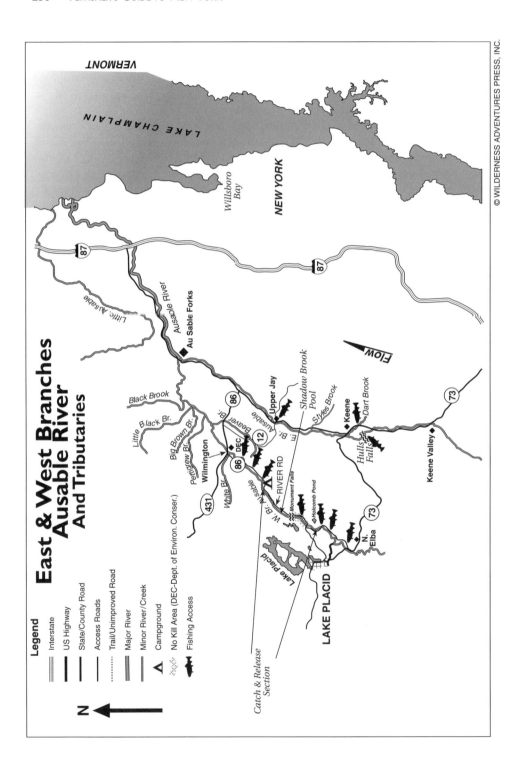

East & West Branches Ausable River And Tributaries

Legend

≡ Interstate
━ US Highway
━ State/County Road
━ Access Roads
⋯⋯ Trail/Unimproved Road
═ Major River
─ Minor River/Creek
△ Campground
▨ No Kill Area (DEC-Dept. of Environ. Conser.)
🐟 Fishing Access

🐟 Catch & Release Section

VERMONT

LAKE CHAMPLAIN

NEW YORK

Willsboro Bay

Little Ausable

Ausable River

Au Sable Forks

Black Brook

Little Black Br.

Big Brown Br.

Petrgew Br.

Beaver Br.

Wilmington

White Br.

W. Br. Ausable

Monument Falls

RIVER RD

Holcomb Pond

Lake Placid

LAKE PLACID

N. Elba

Upper Jay

E. Br. Ausable

Shadow Brook Pool

Styles Brook

Keene

Dart Brook

Hulls Falls

Keene Valley

Flow

87

86

12

431

73

73

DEC

N

rocks. In fact, a size 10 *Isonychia* parachute took a 24-inch brown for Kevin Henebry of Ausable River Sports Shop one autumn. For nymphs, stoneflies and various *Isonychia* imitations will work in fast water. For summer, a few ants and beetles will supplement the stream-born insects.

In addition to fly selection, picking the pockets also requires different tactics than slow water fishing. Initially, all the water looks the same, but with practice anglers will be able to identify the small seams and slicks that are likely to hold trout. Hit every one you find, but keep moving: if a fish hasn't hit after three or four casts, try the next spot. Naturally all the casts in pocket water are short, rarely more than five feet of line plus the leader.

As darkness approaches, matching the hatch is forgotten, and nighttime anglers typically switch to big Wulff patterns in size 10 and 12. And the presentation of these flies is no more delicate than their design. Fran Betters, who developed the Ausable Wulff and runs the Adirondack Sport Shop on the river's bank, strongly advises evening anglers to get the attention of fish by moving these high floating dries with small twitches of the fly line.

The West Branch is heavily stocked by the state, with a substantial stocking by Essex County as well. About 20,000 browns are put in along its length by the DEC. These are supplemented by about 4,300 two-year-old rainbows and browns stocked by Essex County between Elba and the Junction at Ausable Forks. The county fish are float stocked so these trout can be found throughout the river. There is only modest natural reproduction here, except for the wild brookies that come in from some tributaries, and winter ice limits the holdover of browns.

East Branch Ausable River

The East Branch of the Ausable has some pretty good trout fishing, but is not up to the level of its western counterpart. The East Branch rises from a series of lakes in Essex County and flows about 15 miles to its junction with the West Branch at Ausable Forks. The prime flyfishing stretch is roughly between the villages of Keene Valley and Jay. The East Branch is on average a slower, less rocky stream than the west branch, but it still offers stretches of fast moving pocket water—particularly in the steeper upper half—that are ideal for short-line nymphing. One of the best spots is the small gorge below Hulls Falls, off Route 69.

There is access along the upper portion of the East Branch from Route 73, which parallels the stream, and from Route 69 for a few miles. Along the lower portion, Route 9N runs beside the river, offering informal access at various locations. A stretch of dedicated access can be found near the village of Jay on Route 9N, but you'll need to look carefully for the small Public Fishing Rights sign along the road. The fire department in Jay is another good spot, as is the area upstream where Styles Brook enters.

Though the West Branch generally stays cold, the east portion is prone to summer warming, especially in its wider, less canopied water below the village of Jay. Plan to fish it into early July and again in September. In mid-summer, look for faster, shaded water upstream, such as Hulls Falls, since fish gather here. Anglers, on the other hand, are usually not concentrated on the East Branch due to the proximity of the better-known West Branch.

The fish in the East Branch are a mix of stocked browns and rainbows, about 5,000 of each are put in by the state each year. Essex County adds about 1,200 two-year-old rainbows near Keene and another 1,000 downstream in the stretch between Ausable Forks and Jay. There is relatively little holdover of the rainbows, but the browns can remain for several years.

Hulls Falls on the Ausable's East Branch.

The wide Main Stem of the Ausable also holds trout.

Main Branch Ausable River

Below the junction of the two branches in Ausable Forks, the river gets wide and shallow and is not ideal trout habitat. However, trout are stocked here and the fishing can be good. A key is finding the right water, since large portions will be devoid of trout. Concentrate on sections with good structure— particularly pocket water. Even in good looking water, the fishing here can be hit or miss, you'll need some patience and persistence to find the trout.

About 2,700 trout, 1,600 rainbows and the rest browns, are stocked by the DEC from Ausable Forks down to Keeseville; most of these are two-year-old fish. Essex County puts in about 1,000 two-year-old trout below Ausable Forks and another 1,400 two-year-olds, again mixed rainbows and browns, downstream between Clintonville and Keeseville. There are also reports of a small but growing population of wild rainbows in the main stem, mostly small but with a few up to 18 inches.

Despite the stocking, expect the trout fishing to fall off and smallmouth population to grow below Clintonville. For either species, these downstream waters on the main river can be floated in canoes or kayaks.

For its last three miles, from Ausable Chasm to the mouth, the Ausable gets spring and fall runs of landlocked salmon. While not as good as the same fishing in the Saranac or Boquet, the fish can be taken on streamers. Access to the lower end of the stream is limited, but there are a couple of pulloffs along Route 9. There is a large pool where Route 9 crosses the stream, which offers good holding water to fall spawning landlocks.

AUSABLE TRIBUTARIES

Anglers fishing the Ausable should not ignore the tributaries, both as good spots to hit on the river, and as fisheries in their own right. A few are stocked and all have populations of wild brook trout. Fishing for native trout is a staple in the Adirondacks and shouldn't be overlooked.

None of the Ausable tributaries are subject to special regulations, except that 5 extra brook trout of 8 inches or less may be kept—intended to cull the population and allow the wild fish to grow. The following small feeders, listed heading downstream from Wilmington, are worth a look.

White Brook

White is a short stream near Whiteface Mountain. It receives a small stocking of brookies to enhance its wild fish. Route 19 provides access, as does Whiteface Mountain Road upstream.

Beaver Brook

The farthest upstream of a half-dozen closely set tributaries of the lower West Branch, Beaver Brook has wild brook trout and receives a few hundred more through stocking each year. Access is from Route 86 and from Hardy Kilburn Road.

Little Black Brook is one of the many productive small tributaries on the Ausable.

Pettigrew Brook

This unstocked stream enters below Beaver Brook. Access can be found near the mouth at Route 12 and along John Bliss Road.

Black Brook and Little Black Brook

These two streams enter the West Branch about three miles upstream of the junction at Ausable Forks; both are nice small-stream fisheries. Little Black is both narrow and short, running only about four miles from its source at Taylor Pond into the West Branch. It has wild brookies and receives about 1,000 stocked fish each year. There is an impoundment, Newberry Pond, about halfway to the mouth. Access is available at the bottom from Route 12, from the Shaw Dam Road/Route 19 crossing, and near Forestdale Road close to the headwaters.

Black Brook is a longer fishery, running about 10 miles from Clinton County into the Ausable. It holds wild brookies supplemented by stocked brook trout and about 500 browns. Access is again available at Route 12 and upstream where Turnpike Road crosses.

Big Brown Brook

This alliteratively named stream, actually quite small, enters the West Branch just upstream of the two Black Brooks. It is not stocked and the fishing is for wild brook trout (although an occasional brown may enter from the Ausable). As with Little Black Brook, Route 12 and Route 19 are the access points.

Stream Facts: Ausable River

Seasons
- April 1 to October 15; two-mile special regulations section from Holcomb Pond outlet to Monument Falls open all year.
- Migratory section on main stem, below Ausable Chasm, open all year.

Special Regulations
- Two-mile section of West Branch, catch and release, artificials only.
- Below Ausable Chasm, Lake Champlain regulations apply: 3 trout, 2 salmon of 15 inches or more.

Fish
- Stocked and holdover browns, stocked rainbows and some wild brook trout. Smallmouth below Ausable Forks. Downstream of Ausable Chasm, migratory landlocked salmon and a few steelhead.

River Characteristics
- Small mountain stream in headwaters, wide, usually rocky stream in main trout fishing sections, with some sections of slower water. Wider and slower below Ausable Forks.

River Flows
- Usually high in early season, cool and steady through summer most years. Water usually slightly tinged.

Ausable River—Major Hatches

INSECT	J	F	M	A	M	J	J	A	S	O	N	D	FLIES
Blue Winged Olives 14-22				▮	▮					▮	▮		Comparadun, Parachute, Emergers, Pheasant Tail Nymph; Tough to Fish in Early Season
Light & Dark Hendrickson 12-14					▮								Light and Dark Hendrickson, Comparadun, Haystack or Parachute, dark brown Hendrickson Nymph
Caddis Tan Olive Black 14-18						▮							Elk Hair Caddis, Lafontaine Deep Pupa and Emergent Sparkle Pupa, Bead Head Nymphs
Stoneflies Tan, Brown, Black 6-10							▮	▮	▮				Sporadic Hatches; Light and Dark Stonefly Nymphs, Stimulators, Yellow Sallies, Elk Hair Caddis
March Brown 12-14						▮							AuSable Wulff, Comparadun, Haystack
Green Drake10-12						▮							Nymph, Coffin Fly Spinner. Wulff Patterns
Trico 18-24							▮						Trico Spinner, Griffith's Gnat
Slate Drake (Isonychia) 12						▮		▮	▮				Comparadun, Haystack, Parachute, Better's Picket Finn, Zug Bug
Ants, Beetles							▮	▮	▮				Foam Ants, Dubbed Ants, Foam Beetles; Best in Summer
Attractors 6-12					▮	▮	▮	▮	▮				Ausable Wulff and other Wulff patterns
Streamers				▮	▮	▮	▮	▮	▮				Wooly Buggers, White or Black Zonkers, Marabou Patterns; more important in early season and at night

Black Flies

Most hatches bring anglers running to the stream, but one stream-born insect in the Adirondacks drives them away: the notorious black fly. This relentless pest inflicts painful bites and can ruin a fishing trip. But there are some steps angler's can take to avoid their worst effects.

Like traditional midges, the black fly is a member of the Diptera family. The white, somewhat bulbous larva of the black fly attaches to rocks in Adirondack streams and the fly hatches in fast riffles. (Although the larva does nourish stream fish, it is of little use to fly anglers. Imitations will mostly draw minnows and trout fry.) The black flies hatch for about four or five weeks in the Adirondacks; the month of June is generally considered the "black fly season." They will swarm to anyone unlucky enough to be nearby and find any way they can to the victim's skin. Once through the defenses, the biting females will draw blood, leaving a painful wound.

In the past, DDT spraying for black flies had a devastating effect on fish and other wildlife. Today a generally safe pesticide (actually a bacterium) called Bti is used. Bti is sprayed within many Adirondack villages and reduces the black flies, but it is not used in the remote areas where most of the fish are.

The simplest form of individual protection against black flies is to schedule a trip before or after their season. Unfortunately, that month-long period encompasses some very good fishing, so if you can't wait the DEC and other experts recommend some protection:

Wear long-sleeved, collared shirts in dull colors. Avoid blue, which seems to attract the flies.

Wear a lightweight head net, available from catalogues and many tackle and outdoor shops in the region. (Black flies typically swarm to a victim's head.)

Use a DEET-based repellent on all exposed skin. Remember to keep it out of eyes, nose and mouth, and observe all precautions on the label. Also, keep it away from your fly line, which it will quickly destroy. (A good trick to protect your line is to use the backs of your hands to apply repellent.)

If the flies get through despite your precautions, put some antiseptic on the bites, and consider topical cortisone for the swelling. The pain, itch and swelling should subside in a few days. And if it's any consolation, remember that the clean water black flies require to breed is also good for the trout.

SARANAC RIVER

The Saranac River runs nearly parallel to the Ausable and is often in that stream's shadow as a trout fishery. In fact, though, the Saranac offers some excellent fishing for wild brookies and a mix of wild and stocked browns in its nearly 60-mile run to Lake Champlain. It also offers very good fishing for landlocked salmon in its last few miles. The Saranac begins as separate branches, north and south, high in the Adirondacks.

South Branch Saranac River

The South Branch essentially begins at Flower Lake in the town of Saranac Lake. Here it is largely a warmwater fishery, with very good fishing for pike right in the town. A small stocking of browns is made just below the dam at Flower Lake and they may be fished for year round (down to the Pine Street Bridge). Much of the South Branch is quickly swallowed up in two large impounds, Franklin Falls Pond and Union Falls Pond, both excellent for smallmouth and pike and both conducive to boat fishing. While not prime trout water, there is some decent pocket water above Franklin Falls Pond, reachable from River Road/Route 18. In addition, big browns are occasionally taken below the Franklin Falls Dam.

The South Branch also offers some good trout fishing in its last few miles before its confluence with the North Branch in the town of Clayburgh. This is typical pocket water fishing for browns and rainbows.

North Branch Saranac River

The North Branch is not dammed and offers more trout fishing than the South Branch. In its small headwaters near Loon Lake, there are native brook trout, accessible at a few spots along Goldsmith Road. Downstream, between the junctions of Alder Brook and Cold Brook (in the village of Riverview), a run of about two miles, lies some of the best water in the entire river. The water is smoother here and unlike rockier water, accurate imitations are often required. This is especially true for the small Tricos and Olives that hatch late in the season. The area is not heavily stocked and contains rainbows, browns and a few brookies. There are reportedly fewer fish here but generally larger ones; local angler Bill Wellman landed a 13-inch brookie near Riverview. Special regulations apply to the river between Alder and Cold brooks: only three fish may be kept, all over 12 inches and fishing is permitted year round. As with much of the river from here down, access is available from Route 3.

Cold Brook itself is an excellent brook trout fishery and can be reached from Cold Brook Road. Alder Brook also has wild brookies, but posted land and the overhanging vegetation that gives it its name make it difficult to fish.

Good fishing for a mix of stocked and wild fish continues down to the junction with the South Branch in the village of Clayburgh. After Clayburgh, the main river offers trout fishing roughly to the village of Saranac, but the larger water and a series of dams make picking the right spot essential. One good place is below the dam in Moffitville. There is parking at the dam and some good water below, includ-

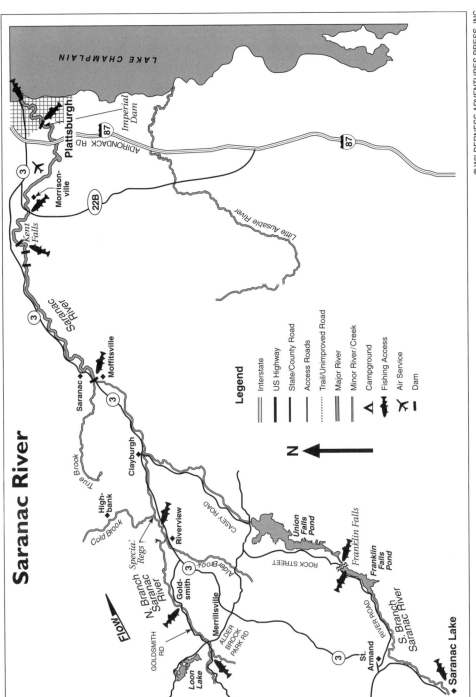

Saranac River

LAKE CHAMPLAIN

Imperial Dam

Plattsburgh

ADIRONDACK RD

87

87

3

Morrison-
ville

22B

Kent
Falls

Little Ausable River

3

Saranac River

Moffittsville

3

Saranac

True Brook

Clayburgh

High-
bank

Cold Brook

Riverview

CASEY ROAD

Union
Falls
Pond

Special
Regs

N. Branch
Saranac
River

Gold-
smith

3

Alder Brook

ROCK STREET

Franklin Falls

Franklin
Falls
Pond

FLOW

GOLDSMITH
RD

Merrillsville

ALDER
BROOK
PARK RD

RIVER ROAD

St.
Armand

3

S. Branch
Saranac River

Loon
Lake

Saranac Lake

Legend

Interstate
US Highway
State/County Road
Access Roads
Trail/Unimproved Road
Major River
Minor River/Creek
Campground
Fishing Access
Air Service
Dam

N

ing where True Brook comes in. Don't ignore the brook itself, which has an excellent population of wild brook trout.

Even better trout fishing can be had by heading well downstream to the Kent Falls Dam—the last of the three closely set dams. Here, for about three or four miles, a mix of flats, runs and pools offer good fishing. There is access along Route 3, including a parking lot provided by NYSEG, which operates the dam.

One important caution for this stretch is that water levels can fluctuate dramatically. It is important to stay aware of flows and leave the water, or at least remain at the edges, if the river is rising.

Hatches on the Saranac are similar to those on the Ausable. Attractors such as members of the Wulff series and Gold-Ribbed Hare's Ear Nymphs will work. You'll want to have some finer imitations for the smaller flies, including Trico spinners and BWO parachutes and comparaduns, along with emergers. Be alert for sporadic caddis hatches as well. The White Fly, sometimes called the White Miller, is important throughout the Saranac and can be imitated by White comparaduns, or White Wulffs in faster water.

Night Fishing

Anglers looking for trophy-sized browns might consider fishing at night on the Saranac. While not for those unfamiliar with the river, or for unsteady waders, night fishing offers a shot at very large trout that rarely if ever are caught in daylight.

Local angler Bruce Handey who lives near the Saranac has been night fishing there for several decades. He finds that most pools on the stream have one lunker brown—the larger pools have two or three—that feeds on baitfish late at night (midnight and beyond). Of course these fish are not easy to catch. Among other challenges, they don't seem to feed every evening, perhaps because of the big meals they eat. However, if you hit the same pool over a week or two, you should have a good chance of hooking the biggest resident. With its more manageable water levels May is a good time.

Landing big browns—fish up to 30 inches have been taken—requires stout gear. Seven-weight rods and 2X leaders are the norm. So are very big flies: Handey uses size 6, 4XL hooks to tie a modified Woolly Worm with a small red tag, black chenille body with matching heavy palmered hackle and a black squirrel tail wing. This or other big streamers should be quartered downstream, drifted on a tight line. Allow the fly to hang at the end of the drift then strip it back slowly. Floating lines are usually the right choice as the browns are chasing minnows in shallow riffles and Handey advises using wide open casting loops, since untangling a leader in the dark is almost impossible. You may catch small rock bass or larger fall fish (up to 16 inches) while night fishing—a good sign that trout will also be feeding in the area. If a brown takes, there will be no doubt and the fight in the dark may be a bit different than the day as the big browns are known to leap when hooked at night.

Obviously all the normal cautions about daytime wading apply even more strongly at night. It is a good idea to scout the pool during the day and have an exit route planned before you enter the stream. And if you go alone, or even with a friend, let someone know which pool you'll hit and don't deviate from the plan. As noted elsewhere, don't wade too deeply or try to go too fast. And stay aware of rising flows from the dams; if the water is getting higher, get out of the stream.

Landlocked Salmon

In addition to the trout and warmwater fishing in its upper end, the last portion of the Saranac provides the opportunity to catch landlocked salmon that migrate in from Lake Champlain. The landlockeds—which are related to Atlantic salmon, and often called that by locals—can be readily targeted with a fly rod in the city of Plattsburgh.

The Saranac can be fished day or night.

Although landlockeds were native to Lake Champlain, the ravages of dams, pollution and overfishing had driven them out by the mid-1800s. Since the 1970s, a steady stocking program has created a fishery on the tributaries, with Saranac probably the best of them. About 30,000 six-inch landlockeds are stocked in the Saranac each year, supplemented by another 30,000 one-inch newborns. There may be some natural reproduction too, though not much. The landlockeds are currently able to run only about three miles upstream to the Imperial Dam behind the State University in Plattsburgh. Plans to build a fish ladder in the dam are close to completion. If successful, the ladder would open up nearly 15 miles of extra fishing and good spawning habitat.

The landlockeds come up the river in spring chasing smelt, their favored baitfish. This migration lasts two to four weeks and, depending on water conditions, occurs from early April to mid-May. Though the fish tend to run smaller in the spring than during fall spawning, they are a bit easier to catch since they are actively feeding. Because the spring-run fish are chasing smelt from the lake, they tend to congregate in the lower half of the stream below Imperial Dam, roughly from the South Catharine Street crossing on down.

Naturally, smelt imitations are the flies of choice. There are dozens, if not hundreds, of these and every angler has a personal favorite. If you don't wish to stock up or spend time tying, local angler and Trout Unlimited director Bill Wellman advises that the standard Grey Ghost remains the most popular choice. Mickey Finns also work, as does a variation called the Mickey Hornburg, which Julie Gossling of Gordon's Marine ties with a barred mallard wing over the bucktail, jungle cock cheeks and big grizzly hackle at the front.

Most local anglers use the same flies during the fall spawning run, even though these fish are not feeding. The fall run landlockeds can begin trickling in as early as late August, but November is usually the best time to try. The run is then near its densest as fall rains raise the water levels, while conditions are milder—at least compared to December. The males come into the river first, followed by larger, heavier females a week or two later. Fish in the 16- to 24-inch range are typical, and unlike Pacific salmon the landlockeds spawn multiple times.

During fall, the fish will be in calmer water and deeper pools than in spring. As with most spawning fish, patience and persistence are required to get non-feeding fish to strike. For both spring and fall fishing, a 7- to 8-weight rod is ideal. The salmon will typically be two to three feet below the surface, so anglers usually rely on small sink tips or intermediate lines with weight on the leader to keep the fly in the strike zone. Flies are cast across and down, with a combination of swinging and stripping. Occasionally, salmon will rise reflexively to a late autumn hatch and will be taken on dries, but this is not something to count on. In addition to the salmon, anglers will occasionally hook browns and rainbows that come in from Lake Champlain.

There is good access at strategic points throughout the three-mile stretch below the dam. Starting at the top, there is access directly below Imperial Dam off Adirondack Road—obviously a good spot, since the fish must stop here. Downstream, there is access next to the high school at the foot bridge off George Angel Drive. The bridge traverses a long mid-stream island, called Webb Island, that offers good pockets on the eastern (far) side. At the downstream end of the island, Allen Street provides access to a deep, popular pool.

Additional good water can be found off South Catharine Street and again behind the police station. At the lower end, the spots just above and below the railroad trestle and foot bridge near the mouth also offer good fishing and the area upstream of the trestle offers access for disabled anglers. The last portion is wide and slow and a small boat can be put in here at the public access and launch on the southern shore near the power plant.

The river is popular during salmon runs, but has nowhere near the crowds of other migratory trout and salmon streams in the state. And, Saranac anglers are generally courteous to each other, even in crowded sections. With closely set access, anglers can usually find some room.

The Saranac River below Imperial Dam is subject to special Lake Champlain regulations. Fishing for trout and salmon is allowed all year, with no more than two 15-inch landlockeds per day allowed (three trout of 12 inches or more may be kept).

Even though Imperial Dam is currently an impassable barrier to landlockeds entering the Saranac, it is possible to catch "resident" landlockeds above the dam. These are stocked fish that will stay in the stream up to two years, then head over the dam to the lake. They grow to decent size—up to about 10 inches—and will readily take dry flies as well as subsurface offerings. Morrisonville Bridge at Route 22B is a good place to try for these fish, along with more typical resident browns and rainbows.

As noted above, the section that includes Morrisonville Bridge, from Imperial Dam upstream to Kent Road Dam, is open to trout fishing all year, with five fish per day of 12 inches or more permitted. Remember that above Imperial Dam the standard landlocked salmon season of April 1 to October 15 applies, with a 15-inch minimum. It is unlikely a juvenile landlocked large enough to keep would be caught above the dam. In any case, better to release them so they can return fully grown.

A silvery landlocked salmon taken at the mouth of the Saranac.

Boats are useful for fishing the Saranac's last few hundred yards.

Stream Facts: Saranac River

Seasons/Regulations
- Trout: April 1 to October 15; five fish any size, plus five brook trout under eight inches.
- South Branch from Flower Lake downstream to Pine Street, open all year.
- North Branch from mouth of Alder Brook downstream to Cold Brook, open all year, three fish of 12 inches or more.
- Main Stem from Kent Falls Dam downstream to Imperial Dam, all year, no extra brook trout allowed.
- Landlocked Salmon: Migratory section downstream of Imperial Dam, open all year; three fish per day, 15 inches or more.

Fish
- Stocked and holdover browns, wild brook trout, small stocked landlocked salmon.
- Downstream of Imperial Dam, migratory landlocked salmon and occasional rainbows and browns.

River Characteristics
- Small mountain stream in headwaters, rocky stream in most trout fishing sections, with slower water above dams.

River Flows
- Usually high in early season, subject to some low water in summer. Dam flows can fluctuate.

Saranac River—Major Hatches

INSECT	J	F	M	A	M	J	J	A	S	O	N	D	FLIES
Blue Winged Olives 14-22													Comparadun, Parachute, Emergers, Pheasant Tail Nymph; Tough to Fish in Early Season
Light & Dark Hendrickson 12-14													Light and Dark Hendrickson, Comparadun, Haystack or Parachute, dark brown Hendrickson Nymph
Caddis Tan Olive Black 14-18													Elk Hair Caddis, Lafontaine Deep Pupa and Emergent Sparkle Pupa, Bead-Head Nymphs
Stoneflies Tan, Brown, Black 6-10													Sporadic Hatches; Light and Dark Stonefly Nymphs, Stimulators, Yellow Sallies, Elk Hair Caddis
Trico 18-24													Trico Spinner, Griffith's Gnat
White Fly 12													White Wulff, Comparadun
Slate Drake (Isonychia) 12													Comparadun, Haystack, Zug Bug
Ants, Beetles													Foam Ants, Dubbed Ants, Foam Beetles; Best in Summer
Attractors 6-12													Wulff patterns, Modified Wooly Worms at night
Streamers													Wooly Buggers, White or Black Zonkers, Marabou Patterns; more important in early season and at right Gray Ghost and smelt imitations for landlocked salmon

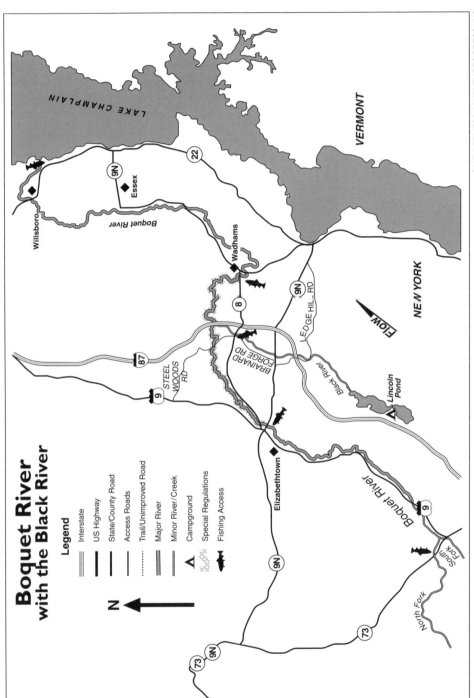

BOQUET RIVER

Along with the Saranac, the Boquet offers the best landlocked salmon run in the region. It also has trout fishing (although not as good as that in the other two major rivers) and some summer angling for smallmouth bass. The Boquet (pronounced "Boket") begins as a small stream in Elizabethtown and flows northeast more than 20 miles before emptying into Lake Champlain at Willisboro, about 10 miles south of the Ausable. About four miles from the mouth, the North Branch of the Boquet enters.

Trout

The trout water on the Boquet is roughly from Elizabethtown downstream (northeast) to the village of Wadhams. Access is good along most of this run; Route 9 parallels the river for its eight plus miles in Elizabethtown, and Routes 8 and 10, along with several crossings, offer access downstream to Wadhams.

The stream is heavily stocked by the state, with additional fish put in by Essex County. Most of the fish are brookies and browns—about 9,000 of each, including some two-year-old browns (mostly added by Essex County)—along with about 7,000 rainbows.

The North Branch, a small mountain flow, receives its own stockings by the state and county—about 3,000 browns supplemented by 1,000 brookies. It can be reached from several road crossings: Route 9 in the upper half and Route 68 and Mountain Road nearer the junction with the main river.

Perhaps due to acidity, the Boquet does not have overwhelming hatches. A selection of Wulffs and Elk Hair Caddis along with basic mayfly nymphs and caddis pupa and larva should be sufficient. High floating flies are essential in the stream, which is largely pocket water.

The Boquet is subject to the standard trout season, but only trout of nine inches or more may be kept between Route 9N in the village of Elizabethtown downstream to Wadham Falls in Wadham (and no additional small brook trout are allowed in this section).

The Black River (unrelated to the larger river in the west that flows into Lake Ontario) joins the Boquet about two miles upstream of Wadhams. It receives its own stocking of trout—about 2,000 brook trout and half as many browns. Brainards Forge Road parallels the stream and Routes 9N and 8 cross it along its roughly six-mile run. No special regulations apply.

Landlocked Salmon

The premier fishing on the Boquet is for landlockeds. There are good spring and fall runs here that can be fished on foot or from a boat. The river runs for approximately 2.5 miles downstream from the dam in Willisboro. In addition, the dam now has a fish ladder, operating only in fall to try to increase natural spawning. However, according to reports, fewer than 100 spawners make it upstream so anglers have much better odds on the lower river for both runs.

The spring run on the Boquet brings in large numbers of salmon from the lake. These fish, which are smaller than the fall spawners, are chasing food into the warmer river water. The run begins a week or two after ice-out, typically in late March, and continues for 4 to 5 weeks (though it can last nearly two months if rains keep the river up). Since the fish are actively feeding they take flies readily, and imitations of smelt are the best choice. The Grey Ghost is popular here, as are the Winnapasauki Smelt and Black-Nosed Dace. Jim Hotaling of Champlain Guide Service also recommends swinging traditional salmon patterns such as The Jock Scott, Green Butt Skunk and steelhead patterns like the Purple Peril.

In spring, the lower half of the stream is probably the better section and a boat is useful here. Unlike the Saranac, a long stretch of the Boquet is conducive to boating. Small boats and canoes can be put in about two miles upstream at School Street in Willisboro. For wading anglers, the two big pools downstream of the dam are the main focus, but they are not as productive in spring.

In the fall, large spawning fish come into the river. The spawning run on the Boquet is a bit earlier than the Saranac, beginning around Labor Day and continuing until mid-November. The fall spawners move up the river in stages, but they eventually will be found all the way to the dam. Because they are not actively feeding, persistence is essential. Experienced anglers will continue to use smolt imitations, particularly in the lower river, then switch to big nymphs or salmon/steelhead flies upstream. Effective nymphs include black stoneflies, large Hare's Ears and— even though they don't live in the stream—Green Drake nymphs. While sunshine in spring warms the water and makes fish more active, the opposite applies in early fall. Plan to fish in morning or evening during the first part of the spawning run. As the weather cools in October, the midday period becomes more productive.

Although the spawning runs are over by the end of May, landlockeds do occasionally come into the lower river in summer. Hotaling reports that cool summer rains that quickly lower the river's temperature can bring fish into the Boquet. You'll need lucky timing or good information from a local source; these brief runs last only a couple of days.

Like all other Champlain tributaries, special regulations apply to the Boquet up to the Willisboro dam. Fishing for landlocked salmon is permitted all year; two fish of 15 inches or longer may be kept.

Smallmouth

From mid-June through July, good-sized smallmouth come into the lower Boquet from Lake Champlain. The lower, floatable portion of the river is the best section for these bass. Muddler Minnows, Woolly Buggers—especially in crayfish colors of brown and rust—and marabou patterns in white and yellow are good flies for the smallmouth. These fish typically weigh a pound or two, although four-pounders are not uncommon. A 5- or 6-weight rod should work fine.

Champlain regulations apply to smallmouth fishing below the dam: the season begins on the second Saturday in June (one week earlier than standard bass season) and ends on November 30. Anglers are allowed five fish of 10 inches or more.

GREAT CHAZY RIVER

This river, better known as a warmwater fishery for bass and muskies, has some trout in its upper section. The Great Chazy is formed by two branches that run east in Clinton County near the Canadian border and join near the village of Mooers Forks before continuing to Lake Champlain. The trout fishing is essentially limited to the North Branch, which runs about 18 miles from its headwaters to the junction. About 9,000 trout are stocked here each year; more than half browns the rest rainbows.

Route 11 parallels all but the uppermost five miles of the North Branch, and there are access points along the stream, including at Ellenburg at the upper end, near the village of Forest and a few miles downstream where Graves Brook enters. The trout section has typical mountain pocket water. Attractor patterns such as Wulffs and Haystacks along with generic nymphs like Hare's Ears and some bead-head caddis imitations should be sufficient.

The main stem of the river is wide and slow moving—primarily a warmwater fishery—but does get a modest stocking of browns. It also gets a substantial stocking of muskies.

There are no special regulations on the North Branch of the Great Chazy. Well downstream on the main stem, a portion of the stream is closed to all fishing until mid-March to protect spawning walleye.

The Great Chazy River
and the Little Chazy River

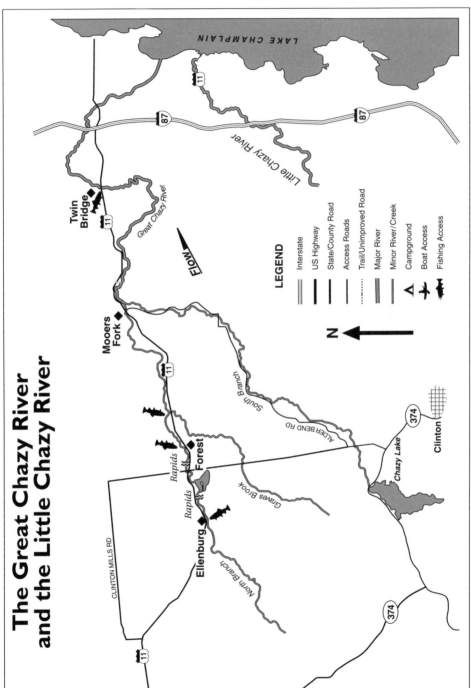

LAKE CHAMPLAIN

Little Chazy River

Great Chazy River

Twin Bridge

Mooers Fork

FLOW

LEGEND

Interstate
US Highway
State/County Road
Access Roads
Trail/Unimproved Road
Major River
Minor River/Creek
Campground
Boat Access
Fishing Access

N

South Branch

ALDER BEND RD

Forest

Rapids

Rapids

Graves Brook

Chazy Lake

Clinton

CLINTON MILLS RD

Ellenburg

North Branch

374

374

© WILDERNESS ADVENTURES PRESS, INC.

The Great Chazy's North Branch where Graves Brook enters.

Little Ausable River

This small to medium-sized stream, despite its name, is not a tributary to the larger river. Instead, it heads south toward the Ausable, then makes a U-turn and runs north into Lake Champlain a bit north of its namesake. Along the way it offers fishing for some brook trout and stocked browns. The better fishing here will be in the upper half of the stream. This portion is accessible first from Clintonville Road, then from River Road, both of which parallel the stream. Substantial overgrowth and a number of downed trees require careful casting, or dapping, to take fish. Like most Clinton County waters, the normal trout season applies and an additional five brookies under eight inches may be kept.

The lower end of the Little Ausable, which enters Lake Champlain near Ausable Point, also gets a small run of landlocked salmon. This section of the stream can be reached from Route 9. Lake Champlain tributary regulations apply to the salmon fishing.

Brush and downed trees can make the Little Ausable tough to fish.

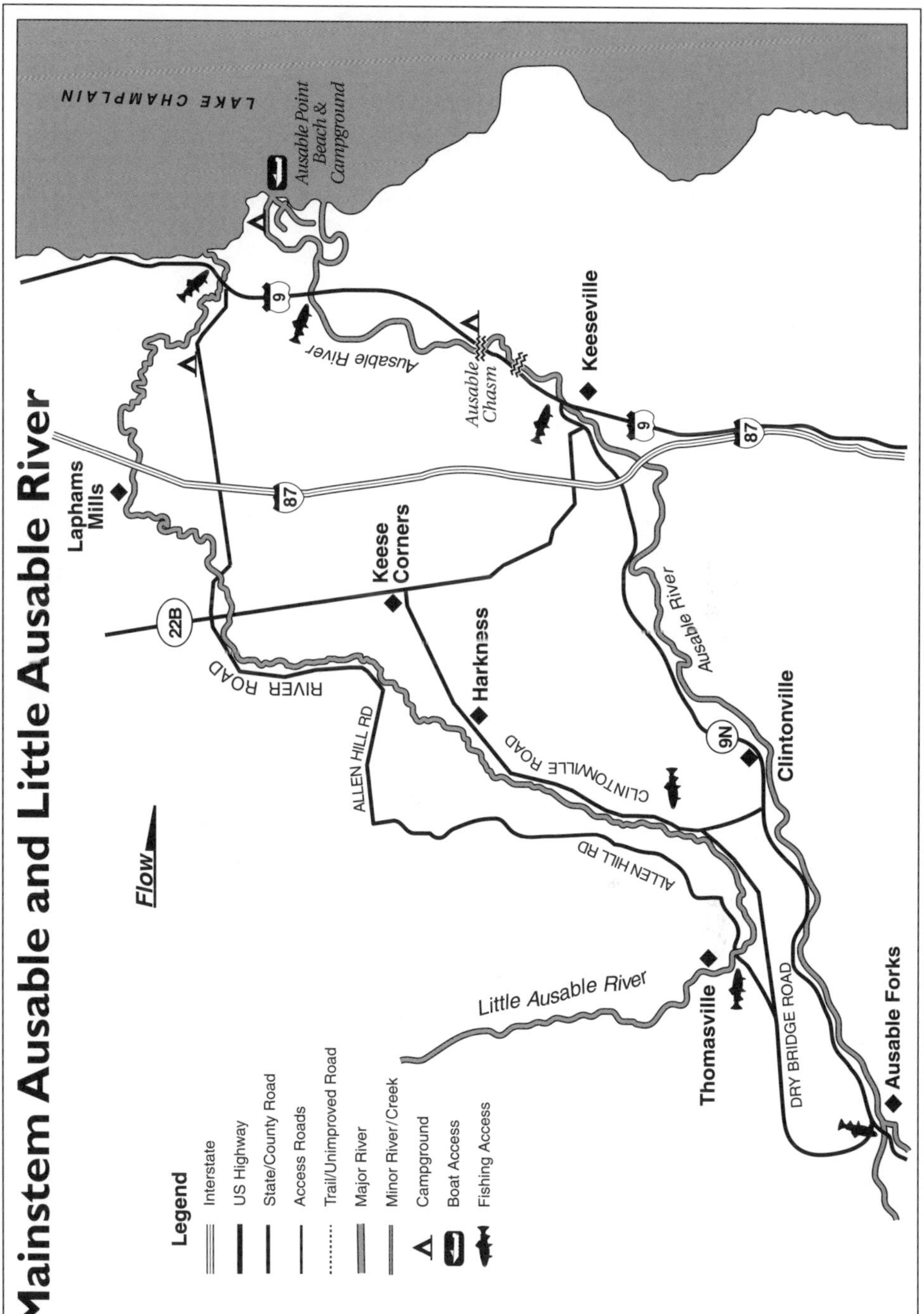

Mainstem Ausable and Little Ausable River

Legend

Interstate
US Highway
State/County Road
Access Roads
Trail/Unimproved Road
Major River
Minor River/Creek
△ Campground
◢ Boat Access
🐟 Fishing Access

N

Flow

LAKE CHAMPLAIN

Ausable Point
Beach &
Campground

9

Ausable River

Ausable Chasm

Keeseville

87

9

87

Laphams Mills

22B

RIVER ROAD

Keese Corners

Harkness

ALLEN HILL RD

CLINTONVILLE ROAD

Ausable River

9N

Clintonville

ALLEN HILL RD

Little Ausable River

Thomasville

DRY BRIDGE ROAD

Ausable Forks

SALMON RIVER

The Salmon River runs east into Lake Champlain south of Plattsburgh, between the Saranac and the Little Ausable. Not to be confused with the migratory fishery on Lake Ontario or the larger Adirondack river in Franklin County that drains north, Salmon is a fairly small flow.

The Salmon is stocked with about 5,000 small brown trout each year. There are probably some small brook trout in its upper reaches as well. The fishing and hatches are typical of the region, with the section near Peasleyville reportedly worth seeking out. Peasleyville Road and Norrisville Road track this upper portion of the stream. The standard trout season applies, with the additional five small brook trout allowed.

LAKE CHAMPLAIN

This long body of water is sometimes called the sixth great lake, and it is exceeded in size among U.S. waters only by the original five. The lake's size and depth make it a difficult place for flyfishing. Instead, fly anglers more typically catch the lake's offerings, particularly landlocked salmon and smallmouth, in tributaries like the Saranac and Boquet. But there is some flyfishing directly in Lake Champlain, including for landlocked salmon and smallmouth bass.

Landlockeds can be taken in the lake on trolled streamer patterns. Spring is the best time and sink tip and full sinking lines are essential as the fish will be anywhere from a few feet to 30 feet deep. As elsewhere, fly anglers trolling from canoes are best off using oarlocks to keep up a constant speed. Landlockeds gorge on smelt in Lake Champlain and imitations of this baitfish are the best choice. Lake and stream guide Jim Hotaling recommends Joe's Smelt in regular and orange colored varieties as well as Winnapasauki Smelt and the ubiquitous Grey Ghost.

Stream mouths, including the Saranac (in Plattsburgh), Ausable (Keeseville) and Boquet (Willisboro), and bays in these areas are the focal points for flyfishing. Willisboro Bay is particularly worth trying and has a public boat launch. In summer, the landlockeds generally go deep—below 50 feet—and aren't accessible to fly rodders. Still, on occasion strong, cool winds will reduce surface temperatures to the low 60s and bring fish up. These events are unpredictable, though, so you'll need a local contact.

Smallmouth can also be taken by trolling in the lake using smelt patterns supplemented by Woolly Buggers and other marabou streamers. The season begins on the second Saturday in June and fishing should be at its best for six to eight weeks. As with salmon, focus on bays and stream mouths. In addition to the streams mentioned above, locals report Scomotion Creek (sometimes listed as Dead Creek), which enters the lake just above Plattsburgh, has smallmouth at its outflow, and its slow moving lower section can be floated.

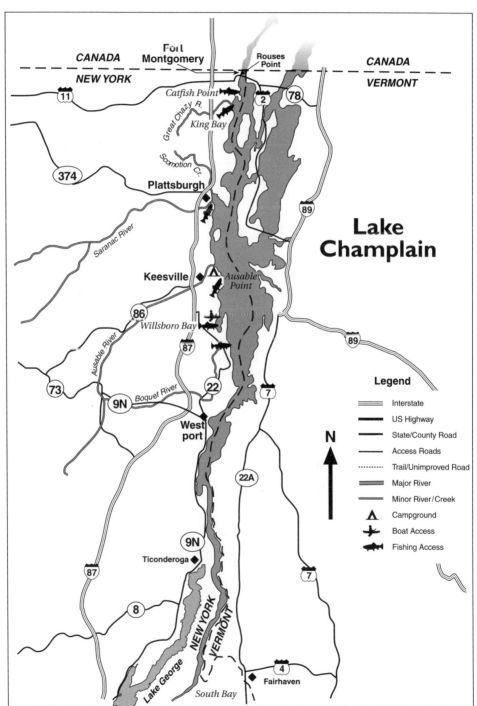

CANADA
NEW YORK

Fort Montgomery

Rouses Point

CANADA
VERMONT

11

Catfish Point

2

78

Great Chazy R.

King Bay

374

Scomotion Cr.

Plattsburgh

89

Saranac River

Lake Champlain

Keesville

Ausable Point

86

Willsboro Bay

Ausable River

87

89

73

Boquet River

22

7

9N

West port

22A

N

Legend

Interstate
US Highway
State/County Road
Access Roads
Trail/Unimproved Road
Major River
Minor River/Creek
Campground
Boat Access
Fishing Access

87

9N

Ticonderoga

8

7

Lake George

NEW YORK

VERMONT

4

Fairhaven

South Bay

© WILDERNESS ADVENTURES PRESS, INC.

In addition to these more traditional targets there is a very unusual angling opportunity in Champlain: flyfishing for bowfin. This denizen of the lake is ugly to most—except those who like strong, hard-hitting gamefish.

The bowfin, which can be traced to prehistoric times, will take flies aggressively in the shallow, swampy sections of Lake Champlain easily reached by canoes. Bowfins, which run 18 -24 inches, hold in heavy cover and can usually be spotted by the long rippling dorsal fin that gives the fish its name. They are not shy and will sometimes even come up to the shaded sides of a boat. A 7- to 9-weight rod is typical and a 20-pound bite tippet is essential for the bowfin's sharp teeth (and some will still bite through the leader). Floating lines are usually enough as the fish generally feed near the surface. Local angler Bruce Handey has found that bendback-style streamers, like those used for bonefish, are the best way to avoid hanging up in the heavy cover where bowfin hide.

From 6-7 p.m. until dark is prime time, with July and August the prime months. Some spots on the New York side of the lake with the right kind of marshy water include Ausable Point, Kings Bay, Catfish Point and Fort Montgomery. Anglers should be prepared for the explosive take—it has been compared to a depth charge and fierce fight of the bowfin. They should also be wary of the fish's sharp teeth. Because the body is supported by cartilage, rather than a skeleton, the fish can turn its head and leave a nasty bite even on a hand holding its midsection.

The mouth of Scomotion Creek is a good place for smallmouth bass.

Fishing Adirondack Ponds

The Adirondacks are a paradise for the stillwater flyfisher. It's a cliché to say that there are more trout ponds here than the average angler could fish in a lifetime, but it is probably true.

The ponds vary in size and remoteness: some are right near roads, others require a day or overnight trip with a canoe. Most are located among the high peaks at the heart of the Adirondacks—in Essex County, upper Hamilton County and lower Franklin County. But there are also good ponds in the north, south and west. Brook trout are the primary quarry in the ponds, but some have brown trout, lake trout, splake (the brookie/laker hybrid) and a few offer landlocked salmon.

It is possible to catch fish in the ponds from shore or by wading, though a boat will dramatically improve the chance of hooking up. In the Adirondacks, a boat usually means a canoe, although kayaks are seen as well. Whichever you choose— and there are plenty of places to rent watercraft—make sure it is a stable one, as whitecaps up to three feet are not unknown on Adirondack lakes when the wind kicks up. Life vests are required and should be worn at all times. Float tubes are not often seen on the region's ponds. They will work but require obvious caution in choppy water; a pontoon or kick boat is preferable as a solo craft.

Casting from the canoe is the obvious technique. Most of the ponds have good mayfly hatches, and many are particularly well populated with large flies like March Browns, Quill Gordons, Brown and Green Drakes and *Isonychia* in sizes 8-12. Caddis are common as are chironomid midges. Damselflies and dragonflies are also found in many lakes; nymphs are the more important stage for these insects. While some hatches do occur during the day, late afternoon to evening seems to be prime time for insects, and even more for rising fish. Generally a fly close in size and color will be good enough—large dries with gray or brown bodies and Elk Hair Caddis in various colors will usually fool pond trout. Occasionally, you'll need to resort to midges on the surface or in pupa form (alone or as a trailer). Chris Williamson of Jones Outfitters recommends a Griffith's Gnat as an imitation of the plentiful pond midges (these are usually the first insects to hatch after ice-out). On the other end of the spectrum he notes that a Montana Nymph—which is mostly an attractor but does resemble a dragonfly nymph—will take fish when cast into riseforms.

Non-insect life is especially important on most ponds. Various minnows can be imitated with Grey Ghosts, Hornburgs (and the hybrid Mickey Hornburg) and Woolly Buggers in black or olive. If you have a preferred baitfish imitation, don't hesitate to try it. Long but sparse streamers are the goal, and if you are tying your own, a trailer hook is a good idea. A nymph trailed a foot or two from the streamer can also improve your odds. Leeches are not nature's most endearing creatures, but pond trout do eat a lot of them. There are various leech patterns, but a black Woolly Bugger will work. Local angler Mike Lagree recalls using a Woolly Bugger in the St. Regis Canoe Area to take a 19-inch splake that had gorged on leeches.

The Adirondack high peaks offer plenty of good stillwater fishing.

Minnows and leech imitations can be cast and retrieved around shorelines and rocky outcroppings. A floating line will often work, but a short sink tip, 5 to 10 feet, will help (intermediate lines are another possibility). The fish will often be in 3 to 6 feet of water. Streamers can also be trolled using a fly rod and this is an especially effective way to take pond fish. Serious trollers have oarlocks on their boat, as it is tough to maintain a steady speed with paddles. Giving the line an occasional abrupt twitch when trolling can draw hard strikes. Early morning and evening seem to work best for streamer fishing.

Spring is prime time for pond fishing, and many anglers try to hit the water within a week of ice-out. Depending on altitude and the weather, this can occur from mid-April to mid-May. Don't ignore summer, though, as many of the lakes are high up and kept cool by underwater springs. In July and August be ready to rig up longer sink tips or full sinking lines to get down to the fish.

Ideally, a pond angler would have two rods, a lighter 5- or 6-weight rod for casting dries or nymphs and a 7-, 8- or even 9-weight for trolling and casting big streamers. A 6- or 7-weight is a good compromise, but be sure to have extra reel spools loaded with sink tips, intermediates and/or full sinking lines.

Fishing is only part of the attraction in Adirondack ponds. The settings are beautiful and remote. In the wilderness areas it isn't unusual to have an entire pond to yourself for an afternoon or a week. Night brings the haunting sounds of loons and the screech of barred owls. There are sights as well as sounds: the northern lights are sometimes visible to campers, and the stars are always magical in the mountains.

Below are some notes on particular ponds. With so many stillwaters, what follows is necessarily a partial list, but don't limit yourself—local tackle shops and the DEC can provide additional suggestions. (For all trips, be sure to read the precautions at the end of this section, and get advice from experts before you go.)

St. Regis Canoe Area

More than 50 ponds are located in this 18,000-acre wilderness area owned by New York State. Located in Franklin County, all of the waters in the canoe area are limited to non-motorized craft, which gives even the more accessible lakes a quiet, remote feel. Day trips can be made to some ponds, but paddling and camping (with occasional portages) bring out the best in this part of the Adirondacks.

There are two main canoe accesses to the St. Regis Canoe Area. The more popular is the eastern entrance at the edge of Little Clear Pond near the state fish hatchery. About a half-mile portage brings you to a walkway on the pond, which is off limits to fishing as a brood stock area for landlocked salmon. The portage route is well maintained by students from Paul Smith College, but it can be rough very early in the season. Regular users recommend portable wheels for the canoe.

Once across Little Clear Pond, a short carry brings you to Saint Regis Pond, a relatively large stillwater with good fishing for brookies and splake. St. Regis can be fished for the day, and can take you to nearby Green and Little Long ponds. Another good route is to float down the short outlet into Ochre Pond (the flow is gentle enough to come back the same way). You might need to carry the boat around a few beaver ponds (where you may encounter the odd brookie). Ochre is a small pond that offers good brook trout fishing.

The other main access for the St. Regis area is farther west at Hoel Pond, off Hoel Pond Road. This pond can be fished—it offers brookies, lakers and landlocked salmon—and is adjacent to Turtle Pond and Slang Pond. A hefty walk from Turtle Pond will get you some solitude on Clamshell Pond. From there, the especially ambitious can make another long carry to Fish Pond (sometimes called Big Fish Pond), a good and remote pond for brookies, splake and lakers. A small connecting stream will take you to Little Fish Pond, also an excellent fishery.

In addition to these two entrances there is parking just outside the canoe area at the southern shore of Upper St. Regis Lake (off Route 30). A one to two mile paddle and a short portage brings you to Bear Pond, a small brook trout fishery. A second short carry away from Bear is Little Long Pond, which offers rainbows and some splake in addition to brookies. Green Pond, with brook trout, browns and splake, can be reached easily from Little Long Pond.

The shorelines of most of the ponds in the St. Regis area have campsites. There are also some lean-tos that are much sought after. No fees are charged, except when camping for more than three nights or with groups of 10 or more. Rollins Pond, Fish Creek and Saranac Lake Islands campgrounds do require fees, and reservations can be made at 800-456-CAMP (2267). Region 5 of the DEC can provide a map and information on the St. Regis Canoe Area.

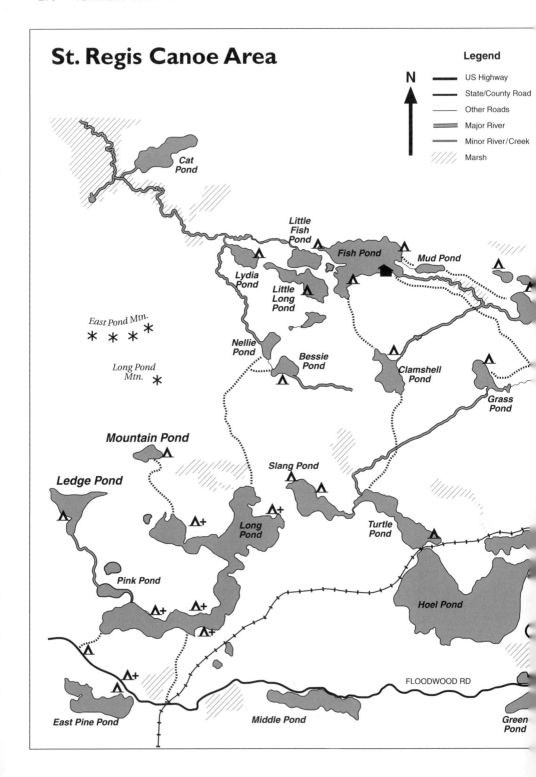

St. Regis Canoe Area

Legend

N

US Highway
State/County Road
Other Roads
Major River
Minor River/Creek
Marsh

Cat
Pond

Little
Fish
Pond

Fish Pond

Mud Pond

Lydia
Pond

Little
Long
Pond

East Pond Mtn.

Nellie
Pond

Bessie
Pond

Clamshell
Pond

Grass
Pond

Long Pond
Mtn.

Mountain Pond

Slang Pond

Ledge Pond

Long
Pond

Turtle
Pond

Pink Pond

Hoel Pond

FLOODWOOD RD

East Pine Pond

Middle Pond

Green
Pond

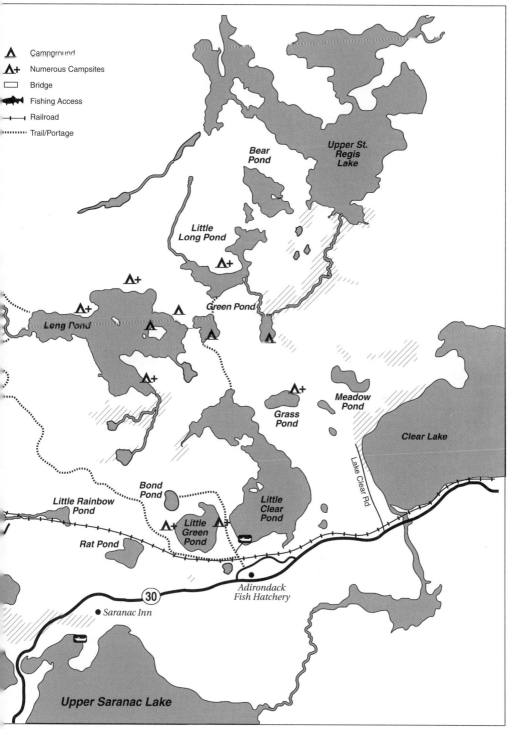

Whey Pond

This small pond adjacent to the Rollins Pond public campground (south of the St. Regis Canoe Area) is a good rainbow fishery. The fish grow well here; rainbows up to 20 inches have been caught. In addition, the pond is home to a restored heritage strain of brook trout. Because of its proximity to the road, Whey is a good place for a day trip. The pond has fairly shallow water and can be waded, but a canoe is obviously more versatile. Due to the lack of depth, Whey is best fished early, generally from ice-out through Memorial Day.

Whey Pond is subject to the normal trout season, but special regulations apply. Only three rainbows of 12 inches or more may be kept, and all brook trout must be released.

Mountain Pond

Just off Route 30, near the village of Paul Smiths, Mountain Pond is a small body of water that nevertheless offers a good population of rainbows and a heritage strain of brookies. Reportedly, some of the state's retired brood stock is put in here, so there is the chance of catching very large fish. Another good spot for a day trip, the shallow water of Mountain Pond stays cool most of the season thanks to underwater springs.

Like Whey Pond, Mountain is subject to special regulations: fishing is permitted until November 30 and all trout (brookies and rainbows) must be released.

Moose Pond

This pond in the Essex County town of St. Armand (not to be confused with another pond of the same name in the southwest corner of the county) offers two types of trout: it is stocked with both rainbows and brookies. It also receives a small number of landlocked salmon and lake trout each year. The northern end of the pond, where a boat can be put in, is reachable from Moose Pond Road off Route 18. Moose Pond is subject to the normal trout season and regulations, except that a smaller 15-inch minimum applies to the lake trout.

Little Tupper Lake and Vicinity

Little Tupper Lake and the smaller nearby Rock Pond and Bum Pond offer anglers a chance to fish for a distinct strain of heritage brook trout. The Little Tupper Lake strain, native to these three waters, is a genetically distinct strain of brook trout believed to descend from the original fish left after the glaciers receded from the mountains about 12,000 years ago. The three impoundments, along with Lilypad Pond and Little Salmon Lake, are located in the William C. Whitney Wilderness, a 15,000-acre logging tract in Hamilton County purchased by the state in 1997.

As in the St. Regis Canoe Area, boating here is limited to non-motorized craft. Parking and boat access are permitted only at the headquarters on Sabattis Road/Route 10A. Little Tupper Lake is about six miles long; at its end the Rock Point Outlet takes canoes most of the way to Rock Pond, with a short carry at the

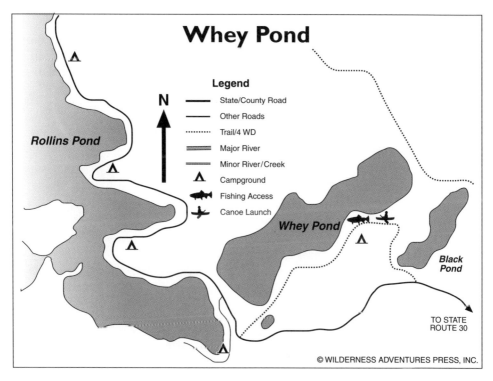

Whey Pond

Legend

State/County Road	
Other Roads	
Trail/4 WD	
Major River	
Minor River/Creek	
Campground	
Fishing Access	
Canoe Launch	

Rollins Pond

Whey Pond

Black Pond

TO STATE ROUTE 30

© WILDERNESS ADVENTURES PRESS, INC.

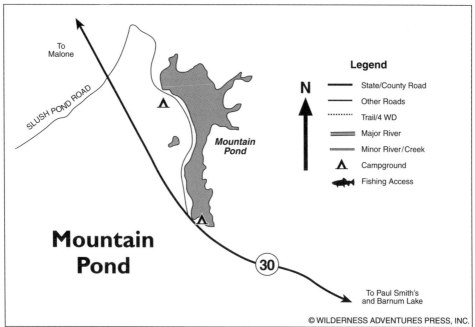

To Malone

SLUSH POND ROAD

Mountain Pond

Legend

State/County Road	
Other Roads	
Trail/4 WD	
Major River	
Minor River/Creek	
Campground	
Fishing Access	

Mountain Pond

30

To Paul Smith's and Barnum Lake

© WILDERNESS ADVENTURES PRESS, INC.

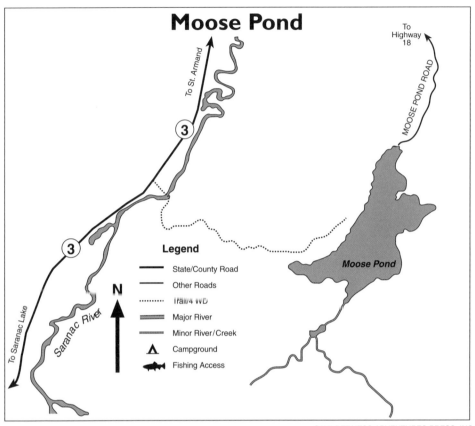

Moose Pond

To
Highway
18

To St. Armand

MOOSE POND ROAD

3

3

To Saranac Lake

Saranac River

Moose Pond

Legend

——	State/County Road
——	Other Roads
········	Trail/4 WD
≈≈≈	Major River
~~	Minor River/Creek
Λ	Campground
🐟	Fishing Access

N

end. To preserve the heritage strain, these two ponds and the connecting stream are catch and release only, with fishing permitted April 1 to October 15. The Charley Pond Outlet, which enters Little Tupper at its lower end near the Rock Pound outlet, is closed to fishing from July 1 to September 15 to allow brook trout spawning. Bum Pond does not have ready canoe access and would be difficult to reach except on foot. Campsites are available on Little Tupper and Rock Pond (and its outlet).

A canoe carry trail is currently planned for the southwestern end of the lake that would give ready access to Lilypad Pond and Little Salmon Lake. Both of these contain brook trout, but not the unique strain found in the other three waters.

All the normal precautions for boating apply to canoeing in the Whitney area. In particular, the size and relative shallowness of Little Tupper Lake make it susceptible to whitecaps. Boaters need to keep this in mind and keep near shore if the wind picks up. In addition, be aware that there is private land adjacent to some of the water, including several of the pond outlets.

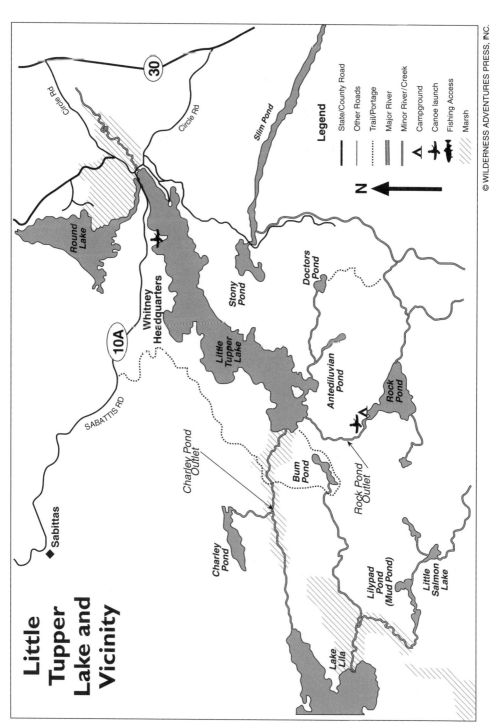

Little
Tupper
Lake and
Vicinity

Legend

State/County Road
Other Roads
Trail/Portage
Major River
Minor River/Creek
Campground
Canoe launch
Fishing Access
Marsh

N

© WILDERNESS ADVENTURES PRESS, INC.

30

Circle Rd
Circle Rd

Slim Pond

Round
Lake

Whitney
Headquarters

10A

SABATTIS RD

Stony
Pond

Doctors
Pond

Little
Tupper
Lake

Antediluvian
Pond

Rock
Pond

Sabittas

Charley Pond
Outlet

Rock Pond
Outlet

Bum
Pond

Charley
Pond

Lilypad
Pond
(Mud Pond)

Little
Salmon
Lake

Lake
Lila

© WILDERNESS ADVENTURES PRESS, INC.

Adirondack lakes and ponds provide solitude and good fishing.

Lake Ozonia and Clear Pond

Although the northern end of the state is not as studded with lakes as the heart of the Adirondacks, there are some stillwaters worth seeking out here. Lake Ozonia, located in the St. Lawrence County town of Hopkinton, is a small to medium-sized pond with stocked rainbow trout and splake. The lake is deep, up to 70 feet, so flyfishing early in the season and at low light is important. Ozonia is just off Lake Ozonia Road where there is a public launch. Motors up to 10 horsepower are permitted. Ozonia is open to fishing all year with five trout of nine inches or better and three landlockeds of 15 inches allowed.

Clear Pond is a small stillwater west of Ozonia in the town of Parishville. It receives a small stocking of brook trout that hold over and grow well. Clear is reportedly less susceptible to winds than other ponds; this and its small size make it more conducive to float tubes, though caution is still in order. Boats and tubes can be brought close to the shore on a roughly two-mile dirt road off White Hill Road. No special regulations apply to Clear Pond.

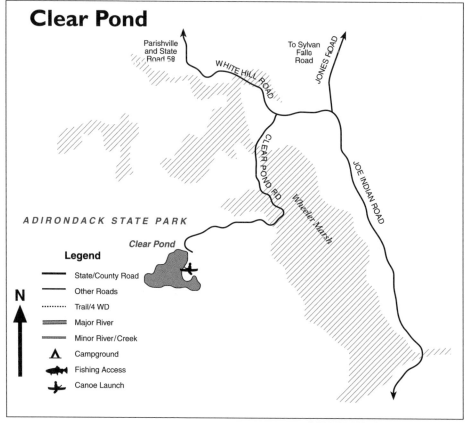

Massawepie Area

This area in the town of Piercefield in southern St. Lawrence County offers ready access to five small to medium-sized ponds: Massawepie Lake, Town Line Pond (not to be confused with Line Pond to the northeast), Pine Pond, Long Pond and Deer Pond. Pine Pond can be reached by paddle across Massawepie, the others are all accessible by road.

All contain brook trout; Town Line and Long Pond are stocked, the others are wild. Deer Pond yielded a state record brook trout of 21 inches and nearly five pounds in 1992.

SIAMESE PONDS WILDERNESS AREA

This area, in Warren County at the southern end of the Adirondacks, contains more than half a dozen ponds and offers a wilderness experience similar to that more typically found farther north.

Siamese Ponds

These adjacent ponds (sometimes called Twin Siamese Ponds) are both very small; the larger lower pond covers less than 50 acres. Despite their diminutive size, they offer excellent fishing. Both have brook trout, and the lower pond, which is over 70 feet deep in its center, also offers sizeable lake trout and some hefty whitefish.

Like most Adirondack ponds, the best fishing is in spring. The ponds can be trolled with a variety of streamer patterns. Victor Sasse of North Country Sports also recommends trolling nymphs such as Hare's Ears and Prince Nymphs, small gray scud imitations, and traditional winged wet flies like the Black Gnat and Blue Quill. Casting to risers in late afternoon and evening will also take trout and is a bit more productive than on many larger ponds.

The biggest challenge to anglers here may be getting to the ponds. There are two entrances: one at the northern end of the wilderness area on Thirteenth Lake (Thirteenth Lake Road), the other in the east on Route 8 south of Bakers Mills. From either direction, there is four to five miles of hiking, or portage if you bring a canoe. Obviously, the ponds are for the sturdy and for those who plan to stay for the night, and more typically two or three nights.

There are no special regulations for the Siamese Ponds.

Hour Pond

This small, shallow pond in the northern end of the wilderness is reached by a roughly four-mile hike. It offers brook trout fishing for stocked and wild fish.

Peaked Mountain Pond

Another small pond, this one is about three miles in, although the first mile or so of that distance can be floated on Thirteenth Lake. Peaked Mountain Pond is not currently stocked, offering fishing for wild brookies. Local anglers do report average trout size here has declined a bit over the years.

Massawepie Area

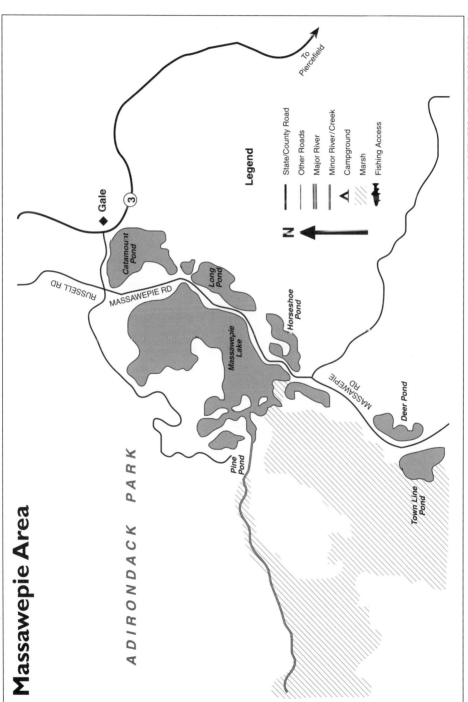

ADIRONDACK PARK

Pine Pond

Massawepie Lake

Catamount Pond

Long Pond

Horseshoe Pond

Deer Pond

Town Line Pond

RUSSELL RD

MASSAWEPIE RD

MASSAWEPIE RD

Gale

③

To Piercefield

Legend

State/County Road

Other Roads

Major River

Minor River/Creek

▲ Campground

Marsh

Fishing Access

N

Siamese Pond Wilderness Area

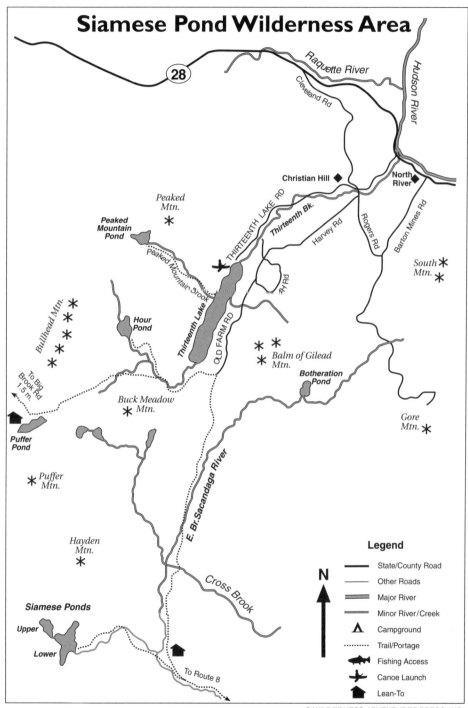

Raquette River

Cleveland Rd

Hudson River

28

THIRTEENTH LAKE RD

Christian Hill ◆

North River ◆

Peaked Mtn. ✳

Peaked Mountain Pond

Thirteenth Bk.

Harvey Rd

Rogers Rd

Barton Mines Rd

Peaked Mountain Brook

South Mtn. ✳ ✳

Bullhead Mtn. ✳ ✳ ✳ ✳ ✳ ✳ ✳

Hour Pond

Thirteenth Lake

7H Rd

OLD FARM RD

Balm of Gilead Mtn. ✳ ✳ ✳

Botheration Pond

To Big Brook Rd 1.5 m.

Buck Meadow Mtn. ✳

Gore Mtn. ✳

Puffer Pond

Puffer Mtn. ✳

E. Br. Sacandaga River

Hayden Mtn. ✳

Cross Brook

Legend

N

▬▬▬	State/County Road
───	Other Roads
▬▬▬	Major River
───	Minor River/Creek
▲	Campground
⋯⋯	Trail/Portage
🐟	Fishing Access
✈	Canoe Launch
🏠	Lean-To

Siamese Ponds

Upper

Lower

To Route 8

© WILDERNESS ADVENTURES PRESS, INC.

Puffer Pond

This small, shallow pond offers good fishing for stocked and wild brookies. It can be reached by a long hike from the Thirteenth Lake access point or a roughly 1.5-mile walk from the access off Big Brook Road on the western side of the wilderness area.

Thirteenth Lake

This medium-sized lake is at the edge of the wilderness area and offers good fishing with a short portage (roughly 100 yards). The entrance is at the wilderness area's northern access on Thirteenth Lake Road.

Unlike most other mountain ponds, the primary targets here are stocked and holdover browns and rainbows, along with landlocked salmon, rather than brookies. Flies can be cast or trolled here; the western shore near where Peaked Mountain Brook enters, the outlet at the northern end and the southern shore are said to be the prime spots. Thirteenth Lake is larger than the other ponds in the wilderness area, which puts a premium on finding the fish. In addition to boat fishing it is possible to wade and cast along the shore, though this is obviously less productive. A great hatch here for waders or boaters is the big *Hexagenia* that comes off in late June and early July. These large, light colored flies will bring fish to the surface at night. A Wulff pattern with cream body and pale wings, in size 6 or 8 will work, as will a similar sized light brown nymph.

Thirteenth Lake is open for an extended season—to November 30—and is subject to a three fish, 15-inch minimum for landlocked salmon, with five trout of any size permitted .

PHARAOH LAKE WILDERNESS AREA

This is another wilderness area toward the southern end of the Adirondacks. Straddling Warren and Essex counties, it is situated between Schroon Lake on the west and Lake George on the east. It contains more than a dozen ponds and lakes. Some, including Pharaoh itself, require a long hike, others are near the wilderness area's boundaries.

Pharoah Lake

The lake that gives the wilderness area its name is primarily a brook trout fishery. It is a long hike in from the western access at the Putnam Pond Campground. In addition to hiking and portaging, horses are permitted on two trails from the southern boundary up to the lake.

Crane Pond

This medium-sized pond is near the western edge of the Pharaoh area and can be reached with a four-wheel-drive vehicle via a dirt road at the end of Crane Pond Road. Crane Pond is stocked with rainbows and a small supply of lake trout. Rainbow fishing is subject to the normal season, but lakers may be targeted all year, with a three fish, 15-inch minimum size limit.

Pharaoh Lake Wilderness Area

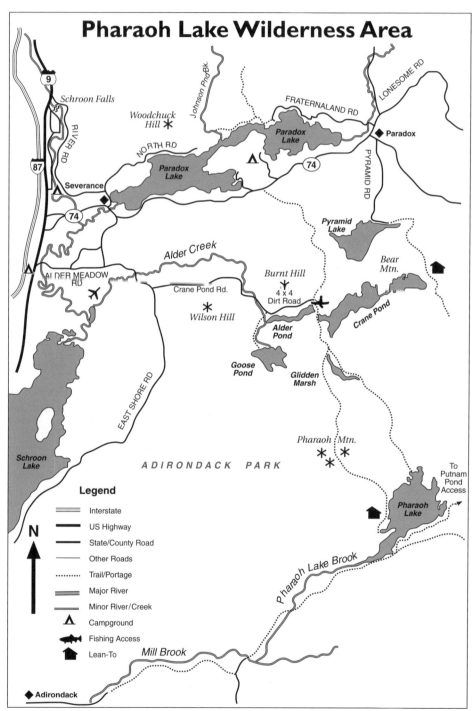

Schroon Falls

Woodchuck Hill ✳

Johnson PndBk.

FRATERNALAND RD

LONESOME RD

Paradox Lake

◆ Paradox

NORTH RD

RIVER RD

Paradox Lake

△

74

PYRAMID RD

Severance

74

Pyramid Lake

Bear Mtn.

Alder Creek

Burnt Hill

4 x 4 Dirt Road

Crane Pond

ALDER MEADOW RD

Crane Pond Rd.

✳ Wilson Hill

Alder Pond

Goose Pond

Glidden Marsh

EAST SHORE RD

Pharaoh Mtn.
✳ ✳
✳ ✳

Schroon Lake

A D I R O N D A C K   P A R K

To Putnam Pond Access

Pharaoh Lake

Legend

≣	Interstate
▬	US Highway
▬	State/County Road
—	Other Roads
····	Trail/Portage
▬	Major River
▬	Minor River/Creek
△	Campground
🐟	Fishing Access
⬠	Lean-To

N

Pharaoh Lake Brook

Mill Brook

◆ Adirondack

Goose Pond

Goose Pond is a modest hike in from the same dirt road that gives access to Crane Pond. The pond receives both brookies and rainbows, as well as a small stocking of splake. The normal season and regulations apply to Goose Pond.

Paradox Lake

This medium-sized lake is at the edge of the Pharaoh area and is comprised of two basins, east and west. Readily accessible from Route 74, Paradox is well stocked with brookies, rainbows and lake trout. The trout may be fished for all year; normal limits apply to the trout, three lakers of 18 inches or better may be kept.

Jabe Pond and Little Jabe Pond

These two ponds are near Lake George, a bit east of the Pharoah area. Four-wheel-drive vehicles can be taken to the main pond on two roads, one leading to the eastern edge, the other at the northern end (Jeep Road). Without an off-road vehicle, a substantial carry is required. Jabe is stocked by the state with both rainbow and brook trout, with Warren County adding some rainbows; Little Jabe receives a small brook trout supply. The main pond is reported to have good caddis, Hendrickson, Green Drake and Sulphur hatches in addition to various minnows. There are numerous islands in Jabe Pond; these, along with the southern end, are good spots to hit. For both ponds, only three trout in combination may be kept, all must be at least 12 inches.

Fishing turns on when the ice breaks up on Adirondack ponds.

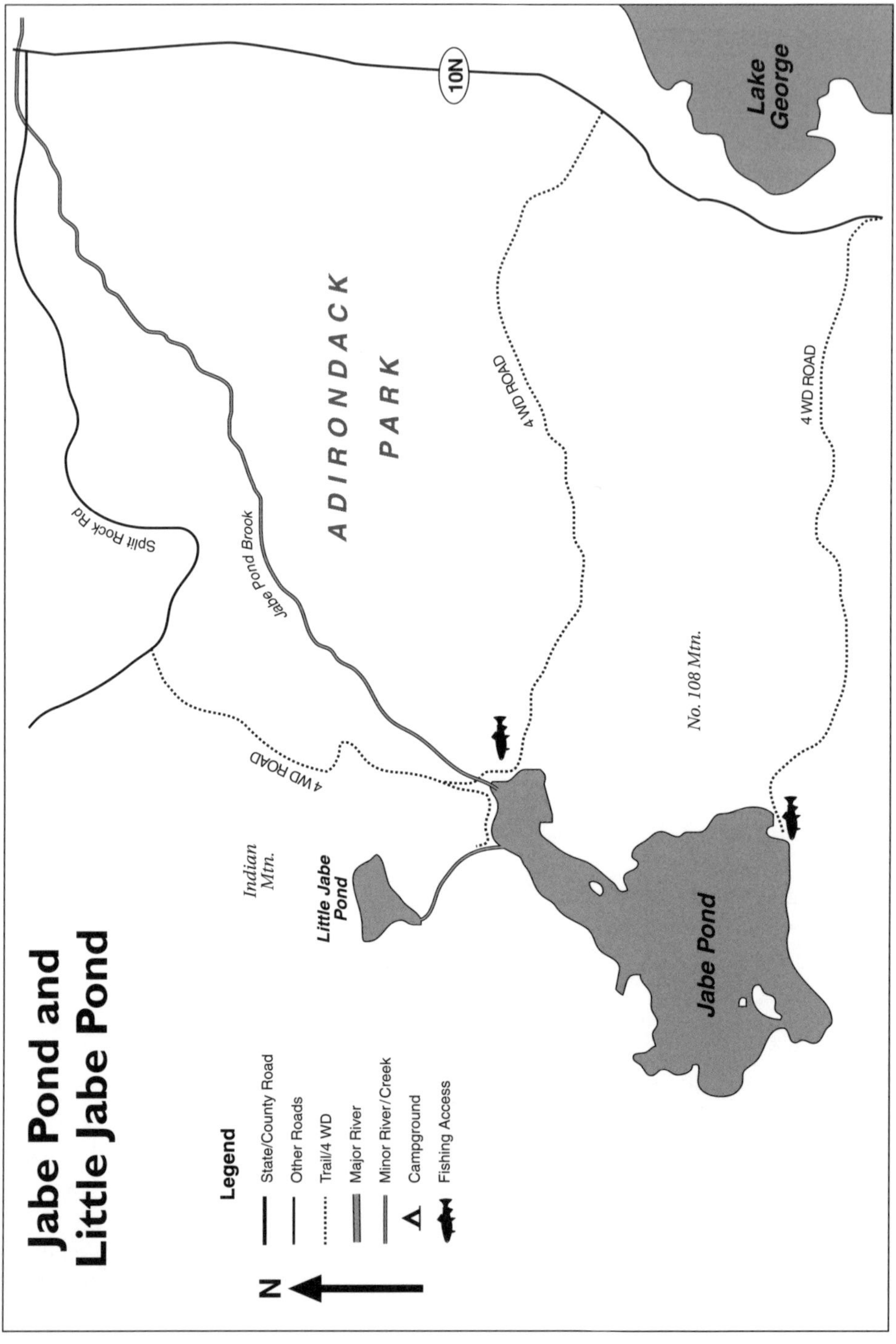

Jabe Pond and
Little Jabe Pond
N
Legend
State/County Road
Other Roads
Trail/4 WD
Major River
Minor River/Creek
Campground
Fishing Access
10N
Lake George
ADIRONDACK
PARK
Split Rock Rd
Jabe Pond Brook
4 WD ROAD
4 WD ROAD
4 WD ROAD
No. 108 Mtn.
Indian Mtn.
Little Jabe Pond
Jabe Pond
© WILDERNESS ADVENTURES PRESS, INC.

Safety For Hikers And Boaters

Anyone entering remote areas, especially any of the wilderness areas, should take basic precautions. This applies whether you are hiking or boating for the day, or staying overnight. The following is good advice, but it is only a start. Anyone planning a trip should read appropriate guidebooks and consult outfitters or mountain clubs for additional detailed information.

Gear and Clothing

Plan to carry a first-aid kit, waterproof matches, pocket knife, whistle, a tarp, a flashlight with extra batteries, some quick energy food and water. Bring a tent, as lean-tos on the lakes may be already occupied. Layered clothing of wool or synthetics and rainwear are also essential (a space blanket is useful, too).

Contact

Whether traveling alone or in a group, leave word of where you'll be and when you'll return. The same goes for the registration books found at trail-heads. In these days of modern communications, a cell phone is not a bad idea, either, although don't expect it to work in every area.

Navigating

The DEC produces useful brochures and maps on various wilderness and park areas. However, they emphasize that these are not intended for navigation. Anyone planning a trip should bring detailed topographical maps, such as those available from the USGS and private vendors. (One good source for guides and maps is the Adirondack Mountain Club; they can be reached weekdays at 800-395-8080 or online at www.adk.org.) A compass is also essential equipment for backcountry trips; take along your GPS receiver if you have one.

Canoe Rentals

Many fly and tackle shops listed in the Northeast Adirondack Hub Cities rent canoes and kayaks. In addition, these outfitters, among others, also rent watercraft:

NORTHERN

Mountainman Outdoor Supply, Route 28 Inlet, NY 13360; 315-357-6672, Route 28, Old Forge, NY 13420; 315-369-6672

St. Regis Canoe Outfitters, Floodwood Road, Lake Clear, NY 12945; 518-891-1838

Adirondack Lakes and Trails, 168 Lake Flower Ave, Saranac Lake, NY 12983; 518-891-7450

SOUTHERN

Lake George Kayak Co., Main St, Bolton Landing, NY 12814; 518-644-9366

Whitewater Challengers, Route 28, Old Forge, NY 13420; 315-369-6699

Adirondacks Hub Cities

Saranac Lake/Lake Placid/Loon Lake/Wilmington

ACCOMODATIONS PRICE KEY

$	Up to 60 dollars per night
$$	61 to 99 dollars per night
$$$	100 to 150 per night
$$$$	151 and up per night

HOTELS/MOTELS

Lake Flower Inn, 15 Lake Flower Avenue, Saranac Lake, NY 12983 / 518-891-2310 / $-$$ / On lake / Pool, docks / Near Saranac headwater

Hotel Saranac, 101 Main Street, Saranac Lake, NY 12983 / 518-891-2200 / $$

Adirondack Inn, 217 Main Street, Lake Placid, NY 12946 / 518-523-2424 / $$-$$$

Lake Placid Lodge, Whiteface Inn Road, Lake Placid, NY 12946 / 518-523-2700 / $$$$

CAMPGROUNDS/RVs

This is just a partial listing. For tent camping there are dozens of campsites on New York State land in the Adirondacks. For information and reservations call 1-800-456-CAMP

Junction Campsite, off Highway 30, Saranac Lake, NY 12983 / 518-891-1819 / 31 sites / 24 full

Meadowbrook Campground, Adirondack State Forest, Highway 86 / 518-891-4351 / No hookups

Baker's Acres Campground, Saranac, NY 12981 / 518-293-6471 / On Saranac River

Wilmington Notch Public Campground, Route 86 (8 miles east of Lake Placid) / 518-946-7172 / Near Ausable at Whiteface Mountain

Saranac Lake Islands Public Campground, Route 3 (6 miles west of Village of Saranac Lake) / 518-891-3170 / On various islands in Lower and Middle Saranac Lakes / Boat access, tenting only

RESTAURANTS

A P Smith Restaurant (at Hotel Saranac), 101 Main Street, Saranac Lake, NY 12983 / 518-891-2200

Averill Conwell Dining Room (at Mirror Lake Inn) / 5 Mirror Lake Drive, Lake Placid, NY 12946 / 518-523-2544

Red Fox Motel & Restaurant, Route 3, Saranac Lake, NY 12983 / 518-891-2127

McKenzie's Grille, 148 Lake Flower Avenue, Saranac Lake, NY 12983 / 518-891-2574 / Breakfast, lunch only / Opens 6 a.m.

FLY SHOPS

Adirondack Sports Shop, Route 86 Wilmington, NY 12997 / 518-946-2605 / www.adirondackssportshop.com / On Ausable West Branch

Ausable River Sports Shop, Route 86, Wilmington, NY 12997 / 518-946-1250 / www.ausableriversportshop.com; fly shop, guide service

Blue Line Sport Shop, 82 Main Street, Saranac Lake, NY 12983 / 518-891-4680 / Saranac Lake (Cortland)

The Hungry Trout, Route 86, Whiteface Mountain, NY 12997 / 518-946-2217 / www.hungrytrout.com, fly shop, guide service, motel/restaurant, near Lake Placid on Ausable West Branch

Jones Outfitters Ltd., 331 Main St, Lake Placid, NY 12946 / 518-523-3468, www.jonesoutfitters.com / Orvis dealer / Guiding, flyfishing school, boat rentals

AUTO REPAIR

K & M Service, 92 Broadway, Saranac Lake, NY 12983 / 518-891-0010

AIRPORT

Adirondack Regional Airport, Lake Clear Road, Saranac Lake, NY 12983 / 518-891-4600

HOSPITAL/CLINIC

Adirondack Medical Center, Lake Colby Drive, Saranac Lake, NY 12983 / 518-891-4141

Plattsburgh

HOTELS/MOTELS

Days Inn, 8 Everleth Drive, Plattsburgh, NY 12901 / 518-561-0403 / $-$$

Best Western (Inn at Smithville), 446 Cornelia Street, Plattsburgh, NY 12901 / 518-561-943 / $$

Baymont Inns, 16 Plaza Blvd, Plattsburgh, NY 12901-6439 / 518-562-4000 / $$

CAMPGROUNDS/RVS

Cumberland Bay State Park, Highway 314, Plattsburgh, NY 12901 / 518-563-5240

Shady Oaks RV Park, 70 Moffit Road, Plattsburgh, NY 12901 / 518-562-0561 / 94 full / Tents

Ausable Point State Campground, Route 9 (12 Miles South of Plattsburgh) / 518-561-7080 / 123 sites / 43 elec. / On Lake Champlain

RESTAURANTS

Anthony's Restaurant & Bistro, 538 State Route 3, Plattsburgh, NY 12901 / 510-561 6420

Irises Cafe and Wine Bar, 20 City Hall Place, Plattsburgh, NY 12901 / 518-566-7000 / Good food and wine list

FLY SHOPS

Gordon's Marine, 1428 Route 3, West Plattsburgh, NY 12962 / 518-561-2109 / Good fly selection

Hook & Hackle Co, Kaycee Loop Road, #7, Plattsburgh NY, 12901 / 518-561-5893 / www.hookhack.com

Outfitters Plus, 1135 Cook Street, Dannemora, NY 12929 / 518-492-2086

VERMONT

The Classic Outfitters, 66 Champlin Mill, Winooski, VT 05404 / 802-655-7999

CANADA

Boutique Salmo Nature, 110 McGill Street, Montreal, Quebec, H2Y 2E5 / 514-871-8447

Green Drake Outfitters, 342 Richmond Road, Ottawa, Ontario, K2A 0E8 / 613-828-1915 / www.greendrake.com

Grand River Troutfitters, 790 Tower Street, Fergus, Ontario, N1M 2R3 / 519-787-4359 / www.grandrivertroutfitters.com

Brightwater Flyfishing, 336 Cumberland Street, Ottawa, Ontario / 613-241-6798

Ben La Mouche, 5926 Rue Hochelaga, Montrial, Quebec / 514-252-1225

Boutique Classique Angler, 414 Rue Mcgill, Montreal, Quebec / 514-878-3474

Le Baron Outdoor Products, 1 Stafford Road, Ottawa, K2H9N5 / 613-596-4415

GUIDES
Lake Champlain Anglers (Jim Hotaling), 1 Bay Rd, Willsboro, NY 12996 / 518-963-8266

AUTO REPAIR
T M Auto Repair, 31 Riley Avenue, Plattsburgh, NY 12901 / 518-563-4263

AIRPORT
Clinton County Airport, 11 Airport Rd, Plattsburgh, NY 12901 / 518-565-4795

HOSPITAL/CLINIC
Bayside Wellness Center, 427 Margaret Street, Plattsburgh, NY 12901 / 518-562-2738

St. Regis River
Includes Deer River

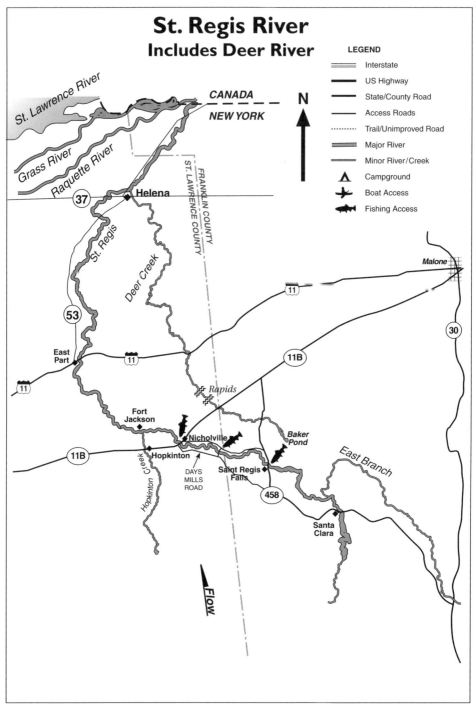

LEGEND

═══	Interstate
▬▬▬	US Highway
━━━	State/County Road
────	Access Roads
··········	Trail/Unimproved Road
▬▬▬	Major River
══════	Minor River/Creek
▲	Campground
✈	Boat Access
🐟	Fishing Access

St. Lawrence River

CANADA
NEW YORK

N

Grass River

Raquette River

37 Helena

St. Regis

Deer Creek

FRANKLIN COUNTY
ST. LAWRENCE COUNTY

Malone

53

11

East Part

11

11B

30

11

Rapids

Fort Jackson

Nicholville

Baker Pond

11B

Hopkinton

DAYS MILLS ROAD

Saint Regis Falls

East Branch

458

Santa Clara

Flow

Northwestern Adirondacks

Many visitors to the Adirondacks never fish the streams in the northwestern part of the region. That's a shame since the waters here, which generally run north to the St. Lawrence, offer some very good fishing, and some of them have excellent populations of wild fish. The westernmost streams here are in the most sparsely populated part of New York; all of them are less pressured than the better known eastern flowing streams.

St. Regis River

For anglers, there are two distinct sections of this north flowing river. The first is located within the Santa Clara Tract of the newly opened Northern Flow Wilderness Area. (The river's east branch is also located within this tract.) The second section is downstream, running about eight miles from St. Regis Falls to the village of Fort Jackson and offers more traditional fishing for stocked and wild trout. From Fort Jackson downstream to the St. Lawrence the water is generally too warm for trout.

Santa Clara Tract

This section of the river is located within land in the enormous Northern Flow area. (In this tract, it is sometimes called the Main Branch or Middle Branch, to distinguish it from the East Branch which joins downstream of the village of Santa Clara.) New York State acquired a combination of easements and ownership here from the Champion International Paper Company in 1999 and first opened it to fishing the following year. The water primarily holds warmwater species such as smallmouth bass. However, tributaries in this section are known to have wild brook trout and there are undoubtedly brookies in the East Branch and the main river on the tract. Some of these wild trout are said to be good-sized, and there is also reported to be a small self-sustaining population of rainbows.

Downstream of St. Regis Falls

Below (north) of the village of St. Regis Falls, the river is heavily stocked with browns and rainbow trout, with the main trout fishing down to Fort Jackson. This portion offers classic pocket water fishing along with a few more gentle sections. A number of road crossings combined with ample public fishing rights make most of the river accessible to wading anglers. Accessible doesn't mean easy, however, as the pocket water here is among the toughest wading in the region. The same precautions applicable elsewhere—felt soles, wading staffs, fishing with a friend and using common sense—are at least as important here.

There is a fair amount of pressure, but much of it is at the access points near St. Regis Falls and at the Days Mills Bridge downstream. Anglers on other parts of the stream will find more space to fish. As guide Tim Damon points out, space is important here, because anglers should not stay in one place too long; they need to move and hit a succession of pockets to find fish.

This river will warm faster than some nearby streams, such as the Raquette or Chateaugay, and can usually be fished by late April. This also means the fishing is best in May to June and again in September. Hatches are similar to other good Adirondack streams. The large dark and light stoneflies common to the stream are particularly worth imitating. Except for the few sections of slower water, this stream is suited to large, bushy dry flies, big nymphs to match the stoneflies, and streamers. For the streamers, Woolly Buggers in olive or black, Muddler Minnows and Marabou Muddlers all work well. A 9-foot 5-weight rod is standard on the St. Regis.

The state stocks the St. Regis with browns and rainbows: About 5,400 browns and 4,400 rainbows in the St. Lawrence County portion of the stream, with the proportions reversed—about 4,500 browns and 5,400 rainbows—upstream in Franklin County. The warm summer temperatures tend to limit holdover, but in mild years it can be substantial.

The St. Regis is subject to a patchwork of regulations in the prime water below St. Regis Falls. The first part of that section, from St. Regis Falls to the Franklin County line is subject to a shortened season of April 1 to September 30 (applicable to most waters in Franklin County), with five additional brook trout of eight inches or less permitted. From the Franklin-St. Lawrence County boundary down to Days Mills Road in Hopkington, the normal trout season and regulations apply. Then, from Days Mills Road downstream to Fort Jackson, trout fishing is permitted all year and five fish of any size may be kept. Normal regulations apply below that, but as already noted, trout fishing falls off downstream of Fort Jackson.

Hopkinton Brook

This small tributary of the St. Regis enters the river in the town of the same name. It can be fished for trout and receives an annual stocking of about 600 browns. No special regulations apply.

Northwestern Adirondacks—Major Hatches

INSECT	J	F	M	A	M	J	J	A	S	O	N	D	FLIES
Blue Winged Olives 14-22													Comparadun, Parachute, Emergers, Pheasant Tail Nymph
Light & Dark Hendrickson 12-14													Light and Dark Hendrickson, dark brown Hendrickson Nymph
Caddis Tan Olive Black 14-18													Elk Hair Caddis, Bead-Head Pupa Imitations
Stoneflies Tan, Brown, Black 6-10													Sporadic Hatches; Light and Dark Stonefly Nymphs, Stimulators, Yellow Sallies, Elk Hair Caddis
Sulphurs/Cahills													Comparaduns, Parachutes, standard dries; Hare's Ear Nymphs, Pheasant Tail Nymphs
Trico 18-24													Trico Spinner, Griffith's Gnat
Slate Drake (Isonychia) 12													Comparadun, Haystack, Parachute, Better's Picket Finn, Zug Bug
Ants, Beetles													Foam Ants, Dubbed Ants, Foam Beetles; Best in Summer
Attractors 6-12													Ausable Wulff and other Wulff patterns
Streamers													Wooly Bugger's, White or Black Zonkers, Marabou Patterns; more important in early season and at night

SALMON RIVER (FRANKLIN COUNTY)

The Salmon River runs through Franklin County should not be confused with the salmon and steelhead fishery in Oswego County. That doesn't make it secondary, though, as it is widely considered one of the better trout streams in the North Country.

The Salmon River rises in the northern Adirondacks around Titus Mountain and flows north until it crosses the Canadian border. From near its headwaters downstream to roughly Westville—a run of about 15 miles—the Salmon offers fishing for a mix of wild and stocked browns and rainbows, along with brook trout in the upper reaches. The area below Chasm Falls has a good population of wild fish.

Although the stream has typical mountain pocket water, it offers more easily waded stretches of flat water than many others in the area. At these points, anglers can cast smaller, hatch-matching offerings to rising fish without the added effort of picking pockets. The Flat Rock area, off Flat Rock Road downstream (north) of Malone in particular has flat water conducive to dry fly fishing. There are good holdovers downstream of Malone, along with some small wild browns.

There a number of dams on the Salmon (many run by Niagara Mohawk's successor Orion Power), although the flow levels are said to be fairly consistent. The areas behind these dams offer good dry fly fishing just where the current enters the heads of the pools.

The Salmon runs a bit colder than nearby streams such as the Chateaugay or St. Regis, so it is a good stream to seek out in July and August. In addition to the dry fly fishing, streamers are a good bet here to bring up some of the big browns that inhabit the stream. The fall *Isonychias* also brings up big fish, so dries that imitate the hatch (and Zug Bugs for the nymphs) are important. There are also sporadic Green Drakes, which come off here in June, along with some caddis and stoneflies.

There is good access at most of the dams, at Kings Falls Park near Malone, and at various pulloffs along River Road above (south) Malone and Route 122 below. The Ballard Mills Dam right in Malone also offers disabled access.

The state stocks the Salmon substantially with rainbows and browns, mostly in the town of Malone (from Titus Mountain to around Route 28). Over 20,000 browns and about 7,500 rainbows are stocked. In addition, the state puts in a few hundred small tiger muskies in the warmer water near Ft. Covington. There are no special regulations on the Salmon, but it is subject to the earlier closing date of September 30 applicable to most Franklin County waters.

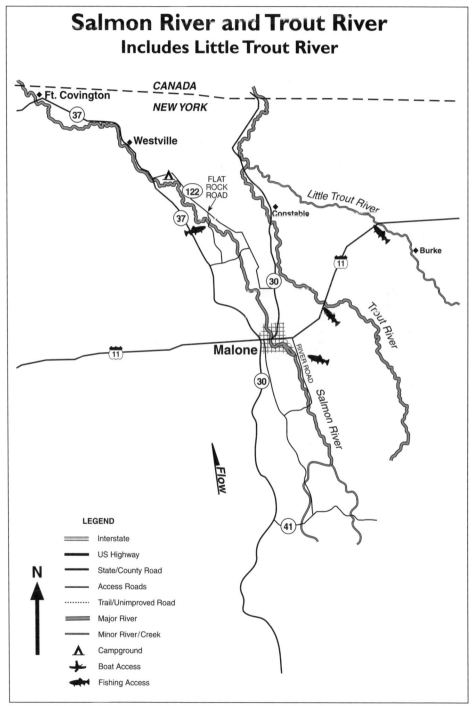

Salmon River and Trout River
Includes Little Trout River

CANADA

NEW YORK

Ft. Covington

37

Westville

FLAT
ROCK
ROAD

122

37

Little Trout River

Constable

Burke

11

30

11

Malone

RIVER ROAD

30

Trout River

Salmon River

Flow

41

LEGEND

Interstate

US Highway

State/County Road

Access Roads

Trail/Unimproved Road

Major River

Minor River/Creek

▲ Campground

Boat Access

Fishing Access

N

© WILDERNESS ADVENTURES PRESS, INC.

The Salmon River, which flows right through Malone, is a fine trout stream.

The brawny Chateaugay River is one of several good north-flowing streams.

THE CHATEAUGAY RIVER

The Chateaugay is a brawling, north-flowing stream that provides good fishing for trout. Beginning at Lower Chateaugay Lake near the village called The Forge, the Chateaugay flows about 11 miles until it crosses the Canadian border and continues to the St. Lawrence.

All three species of trout are stocked in the Chateaugay (from the nearby state hatchery), though stocked brookies and rainbows greatly outnumber the browns (about 20,000 trout are put in). The relatively small number of stocked browns is said to be supplemented by a fairly good self-sustaining population particularly upstream of Route 11. Hatches are also good in the river, with Green Drakes particularly strong.

Dedicated public access in the form of public fishing easements is extensive on the Chateaugay. It begins just below the lake and continues through Brainardsville and Cooks Mill (where the Marble River joins) and ends less than a mile from the Canadian border, covering one or both banks virtually the entire way. There are some fast, treacherous sections that waders should be aware of in the upper half upstream (south) of Pulpmill Road and again in the chasm downstream of Route 11. If fishing the lower (northern) end of the river, be sure to hit the large, productive pool just before the Canadian border. The standard trout season applies here, with five additional brookies allowed.

MARBLE RIVER

A fine little stream, the Marble River runs about eight miles from the town of Clinton in Clinton County northward through the corner of Franklin County and into the Chateaugay River near Cooks Mills. Ironically, the stream has the Chateaugay State Fish Hatchery on its banks, but its own fish are entirely wild; brookies, browns, and rainbows all reproduce naturally here. They are mostly on the small side, but plentiful in the small pools and rocky pockets.

In addition to good habitat, the stream offers plentiful and varied insects. Turn over any rock in the stream and you will likely find cased green caddis along with stonefly and mayfly nymphs. This ample buffet gives the small wild trout here a bit more heft than usual. The Marble has a lot of brush and closely set trees, so use a small rod if possible and watch the back casts. If nothing is hatching, try a green dubbed caddis larva imitation with a wire rib and gold beadhead.

With bridge crossings and state acquired fishing rights, there is ample access to the Marble River. From the Franklin County Line downstream, the majority of the river is open to fishing. Parking and fishing is permitted on the hatchery property from 9 a.m. to 3 p.m., and a set of stairs is conveniently provided. (If you park inside the hatchery gate, remember that you'll be locked in shortly after 3 p.m.) Visitors are welcome to view the hatchery, but because whirling disease has been found in the stream, anglers should not approach the fish tanks after being in the water. In addition to informal pulloffs along Route 11 and Route 35, which parallel

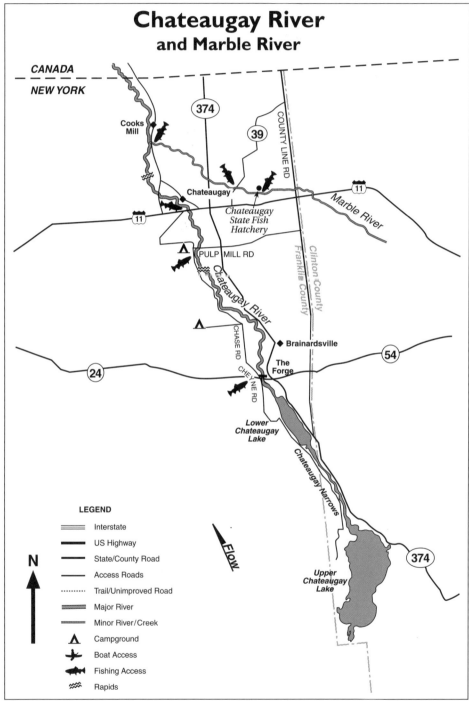

Chateaugay River
and Marble River

CANADA

NEW YORK

374

39

Cooks
Mill

COUNTY LINE RD

11

Chateaugay

Marble River

*Chateaugay
State Fish
Hatchery*

PULP MILL RD

11

Chateaugay River

Clinton County
Franklin County

♦ Brainardsville

54

CHASE RD

The
Forge

24

CHEYNE RD

*Lower
Chateaugay
Lake*

Chateaugay Narrows

LEGEND

N

Flow

═══ Interstate

── US Highway

── State/County Road

── Access Roads

········ Trail/Unimproved Road

═══ Major River

── Minor River/Creek

Λ Campground

✈ Boat Access

🐟 Fishing Access

〰 Rapids

*Upper
Chateaugay
Lake*

374

© WILDERNESS ADVENTURES PRESS, INC.

the stream, there is dedicated parking where Route 39 crosses, about three-quarters of a mile downstream of the hatchery. There are no special regulations on Marble Creek, but as with any wild stream, catch and release is highly recommended.

DEER RIVER

The Deer River is formed at swampy headwaters in the town of Brandon in Franklin County and runs more than 20 miles before meeting the St. Regis near the village of Helena in St. Lawrence County. Primarily a put-and-take fishery, the river is heavily stocked with browns from near its headwaters to the St. Lawrence County Line.

TROUT RIVER

This stream runs north in Franklin County just east of the Salmon River. It runs about 15 miles from its swampy headwaters in the town of Belmont to the Canadian border. The stream is similar to the riffly water of the Salmon River, but smaller. It is stocked with about 3,000 browns a year.

Little Trout Brook runs west and north from near the village of Burke and joins the larger stream a few miles south of the border near the village of Constable. Little Trout is stocked with browns and has a good population of wild fish.

Route 30 parallels the main river, and numerous road crossings also give access. Little Trout can be reached from Route 122. and where Route 11 crosses near the village of Burke Center. No special regulations or seasons apply to either stream, except that an extra five small brook trout may be kept.

Little Trout Brook is another good stream that flows north.

GRASSE RIVER

The river (sometimes spelled "Grass") is composed of two branches, north and south, which meet in the small village of Palmerville. For trout it is the longer south branch and the main river that are of interest. Both are mostly put-and-take fisheries: the Grasse receives a stocking of about 2,000 small browns a year in the main river and another 800 are put in the South Branch in the town of Clare. Access is good along most of the stocked sections. The South Branch runs along the Degrasse State Forest and there is access along Route 17, including at the bridge in the village of Russell. Most of the South Branch, from the Clare Town Line upstream, is catch and release only. Care should be taken when wading the South Branch, which has several stretches of rapids.

Plumb Brook, a tributary of the Grasse receives a stocking of nearly 4,000 small browns every year. It can be reached from the Whippoorwill Corner and Silver Hill state forests off Route 17.

Muskellunge

The Grasse River has a naturally reproducing muskellunge population that is underfished by anglers. According to local guide Tim Damon, fly anglers can often take two or three muskies a day in the 10- to 15-pound range here.

A few larger fish can be had toward the lower end of the stream near Canton, New York. Farther upstream, the fish are smaller but more plentiful. Access is at various bridge crossings and wading anglers can take muskie in the river. For more chances at these voracious feeders, the Grasse River can be floated in kayaks or canoes (Damon employs a pontoon boat for guided trips). Typical floated stretches are from the village of Morley (Route 27 Bridge) downstream to the village of Bucks Bridge (Route 34 crossing), Bucks Bridge to the Route 345 crossing in Madrid, and Madrid down to Town Line Road in Chase Mills.

Even though they are not trophy-sized muskies, these fish still demand large flies and big rods. A 9-by-9 rod with a floating line and a mini-sink tip (or interchangeable looped weighted tips) is the standard rig. Nylon coated bite tippet is also required. At the end of the tippet, put on a big fly like a Deceiver or rabbit strip streamer pattern, the bigger the better. Damon ties a large but simple streamer of Big Fly Fiber lashed to big hooks (3/0 and up) with a white underwing and overwings of black, red or blue. He leaves the fiber long—about 12 inches—and ties a stinger hook in back. He finds about half the hookups come on the rear hook. Late in the day, the fish will sometimes feed at the surface, and this is the time for big Dahlberg Diver patterns.

The muskies will be in downed trees and other structure in daytime, and will move into the shallows as the sun sets. Plan to experiment with various flies and retrieves. And be prepared for a fight; unlike the similar-looking northern pike, which are also found in the Grasse River, muskies battle from the time they are hooked to the moment they are landed.

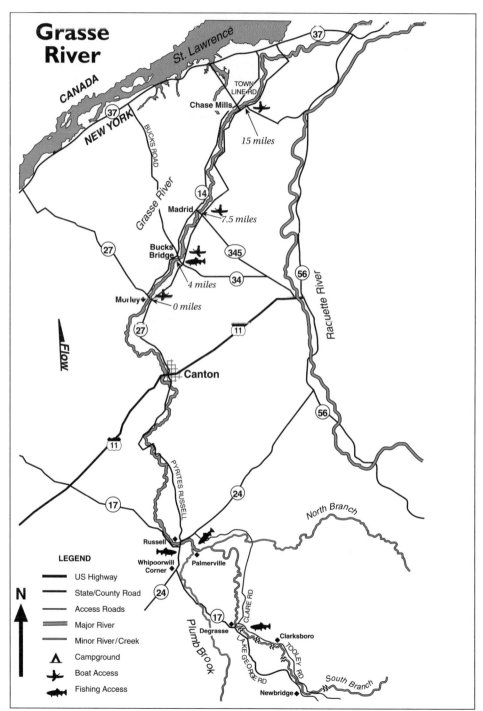

© WILDERNESS ADVENTURES PRESS, INC.

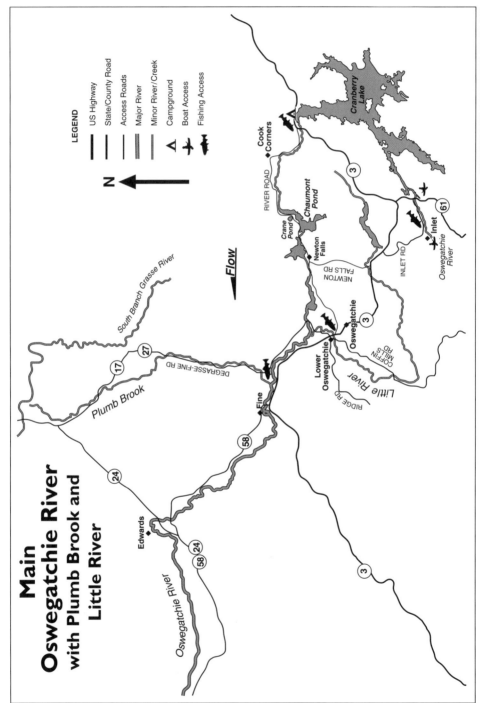

Main
Oswegatchie River
with Plumb Brook and
Little River

LEGEND
US Highway
State/County Road
Access Roads
Major River
Minor River/Creek
Campground
Boat Access
Fishing Access

N

Flow

South Branch Grasse River

Plumb Brook

DEGRASSE-FINE RD

17
27
24

Edwards

Oswegatchie River

58
24

58

Fine

RIVER ROAD
Cook
Corners

Crane
Pond

Chaumont
Pond

Newton
Falls

NEWTON
FALLS RD

3

Cranberry
Lake

61

Inlet

Oswegatchie
River

INLET RD

Lower
Oswegatchie

Oswegatchie

RIDGE RD

Little River

COFFEIN
MILLS
RD

3

3

© WILDERNESS ADVENTURES PRESS, INC.

OSWEGATCHIE RIVER

This stream in St. Lawrence and Lewis counties is composed of two branches: the western-running main river and a northern-flowing west branch that joins the main flow.

Main River

There are three trout stretches of the main Oswegatchie, all at its upper end. The first is the short inlet to Cranberry Lake in the town of Fine. This portion runs less than two miles and holds a good population of small wild brook trout. The section can be floated and a boat may be put in at the upper end in the village of Inlet, or at the lower end at Cranberry Lake. Wading access is from the appropriately named Inlet Road and Route 61, which crosses the stream near the lake.

The next trout fishing on the Oswegatchie is found in the roughly six-mile run from the river's source at Lake Cranberry to Crane Pond and Chaumont Pond. It is the first couple of miles below Cranberry that are most popular.

After passing through a series of ponds, the Oswegatchie emerges from a power dam near the village of Lower Oswegatchie, where is offers fishing for another couple of miles (roughly to the village of Fine).

This is a mixed brook trout and brown trout fishery—about 2,000 brookies and 1,300 browns are stocked, including some two-year-old browns.

Both trout stretches of the Oswegatchie below Cranberry Lake are open for an extended trout season of April 1 to November 30, with five fish of any size permitted. Above Cranberry, the normal trout season and regulations apply.

Several tributaries of the Oswegatchie also offer trout fishing.

Little River

This small stream runs north and meets the Oswegatchie in the stretch between Newton Falls and the power dam, near the village of Lower Oswegatchie. (This is a separate stream from the more northerly Grasse River tributary with the same name.) The Little River is about four miles long, and runs parallel to Coffin Mills Road upstream and Ridge Road downstream. About 2,000 small browns are put in here each year. Like the portions of the Oswegatchie below Cranberry Lake, the Little River is open to trout fishing until November 30.

Plumb Brook

Plumb Brook is a long tributary that enters the Oswegatchie from the north. It begins near the Grasse River and runs about 12 miles to the Oswegatchie upstream of the village of Fine. About 3,000 browns are stocked in the Plumb each year, primarily in the last three to four miles of the stream. Degrasse Fine Road/Route 27 runs right next to this section. Plumb Brook trout fishing closes October 15.

Oswegatchie West Branch

The West Branch of the Oswegatchie forms in Herkimer County and flows west then north through Lewis County to meet the main river in the St. Lawrence County town of Edwards. The headwaters offer small stream fishing for some wild brookies, but it is primarily the 10 miles in the Lewis County towns of Croghan (northern half) and Diana that offer trout fishing on the West Branch. Over 1,000 small brookies are stocked and their are some wild fish here as well. Access in this section can be had from various road crossings off of Route 812, and there is access for the disabled where Long Pond Road crosses the river.

Part of the West Branch in Croghan falls within the recently opened Croghan Tract of the Northern Flow area, on land acquired by the state from Champion Paper Company. Portions of the river near Mud Pond are wide and slow and can be canoed. The floatable section can be reached from Long Pond Road in Croghan. No special season or regulations apply to the Oswegatchie West Branch.

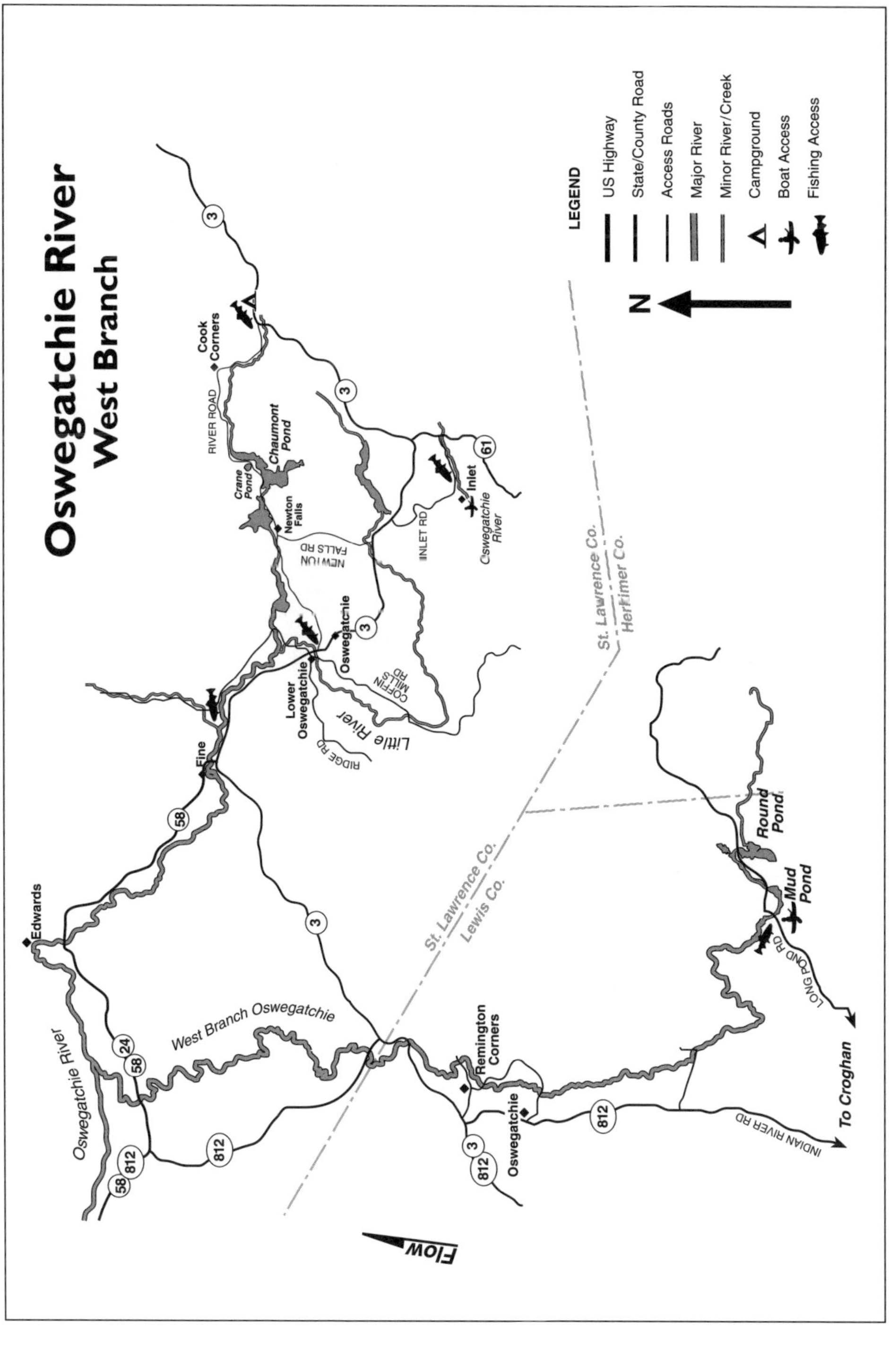

Oswegatchie River
West Branch

LEGEND

US Highway
State/County Road
Access Roads
Major River
Minor River/Creek
Campground
Boat Access
Fishing Access

N

© WILDERNESS ADVENTURES PRESS, INC.

Cook Corners

RIVER ROAD

Chaumont Pond

Crane Pond

Newton Falls

NEWTON FALLS RD

Inlet

61

INLET RD

Oswegatchie River

Oswegatchie

3

COFFIN MILLS RD

Lower Oswegatchie

Little River

RIDGE RD

Fine

58

Edwards

St. Lawrence Co.
Herkimer Co.

St. Lawrence Co.
Lewis Co.

Round Pond

Mud Pond

LONG POND RD

West Branch Oswegatchie

24

58

812

58

812

3

Remington Corners

Oswegatchie

812

3

812

INDIAN RIVER RD

To Croghan

Oswegatchie River

Flow

Fish Creek

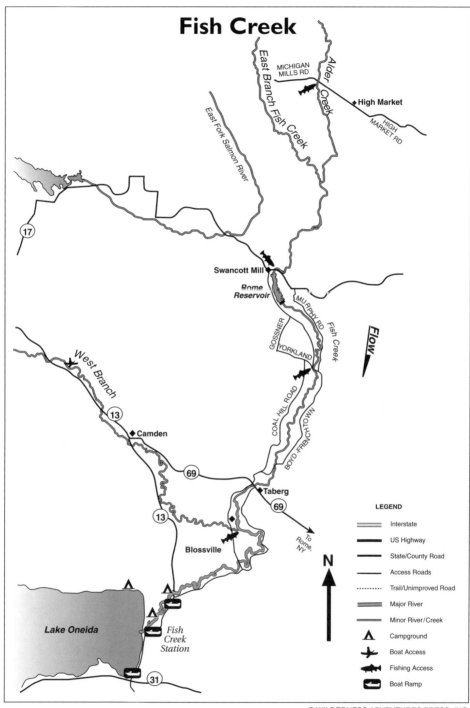

LEGEND

	Interstate
	US Highway
	State/County Road
	Access Roads
	Trail/Unimproved Road
	Major River
	Minor River/Creek
	Campground
	Boat Access
	Fishing Access
	Boat Ramp

© WILDERNESS ADVENTURES PRESS, INC.

FISH CREEK

This promisingly named stream flows about 30 miles south from Lewis County into Lake Oneida, but it is primarily the East Branch near the trout section of the Black River—along with a small stretch of the main creek—that is of interest to fly anglers.

The trout water on the East Branch of Fish Creek begins in the town of Lewis, continuing about five miles until the stream enters the small Rome Reservoir (also known as the East Branch Fish Creek Reservoir) near Swancott Mill. The headwaters, above the town of Lewis, are primarily a small wild brook trout fishery. (Alder Creek enters in this section. This small stream is stocked with browns and may be reached from a series of road crossings along its lower end, and from Michigan Mills Road upstream.) Fish Creek above the impoundment is small but receives a healthy stocking of about 4,000 small trout, a bit more than half browns, the remainder rainbows. In addition, about 4,000 very small browns are put in the reservoir each year. These are said to grow impressively and are sometimes taken upstream. Fish Creek warms up before other area streams, and is a particularly good place for April fishing.

Below the reservoir, the East Branch flows for about eight miles before meeting the West Branch near the Oneida County village of Blossville. Here about 5,000 small browns are stocked. Big browns from the reservoir are sometimes taken downstream of the dam. Murphy Road parallels the stream for several miles below the dam, until Yorkland Road crosses. Downstream, pulloffs on Boyd Road/Frenchtown Road and the crossing at Palmer Road provide access. Stocking of browns continues onto the main creek downstream of Blossville for a few miles, but the water is warmer and wider here.

Both upstream and downstream of Rome Reservoir, Fish Creek is rocky, pocket water fishing that requires tough wading and short casts. There are some big stoneflies in Fish Creek, so large golden and black stonefly nymph imitations are effective here. Don't leave out big stonefly dries; Pat Dando, who guided in the area for many years, took a 24-inch fish on a heavily hackled size 4 stonefly below Rome Reservoir. Caddis are also common, if sporadic, on Fish Creek, including a lime green version with white wings in a size 16 and a small black variety. For dries, Elk Hair Caddis and various Wulffs will be important in the rough water.

A complex set of regulations governs fishing on the East Branch of Fish Creek. Above Rome Reservoir, the normal trout season and regulations apply. Below the reservoir, trout fishing is permitted until November 30, and five fish of any size may be kept. However, below the Route 6 Bridge in Taberg—roughly the last two miles—no fishing of any kind is permitted until the first Saturday in May to protect spawning walleye. The same delayed opening applies to the entire main creek down to Lake Oneida.

Black River

Though perhaps better known as an Ontario steelhead and salmon fishery, the Black River offers the chance to fish for trout from shore or a boat in a big river setting. Hatches are reliable and there is some good holdover of stocked browns and rainbows.

The Black, which runs more than 60 miles, begins as small water on the western edge of Herkimer County (just north of the source of West Canada Creek), then becomes larger as it crosses into northern Oneida. It continues north through Lewis County then turns west and bisects the city of Watertown before reaching Lake Ontario. The headwaters in Herkimer County hold wild brook trout. As the river widens in Oneida County it passes through some swampland and a long impoundment. Downstream, it receives a healthy stocking of browns and rainbows, including some two-year-old browns, as well as a smattering of brook trout. Access in this section is from River Road and Edmonds Road.

Probably the best trout water on the river is from the Lewis County border downstream (north) to Lyons Falls. There are numerous dams in this section and big fish will hold in the impounded water, then move into the shallower flow upstream to feed. In particular, the impoundment just upstream of Port Leyden offers excellent fishing for browns that can grow to 20 inches. The flow here—and before most impoundments—is slow and gentle, ideal for dry fly fishing. Good hatches at this spot, and in the rest of the trout water, include *Isonychia*, caddis and a large *Potomanthus* (Golden Drake) that hatches sporadically in late June, but brings up big fish. There are also small Blue Winged Olives and midges, often imitated locally with small Adams patterns. About 12,000 fish are put in here, more than half rainbows.

Anglers with float tubes or small kayaks and canoes can float segments of the trout section. Toward the upper end, there is access at the new bridge off Norton Road (Bridge Road) just downstream of Port Leyden and again downstream about two miles north, just above the Lyons Falls Dam, allowing this stretch to be floated in either direction.

Throughout the trout water of the Black River, the flow is very wide—50 yards or more on average—so plan to bring a long rod in a 5- or 6-weight. The river is subject to warm summer temperatures; fishing will be best in May and June, then again in September. In summer, the coolness of evening will draw fish out of the deeper water at the impoundments.

The river becomes primarily a warmwater fishery below Lyons Falls, with good fishing here for walleye and northern pike. While it is mostly the province of spin fisherman using jigs and Rapalas, there is no reason a flyfisher couldn't take these fish with Clouser Minnows or other weighted streamers. The seven-mile run from Lowville to Castorland is best for this warmwater fishing. The spot where Route 812 crosses the river about two miles downstream of Lowville is particularly good, as farm irrigation ditches draining near here bring baitfish into the river.

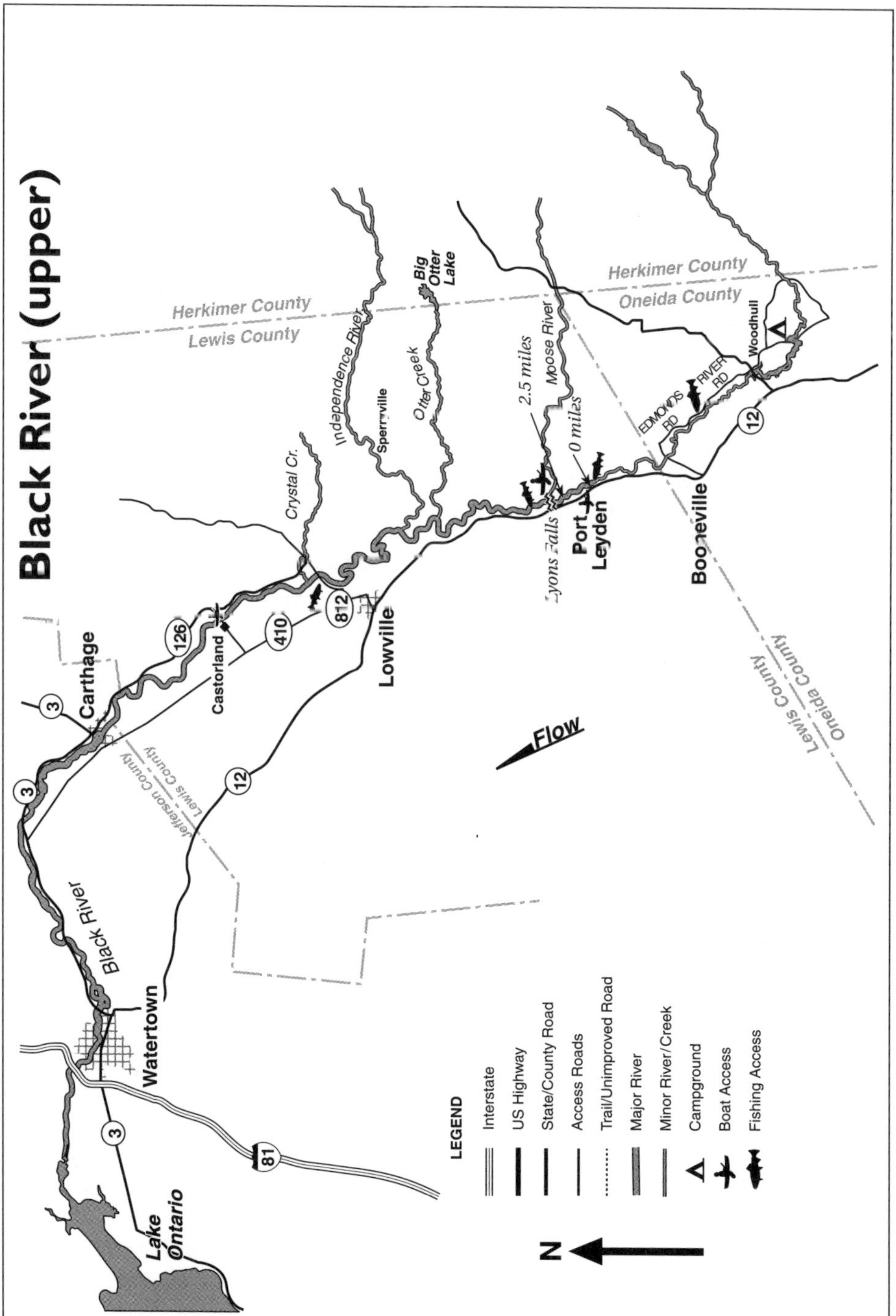

Black River (upper)

LEGEND

	Interstate
	US Highway
	State/County Road
	Access Roads
	Trail/Unimproved Road
	Major River
	Minor River/Creek
	Campground
	Boat Access
	Fishing Access

Herkimer County
Lewis County

Herkimer County
Oneida County

Big Otter Lake

Independence River

Otter Creek

Sperryville

Crystal Cr.

Moose River

2.5 miles

0 miles

Woodhull

EDMONDS RD

RIVER RD

12

Booneville

Lyons Falls

Port Leyden

Carthage

126

410

812

Castorland

Lowville

3

3

3

12

81

Jefferson County
Lewis County

Lewis County
Oneida County

Flow

Black River

Watertown

Lake Ontario

N

© WILDERNESS ADVENTURES PRESS, INC.

Well downstream, the state now stocks some browns, which can be fished for in Watertown itself, above the Mill Street Dam (which marks the upper end of salmon and steelhead fishing). There is access, including disabled anglers, at Eastern Boulevard/Route 3.

Trout fishing on the Black River is open for the normal season, April 1 to October 15, with no special regulations.

Independence River

The Independence is a small but lengthy tributary to the Black River, running almost 20 miles from the headwaters in Herkimer County to its mouth. It is not stocked and offers a quiet setting for presenting flies to wild brook trout. While the stream can be fished to its mouth, the better choice is to head upstream. Bailey Road near Sperryville provides access. Just north of Sperryville, Beach Mill Road ends at the Gleasmans Falls Trail, which offers about a mile hike to a section of water farther upstream. Anglers making the hike will likely have the stream to themselves and can wade up as far as they like. Several miles upstream from the Gleasmans Falls Trail, anglers will hit a series of closely set tributaries called Second, Third and Fourth creeks that can also be fished, as can a series of nearby ponds.

Despite its small size, the Independence usually offers enough room to cast. It also offers a variety of water, smooth sand and gravel stretches, rocky riffles and a few boulders. Undercut banks in various spots will usually hold the largest fish. These are not trophies, rarely more than 12 inches, and more often 5-7 inches. Presentation is more important here than fly selection; these are hungry mountain fish. Local angler Mike Pyrek, who has fished the Independence for more than a decade, often uses a Gray Wulff on top and a dragonfly nymph subsurface. As on most small brook trout streams, you won't be casting far so use a short leader and small rod (unless you like to dap). The first month of the season here usually offers cold water and inactive fish. Beginning in May the fish get moving and fishing continues right through to fall, when brightly colored males can be seen pairing up with their mates to spawn.

No special regulations or season apply to the Independence River, but releasing all trout will help preserve this small, wild fishery.

Otter Creek

Otter Creek, which joins the Black River just in the town which shares its name, offers hybrid fishing: stocked browns in the lower end and wild brookies upstream. The stocked fish—about 2,000 browns including a few hundred two-year-olds—are mostly found in the last mile or so, from roughly Pine Grove Road downstream. The browns are said to grow pretty well in this lower portion.

For the brookies, head well upstream. Partridgeville Road parallels the stream for more than five miles and ambitious anglers can park at its end and hike in all the way to Big Otter Lake (actually fairly small), which is stocked with brook trout.

Crystal Creek, Independence River, and Otter Creek

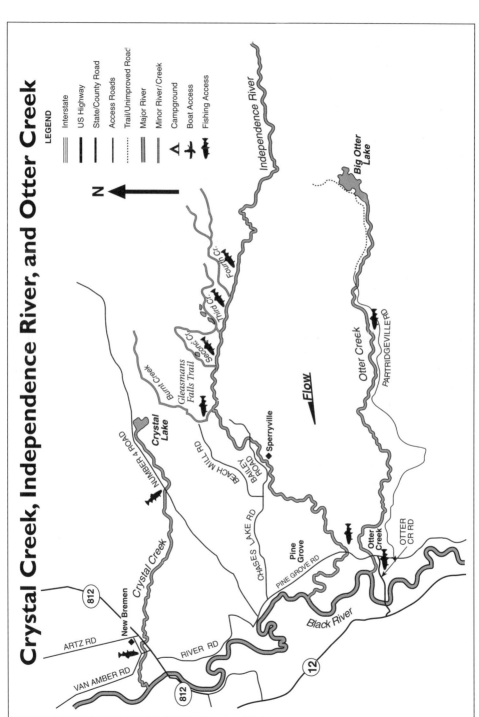

LEGEND

Interstate
US Highway
State/County Road
Access Roads
Trail/Unimproved Road
Major River
Minor River/Creek
Campground
Boat Access
Fishing Access

N

Independence River

Big Otter Lake

Fourth Cr.

Third Cr.

Second Cr.

Gleasmans Falls Trail

Burnt Creek

Crystal Lake

Otter Creek

PARTRIDGEVILLE RD

Flow

NUMBER 4 ROAD

BEACH MILL RD

BAILEY ROAD

Sperryville

CHASES LAKE RD

Pine Grove

PINE GROVE RD

Otter Creek

OTTER CR RD

812

New Bremen

Crystal Creek

ARTZ RD

RIVER RD

VAN AMBER RD

812

Black River

12

© WILDERNESS ADVENTURES PRESS, INC.

Crystal Creek

This small tributary to the Black River is shorter and more accessible than Otter or Independence. Like Otter Creek, Crystal has browns stocked near the mouth—about 1,200 in all. The half-mile or so from the Van Amber Road Bridge downstream to Artz Road in New Bremen is a good place to begin fishing for the browns. The water warms here fairly early, so it can be a good place to hit in the first weeks of the season. Browns grow well here, including in a small impoundment, and fish up to 20 inches are not unknown. One limitation is overhanging brush, which can make fishing difficult. Wild brookies can be found upstream off various side roads of Number Four Road.

Upper Salmon River

Salmon and steelhead anglers may not realize that the upper portion of the famed Salmon River has pretty good fishing for resident trout. This section, an eight-mile run of the river above Redfield Reservoir, offers fishing for stocked and holdover rainbows and brookies, as well as occasional big trout that come up from the reservoir.

The stretch above the reservoir begins as separate east and west forks that join near the Lewis County village of Swancott Mill. Above the junction the streams are very small and hold some wild brookies. Downstream, the Salmon crosses the town of Osceola into Oswego County where it joins the reservoir in Redfield. The section above the reservoir is stocked with about 1,000 rainbows and the same number of brook trout. There are also some wild fish here. Access is primarily from pulloffs on Waterbury Road.

No special regulations or season apply to the upper portion of the Salmon River. Redfield Reservoir itself is open to fishing all year.

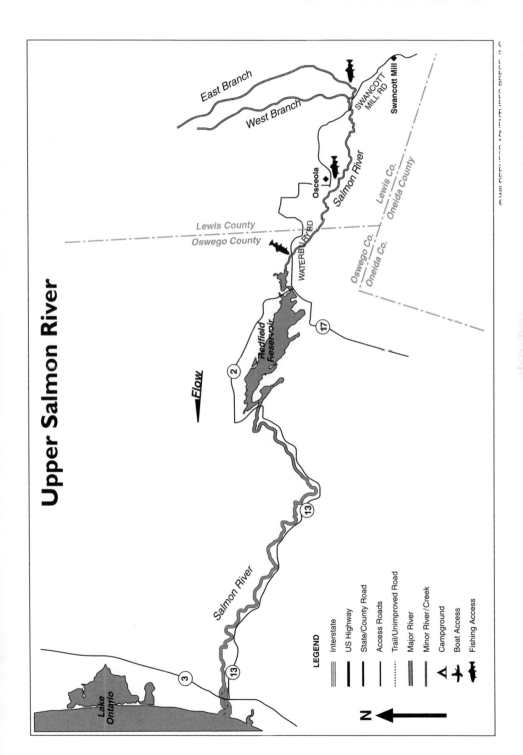

Upper Salmon River

East Branch

West Branch

Swancott Mill

SWANCOTT MILL RD

Salmon River

Osceola

Lewis Co.
Oneida County

Lewis County
Oswego County

WATERBURY RD

Oswego Co.
Oneida Co.

Redfield Reservoir

17

2

Flow

13

Salmon River

13

3

Lake Ontario

LEGEND

Interstate
US Highway
State/County Road
Access Roads
Trail/Unimproved Road
Major River
Minor River/Creek
Campground
Boat Access
Fishing Access

N

ST. LAWRENCE RIVER

This wide, long, dammed flow runs from Lake Ontario all the way to the Atlantic. It offers primarily warmwater fishing for pike, muskies and walleye, although some trout can be found here. The fishing is mostly with spinning gear and mostly from boats, and there are numerous launches along the river.

Trout anglers using flies can also take fish from boats. The river just below the Robert Moses Power Dam on Barnhart Island opposite the city of Massena holds both browns and rainbows. The Massena Municipal Boat Launch north of Route 37 just east of the city provides boat access to the water downstream of the dam. Care must to taken to remain on the New York (U.S.) side of the river; anglers fishing Canadian waters without appropriate licenses may be fined.

At one time, a decent number of stray chinook salmon from Lake Ontario found there way into the St. Lawrence and its tributaries. Since the reduction of lake stocking in 1994, salmon in the river have been rare.

Carp Fishing

Although not usually listed among the top gamefish here, or anywhere else, very big carp live in the St. Lawrence. Not only can they be caught by fly anglers, but in late May and early June these bottom feeders will come to the surface at dusk to gorge on large mayflies.

The fish pod up in the shallows—often close enough to be caught by wading anglers—and feed greedily on the big naturals on the water. Surface feeding carp are not subtle. Because of their downturned mouths, they must roll on their sides as they break the surface to pick insects off the water.

Local angler Dan Yando has been fishing to these risers for several years and has landed carp over 45 pounds. He recommends big gear for these fish: 9-foot, 9-weight rods with a floating line and shock tippet to withstand the violent take. Big bushy flies are more important than matching the hatch; Yando likes Ausable Wulffs or Muddler Minnows in size 10, dead drifted with an occasional small strip. Hooking the fish is not easy, he notes, as there are often missed strikes and the same fish will rarely take again. Also, carp are wary, especially when feeding on top. He advises making long casts and, if possible, staying on the sunny side of the pod, which seems to hide the angler's presence.

These surface-feeding carp can be found in the village of Massena and around several of the locks on the river. Wading is entirely possible, though a shallow-bottomed boat rowed or poled along the shallows will make more fish accessible. But be prepared: Yando has seen big carp actually tow small boats and the biggest fish can take an hour to land.

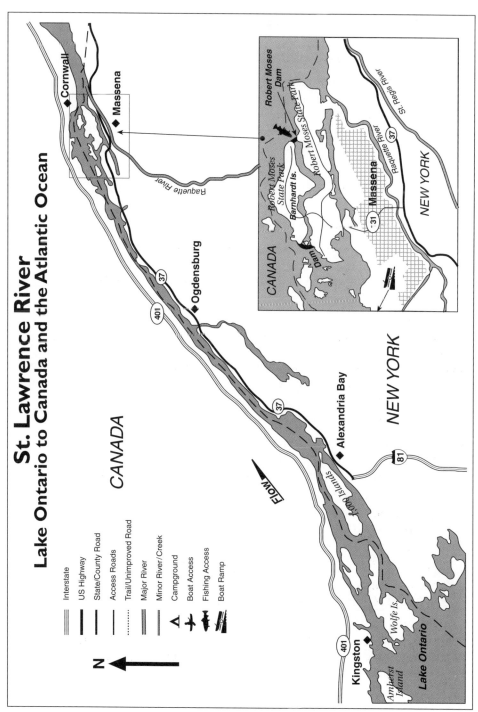

St. Lawrence River
Lake Ontario to Canada and the Atlantic Ocean

N

CANADA

NEW YORK

NEW YORK

Legend:
- Interstate
- US Highway
- State/County Road
- Access Roads
- Trail/Unimproved Road
- Major River
- Minor River/Creek
- Campground
- Boat Access
- Fishing Access
- Boat Ramp

Cornwall

Massena

Raquette River

Ogdensburg

401

37

37

Alexandria Bay

81

1000 Islands

FLOW

Kingston

401

Wolfe Is.

Amherst Island

Lake Ontario

Robert Moses Dam

Robert Moses State Park

Barnhardt Is.

Dam

Massena

Raquette River

St. Regis River

37

31

Northwestern Adirondacks Hub Cities

Ogdensburg/Massena/Potsdam

ACCOMMODATIONS PRICE KEY

$ Up to 60 dollars per night
$$ 61 to 99 dollars per night
$$$ 100 to 150 per night
$$$$ 151 and up per night

HOTELS/MOTELS

Econo Lodge, 15054 Route 37, Massena, NY 13662 / 315-764-0246 / SD 65-95 / $$

Super 8 Motel, 84 Grove Street, Massena, NY 13662 / 315-764-1065 / SD 50-56 / $

Ramada Inn River Resort, 119 West River Street, , Ogdensburg, NY 13669 / 315-393-2222 / SD 60-80 / $$

Quality Inn Gran View, 6765 State Route 37, Ogdensburg, NY 13669 / 315-393-4550 / SD 45-72 / $-$$

CAMPGROUNDS/RVS

Coles Creek State Park, Route 37, Massena, NY 13662 / 315-388-5636 / Tents and trailers

Massena International Kampground, 84 County Route 42, Massena, NY 13662 / 315-769-9483 / 131 / 68 full / 47 w/e

KOA Thousand Islands, 4707 State Route 37, Ogdensburg, NY 13669 / 315-393-3951 / On St Lawrence / 105 sites / 20 full, 63 w/e

RESTAURANTS

Village Inn, 181 Outer Maple St, Massena, NY 13662 / 315-769-6910

Gran View, 6765 State Route 37, Ogdensburg, NY 13669 / 315-393-4550,

FLY SHOPS/TACKLE SHOPS

Sandy's Custom Tackle, 10079 State Highway 37, Ogdensburg, NY 13669 / 315-394-0308

Wear On Earth, 19 Market Street, Potsdam, NY 13676 / 315-265-3178

GUIDES

Tim Damon (Damon Rodworks), 19 Market Street, Potsdam, NY 13676 / 315-265-0174 / www.tpinter.net/damonrod

AUTO REPAIR

B & M Auto Repair, 439 Main Street, Massena, NY 13662 / 315-764-3115

Rishe's Auto Service, 1111 Patterson Street, Ogdensburg, NY 13669 / 315-393-8454

Airport

Massena International Airport, 90 Aviation Road, Massena, NY 13662 / 315-769-7605

Hospital/Clinic

Massena Memorial Hospital, 1 Hospital Drive, Massena, NY 13662 / 315-764-1711

Hepburn Medical Center, 214 King Street, Ogdensburg, NY 13669 / 315-393-3600

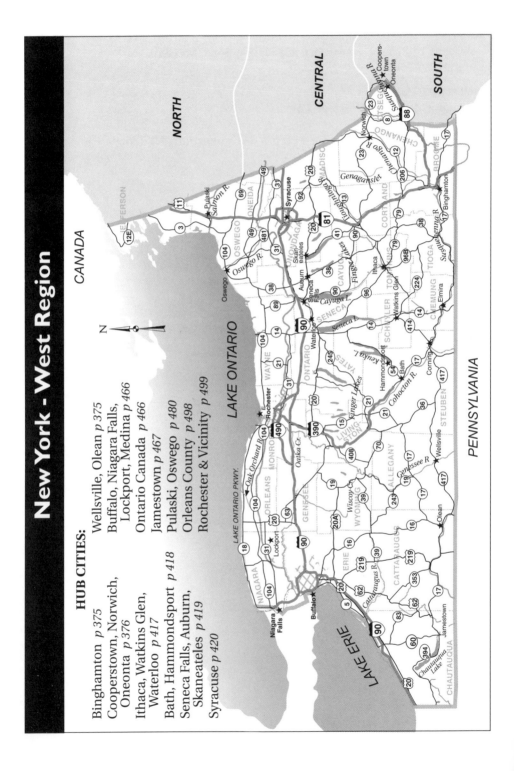

New York - West Region

HUB CITIES:

Binghamton *p 375*
Cooperstown, Norwich,
  Oneonta *p 376*
Ithaca, Watkins Glen,
  Waterloo *p 417*
Bath, Hammondsport *p 418*
Seneca Falls, Auburn,
  Skaneateles *p 419*
Syracuse *p 420*

Wellsville, Olean *p 375*
Buffalo, Niagara Falls,
  Lockport, Medina *p 466*
Ontario Canada *p 466*
Jamestown *p 467*
Pulaski, Oswego *p 480*
Orleans County *p 498*
Rochester & Vicinity *p 499*

West Region

T his area of New York—which for the purpose of this book includes every-thing west of the Catskills and Adirondacks, including the eastern shore of Lake Ontario—covers an enormous territory and a remarkable variety of flyfishing.

The Western portion of New York has terrific fishing from the renowned large salmon and steelhead of Lake Ontario to the topnotch warmwater fishing for smallmouth, pike and even carp in the Susquehanna Valley and Leatherstocking Region. It also hosts fishing for trout and landlocked salmon in the Finger Lakes and their tributaries and an excellent steelhead fishery in Lake Erie. The Oatka and Wiscoy creeks found here are two of the state's best trout fisheries.

The Genegantslet, in the stream's catch and release section.

Leatherstocking Region and Susquehanna Basin

Talk to local anglers in this central part of the state and you'll hear a lot of praise for the local streams, along with apologies for not fishing them more often. With the Ontario tributaries and the Adirondacks to the north, and the Catskills to the southeast, residents can be forgiven for making the relatively short trip to prime fishing a couple of hours away.

Still, there is very good flyfishing in this region. This area hosts some of the state's best warmwater stream fishing opportunities, including the chance to fish for trophy smallmouth. Float fishing opportunities are plentiful on these warmwater streams, which are usually smooth and slow running. There are also good trout streams here. The fish are not usually large, but the streams are lovely freestone waters running through gently rolling farmland.

LEATHERSTOCKING REGION
Otsego, Chenango, and Madison Counties

The Leatherstocking Region is at the northern part of this section and has more of the good trout fishing. The area gets its name from the five novels James Fenimore Cooper wrote between 1823 and 1840, including *The Last of the Mohicans*, collectively known as *The Leatherstocking Tales*. In fact, several of these were set on the shore of Lake Otsego.

GENEGANTSLET CREEK

This small, freestone stream is probably the best trout fishery in these counties. The Genegantslet (pronounced "Jeenaganslet"), runs south about 20 miles from the Chenango County town of Pharsalia into the Chenango River near the village of Greene, and has cool, shaded water and good hatches. As a result, stocked trout grow well here, and equally important, the creek supports considerable natural reproduction of brown trout, along with wild brookies in the upper section.

The headwaters in Pharsalia and the first couple of miles in the town of McDonough offer a chance at wild brook trout, although fallen logs and overgrowth in this section can make wading and casting difficult. Instead, try the seven miles above the village of Smithville Flats, which is probably the best water. Good fishing can be had at the new access on Creek Road in the town of McDonough. A few miles downstream is a one mile catch and release section, which runs from the Route 220 Bridge north of Smithville Flats upstream to the mouth of the stream called Five Streams. Fishing is open on the catch and release section all year. The lower half of the catch and release section is said to be less pressured, and throughout the prime trout section walking or wading to less convenient spots is usually

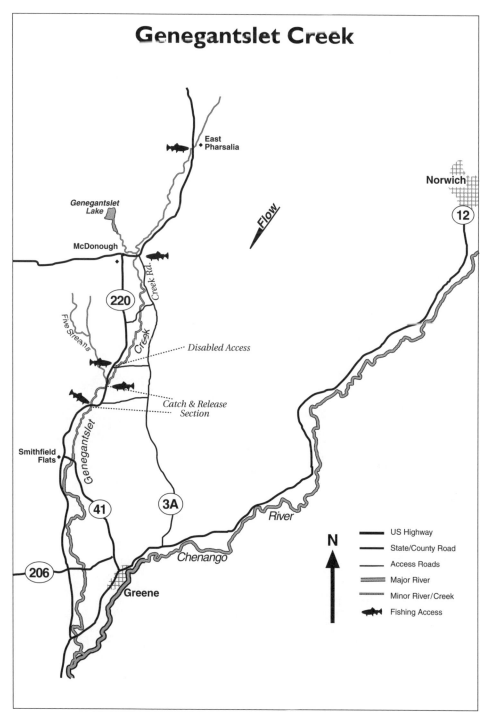

© WILDERNESS ADVENTURES PRESS, INC.

worth the effort. Just above the catch and release section, off Art Lake Road, is a DEC access with a casting platform for disabled anglers and a couple of deep pools that make it a popular spot.

The water below Smithville Flats is warmer and better known for walleye, but some big trout are occasionally taken in this section, and it has the advantage of being lightly fished. Try the area around the Route 206 crossing, for some good browns and easy wading.

The Genegantslet has a mixed array of caddis and a selection of mayflies. Spring Blue Quills and Hendricksons are especially strong and there is a steady supply of small Sulphurs from mid-May to mid-June. There is a good Green Drake hatch in late May and early June. Journalist and local angler Dave Rossie recommends the Green Drake emergence as a chance to catch big fish that are otherwise rarely seen at the surface. An old-fashioned Gray Fox Variant will work for the Green Drake duns—keeping the hackle sparse may make it more effective.

The stream receives a substantial stocking of about 2,000 browns, including about 700 two-year-old fish. There are some big fish in the stream, and anglers report catches of fish in the 16- to 18-inch range. The wild browns typically run 6-12 inches.

Except for the year round catch and release section, the Genegantslet is subject to the normal trout season and regulations, with five additional small brook trout permitted throughout Chenango County.

Some deep pools and access for the disabled can be found just outside the Genegantslet's catch and release section.

Genegantslet Creek—Major Hatches

INSECT	J	F	M	A	M	J	J	A	S	O	N	D	FLIES
Blue Quill 16-18				▮									Blue Quill Dry, Pheasant Tail Nymph
Lt. And Dark Hendrickson 12-14				▮									Light and Dark Hendrickson Parachute, Emergers, Spinners
Sulphurs 14-20					▮								Comparadun, Parachute, Emergers; Smaller sizes more common
Green Drake						▮							Gray Fox Variant, Comparaduns, Compara-Emergers
Caddis Green, Gray, Tan 14-18					▮	▮	▮						Lafontaine Deep Pupa and Emergent Sparkle Pupa, Soft Hackle Wets, Bead-Head Nymphs
Terrestrials						▮	▮	▮	▮				Dubbed and Foam Ants and Beetles, Letort Hoppers and Crickets

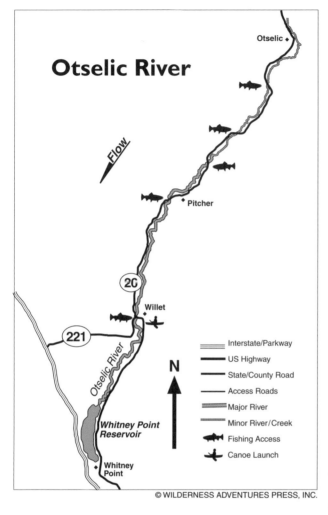

© WILDERNESS ADVENTURES PRESS, INC.

OTSELIC RIVER

Primarily put and take, the Otselic is stocked with about 11,000 brown trout. Despite the less than ideal trout water, the stream is heavily fished, especially by spin anglers in the early season. There is some holdover, and local anglers are hoping to get more fall stocking and float stocking to provide a better fishery. Stabilization of farm banks in the upper portion of the stream is also desired.

Because of the warm water the Otselic is best fished early (although it is probably best to avoid the first week after stocking when it is most heavily hit). The best trout water here is the roughly six-mile stretch from the village of Otselic downstream to the village of Pitcher. There are some good hatches here, including Quill Gordons from mid-April to mid-May, Hendricksons a bit later and some Sulphurs and Cahills in summer. Emergers are said to work particularly well on the Otselic.

Below Pitcher the increasingly warm water makes the Otselic more of a walleye and bass fishery. Route 26 parallels the Otselic and offers access in the trout water. No special regulations apply to trout fishing on the Otselic.

The Otselic offers both trout and warmwater fishing.

Otsego Lake

This 4,000-acre lake hosts good-sized browns and lakers and has recently seen landlocked salmon stocked as well. The lake trout reproduce in Otsego; the browns and landlockeds are almost entirely stocked, but they do grow well.

From April ice-out into early May, streamers can be cast from shore to the fish, particularly landlockeds and browns, that come into the shallows. The western shore is the better half for flyfishing. Threemile Point, not surprisingly located about three miles north of the dam on the western shore, is accessible and offers a good place to cast. Trolling a streamer from a canoe or kayak will give anglers a wider range and a chance to fish later into the season. Threemile is also a good place to start trolling as cartop craft can be put in here and the steep dropoff along the western shore north of this point often holds fish. For larger craft, a formal boat launch can be found at the lake's southern end. Whether casting or trolling, try to imitate the local alewife forage.

Otsego can be fished for any of the three species year round. Only two of these fish—in any combination—may be taken, with a minimum size of 18 inches for trout and landlocked salmon, and 21 inches for the lakers.

Otsego Lake and Tributaries

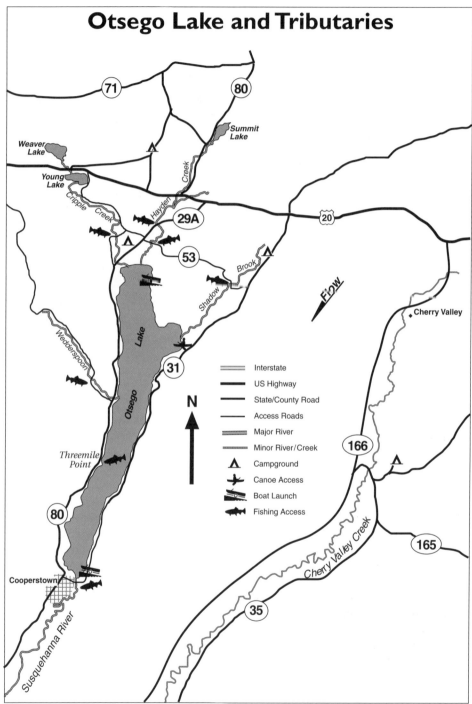

Interstate
US Highway
State/County Road
Access Roads
Major River
Minor River/Creek
Campground
Canoe Access
Boat Launch
Fishing Access

N

© WILDERNESS ADVENTURES PRESS, INC.

HAYDEN CREEK

This small stream runs into Otsego at the lake's northern tip, and can be reached from the crossings at Route 53 and Route 29A. It gets about 500 small browns a year, but also offers the chance to take large lake-dwelling browns ascending the stream in fall. The water tends to run low and warm by that time, but a cool rain may bring fish in. In fact, any of the tiny feeders to Otsego are worth looking at in fall for migrating trout and landlockeds, including Cripple Creek just west of Hayden, Wedderspoon on the western shore and Shadow Brook which enters at Glimmerglass State Park on the eastern side.

JEFFREY POND

This 20-acre pond in the town of North Norwich has been restored as a brook trout pond (about 1,000 small brookies are stocked each year and live baitfish have been banned to preserve the fishery). The water is not very deep, so the fishing is largely put and take. It is located on state forest land and can be reached from Post Road off Route 29 in the town of North Norwich (the portion of the road that runs next to the pond is unpaved). Float tubes or small canoes and kayaks can be carried in and used here.

CHITTENANGO CREEK

Chittenango Creek, the premier trout water in Madison County, flows out of Tuscarora Lake and Cedar Swamp, heading north until it joins Oneida Lake. Although there are some trout above and below, the best fishing for trout is found in the eight miles or so between the villages of Cazenovia and Chittenango.

In its upper reaches, the Chittenango is slow and brushy; trout do hold here but the water is more conducive to spin and bait fishing. From Cazenovia to Chittenango Falls the creek has a moderate gradient, with riffles and pools the typical features. Below the falls, the stream gets steeper and pocket water predominates, particularly in the steep ravine just downstream of the falls.

The Chittenango is heavily stocked with more than 10,000 browns each year, including a couple of thousand two-year-olds. Small brookies are occasionally caught, but they are a minor part of the fishery. Some fishermen assume the Chittenango is strictly put and take, but local anglers do catch fish in winter and early spring in the year round section of the stream. Since this is before the annual stocking, some trout apparently do make it through winter. Still, most fish are stocked and typically are not very selective.

Insects on Chittenango include good populations of Hendricksons in early May, Blue Winged Olives and sporadic caddis. There are also some Green Drakes, which seem to show up in some years but not in others. For the upstream section, normal dries and nymphs are in order, but in the faster water below the falls, high floating dries and big nymphs are better for the pockets. Bob Smith, president of the Madison County Chapter of Trout Unlimited, likes to explore the pocket water with a GC Nymph—a fly similar to a Woolly Worm, tied with a black chenille body and a clipped, palmered hackle.

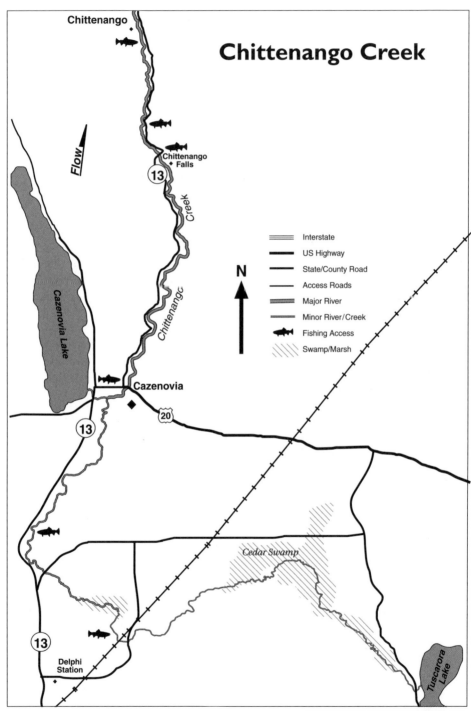

Chittenango Creek

Chittenango

Flow

Chittenango Falls

13

Creek

Chittenango

Cazenovia Lake

N

Cazenovia

20

13

Cedar Swamp

13

Delphi Station

Tuscarora Lake

	Interstate
	US Highway
	State/County Road
	Access Roads
	Major River
	Minor River/Creek
	Fishing Access
	Swamp/Marsh

© WILDERNESS ADVENTURES PRESS, INC.

The Chittenango is well known to local anglers and is heavily hit, especially in the early season. Fly anglers are well advised to skip the first few days after stocking and to wade a bit up or down from popular spots. Moving around is easy on the stream as large swaths of it along Route 13 are open to fishing. Local anglers are trying to get a catch and release section to enhance the fishing. Meanwhile, a few hundred yards in the village of Chittenango are set aside for young anglers, with catch and release requested.

The year round section of Chittenango runs from Route 20 in Cazenovia upstream to the railroad tracks near the small village of Delphi Station. Elsewhere, the stream is subject to the normal trout season and regulations, with five extra small brook trout permitted throughout the stream (and in most of Madison County).

Tioughnioga Creek

The Tioughnioga (pronounced "tyafneeoga") is composed of two branches that merge in the city of Cortland. The trout fishing is primarily in the branches, with the east branch generally considered the better fishery. (A small tributary of the upper East Branch near the village of Cuyler is incorrectly marked as the West Branch on some maps).

The East Branch of the creek runs down from lower Onondaga County, where its small waters hold some native brook trout. Once entering Cortland County the stream is well stocked with fish down to the junction with the East Branch. About 4,000 fish are put in each year, all of them browns. This water can run low and warm in summer, so it is better fished in spring.

Riffled water on the East Branch of the Tioughnioga.

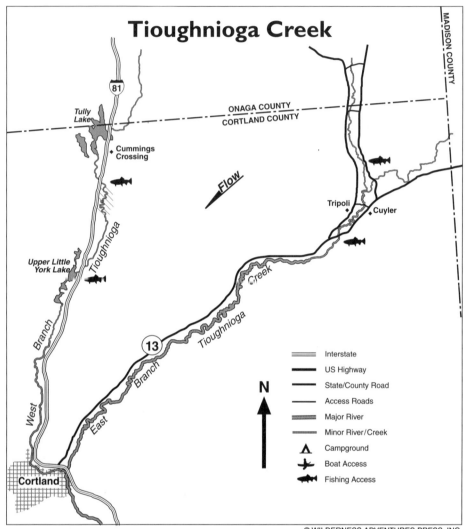

Tioughnioga Creek

ONAGA COUNTY
CORTLAND COUNTY

Tully Lake

Cummings Crossing

Flow

Tripoli

Cuyler

Upper Little York Lake

Tioughnioga

Branch

West

East

Branch

Cortland

Tioughnioga

Creek

MADISON COUNTY

	Interstate
	US Highway
	State/County Road
	Access Roads
	Major River
	Minor River/Creek
Λ	Campground
	Boat Access
	Fishing Access

N

© WILDERNESS ADVENTURES PRESS, INC.

The West Branch has some brook trout in its small headwaters, also in Onondaga County. After crossing south into Cortland County, the flow is interrupted by a series of lakes and some swampy sections. The main trout fishing section, and the portion stocked with brown trout, is in the town of Homer. From here down to the junction, the roughly seven miles receive about 3,500 browns yearly.

Good walleye and smallmouth fishing can be found on the small, wide portion of the Otselic River that flows from Whitney Point Reservoir (sometimes called Dorchester Lake) and down into the main stem of the Tioughnioga at the village of Whitney Point.

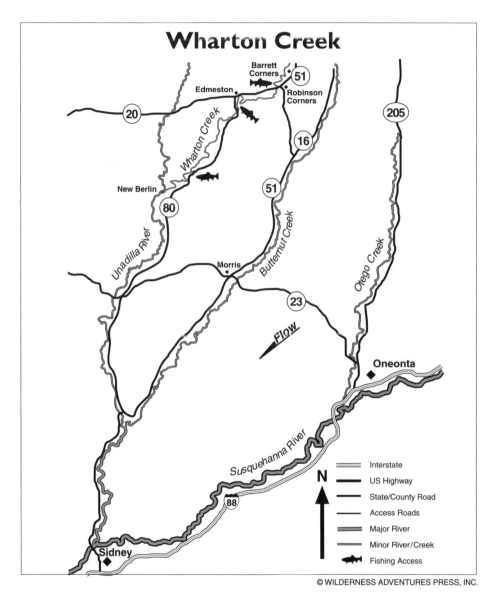

Wharton Creek

© WILDERNESS ADVENTURES PRESS, INC.

WHARTON CREEK

This stream runs south at the western side of Otsego County where it joins the warmwater Unadilla River. The trout water is in the upper portion of the stream, in the towns of Edmeston and Burlington. About 3,000 small browns are stocked. Access can be had from Route 80 and Route 51, which parallel the stream and have several sections of public access, including near the villages of Barrett Corners and Robinson Corners.

COWASELON CREEK

No more than 15-20 feet across, Cowaselon was once popular with locals as a good small trout fishery. Although the water is still good, the access is not and only about a mile between Route 5 and the railroad tracks to the north are open to public fishing. About 1,200 small browns are stocked in this stretch each year, which can be reached off Elm Street just west of downtown Oneida.

Susquehanna Basin

The best-known water here is obviously the Susquehanna itself. It offers outstanding smallmouth and other warmwater fishing and has occasional trout in its upper reaches. The Chenango also has good warmwater fishing and is a good place to fish from a canoe or kayak.

The trout streams here are generally small and of moderate gradient. Flows typically fall off considerably in summer and the temperatures warm, although overhanging brush keeps the waters well shaded in many places. All the streams are stocked with browns and a few have fair to good populations of wild brookies in the upper reaches. These streams generally offer a basic menu of hatches, without the density or variety of their Catskill neighbors.

Mid-stream islands, like these at Grippen Park, are good
places to look for smallmouth on the Susquehanna.

SUSQUEHANNA RIVER

This wide, meandering flow runs more than 80 miles through Chenango, Broome and Tioga counties. It has exceptional fishing for smallmouth bass—much the equal of the fishery downstream in Pennsylvania—along with northern pike, some stocked tiger muskellunge and walleye. Near its source at Lake Otsego, there is seasonal fishing for large browns and landlocked salmon that come over the dam.

Smallmouth Bass

Among the warmwater fish in the Susquehanna, smallmouth bass are definitely the favorite quarry for the fly angler. The river is full of smallies. Fish in the 16-inch range are not uncommon, and even 20-inchers are taken by fly anglers. In all, the Susquehanna population is believed to be both the densest and largest of any stream in the region (if not the state).

The smallmouth fishing comes into its own on the Susquehanna after the stream widens at Sidney in Chenango County. Though the river can be floated in canoes and kayaks, most of the flyfishing for bass is done on foot. On warm summer evenings, you might even want to leave the waders at home. Most of the Susquehanna is open to anglers and anyplace with the right structure will probably hold fish. Not all water is equal, however. As Dave Delillo of Timber Creek Sports Shop notes, in low water smallmouth anglers should concentrate on riffles, and when the water is high, on the V-shaped wake downstream of the many islands in the river. From mid-July on is often the best time, Delillo observes, as lower water levels allow wading in most sections.

Perhaps the best fishing is on the last 30 miles, after the river has made its brief U-turn in Pennsylvania. In this stretch, the city of Binghamton and nearby communities offer excellent fishing. The section at the old Gaudy Coal Plant in Johnson City just west of Binghamton has excellent habitat. Downstream a few miles in Endicott, Grippen Park offers a boat launch and, equally important, a series of small islands behind which the bass congregate. It also has an easily wadeable flow rarely more than five feet deep. This area is particularly good for rising fish on summer evenings. A lot of smallmouth fishing goes on subsurface. Popular and effective streamers include Clouser Minnows with green or chartreuse top wings, small Deceivers and Woolly Buggers in both dark and crayfish colors. Any one of the more specific crayfish imitations would also be a good choice.

Despite the importance of streamers, smallmouth are often caught on top. The big White Fly is a summer staple, but there are also large Cahills and olive-colored mayflies, and some caddis. The Wulff series in different colors, sizes 12-16, supplemented by a few Elk Hair Caddis, will take fish when they are rising. Less delicate, but also effective, are Dahlberg Divers and even mouse imitations fished at the surface. Backcasting is not an issue on the lower Susquehanna, so pick a long rod in 6-

Susquehanna River

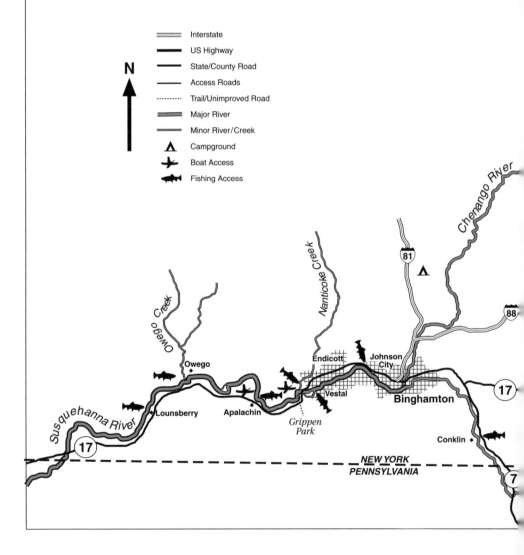

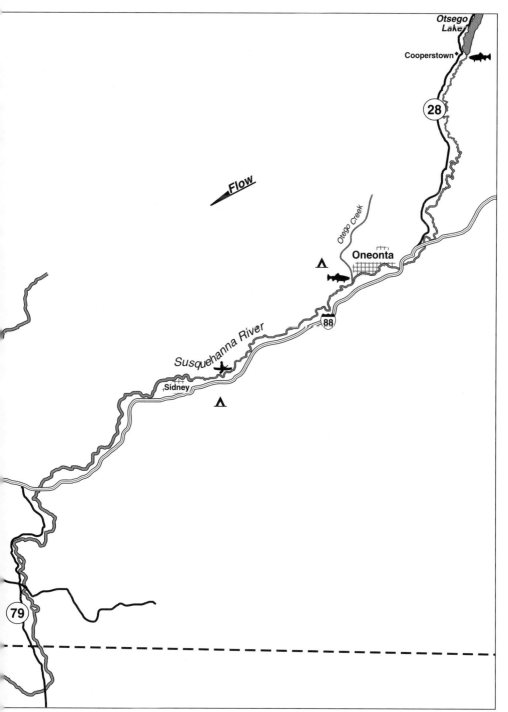

or 7-weight. Floating lines are generally sufficient, but a shorter bug taper will help turn over any of the larger flies.

Good smallmouth fishing continues into Tioga County to the village of Owego. After Owego, deeper water makes flyfishing difficult until the village of Lounsberry. There are a couple of accesses here to a shallow stretch called The Flats, a particularly good spot for evening dry fly action.

Other Warmwater Species

Smallmouth are not the only warmwater target on the Susquehanna. Carp up to 35 pounds can be taken on top in the Susquehanna in the summer and flyfishing for these strong, wary fish is becoming increasingly popular. Big rods—up to 9-weight—are in order. When the fish are rising, any of the same big mayflies that work for bass will take carp, although they are harder to fool. The portions of water at Conklin and downstream at Vestal are two good places to try.

Large pike and stocked tiger muskellunge also live in the Susquehanna. The tiger muskies have been stocked for more than a decade and grow well here; fish up to 20 pounds are occasionally caught. Both pike and tiger muskies are taken in deeper water with 9-weight rods and 5- to 6-inch streamers—blue and white Deceivers in particular. Be sure to include lots of flash in the fly, and use a bite tippet. The deep water right in the lower half of Binghamton and again below Owego are good places to try for pike and muskie, but this is obviously a lower percentage venture than fishing for smallmouth.

New York does not stock true muskies, but Pennsylvania does in the brief section of the river that dips into Pennsylvania before returning to Broome County. The muskies are sometimes caught in the New York water and only one of either species (pure or tiger) may be kept.

Walleye fishing is still mostly done with spinning gear, but they are sometimes taken on flies in the river. The small village of Apalachin in Tioga County has a new boat launch and good deep holes for walleye fishing.

Trout and Salmon

Surprisingly, this famous smallmouth river has trout and even salmon in its upper portion. Even at the headwaters the river is too warm in summer for year round trout or salmon populations. But in fall (generally after the close of the fishing season) large landlocked salmon and browns, and occasional lake trout, wash over the dam at Lake Otsego and hold in the uppermost stretch of the river, right in Cooperstown. The fish can be large; sleek, silvery landlockeds of 24 inches are caught, along with browns in the five-pound range. Beginning with opening day in April, local anglers fish hard here, and at times the anglers may outnumber the fish.

Most of the anglers use spinning gear with live bait or worms, but flyfishers can and do take both species. Fly selection is not complicated: streamers like olive Woolly Buggers, Black-Nosed Dace or Mickey Finns, or large stoneflies or other nymphs. You'll need to get the fly down as the bend pools can be as deep as 15 feet, and the dam usually releases water in spring to lower the level of the lake before ice-out. A floating line with a long leader and some weight usually works, though a sink tip is probably worth bringing along. The first couple of bend pools below the dam (along the hospital parking lot in Cooperstown) are generally considered the best spots. Anglers have been known to sleep in their cars here to beat the competition on opening day. However, a few stray fish make their way downstream as far as the dam in Oneonta.

Stream Facts: Susquehanna River

Seasons/Regulations
- Smallmouth: Third Saturday in June to November 30, five fish per day of at least 12 inches.
- Pike: First Saturday in May to March 15, five fish per day, 18-inch minimum.
- Tiger Muskellunge/Muskellunge: First Saturday in May to March 15, one fish of either species at least 30 inches long.
- Carp: All year, no limit.
- Trout, landlocked salmon and lake trout: April 1 to October 15; browns five fish of any size; landlocked salmon three fish of 15 inches or longer; lake trout three fish of 21 inches or more.

Fish
- Smallmouth bass, pike, stocked tiger muskellunge and stray muskellunge, walleye, carp. Brown trout, landlocked salmon and occasional lake trout from Lake Otsego in first few miles.

River Characteristics/Flows
- Wide, slow, meandering flow, with some deep holes. Riffles and mid-stream islands interspersed.

Susquehanna River—Major Hatches/Flies

INSECT	J	F	M	A	M	J	J	A	S	O	N	D	FLIES
White Fly 12-14 Cahills and Olives 12-16 Caddis 12-16													Comparaduns, White and other Wulffs, Soft Hackle Wet Flies, Elk Hair Caddis
Streamers													Woolly Buggers, Black and/or Olive and Crayfish Colors; Crayfish imitations; Small Deceivers; Clouser Minnows in Chartreuse/White and Green/White, Muddler Minnows
Nymphs													Swimming Nymphs, Large Hare's Ear Nymphs
Popper/Slider													Dahlberg Divers black and purple, Chuggers, Mouse imitations

Oxford is a good place to start or end a float trip on the Chenango.

CHENANGO RIVER

The Chenango, composed of east and west branches that join near the village of Sherburne, is primarily a warmwater fishery, but it does offer trout fishing in its upper portion.

The West Branch is definitely the better trout fishery, and the best section there is well upstream from the junction in the Madison County town of Eaton, about five miles in all. After the stream emerges from the Morrisville Swamp, it offer a good series of riffles and pools. Hendricksons, Cahills and Sulphurs all hatch here. The fish are primarily stocked browns; about 3,500 a year, including 500 two-year-olds.

The East Branch of the Chenango—also called the Sangerfield River—is a more marginal fishery than the West Branch. It emerges from a long swamp and its water is subject to high temperatures in summer. Its roughly five miles of trout water are best fished in spring. The Sangerfield receives about 3,000 browns a year, with a couple of hundred two-year-old fish. No special season or regulations apply to either branch of the Chenango River.

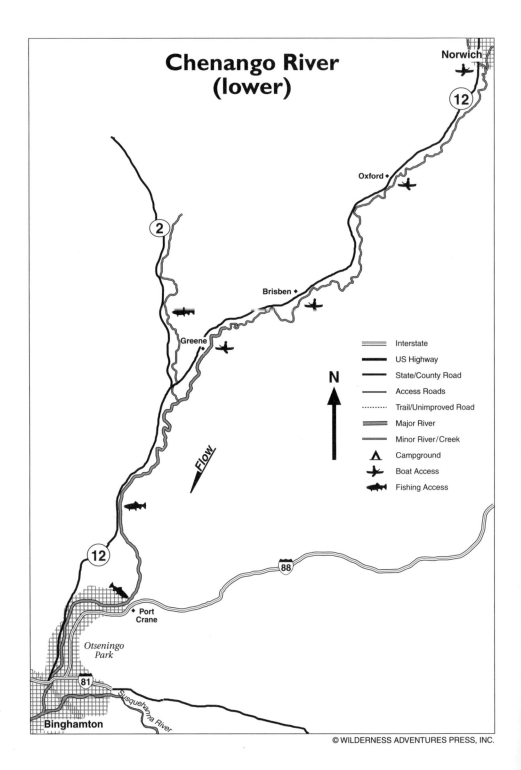

Chenango River (lower)

Norwich

12

Oxford

2

Brisben

Greene

N

Interstate
US Highway
State/County Road
Access Roads
Trail/Unimproved Road
Major River
Minor River/Creek
Campground
Boat Access
Fishing Access

Flow

12

88

Port
Crane

Otseningo
Park

81

Susquehanna River

Binghamton

© WILDERNESS ADVENTURES PRESS, INC.

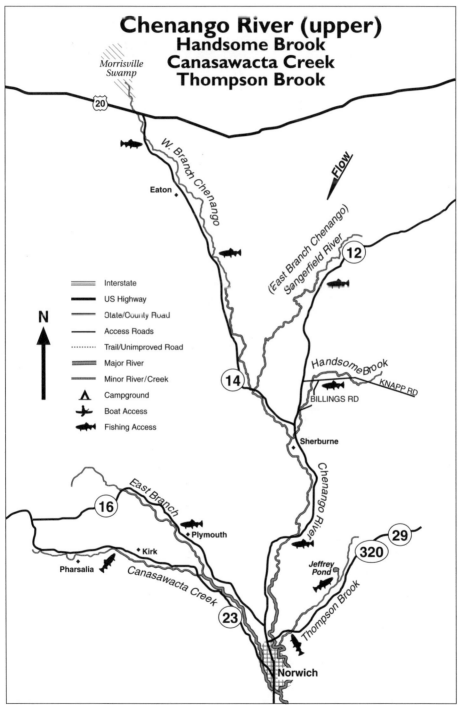

Chenango River (upper)
Handsome Brook
Canasawacta Creek
Thompson Brook

© WILDERNESS ADVENTURES PRESS, INC.

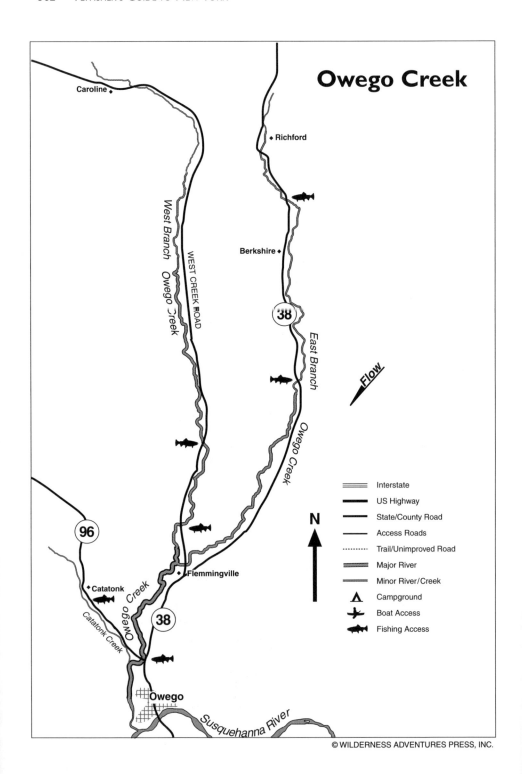

Owego Creek

Caroline ♦

♦ Richford

Berkshire ♦

West Branch Owego Creek

WEST CREEK ROAD

East Branch Owego Creek

38

Flow

96

Owego Creek

♦ Catatonk

Catatonk Creek

Owego Creek

♦ Flemmingville

38

N

	Interstate
	US Highway
	State/County Road
	Access Roads
	Trail/Unimproved Road
	Major River
	Minor River/Creek
▲	Campground
✈	Boat Access
🐟	Fishing Access

Owego

Susquehanna River

© WILDERNESS ADVENTURES PRESS, INC.

Warmwater

Below the confluence of its two branches near Sherburne, the Chenango is a warmwater fishery. This is primarily spin fishing territory, but flyfishers can also try for the river's northern pike and walleye. If you like warmwater flyfishing it may be worth the effort. The fish here can get very large: northerns of 30 inches or better are taken every season, as are six-pound walleyes.

The Chenango's main stem is large and best fished from a boat. There are several good, full day floats available, about seven miles each. The first goes from Norwich downstream to Oxford, the second from Oxford to Brisben and the last from Brisben to Greene. Each of these spots has access points for cartop canoes and kayaks. Also, the water is typically slow enough to paddle back to any access point during a shorter jaunt.

Spin anglers, who predominate here, typically use bucktail jigs so a fly angler would do well to offer various bucktail streamers and Clouser Minnows. The Sparkle Grub, a short fly with dumbbell eyes, sparkle chenille body and marabou tail is a good facsimile of the twister tails that are also successful on spinning gear here. Except on cloudy days, look for pike in deep holes and walleye where riffles run into pools.

Standard northern pike and walleye seasons apply to the Chenango: first Saturday in May to March 15. Five fish of each type may be taken, the pike must be 18 inches, the walleye 15 inches.

In addition, large carp can be taken in the lower Chenango. The flat, riffly water at the small village of Port Crane (along Route 88, a few miles upstream of Binghamton) regularly yields fish of 20 pounds or more. If the carp aren't rising to big mayflies, try a weighted or conehead Woolly Bugger.

Though the nearby Susquehanna is the better smallmouth fishery, the last portion of the Chenango also has good bass fishing. Try the riffly, island-studded water at Otseningo Park in Binghamton. Good-sized smallmouth can be taken here at the surface on summer evenings.

OWEGO CREEK

Owego Creek is composed of a west branch, east branch and a relatively short main stem that all run south through Tioga County before joining the Susquehanna in Owego. Public access is extensive, covering nearly 30 miles of water on the Owego.

The East Branch is the most popular portion of Owego and offers stocked browns and wild brookies. It is mostly brush-lined and usually not more than 10 feet wide, so a shorter rod is in order. Wading is fairly easy on the rocky bottom, but there are some winding meadow sections in the upper reaches where heavy silt can make it difficult to maneuver.

The heavy stocking of browns—nearly 6,000 fish—takes place in the town of Berkshire and there are various access points along Route 38 in this section. However, it is worth starting a bit north, in the town of Richford, which is primarily brook trout water. Don't be surprised to take wild brookies downstream, though; local anglers report that in recent years brook trout are well distributed on the East Branch. At the other end of the East Branch, the last half-mile before the junction with the West Branch (above and below where West Creek Road crosses) is an excellent place for catching brown trout.

The West Branch, which runs from swampy headwaters near the village of Caroline to the junction at Flemingville, doesn't see as many anglers as the East Branch. It too receives a substantial stocking of browns that are said to holdover well here, supplementing a good brook trout population. The West Branch is a bit narrower than the East—20 feet across on average—and flyfishing usually involves a bit of stalking. Access can be had along West Creek Road, which runs parallel.

The Main Stem runs only about five miles from Flemingville to the Susquehanna and gets warmer as it heads downstream. A few thousand browns are stocked here, primarily in the first couple of miles below the junction. Generally, you can expect to find browns upstream of the Route 96 crossing (sometimes called Turner's Bridge). The stream here is much wider, up to 40 yards across. Though less accessible than the two branches, some entry can be found along Route 38. Catatonk Creek enters near the Susquehanna. This tributary receives its own stocking of browns in its upper section in the town of Candor.

Owego has a good complement of mayflies, including a particularly strong Hendrickson hatch at the end of April and a Green Drake hatch that seems to come and go. More reliable is a steady dark summer caddis, well imitated by a size 14 Henryville Special. Habitat on both branches has been improved by digger dams built by local Boy Scout troops with funding from the Al Hazzard and other Trout Unlimited chapters. There are no special seasons or regulations on any portion of Owego Creek, except that five additional small brook trout may be kept (as in most Tioga County waters).

Foliage along Owego Creek can make casting a challenge.

Otego and Butternut Creeks

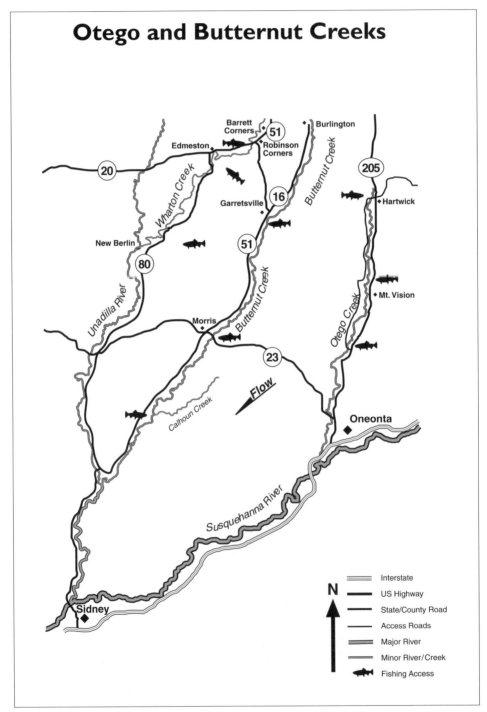

© WILDERNESS ADVENTURES PRESS. INC.

OTEGO CREEK

This small stream runs south about 10 miles to meet the Susquehanna downstream of Oneonta. The upper stretch has a good population of native brookies, though the water here is quite small. Local anglers report catching brookies in the double digits on good days. In addition, browns are stocked in the town of Hartwick (about 1,800 small fish per year). There is some holdover and perhaps some natural reproduction as well. The best stretch for browns is roughly from the village of Hartwick, where Route 11 crosses the creek, downstream to Mt. Vision near Route 46. For brookies, fish from Hartwick upstream. Local anglers report that the Otego seems to fish better in September than in spring.

Informal access is available at road crossings and pulloffs along Route 205 and Route 11, which border the stream. There are fishing easements on Otego from its mouth to its headwaters. Below Mt. Vision, trout fishing begins to taper off and the population is increasingly bass and walleye before the stream joins the Susquehanna. No special regulations apply to Otego Creek.

BUTTERNUT CREEK

Though small, this stream nevertheless supports a good population of native brook trout—including a few of 12 inches or more—supplemented by substantial stockings of small brown trout. Butternut begins in the Otsego County town of Exeter and flows south until it meets the Unadilla River north of Sidney. It is the stretch above the village of Morris that is the main trout water, though browns are occasionally taken downstream (try the mouth of Calhoun Creek, just below Morris). A favorite downstream portion for local anglers is the four-mile run from Garretsville, where Route 51 crosses, down to the village of New Lisbon near Route 12. (See map of Otego, Wharton and Butternut Creeks).

About 4,000 browns are put in each year, all in the town of Burlington; despite the small size of the creek, they are reported to hold over well. Butternut offers a variety of riffles, runs and pools. Casting conditions are tight throughout, so use a small, lightweight rod. Access is good from Route 16 and Route 51, which parallel most of the stream, and from numerous road crossings. No special regulations.

Angling on Thompson Creek requires careful stalking and casting from the bank.

Handsome Brook, Canasawacta Creek, and Thompson Brook

These three tributaries to the Chenango River primarily offer fishing for wild brook trout.(See Chenango River map).

Handsome Brook runs only about four miles before meeting the Chenango River near the village of Sherburne in northern Chenango County. It receives a small annual stocking of browns, in addition to the brook trout, and a few of the native fish grow to good size. It can be reached from Billings Road and Knapp Road.

Thompson Creek, sometimes called Kings Settlement Creek, runs southwest for about five miles and meets the Chenango just above Norwich. It is said to hold some good-sized wild brookies. Access is along Route 320 and upstream along Route 29. The stream is rarely more than four feet across, so casting would be from shore.

Canasawacta is a longer stream that meets the Chenango in Norwich. It divides about six miles upstream of the mouth, with the eastern portion called the East Branch and the other portion just the Canasawacta. It is on the upper reaches that wild brookies can be found (no additional trout are stocked here). In general, look for brookies above the village of Kirk on the main stream and above the village of Plymouth on the East Branch.

Access to the upper Canasawacta can be had along Route 23, including some state land near the village of North Pharsalia. The East Branch runs parallel to Route 16 and there is some state land traversing the stream about two miles upstream of the village of Plymouth.

The normal season applies to all three streams. An extra five small brook trout under eight inches may be kept, but even small wild fish are best taken sparingly.

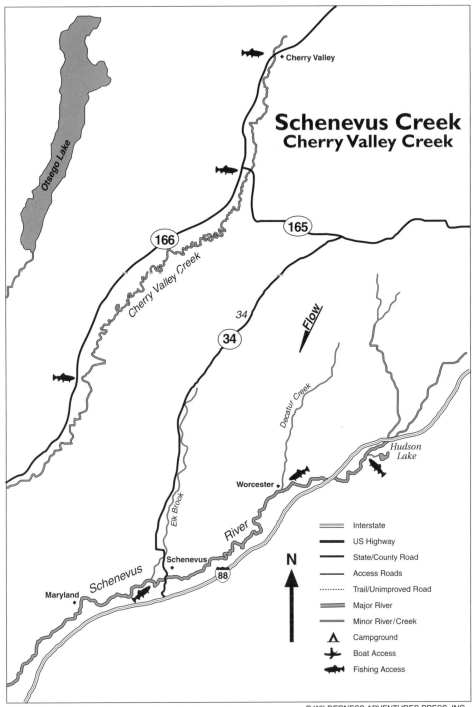

Schenevus Creek
Cherry Valley Creek

Otsego Lake

Cherry Valley

166

165

Cherry Valley Creek

34

34

Flow

Decatur Creek

Hudson Lake

Worcester

Elk Brook

River

Schenevus

Schenevus

88

Maryland

N

Interstate
US Highway
State/County Road
Access Roads
Trail/Unimproved Road
Major River
Minor River/Creek
Campground
Boat Access
Fishing Access

© WILDERNESS ADVENTURES PRESS, INC.

SCHENEVUS CREEK

Among the largest of the area trout streams, the Schenevus cuts south and west across Otsego County before meeting the Susquehanna. The trout fishing is concentrated in the town of Maryland (the town of Worcester on the southern bank), where about 4,500 browns are stocked each year, including about 500 older fish. From the village of Worcester upstream you will find increasing numbers of wild brook trout as well.

A good spot to hit the Schenevus is at the mouth of Elk Brook (sometimes listed as Elk Creek), where Route 34 reaches the stream near the village of Schenevus. There is dedicated parking here and fishing easements in both directions. Don't ignore Elk Brook itself. The tributary receives a healthy stocking of browns, and fish from the Schenevus are sometimes taken in fall as they ascend Elk.

Good hatches on Schenevus include Hendricksons, a moderate Sulphur hatch and *Potomanthus* in late June and early July (said to be particularly good near Elk Creek). In addition to access at Elk Creek, anglers can get on where Route 39 reaches the stream near the mouth of Decatur Creek, and again further upstream at Route 38 (above Hudson Lake).

The Schenevus running through farmland near the mouth of Elk Brook.

CHERRY VALLEY CREEK

This long, narrow creek drains the large valley that provides its name. It isn't stocked, but it does hold wild brook trout in its upper reaches. The stream runs along Route 166; the brook trout are more likely to be found near the village of Cherry Valley and upstream.

NANTICOKE CREEK

This small tributary meets the Susquehanna west of Endicott and is heavily stocked with brown trout—nearly 5,000 fish per year, including some large fish. Unfortunately, it is also heavily fished, and anglers tend to bunch up because access is limited. Anglers can get on at a few road crossings.

OQUAGA CREEK

A small to medium-sized stream, Oquaga runs at the eastern edge of this region. The creek flows south and east, joining the West Branch of the Delaware a couple of miles below the Cannonsville Dam. Despite its location, it is more often fished by locals than visitors to the Catskills.

The stream gets a fairly heavy stocking of about 4,000 brown trout, and there is reportedly some good natural reproduction of browns as well. Oquaga also holds a decent population of wild brookies. The bottom is rocky, but wading is relatively easy. Hatches on Oquaga are similar to Catskill streams, though not as dense.

Access is available along Route 41, and there is access for disabled anglers at Fireman's Park in Deposit. There is also a three-mile long catch and release section on the Oquago running roughly from the village of McClure downstream to the Route 17 Bridge near the mouth. The mouth of the stream on the West Branch presents an interesting opportunity to catch Delaware fish. When very cold water is coming out of the Cannonsville Dam, West Branch trout will congregate at the warmer mouth of the Oquaga—a warmwater refuge, instead of the usual coldwater variety.

Except for the catch and release section on the lower stream in which fishing is permitted year round, normal trout season and regulations apply to the Oquaga. Five additional brook trout under eight inches may be taken, which applies throughout Broome County.

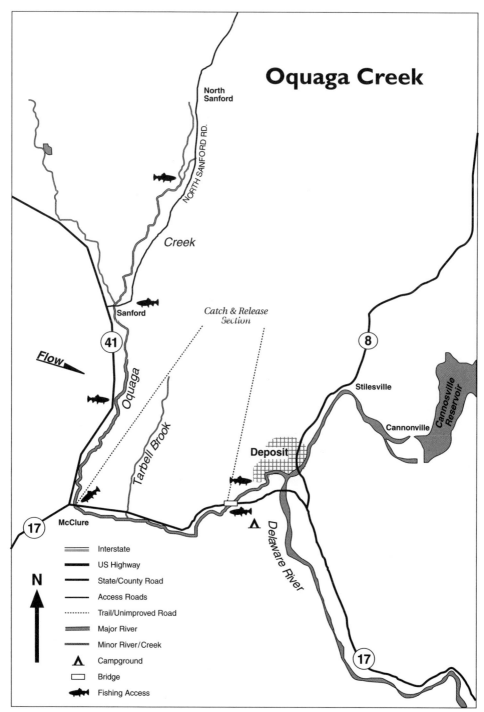

Oquaga Creek

North
Sanford

NORTH SANFORD RD.

Creek

Sanford

Catch & Release
Section

41

Flow

Oquaga

Tarbell Brook

8

Stilesville

Cannonville

Cannosville
Reservoir

Deposit

McClure

17

Delaware River

17

Interstate
US Highway
State/County Road
Access Roads
Trail/Unimproved Road
Major River
Minor River/Creek
Campground
Bridge
Fishing Access

N

© WILDERNESS ADVENTURES PRESS, INC.

Susquehanna Valley Region—Major Hatches/Flies

INSECT	J	F	M	A	M	J	J	A	S	O	N	D	FLIES
Blue Quill													Blue Quill Dry, Pheasant Tail Nymph
Lt. And Dark Hendrickson 12-14													Light and Dark Hendrickson Parachute, Emergers, Spinners
Caddis Green, Gray, Tan 14-18													Lafontaine Deep Pupa and Emergent Sparkle Pupa, Soft Hackle Wets, Bead-Head Nymphs
Blue Winged Olives 16-22													Parachute, Emergers, Spinners
Sulphurs 14-20													Comparadun, Parachute, CDC Emerger, Compara-Emerger, Pheasant Tail Nymph
Light Cahill\White Fly 12-16													Cream Variants, Comparaduns, Cahill Wet Fly, Light Hare's Ear Nymph
Trico 22-26													Trico Spinner, Griffith's Gnat
Terrestrials													Dubbed and Foam Ants and Beetles, Letort Hoppers and Crickets

Leatherstocking and Susquehanna Region Hub Cities

Binghamton

Accomodations Price Key

$ Up to 60 dollars per night
$$ 61 to 99 dollars per night
$$$ 100 to 150 per night
$$$$ 151 and up per night

Hotels/Motels

Comfort Inn, 1156 Front Street, Binghamton, NY 13905 / 607-722-5353 / $$-$$$
Motel 6, 1012 Front Street, Binghamton, NY 13905 / 607-771-0400 / $
Holiday Inn Arena, 2-8 Hawley Street, Binghamton, NY 13901 / 607-722-1212 / $$

Campgrounds/RVs

Chenango Valley State Park, Pigeon Hill Road, Binghamton NY, 13905 / 607-648-5251 / No hookups / 51 elec.
Pine Valley Campground, 600 Boswell Road, Endicott, NY 13760 / 607-785-6868

Restaurants

Argo Restaurant, 117 Court Street, Binghamton, NY 13905 / 607-724-4692 / 6 a.m. to 9 p.m.
Spot Diner, 1062 Front Street, Binghamton, NY 13905 / 607-723-8149, 24 Hours
Lost Dog Cafe, 222 Water Street, Binghamton, NY 13901 / 607-771-6063

Fly Shops

Timber Creek Sports Shop, 100 Rano Boulevard, Vestal, NY 13850 / 607-770-9112 / www.timbercreeksports.com / Orvis dealer / Full service fly shop, guiding

Cooperstown/Norwich/Oneonta

HOTELS/MOTELS

Best Western Inn & Suites, 50 Commons Drive, Cooperstown / NY 13326 /
607-547-9439 / $$$

Super 8 Motel, 4973 Route 23, Oneonta, NY   13820607 / 432-7483 / $$

CAMPGROUNDS/RVs

Cooperstown KOA Campground, Cooperstown, NY   13326 / 800-562-3402

RESTAURANTS

Gabriella's on the Square, 161 Main Street, Cooperstown, NY 13326/
607-547-8000

Silo City Club Restaurant, 75 North Broad Street, Norwich, NY   13815 /
607-337-7456

Nardi's Café, 6798 Route 20, Bouckville, NY 13310 / 315-893-7902

FLY SHOPS

Stevens Hardware, 153 Main Street, Oneonta, NY 13820 / 607-432-2720 / Good
selection of flies.

TACKLE SHOPS

Mayhood's Sporting Goods,102 Gilmore Lane Route 12, Norwich, NY /
607-334-2001 / www.mayhoods.com

The Finger Lakes Region

The Finger Lakes—11 long, thin bodies of water carved by glaciers —occupy the heart of the western portion of New York State. They stretch across more than 80 miles, from Conesus in the west to Otisco in the east. The largest, Cayuga and Seneca, are more than 35 miles long and 400 feet deep.

For fly anglers it is the area around the lakes rather than the large stillwaters themselves that are most important, but some flyfishing does take place on the lakes. Most of the inlets have runs of migratory fish—landlocked salmon, rainbow and brown trout, and some smallmouth. A few of the outlets also offer fishing for trout. Several streams in the region not connected to the lakes, most notably the Cohocton, offer very good flyfishing as well. Beyond the fishing, there are myriad tourist opportunities in the region, from gliding to a thriving wine industry, which makes it an appealing destination even for non-anglers.

The Cohocton at the Veterans Administration Bridge, downstream of the upper special regulations area.

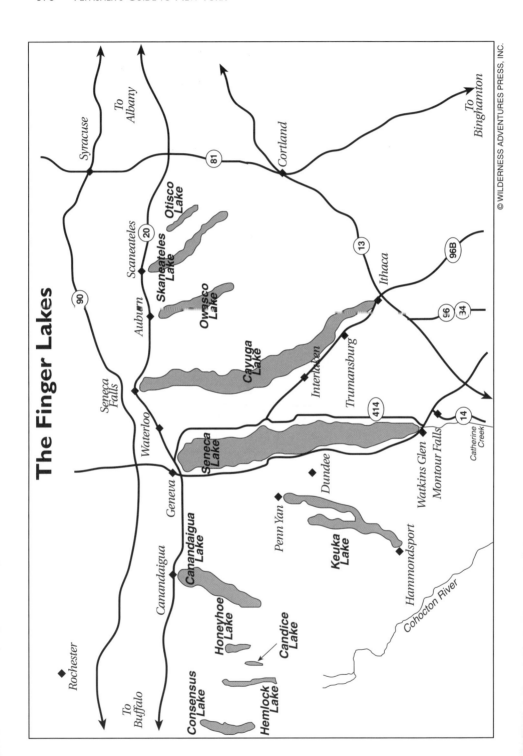

The Finger Lakes

To Buffalo

To Albany

Syracuse

To Binghamton

Cortland

81

Rochester

90

Otisco Lake

Scaneateles

20

Skaneateles Lake

13

96B

Ithaca

96

34

Auburn

Owasco Lake

Seneca Falls

Cayuga Lake

Trumansburg

Interlaken

Waterloo

Canandaigua

414

Seneca Lake

14

Watkins Glen

Montour Falls

Catherine Creek

Geneva

Dundee

Canandaigua Lake

Penn Yan

Keuka Lake

Hammondsport

Honeyhoe Lake

Candice Lake

Cohocton River

Consensus Lake

Hemlock Lake

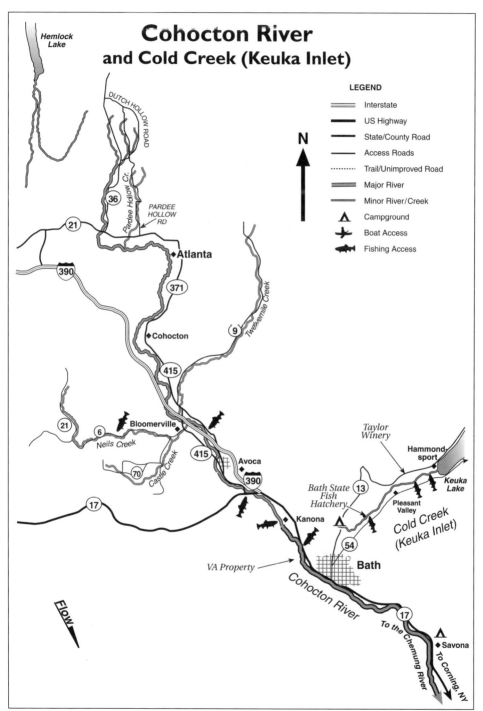

Cohocton River
and Cold Creek (Keuka Inlet)

Hemlock
Lake

DUTCH HOLLOW ROAD

Pardee Hollow Cr.

36

21

PARDEE
HOLLOW
RD

◆Atlanta

390

371

Twelvemile Creek

9

◆Cohocton

415

21

6

Bloomerville◆

Neils Creek

415

70

Castle Creek

Avoca◆

390

Taylor
Winery

Hammond-
sport

Keuka
Lake

Bath State
Fish
Hatchery

13

Pleasant
Valley

Cold Creek
(Keuka Inlet)

17

Kanona

54

VA Property

Bath

Flow

Cohocton River

To the Chemung River

17

To Corning, NY

Savona

LEGEND

Interstate

US Highway

State/County Road

Access Roads

Trail/Unimproved Road

Major River

Minor River/Creek

▲ Campground

✈ Boat Access

🐟 Fishing Access

N

COHOCTON RIVER

The Cohocton rises near the village of Atlanta, flows through swampland, then emerges to run about 30 miles until it drains into the Chemung River. This rich water offers good food to native brookies and a mix of stocked and wild browns. (Usually written as "Cohocton," the river's proper spelling is actually "Conhocton," an Native American word meaning "log in the water." With due apologies to purists, the corrupted spelling will be used here to make identification easier for anglers.) The primary trout water of the Cohocton runs from the village of Cohocton to the town of Bath. Occasional trout are also taken all the way to the river's junction with the Chemung.

The Cohocton's water has a high mineral content and this provides a rich abundance of insect life to the fish. In fact, the banquet allows much feeding to be done on nymphs and local anglers say that rising fish can be a bit hard to find on the stream. Still, dry fly fishing does work. There are some good small black stoneflies, followed by heavy hatches of Hendricksons, March Browns, Gray Fox, Blue Winged Olives and good summer and fall Tricos. Caddis hatch prolifically at times, enough that Milt Nehrke, who runs a shop and teaches flyfishing in the area, considers an Elk Hair Caddis the ideal searching fly for this water. For subsurface fishing, a Hare's Ear is his first choice.

In addition to the insects, DEC biologist Brad Hammers notes that the river hosts dace (both black and long nosed), sculpins, common shiners and white suckers. Basic imitations of these should take fish, though it is the wider portions of the stream—from Avoca on down—that are most conducive to throwing and retrieving streamers. A five-weight is all you will need on the stream, and many anglers drop down to a four or even a three-weight. Though fish average 10-12 inches, each year 4- to 5-pound fish are taken here, especially by those willing to fish at night with big, bulky flies.

The Cohocton receives substantial stocking along most of its length, and the river has some good spots for stocked fish to hold over. There is also natural reproduction here—including at the two special regulations sections, which are known to hold wild fish up to about 14 inches. The naturally reproducing browns are believed to reproduce in the various tributaries, including Neils Creek (and its tributary Castle Creek) which joins at the upper end of the first special regulations section at Avoca, and Twelvemile Creek a bit farther upstream. There are also some wild brook trout in the uppermost section of the stream, above the village of Atlanta, and again where some springs enter around the village of Cohocton.

The river and some of its feeders have suffered from bank erosion and the Conhocton Chapter of TU (which understandably insists on the stream's proper spelling), along with other local organizations, have done extensive restoration work to limit the problem. The stream can still get muddy and silty after rain and typically stays that way for several days.

Fishing is open all year, but the river will freeze over in the winter. The two special regulations sections, limited to three fish of 12 inches or more per day, are upstream near Avoca and downstream near the Veterans Administration property outside Bath. The upper section runs about 2.5 miles from the northern boundary of the village of Avoca upstream to the mouth of Neils Creek, the lower one about two miles from the upstream boundary of the Veterans Administration Center property up to Route 415. The Conhocton TU chapter and others are trying to get the upper section made entirely catch and release, so keep an eye on future regulations. All other parts of the stream have the standard five fish limit.

Neils Creek

This tributary to the Cohocton runs about five miles from its headwaters to the river. Insect life is similar to the Cohocton, but the stream is smaller so a shorter rod, say 7 or 8 feet, will be helpful. There is good reproduction in Neils and, as noted, some of the wild fish on the Cohocton spawn here. Access is available along Route 6. The normal trout season of April 1 to October 15 applies to Neils Creek, as does the standard five fish limit. However, catch and release is strongly encouraged as this is a good nursery for wild fish.

Neils Creek is a tributary to the Cohocton that is also worth fishing.

Stream Facts: Cohocton River

Season
- Open all year.

Special Regulations
- Two special regulations sections, catch and release and artificials only: first from Neils Creek downstream to north border of village of Avoca, second from Route 415 downstream to north boundary of Veterans Administration property.

Fish
- Mostly brown trout, some brookies in upper reaches.

River Characteristics
- Small meandering stream near headwaters, medium-sized in main trout sections.

River Flows
- High in spring, subject to low water in summer. Takes time to clear after rains.

Cohocton River—Major Hatches

INSECT	J	F	M	A	M	J	J	A	S	O	N	D	FLIES
Black\Brown\Yellow Stone 14-18				▬									Soft Hackle Wet, Stonefly Nymphs
Blue Winged Olives 16-22				▬▬▬▬▬▬▬▬▬▬									Parachute, Emergers, Spinners
Blue Quill 18				▬									Blue Quill Dry, Pheasant Tail Nymph
Lt. And Dark Hendrickson 12-14				▬									Light and Dark Hendrickson Parachute, Emergers, Spinners
Gray Fox 12					▬▬								Comparadun, Extended-Body Dry Flies,
March Brown 12					▬▬								Comparadun, Extended-Body Dry Flies, Rusty Spinner
Caddis Gray, Brown, Tan 12-18				▬▬▬▬▬▬									Elk Hair Caddis, Lafontaine Deep Pupa and Emergent Sparkle Pupa, Soft-Hackle Wets, Bead-Head Nymphs
Sulphurs 14-18					▬▬▬▬								Comparadun, Parachute, CDC Emerger, Compara-Emerger, Pheasant Tail Nymph, Hare's Ear Nymph
Slate Drake (Isonychia) 14						▬▬		▬▬					Comparadun, Leadwing Coachman, Zug Bug
Trico 22-26							▬▬▬▬						Trico Spinner, Griffith's Gnat
Streamers	▬▬▬▬▬▬▬▬▬▬▬▬▬▬▬▬▬▬▬▬▬▬▬▬												Bucktail Patterns, Muddler Minnow

CAYUTA CREEK (SHEPHARD'S CREEK)

Like the Cohocton, Cayuta Creek is near the Finger Lakes but not connected to any of them. Running about 30 miles from its source at small Cayuta Lake to the Pennsylvania border, Cayuta, sometimes called Shephard's Creek, offers good hatches and some nice holding water. These combine to provide flyfishing for stocked and holdover browns with some wild fish mixed in.

Trout fishing on Cayuta begins near its source at Cayuta Lake in Schuyler County, where there is access from Oak Hill Road and Route 224. Cayuta is a warmwater lake, so the water actually cools, and the fishing gets better, a bit downstream near the village of Alpine Junction. There is access in Alpine Junction and again near Varney Hill Road.

A substantial number of browns are stocked along the entire length of Cayuta as it runs through Schuyler, Chemung and Tioga counties. About 13,500 browns are put in, including about 2,300 two-year-olds. In the best sections of Cayuta, local fishing and conservation groups have teamed up with the DEC to float stock, spreading the fish out and assuring that more of them make it well past opening day.

Perhaps the most productive section of Cayuta is the roughly four-mile stretch from the village of Swartwood to the village of Van Etten. Beginning below Swartwood and running about two miles in all, is a special regulation section limited to three fish of 12 inches or better. (There has been discussion of extending the special regulation section upstream.) Like the entire creek, this section is open to fishing year round. The largest fish in Cayuta are often found in the deep holes in this section, which provide refuge through the summer. The last half-mile or so of the special regs section, through farmland known as Mormon Valley, is particularly good. (Wyncoop Creek, which marks the beginning of the special regulation section, is also fishable and receives a small stocking of about 300 browns each year.)

Insect life on Cayuta is plentiful, with particularly good hatches of caddis and Blue Winged Olives. An Elk Hair Caddis is a good searching dry fly here, while a beadhead Hare's Ear will work well in the deep holes and undercut banks. Don't ignore the post-hatch phase of local mayflies. Jake Trimmer, of the Chemung Federation of Sportsmen, took an 18-inch Cayuta brown on a rusty spinner. Cayuta has a great deal of overhanging foliage that can make casting tricky but also makes summertime terrestrials useful. The water does slow down and warm in summer. It is still fishable, but plan to look for deep holes or tributary mouths, and avoid fishing when the water reaches 70 degrees.

Except for the special regulations section, Cayuta anglers can keep five fish per day of any size. The entire stream is open all year.

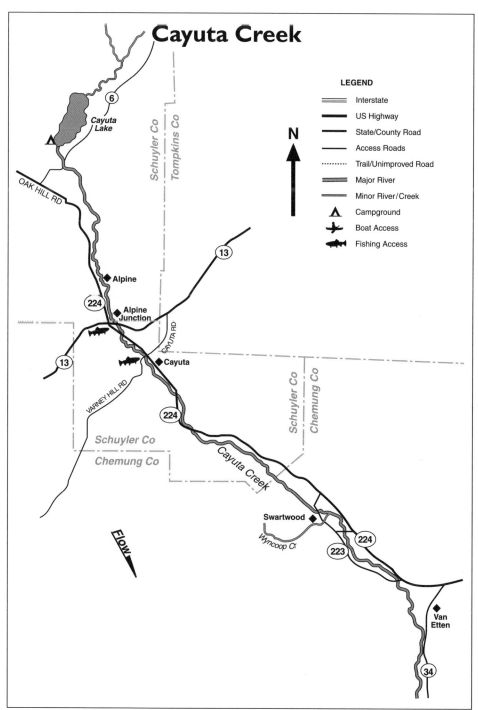

Cayuta Creek

LEGEND

≡≡≡	Interstate
▬▬▬	US Highway
━━━	State/County Road
───	Access Roads
·······	Trail/Unimproved Road
▬▬▬	Major River
━━━	Minor River/Creek
⛰	Campground
✈	Boat Access
🐟	Fishing Access

N

Cayuta Lake

Schuyler Co

Tompkins Co

OAK HILL RD

6

13

Alpine

224

Alpine Junction

CAYUTA RD

13

Cayuta

VARNEY HILL RD

224

Schuyler Co

Chemung Co

Schuyler Co

Chemung Co

Cayuta Creek

Flow

Swartwood

Wyncoop Cr

223

224

Van Etten

34

Stream Facts: Cayuta Creek

Seasons
- Open all year.

Special Regulations
- Roughly two mile section from Wyncoop Creek Road to Route 223 in Chemung County town of Van Etten, artificials only, three fish per day of 12 inches or more.

Fish
- Stocked browns, good holdover, some wild fish.

River Characteristics
- Small to medium-sized, mostly slower moving meadow stream in prime stretches.

River Flows
- Best in fall and late spring, can be high and dirty during early spring thaw.

Trees along Cayuta Creek may be bare in late winter, but the fishing is open all year.

Cayuta River—Major Hatches

INSECT	J	F	M	A	M	J	J	A	S	O	N	D	FLIES
Lt. And Dark Hendrickson 12-14				▮	▮								Light and Dark Hendrickson Parachute, Emergers, Spinners
Blue Winged Olives 16-22				▮	▮	▮	▮	▮	▮				Parachute, Emergers, Spinners
Caddis Gray, Brown, Tan 12-18					▮	▮	▮	▮					Elk Hair Caddis, Lafontaine Deep Pupa and Emergent Sparkle Pupa, Soft Hackle Wets, Bead-Head
Trico 22-26							▮	▮	▮				Trico Spinner, Griffith's Gnat
Terrestrials	▮	▮	▮	▮	▮	▮	▮	▮	▮	▮	▮	▮	Foam and dubbed ants, beetles, hoppers

Newtown Creek

Newtown Creek, a small flow that runs near Elmira and flows into the Chemung River a few miles west of Cayuta Creek, offers fishing for brown trout. About 400 browns are stocked each year in the vicinity of Horseheads, north of Elmira. In addition, there is some natural reproduction of browns here. Access is available where Mill Street crosses the stream and at other road crossings.

Mill Street Pond

Anglers looking to teach youngsters to flyfish for trout should seek out Mill Street Pond in Horseheads (east of Newtown Creek). This small, spring-fed pond on Mill Street is restricted to children 14 or under, seniors and those with physical disabilities. The pond is stocked with rainbows that grow nicely by feeding on insects in the cool water.

Canaseraga Creek

Though not on par with Cohocton or Cayuta, this stream and its tributaries all located west of the Cohocton— offer decent fishing in the vicinity of Dansville. The Canaseraga receives about 3,000 browns per year, including some two-year-old fish, and there are a few wild fish in its headwaters. No special regulations apply.

Mill Creek

Mill Creek, which is close to the headwaters of the Cohocton, joins the Stony Brook near Perkinsville, and its waters ultimately flow into Canaseraga Creek. The stream is not stocked, but it supports a good population of small wild brown trout. Access can be found right in Perkinsville and again upstream where Quarz Road/Route 90 crosses. Mill Creek is open to fishing all year.

Sugar Creek

This creek joins the Canaseraga near Dansville and supports some wild fish, in addition to receiving a small stocking of browns, with normal season and regulations.

Flint Creek

Flowing along Italy Valley, Flint Creek runs nearly 25 miles from its source in southern Yates County to the village of Phelps where it empties into the Canandaigua Outlet. It is the first eight miles from its headwaters to a swampy section near the village of Middlesex, however, that is of interest to trout anglers.

The water is not stocked but hosts a self-sustaining population of mostly small rainbows. The stream is about 15 feet wide, and never very deep—hip boots are usually enough for waders. Access can be had along Route 18, which parallels the creek. No special regulations apply.

Newtown Creek

Newtown Creek, a small flow that runs near Elmira and flows into the Chemung River a few miles west of Cayuta Creek, offers fishing for brown trout. About 400 browns are stocked each year in the vicinity of Horseheads, north of Elmira. In addition, there is some natural reproduction of browns here. Access is available where Mill Street crosses the stream and at other road crossings.

Mill Street Pond

Anglers looking to teach youngsters to flyfish for trout should seek out Mill Street Pond in Horseheads (east of Newtown Creek). This small, spring-fed pond on Mill Street is restricted to children 14 or under, seniors and those with physical disabilities. The pond is stocked with rainbows that grow nicely by feeding on insects in the cool water.

Canaseraga Creek

Though not on par with Cohocton or Cayuta, this stream and its tributaries— all located west of the Cohocton— offer decent fishing in the vicinity of Dansville. The Canaseraga receives about 3,000 browns per year, including some two-year-old fish, and there are a few wild fish in its headwaters. No special regulations apply.

Mill Creek

Mill Creek, which is close to the headwaters of the Cohocton, joins the Stony Brook near Perkinsville, and its waters ultimately flow into Canaseraga Creek. The stream is not stocked, but it supports a good population of small wild brown trout. Access can be found right in Perkinsville and again upstream where Quarz Road/Route 90 crosses. Mill Creek is open to fishing all year.

Sugar Creek

This creek joins the Canaseraga near Dansville and supports some wild fish, in addition to receiving a small stocking of browns, with normal season and regulations.

Flint Creek

Flowing along Italy Valley, Flint Creek runs nearly 25 miles from its source in southern Yates County to the village of Phelps where it empties into the Canandaigua Outlet. It is the first eight miles from its headwaters to a swampy section near the village of Middlesex, however, that is of interest to trout anglers.

The water is not stocked but hosts a self-sustaining population of mostly small rainbows. The stream is about 15 feet wide, and never very deep—hip boots are usually enough for waders. Access can be had along Route 18, which parallels the creek. No special regulations apply.

Canaseraga Creek

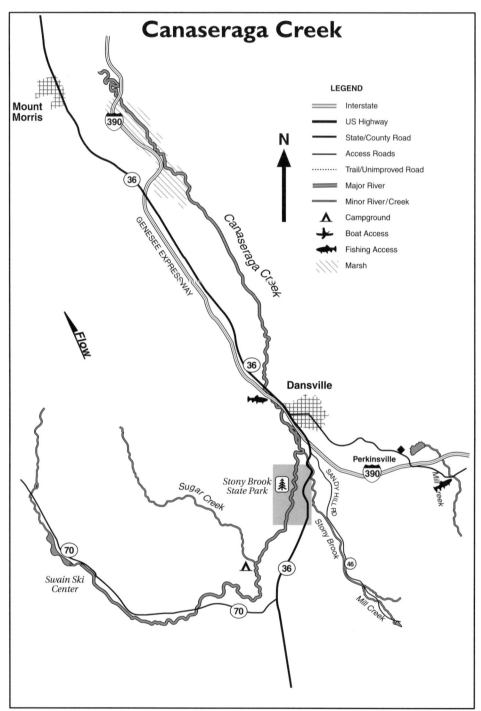

LEGEND

≣	Interstate
▬	US Highway
━	State/County Road
—	Access Roads
····	Trail/Unimproved Road
▬	Major River
═	Minor River/Creek
⚑	Campground
✈	Boat Access
🐟	Fishing Access
⁄⁄⁄	Marsh

Mount Morris

390

36

Genesee Expressway

Canaseraga Creek

Flow

36

Dansville

Perkinsville

390

Mill Creek

Sugar Creek

Stony Brook State Park

Sandy Hill Rd

Stony Brook

70

Swain Ski Center

Λ

36

46

70

Mill Creek

Flint Creek
Naples Creek

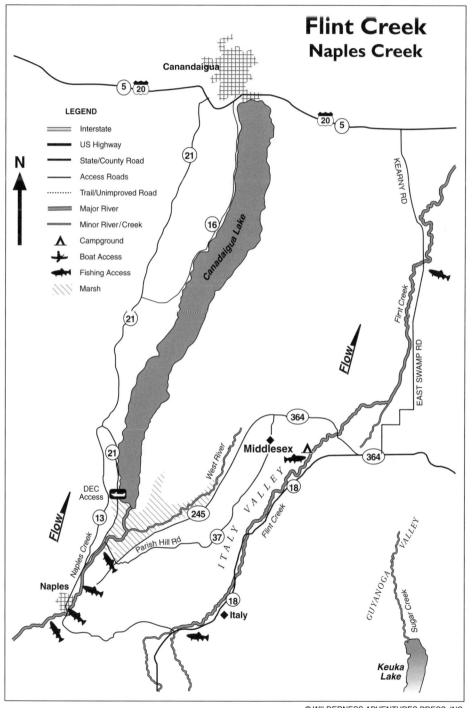

LEGEND

≡≡≡	Interstate
▬▬▬	US Highway
▬▬▬	State/County Road
────	Access Roads
········	Trail/Unimproved Road
▬▬▬	Major River
≡≡≡	Minor River/Creek
⛺	Campground
✈	Boat Access
🐟	Fishing Access
///	Marsh

Canandaigua

Canandaigua Lake

Kearny Rd

Flint Creek

East Swamp Rd

Flow

364

Middlesex

West River

DEC Access

245

13

37

Parish Hill Rd

ITALY VALLEY

Flint Creek

Flow

Naples Creek

Naples

18

Italy

GUYANOGA VALLEY

Sugar Creek

Keuka Lake

N

© WILDERNESS ADVENTURES PRESS, INC.

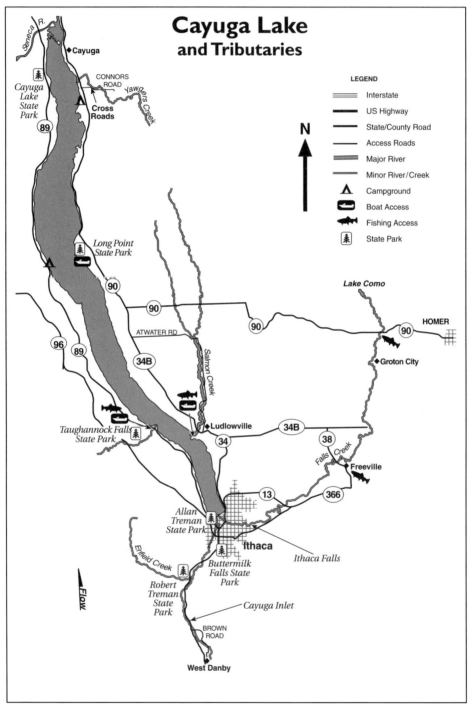

Cayuga Lake
and Tributaries

LEGEND

≡≡≡	Interstate
▬▬	US Highway
▬	State/County Road
—	Access Roads
▬	Major River
▬	Minor River/Creek
Δ	Campground
🛥	Boat Access
🐟	Fishing Access
🌲	State Park

N

Seneca R.

◆Cayuga

🌲 Cayuga Lake State Park

CONNORS ROAD

Yawgers Creek

Δ Cross Roads

89

Long Point State Park Δ 🛥

Lake Como

90

90

90

HOMER

ATWATER RD

🐟

96   89

34B

Salmon Creek

◆Groton City

🛥

Taughannock Falls State Park 🌲

🛥

◆Ludlowville   34B   38

🐟

34

Falls Creek

◆Freeville

🐟

13   366

Allan Treman State Park 🌲

Enfield Creek

🌲 Ithaca

Ithaca Falls

Flow

🌲 Buttermilk Falls State Park

Robert Treman State Park

Cayuga Inlet

BROWN ROAD

West Danby

© WILDERNESS ADVENTURES PRESS, INC.

THE FINGER LAKES

The 11 Finger Lakes contain a wide variety of fish. Rainbow trout, browns, and lakers swim in most of the lakes, and about half have landlocked salmon as well. There are also plenty of warmwater fish like smallmouth bass and pike and some tiger muskellunge.

As with any big stillwaters, the presence of gamefish and the opportunity to catch them on a fly rod are two different things. The Finger Lakes are relatively narrow but still wide enough to make shore casting a low percentage technique. Get out on the lake in a boat or float tube and the problem becomes depth—the water is well over 100 feet deep in a number of these lakes and several times that deep in Seneca and Cayuga. As might be expected, it is trolling and deep spin fishing that are the methods of choice in these waters.

Still, a fly rod is not useless on the Finger Lakes. First, the mouths of the feeders can offer fishing for trout and landlocked salmon heading upstream to spawn and for fish chasing baitfish, typically smelt. This can be done from shore or from a boat or float tube. Beyond the stream mouths, the lakes can be fished by casting and by trolling.

One recent problem for the lakes is the decline in the smelt population. Though not conclusively established, the drop is widely suspected to be the fault of zebra mussels. Whatever the cause, the decline has so far caused a noticeable drop in the numbers and size of lake trout in the Finger Lakes. While browns, rainbows and landlockeds seem better able to adapt, the smelt decline and zebra mussel infestation may take a toll on them as well.

A few determined anglers do flyfish from shore on the Finger Lakes. This generally involves casting streamer patterns for landlockeds and browns, though lakers are also sometimes caught this way. It is a lot like saltwater flyfishing—as much a matter of finding fish close to shore as of technique or fly selection. A few of the lakes have particular fishing opportunities worth noting.

Cayuga Lake and Seneca Lake

These two large lakes can be flyfished for landlockeds, browns and lakers. John Gaulke, who lives between the two and fishes both, says he takes more landlockeds on Cayuga and more browns and lakers on Seneca. The best fishing is from late fall through early spring, generally peaking in late March and early April. After that, most of the resident fish go deep—out of the reach of fly gear.

Gaulke recommends casting from points of land on the lakes—including Taughannock Point and Myers Point on Cayuga and Plum Point, Glenora and Lodi Point on Seneca. In winter, the lakes are usually drawn down about 5 feet, which makes walking and casting along the shoreline much easier.

Naturally, casting can also be done from a boat, provided the weather cooperates. Boat access on Seneca can be found at Geneva on the north end, Watkins Glen at the south, and Dresden and Clark Point along the western shore, and Sampson State Park on the eastern shore. For Cayuga, boaters can use Ithaca and Geneva at

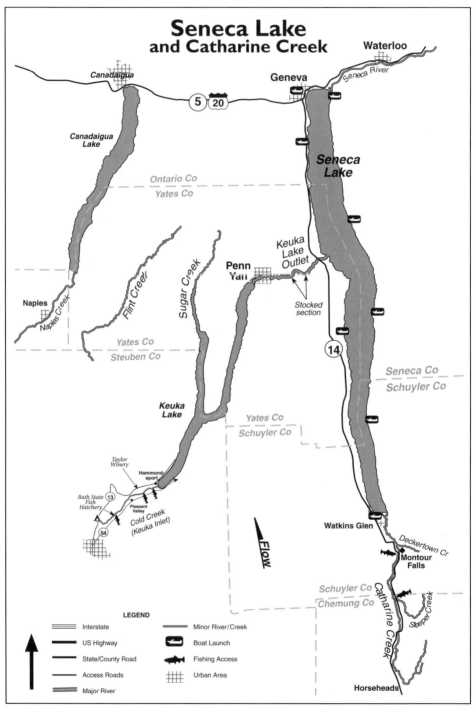

© WILDERNESS ADVENTURES PRESS, INC.

the two ends along with Long Point State Park and Myers Point on the eastern shore and Taughannock Point and Willow Creek Point on the western side.

A fast action 6- or 7-weight rod is in order for flyfishing the Finger Lakes. Floating and intermediate lines will work, but Gaulke often goes to a sinking line that descends about four inches per second. Streamers such as Deceivers and Clousers should imitate resident smelt or alewives, with the latter becoming increasingly important as the smelt have declined. The fish sometimes feed on top and a Gartside Gurgler pattern is a durable and effective fly for rising fish.

Whether from a boat or from shore, fishing for landlocked salmon, brown trout and lakers is open all year on the Finger Lakes. Five fish in combination may be taken, which may include no more than three landlockeds or lakers. Fish must be 15 inches, except for landlockeds on Cayuga, which must be 18 inches.

Skaneateles Lake

Skaneateles ("Skaneeatlas") Lake, on the eastern side of the region, has an excellent hatch of Brown Drakes that bring up big rainbows and landlockeds. And, unusual for one of the Finger Lakes, it also brings out a large number of flyfishers. Beginning around the third week in June and continuing for about two weeks, fly anglers can be found casting to rising fish. The drakes hatch in the evenings, starting about 7:30 p.m. and rising fish can be found anywhere from shallow shoreline areas to water over 40 feet deep. Extended body imitations or long comparaduns in sizes 10 to 12 are the flies recommended by Mike DeTomasso of nearby Royal Coachman Fly Shop.

After the brown drakes are done, a slightly larger creamy yellow drake hatches for another two to three weeks and continues to bring up trout and salmon (lakers, bass and even catfish are also occasionally taken on both hatches). This hatch starts about a half-hour later each evening, leaving only a relatively short time to fish before dark.

Fishing with these big mayfly imitations is done mostly from boats. There is only one public boat launch on Skaneateles, on Route 41A/West Lake Shore Road near the northwest corner of the lake. (Conveniently, the area around the launch often holds rising fish.) Parking is limited, and prohibited on the road, so anglers should arrive well before these popular hatches.

Western Finger Lakes Smallmouth

The seven western Finger Lakes (Conesus, Hemlock, Canadice, Canandaigua, Honeoye, Keuka and Seneca) now have early season fishing for bass on a catch and release basis. The extended season is the six-week period from the first Saturday in May until the third Saturday in June (when normal season opens for black bass).

This catch and release period is ideal for fly anglers seeking smallmouths since the bass tend to go deep by the time the standard season begins. This fishing is best done from a boat, and local anglers suggest targeting structure like docks and rock piles. The fishing is mostly subsurface with Clouser Minnows imitating smelt and alewives, along with crayfish patterns. However, in early season, aggressive smallmouth holding well beneath the surface will sometimes come up to hit poppers.

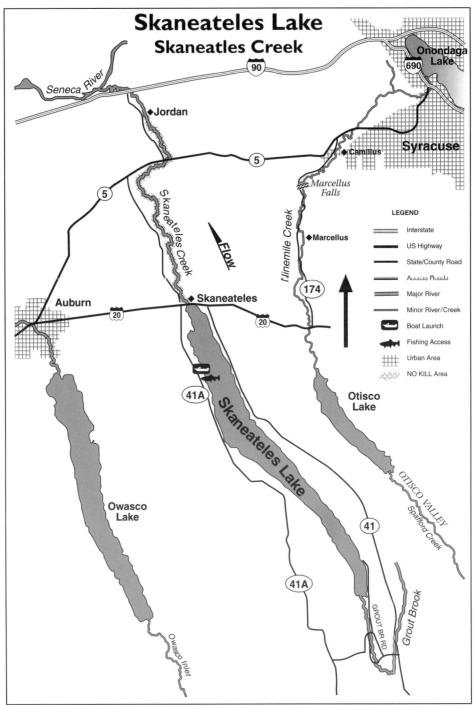

© WILDERNESS ADVENTURES PRESS, INC.

Smallmouth can be fished for during an extended season on Canandaigua and other western Finger Lakes.

Otisco Lake Tiger Muskies

Otisco Lake, primarily a warmwater fishery, is a good place to cast to tiger muskellunge. About 7,500 small hybrids are put in annually and they grow well on the forage here. Fish over 30 pounds have been caught on Otisco, but flyfishers should expect their biggest fish to be about half that size. In summer, the tiger muskies are found around structure, but at the beginning of the season in May they can sometimes be spotted sunning themselves over sandy bottom in shallow water. Alewife imitations are recommended, along with heavy leaders and bite tippets. A 9- or even 10-weight rod is in order to bring the fish up when they dive at the end of their fight.

Trolling

In addition to casting it is possible to take trout and salmon in the Finger Lakes by trolling streamers. Randy Weidman, a doctor who lives near Keuka, trolls the lake from a kayak and reports catching landlockeds, browns and rainbows, along with the occasional lake trout.

Weidman's technique is to place the fly rod—he uses a 9-foot, 6-weight—at right angles to the kayak trailing a streamer pattern on a full sinking line. When a fish takes, the rod tip bends abruptly and he rows hard to keep slack out of the line before taking hold of the rod. For flies, he picks smelt imitations such as the

Winnapasauki Smelt, Nine-Three or Thunder Creek patterns. (He notes, though, that the decline in smelt may make imitations of alewives—another Finger Lakes baitfish—an increasingly useful alternative.)

This technique only works, Weidman has found, when there is enough wind to put a chop on the water—calm days are unproductive. Points and stream mouths are the places to key on, and November to May is the best time as all the salmonids, especially the lakers, go deep in summer.

While Weidman has focused on Keuka near his home, there is no reason the same approach wouldn't work on other area lakes. Hemlock, one of the smaller Finger Lakes on the western side of the region, would offer a particularly pleasurable boating experience since its shoreline remains completely undeveloped (it is part of Rochester's water supply). Hemlock gets modest stockings of browns, landlockeds and lake trout, along with rainbows that reproduce well in the lake.

Trout and salmon, including lakers, may be fished for all year on all the Finger Lakes. On Keuka and Hemlock, all fish must be the standard Finger Lakes minimum of 15 inches, with five fish allowed in any combination, and no more than three landlocked salmon or lakers.

An Unusual Fly Shop

Anglers visiting the new flyfishing shop on West Seneca Street in Ithaca may not realize they are in a unique place. The rods, reels, lines and leaders are all typical, but this is a fly shop managed and staffed by local high school students. And the shop is only one part of The Community Fly Fisher, a not-for-profit program that gets teenagers, including those from low and moderate income backgrounds, interested in flyfishing and the environment.

The Community Fly Fisher was founded in 1989 as part of the SAREP program, a 4-H sponsored sportfishing education program operated throughout New York State. After starting with an apprentice/mentor flyfishing program, CFF began planning an ambitious expansion in the mid-1990s, to include a permanent home with an environmental education center and shop. A HUD grant—part of a waterfront redevelopment in Ithaca—was received in 1996 and that year CFF joined forces with the Cornell Cooperative Extension.

The fly shop, located at the confluence of Sixmile Creek and Cayuga Inlet, will offer a full array of gear and flies—including some imitations tied by local teens participating in CFF. The store will also offer flyfishing lessons and referrals to local guides. Both paid and volunteer youth will work in the store, but their role goes well beyond that. According to CFF program manager Shahab Farzanegan, they have also been involved in business planning, design, and construction of the store and staffing decisions. Proceeds from the store will be put back into CFF and its apprenticeship and environmental programs; the goal is to help make the CFF self-sufficient.

The CFF Shop is located at 1015 West Seneca Street in Ithaca. Anyone interested in the store or other CFF programs can call 607-697-0053, or visit their Web site at www.cce.cornell.edu/tompkins/environment/community-fly-fisher.

Finger Lakes Tributaries

The Finger Lakes tributaries offer excellent flyfishing for trout and salmon. The spawning rainbow trout that ascend in spring are the prime targets of this feeder stream fishing, but migrating browns and landlockeds in fall are also caught on flies. The main tributaries enter at the southern ends of the lakes, although some feeders also come in farther up the shorelines.

Rainbows

The spawning rainbows, sometimes referred to as steelhead, come up the main feeders in late winter or spring, depending on weather and snow melt. Mid-March to the end of April is the prime time, and it is important to remember that general Finger Lakes tributary regulations bar fishing before April 1.

The males come into the stream first and stay later than the egg-bearing females. Not all these streams support natural reproduction of rainbows; the best are Catharine Creek (Seneca Lake), Naples Creek (Canandaigua Lake), Cold Brook (Keuka Lake), Cayuga Inlet (Cayuga Lake) and Springwater Creek (Hemlock Lake). Where spawning does occur, it may take place as much or more in smaller tributaries to the main stream. The newborn rainbows will remain in the stream for at least a year before dropping back to the lake. Unlike Pacific salmon, the parents can spawn more than once and will also return to the main lake.

The primary fishing method for spawning rainbows is spin fishing, or a hybrid rig—a fly rod and reel loaded entirely with monofilament line. However, short-line nymphing with a fly rod is an effective way to target the spawners. Exact gear will vary somewhat based on the size of stream, but figure a 6- to 8-weight rod up to 9 feet long with a 9- to 11-foot leader. Flies are all the obvious staples: individual egg and egg cluster patterns (real egg sacks are the first choice of bait fishermen), along with nymphs and Woolly Buggers.

Browns and Landlocked Salmon

Most of the Finger Lakes contain brown trout, and six of them (Skaneateles, Cayuga, Seneca, Owasco, Keuka and Hemlock) are stocked with landlocked salmon as well. Both species move up the streams in fall, anywhere from October to December (remember that the season ends on December 31). The runs of both fish are generally sparser than the best rainbow migrations, and the fishing is correspondingly difficult. On the other hand, because the fishing is slower, and because it competes with hunting in the fall, anglers are likely to have more room to themselves.

Finger Lakes Tributary Regulations

Like the Great Lakes and Champlain tributaries, the tributaries to the Finger Lakes are subject to special regulations. The rules for these tributaries apply up to the first impassable barrier and cover brown and rainbow trout, landlocked salmon and lake trout. Fishing is permitted April 1 to December 31. On most of the streams, all fishing is prohibited outside of this season, and fishing is permitted during daylight hours only from opening day to May 15, and between October 1 and the end of the season. Three fish in any combination may be taken, with all fish at least 15 inches, except that trout may be nine inches in tributaries to Owasco, Skaneateles and Otisco, and landlockeds must be 18 inches from Cayuga tributaries.

CATHARINE CREEK

Seneca Lake has an excellent, self-sustaining population of rainbows. As a result, its main tributary Catharine Creek gets very good runs of wild spawning rainbows in spring, as well as some landlockeds and browns in the fall. The rainbow runs in particular can be fished over a long stretch of the stream, and on several good feeders.

Catharine runs from its swampy headwaters near Horseheads to Seneca Lake in the town of Watkins Glen. Ten or more miles of the creek are fishable for the spring run of rainbows, which are known to go all the way into the swamp. Access is plentiful from Route 14, which parallels the stream for most of its run.

All the rainbows here are naturally reproducing, descended from fish brought from California's American River more than 50 years ago. Though the spawners are not steelhead, they do take on a silvery color when fresh from the lake, becoming darker over time.

Depending on runoff and water temperatures, the run can begin as early as mid-March, but fishing opens on April 1. Unless you enjoy crowds, the first day of

Anglers looking for spawning rainbows on Catharine Creek.

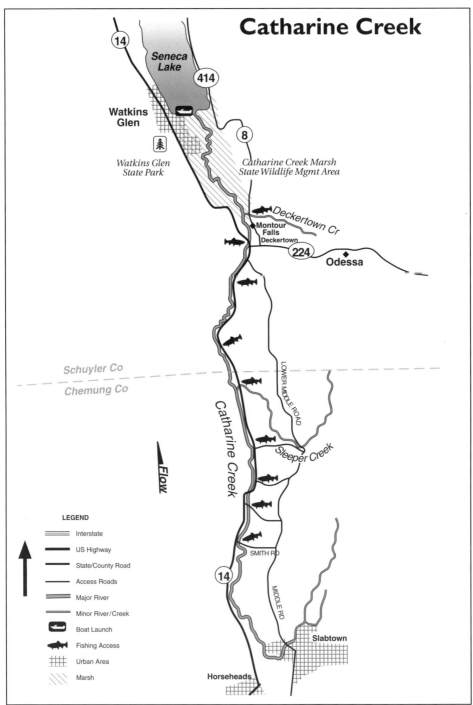

Catharine Creek

14

Seneca
Lake

414

Watkins
Glen

8

Watkins Glen
State Park

Catharine Creek Marsh
State Wildlife Mgmt Area

Deckertown Cr

Montour
Falls
Deckertown

224

Odessa

Schuyler Co

Chemung Co

LOWER MIDDLE ROAD

Catharine Creek

Sleeper Creek

Flow

LEGEND

Interstate

US Highway

State/County Road

Access Roads

Major River

Minor River/Creek

Boat Launch

Fishing Access

Urban Area

Marsh

SMITH RD

14

MIDDLE RD

Slabtown

Horseheads

April is a good day to avoid Catharine Creek. In fact, despite its length, Catharine suffers from overcrowding during much of the rainbow run. Any warm spring day will find multiple cars at every pulloff and bridge crossing. The best strategy for finding a bit more room is to wade up and downstream from access points and to check feeder creeks. Among the best feeders is Sleeper Creek, which joins Catharine about a mile south of the Schuyler/Chemung county line, and Deckertown Creek, which enters near the village of Mountour Falls.

On the main creek and its feeders, the rainbow run can continue to about the third week of April. At the run's peak, the stream will be filled with fish. The spawners can run up to 10 pounds, though 3 to 4 pounds is more common, and locals say the fish have gotten smaller over the last 30 years.

Catharine Creek is mostly hit by spin fisherman, but the creek's narrow flow makes it ideal for short-line, dead-drift nymphing. A 9-foot, 7-weight rod is a good choice, but lighter or heavier lines will also work. Generally you will be fishing only with the leader, so plan to make it in the 9- to 12-foot range, around 3X or 4X.

Fly choices include single eggs in the usual cheese, pink and chartreuse and egg clusters in the same hues. The rainbows will also take a San Juan Worm. There is a spawning run of large suckers from the lake that arrives just behind the rainbows, and catching suckers instead of rainbows can be infuriating. Oddly, the Sucker Spawn pattern—so popular on Ontario and Erie tributaries—has not caught on here yet. It is certainly worth trying. Whatever the pattern, be prepared to drift it repeatedly through the same spots. Like all spawning fish, rainbows can take dozens of looks before hitting a fly.

The water of Catharine can run very clear, sometimes allowing anglers to sight fish. But according to Don Walker, an avid angler who lives nearby, fishing improves when the water is slightly off color. In either case, the water is rarely more than four feet deep, and you will often be fishing from shore so hip boots are enough. Because of its gravel bottom the bed of Catharine Creek shifts often, so good spots one season may not be productive a year later.

Catharine Creek suffered badly from 1996 flooding and subsequent cleanup work, losing sections of its canopy of trees and many of its natural pools. The former will take time to grow back, but along with bank restoration, 13 "digger dams" are being created on Catharine Creek and a few of its tributaries by state and county officials (with the help and encouragement of local conservation groups). These wooden miniature dams create pools in which spawning rainbows rest while ascending the stream. During the run, you may catch the amazing sight of rainbows leaping one of these dams. Equally important, the dams provide habitat for newborn rainbows so they can stay for two years and grow to healthy size before returning to the lake. (If they drop back too soon, they are quickly eaten.)

Rainbow fishing does not have to end with the spawning run. Though there is not a true resident population of trout in Catharine Creek, the young rainbows, 4-10 inches and occasionally bigger, will be in the stream all spring. The fish will take dries, but these are swallowed so aggressively they become hard to remove; try a small yellow soft hackle instead. Crimped barbs and catch and release are strongly recommended to allow these wild fish to make it back to the lake.

Landlockeds and Browns

Though not as strong as the rainbow run, there are spawning runs of both landlockeds and browns in Catharine Creek. November and December are the right months, and locals report that the week between Christmas and New Year's is a good time (remember that all Finger Lakes tributaries close at year's end). As with rainbows, egg patterns, single or cluster, along with some stonefly nymphs and pulsating patterns like Zonkers or Woolly Buggers, should work. One major difference from the rainbow run is that the fall spawners don't go very far upstream. Generally, figure on fishing no more than the last two miles above the marshy mouth of the creek.

Stream Facts: Catharine Creek

Seasons

- Finger Lakes tributary regulations apply to the first impassable barrier—April 1 to December 31, with fishing limited to daylight hours until May 15.

Regulations

- Three fish in any combination, 15 inches or more.

Fish

- Spawning and young rainbows in spring, sparser spawning landlocked salmon and browns in late fall.

River

- Characteristics: Narrow and relatively shallow with rocky and gravel bottom.

River Flows

- Generally steady and clear during spawning season—easier to fish when slightly cloudy.

Sleeper Creek is one of several good tributaries to Catharine Creek.

CAYUGA LAKE TRIBUTARIES

Cayuga Lake (see Cayuga Lake map) has good populations of brown and rainbow trout and landlocked salmon—stocked fish supplemented by natural reproduction—all of which run into the lake's tributaries. The three main tributaries, in descending order of length, are Cayuga Inlet, Salmon Creek and Fall Creek. All three get runs of spawning rainbows and feeding landlockeds in spring, as well as fall spawning runs of landlockeds and, to a lesser extent, spawning browns.

Anglers in the area gravitate to the best fishing, so all the streams receive considerable pressure. Typical gear is a 9-foot rod with 6- or 7-weight line. Flies are the standards: for spring spawning rainbows, egg or egg sack imitations, Woolly Buggers and stoneflies. The same will work for fall spawning browns. For spring landlockeds the obvious choice remains smelt imitations—since that is what they are eating. Remember that the spring landlockeds do not head as far upstream as spawning rainbows. For landlockeds in fall, eggs, Buggers and stoneflies will work. Classic salmon flies add a nice touch of tradition—and are effective. Locals say that green or chartreuse flies out-produce others during the fall landlocked run. At least one area angler uses only a Green Highlander for spawning salmon.

There is also an unusual run of spawning smallmouth bass from the lake. Though not easy to catch, these fish sometimes approach two feet in length. Their timing is poor, at least for anglers: the run often peaks before the smallmouth season begins. Still it is worth checking out the streams for this run during the first week of the season, which begins on the third Saturday in June. Woolly Buggers, stoneflies and Clousers are all useful if the fish are there, and local angler Phil Koons has had success with the Murray's Mad Tom streamer pattern originally devised for the Shenandoah River in Virginia.

Cayuga Inlet

With no natural barriers, Cayuga Inlet is by far the longest of the three major Cayuga tributaries. The stream can be fished for nearly 10 miles from the lake upstream to the small village of West Danby. Fish do run all the way up and the upper end sometimes has 20-inch rainbows taken from water no more than six feet wide. Despite its length, there is good access on most of the stream, including five dedicated angler access sites. The Cayuga can be tricky to fish in places due to brushy banks and deadfalls and the long run makes it essential to be where fish are.

The mouth of the inlet is a flood control channel. At the top of the channel, a couple of miles upstream, there is a collection point—sometimes referred to as the fish ladder. Here the DEC harvests fish eggs, but the migratory fish have no difficulty heading upstream. The inlet is by far the main nursery for those wild fish in Cayuga that supplement the stocking—by some estimates 90 percent of the wild rainbows in the lake come from the inlet. (This is also the only Cayuga tributary that receives landlocked stocking directly in the stream; the others depend on lake-stocked fish for their runs.)

Enfield Creek, which enters Cayuga Inlet about four miles up from the lake, is also a spawning stream and can be fished within Treman State Park. Cayuga itself can be fished from Buttermilk State Park and along Route 34 and Brown Road, both of which offer dedicated access.

Salmon Creek

Unlike the other two main tributaries, Salmon Creek (see map page 394) enters Cayuga Lake not at Ithaca but about five miles up the eastern shore. The migratory section of the stream runs about two miles from the lake to the falls in the village of Ludlowville. Access is available for all this length along easily remembered Salmon Creek Road.

Above the Ludlowville Falls, Salmon Creek has some stocked and resident brown trout. The stream is frequently slowed by beaver dams, but these temporary impoundments do make good places to fish for browns.

Fall Creek

This very short stream runs right through downtown Ithaca where it joins the lake just east of Cayuga Inlet. It gets good runs of fish, which are necessarily concentrated in its roughly one mile length from Ithaca Falls. The entire run has public access—flowing through a park and schoolyard among other settings. This level of access and its size make it heavily pressured.

In addition to the migratory fish, Fall Creek holds some brook trout near its source at Lake Como. Most of these are stocked fish put in at the town of Summer Hill and can be found primarily between the lake and the Route 90 crossing. Below Route 90 there are still some brookies, and anglers may also hit a few wild rainbows. Downstream, in the town of Groton in Tompkins County, the creek also receives a stocking of small brown trout. A roughly five-mile section here, from the Route 38 Bridge in the village of Freeville upstream to the bridge at the village of Groton City, is open to fishing all year. The remainder of the upper portion of Fall Creek is governed by the standard trout season.

Taughannock Creek

Though not as well known as the big three, this Cayuga tributary does get runs of fish at its lower end in Taughannock Falls State Park on the lake's western shore. The fish can run about 1.5 miles up to the dramatic falls (which has a longer drop than Niagara). The outlet of the stream on the lake is known as a good place for rainbows and browns in mid-winter. It can be fished from shore, but a sink tip line is usually necessary as the lake quickly gets deep.

Yawgers Creek

This small tributary enters Cayuga on its eastern shore about five miles from the lake's northern tip. It can get some runs of fish in spring and again in fall if there is enough water. Yawgers can be reached from Connors Road near the small village of Cross Roads.

The spring rainbow run brings many anglers to Naples Creek, the inlet to Canadaigua Lake.

OTHER FINGER LAKES TRIBUTARIES

Owasco Inlet

This inlet, along with several of its tributaries, offers good fishing for spawning rainbows in spring. Landlocked salmon are not stocked in large numbers in the stream and there is not much of a salmon run here; however, there are some large spawning brown trout from the lake that will hit streamers in fall.

With no artificial barriers, Owasco has about 12 miles of fishable water, though it is mostly the rainbows that travel far upstream. For these spring spawners, look for fish upstream between Groton and Locke. In fall, the browns are generally found closer to the mouth in Moravia. The entire length of Owasco Inlet has good access and can be reached along Route 38 and from side streets.

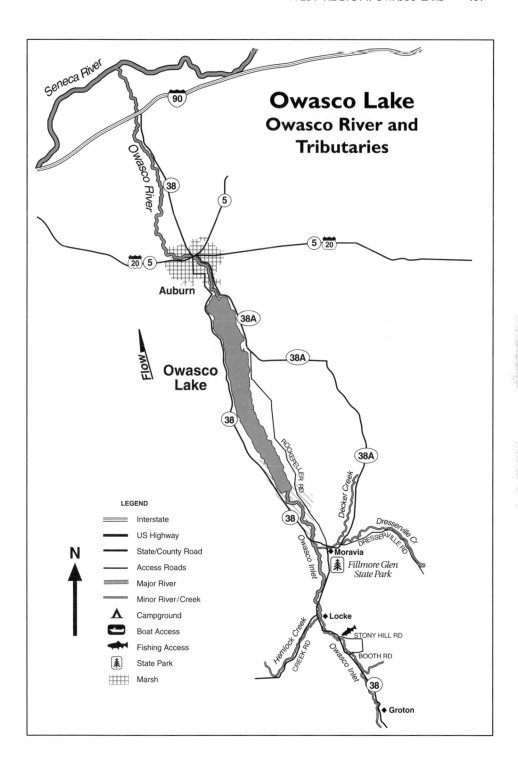

Owasco Lake
Owasco River and
Tributaries

Seneca River

Owasco River

90

38

5

5 20

20 5

Auburn

38A

Flow

Owasco Lake

38A

38

Rockefeller Rd

Decker Creek

38A

LEGEND

Interstate
US Highway
State/County Road
Access Roads
Major River
Minor River/Creek
Campground
Boat Access
Fishing Access
State Park
Marsh

N

38

Dresserville Cr

Dresserville Rd

Moravia

Fillmore Glen
State Park

Owasco Inlet

Locke

Stony Hill Rd

Hemlock Creek

Creek Rd

Owasco Inlet

Booth Rd

38

Groton

Hemlock Creek and Dresserville Creek

These two feeders to the Owasco Inlet are the primary nurseries for the inlet's spawning rainbows and both offer good fishing. They are also good streams to hit when the inlet is running high and off-color, as it sometimes does in spring.

Hemlock enters the inlet at Locke and runs parallel to Creek Road. Dresserville Creek (sometimes referred to as Peg Mill Creek) runs into Owasco Inlet at Groton and runs beside Dresserville Road. It can be fished for about one mile up to the falls near where Route 38A crosses. Just below this barrier, Decker Creek enters Dresserville Creek, and this tributary also gets a run of fish.

Grout Brook

Grout Brook, the primary tributary to Skaneateles Lake, gets a pretty good run of spawning rainbow trout and some fall landlocked salmon. Its very small size makes it difficult to flyfish. Those willing to try can look for access along Grout Brook Road.

Naples Creek

Naples, the main tributary to Canandaigua Lake, offers good fishing for wild spawning rainbows in spring and gets among the best runs of spawning landlocked salmon in fall. Like Catharine Creek, Naples was damaged in the 1996 floods and bank restoration and other habitat improvements have recently begun here.

In spring, Naples is heavily hit by spin fisherman at the numerous bridge crossings in the village of Naples and at a couple of formal DEC access sites downstream. Still, the healthy runs make it a good place to wade up or down from an access point and try your luck for rainbows with the usual array of flies imitating eggs and egg clusters.

In fall, the landlocked salmon run brings out fewer anglers. Flyfishers should plan to fish close to the lake—such as the Parrish Road crossing and the DEC access sites upstream. Locals recommend using stonefly nymphs and steelhead patterns. Naples also gets a modest run of spawning browns in October and November, but nothing like the spring run of rainbows.

The small headwaters of Cold Creek, the inlet to Keuka Lake.

COLD CREEK (KEUKA INLET)

Cold Creek, the main inlet to Keuka Lake, is a short but productive stream for spawning rainbows, and offers good access along its three to four miles of fishable water.

Beginning outside Bath, Cold Creek runs through Hammondsport to the lake. The creek is small but fishable in its upper reaches. There is public access here both at the Bath State Fish Hatchery (limited to daylight hours) and at another parking spot just downstream (north) of it. Here the stream is less than a rod length across and angling will mostly be done from the banks.

The stream widens toward the village of Pleasant Valley, though it is still not more than 15 feet across. Extensive access is available here in Taylor Park and at the large parking lot nearby (the former home of the Taylor Winery), which bears a sign permitting anglers. The stream in this area has sometimes overrun its banks and caused serious erosion, but bank supports put in by Conhocton Trout Unlimited has helped limit this problem.

Downstream from Taylor, access can be had at Hammondsport (just upstream of the schoolyard). From here down the stream mouth is slow and wide—more suited to spin and bait fishing. However, by starting here or at the very bottom in Hammondsport a fly angler in a float tube or kayak could cover this stretch with a streamer. Cold Brook also offers smaller runs of landlockeds and browns in fall.

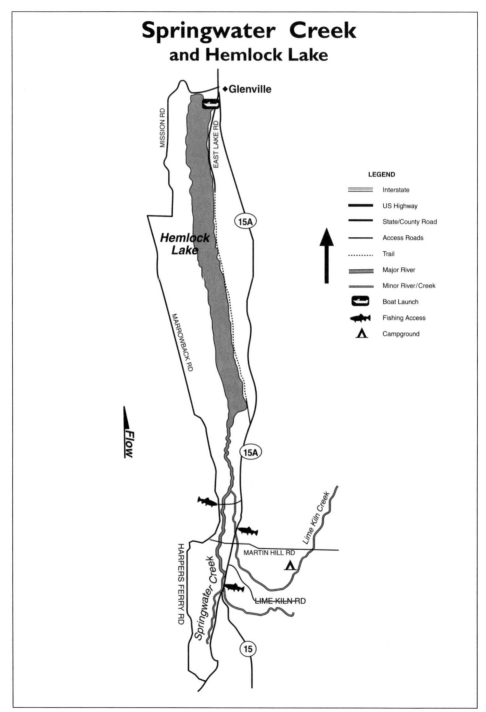

Springwater Creek
and Hemlock Lake

◆Glenville

MISSION RD

EAST LAKE RD

LEGEND

Interstate

US Highway

State/County Road

Access Roads

Trail

Major River

Minor River/Creek

Boat Launch

Fishing Access

Campground

15A

Hemlock Lake

MARROWBACK RD

Flow

15A

Lime Kiln Creek

HARPERS FERRY RD

MARTIN HILL RD

Springwater Creek

LIME KILN RD

15

© WILDERNESS ADVENTURES PRESS, INC.

Springwater Creek

Among the smaller of the Finger Lake feeder streams, Springwater gets a very good run of rainbows from Hemlock Lake, which holds a healty population of wild fish. Access to the stream is readily available along Route 15, including DEC access sites near East Road and farther downstream where Route 15A branches off. Springwater's tributary Limekiln Creek, which enters about a mile from the lake, can also be fished. Because of its narrow size, Springwater (and Limekiln) can be tricky to flyfish, but short-line drifting of nymphs should be possible.

Finger Lake Outlets

Several of the Finger Lake outlets offer fishing, both for resident trout and for lake fish that wash over the dams into the streams. All the outlets, including those discussed below, exit the lakes at their northern ends.

Keuka Outlet

The outlet of Keuka passes over a series of old dams on its 6 mile trip to the western shore of Seneca Lake at Dresden. This stream was not stocked for many years, but with the encouragement of the Finger Lakes Trout Unlimited Chapter, the DEC has begun putting in one- and two-year-old browns since the late '90s. The state stocks about 1,100 fish in all.

The stocking—and the fishing—is roughly in the 1.5-mile section from Seneca Mills downstream to Cascade Mills. The water from Keuka Lake is warmer than trout like—one of the reasons stocking was suspended—but this section is actually colder than the outflow, apparently from underwater springs. The stocked fish hold over fairly well here, and are occasionally supplemented by large stray rainbows and browns that wash out of the lake. High water can be a problem for anglers on the outlet as water is released from the lake to maintain its level.

Access is good along the abandoned railroad tracks that parallel the stream and have been converted into the Keuka Outlet Trail, a hiking and riding path. (There is also an information pavilion and picnic area at Cascade Falls.) About 20 feet across, Keuka Outlet has a rock and gravel bottom and some good mayfly hatches including March Browns and Hendricksons in early season and Blue Winged Olives later on. A tan caddis also comes off in summer.

As noted, the outlet drains into Seneca Lake. There is a culvert at the bottom that often prevents lake fish from ascending the stream, but in high water large rainbows, and even a few lakers, can make it up into the outlet.

The prime trout section of Keuka Outlet is open for year round fishing, with five trout of any size permitted. However, farther downstream from the first impassable barrier before Seneca Lake (above the culvert) to the mouth, Finger Lakes regulations apply: fishing is open April 1 to December 31.

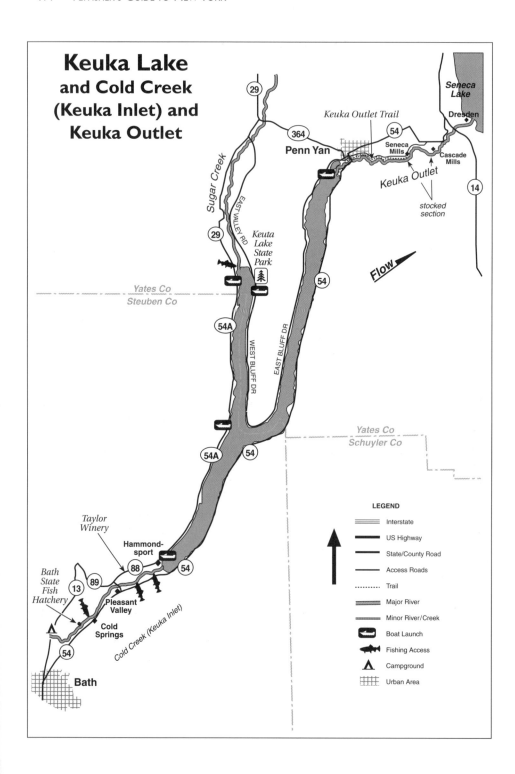

Keuka Lake
and Cold Creek
(Keuka Inlet) and
Keuka Outlet

Seneca Lake

Keuka Outlet Trail

Dresden

Penn Yan

Seneca Mills

Cascade Mills

Keuka Outlet

stocked section

Sugar Creek

EAST VALLEY RD

Keuta Lake State Park

Flow

Yates Co
Steuben Co

54A

WEST BLUFF DR

EAST BLUFF DR

Yates Co
Schuyler Co

54A

Taylor Winery

Hammond-sport

Bath State Fish Hatchery

Pleasant Valley

Cold Springs

Cold Creek (Keuka Inlet)

Bath

LEGEND

Interstate
US Highway
State/County Road
Access Roads
Trail
Major River
Minor River/Creek
Boat Launch
Fishing Access
Campground
Urban Area

Skaneateles Creek

Skaneateles Creek, the outlet of Skaneateles Lake, runs about 12 miles to the Seneca River/Erie Canal. This small stream is a fine fishery for naturally reproducing brown and rainbow trout. Except for a modest annual stocking of browns, all the fish here are wild, and some of the browns get to 20 inches. The stream is no more than 10-15 feet wide, and except for a mile or two at each end is entirely catch and release.

The creek is well shaded, with a sand and gravel bottom, and stays reasonably cool thanks to minimum flows released from the lake. There are a wide variety of mayflies, including Hendricksons, March Browns and Quill Gordons. Caddis are also plentiful and the overhanging foliage makes terrestrials effective in summer.

The toughest part of fishing the creek is finding access. Virtually the entire run is through private land and except for a heavily hit town park near the source in the town of Skaneateles, there is no formal public access. Anglers must look for access at road crossings off Route 31C in the lower portion of the stream and Fennell Road close to the lake.

The normal trout season applies to the Skaneateles Creek, and as noted there is a catch and release section covering most of the stream. The catch and release section runs from the Old Seneca Turnpike Bridge in the village of Skaneateles (about one mile from the lake) downstream roughly 10 miles to the bridge at Jordan Road in the village of Jordan (about two miles from the mouth). Outside of the catch and release section, five fish of any size may be kept.

Owasco River (Owasco Outlet)

This wide stream, which runs out of Owasco Lake through the city of Auburn on into the Seneca River, has the potential to become a fine urban fishery. Currently, the stream is not stocked, but gets a steady smorgasbord of fish that wash over the dam at the mouth of the lake, including browns, rainbows and a few lake trout (in addition to smallmouth bass and walleye). Anglers in the area, including the local chapter of the Federation of Fly Fishers, have been working on cleaning and monitoring the stream. They have found small rainbows here that might be stream-bred fish. A formal DEC survey is expected soon, so this is a stream to keep an eye on for trout fishing.

At the moment, Owasco River is subject to the same regulations as the lake itself, meaning trout and salmon can be targeted all year, no more than five fish in combination, with a 15-inch minimum for landlocks, browns and lakers and the smaller 9-inch minimum that applies to rainbows on Owasco.

Ninemile Creek

The outlet of Otisco Lake, Ninemile Creek runs about 15 miles to Onondaga Lake. Substantial segments of Ninemile—particularly the portion in the towns of Camillus and Marcellus—remain cool all summer thanks to a multitude of underwater springs. (In fact, unlike most tailwaters, temperatures here actually drop when flows from the dam at Otisco Lake are reduced.)

Though the stream can and does support some natural reproduction, the fish here are largely stocked browns. It is very heavily stocked with more than 10,000 fish each year. It is also heavily hit, in large part due to its proximity to the city of Syracuse.

The cold spring water of Ninemile supports a good supply of mayflies, including the big White Fly that hatches in late July and August. There is also a healthy supply of scuds, mostly in gray and olive. These run on the small side—size 16 to 18. In addition to scud patterns, small flashback Hare's Ear Nymphs will work. Streamers fished in the evenings, including Woolly Buggers and Black-Nosed Dace, can be effective. No special season or regulations apply to Ninemile Creek.

Finger Lakes Region Hub Cities

Ithaca/Watkins Glen/Waterloo

ACCOMODATIONS PRICE KEY
$ Up to 60 dollars per night
$$ 61 to 99 dollars per night
$$$ 100 to 150 per night
$$$$ 151 and up per night

HOTELS/MOTELS
Best Western University Inn, 2271 Kraft Road, Ithaca, NY 14850 / 607-387-9225
Falls Motel, 239 North Genesee Street, Watkins Glen, NY 14891 / 607-535-7262

CAMPGROUNDS/RVs
Buttermilk Falls State Park, Highway 13, Ithaca, NY 14850 / 607-273-5761 / 46 sites / Lake fishing / No hookups
Spruce Row Campsite, 2271 Kraft Road, Ithaca, NY 14850 / 607-387-9225 / 200 sites / 10 full / 160 elec.

RESTAURANTS
Glenwood Pines Restaurant, 1213 Taughannock Boulevard / 607-273-3709
Curly's Family Restaurant, 2780 Route 14, Watkins Glen, NY / 607-535-4383

FLY SHOPS
Badger Creek Fly Tying, 1408 Hanshaw Road, Ithaca, NY 14850 / 607-266-0736 / www.mwflytying.com / Materials, accessories, gear
Community Fly Fisher, 1015 West Seneca Street, Ithaca, NY 14850 / 607-697-0053 / Shop run by a non-profit organization promoting flyfishing to youngsters

AUTO REPAIR
Goodyear Auto Service Center, 227 Elmira Road, Ithaca, NY 14850 / 607-273-4580

AIRPORT
Tompkins County Airport, 72 Brown Road, Ithaca, NY 14850 / 607-257-0456

HOSPITAL/CLINIC
Cayuga Medical Center, 101 Dates Drive, Ithaca, NY 14850 / 607-274-4011

Bath/Hammondsport

HOTELS/MOTELS

Days Inn, 330 West Morris Street, Bath, NY 14810 / 607-776-7650 / $$

Village Tavern Inn / 30 Mechanic Street, Hammonsport, NY, 14840 / 607-569-2528 / $$-$$$ / Restaurant, see below

CAMPGROUNDS/RVS

Hickory Hill, 7531 Mitchellsville Road, Bath, NY 14810 / 607-776-4345 / 185 / 95 full / Tenting

Keuka Lake State Park, 3370 Pepper Road, Bluff Point, NY 14478 / 315-536-3666 150 / 53 elec. / Tents

RESTAURANTS

Chat-A-Whyle Restaurant, 28 Liberty Street, Bath, NY 14810 / 607-776-8040 / Famous sticky buns

Village Tavern Restaurant, 30 Mechanic Street, Hammonsport, NY, 14840 / 607-569-2528

Pleasant Valley Inn, 7979 State Route 54, Hammondsport, NY 14840 / 607-569-2282

Snug Harbor, 144 West Lake Road, Hammondsport, NY 14840 / 607-868-3488,

FLY SHOPS

Nehrke's Fly Shop, 34 Robie Street, Bath, NY 14810 / 607-776-7294 / materials, accessories, and gear / near Cohocton River / (by appointment)

Pinewood Flies, 185 Pine Valley Road, Pine Valley, NY / 607-739-4348 / www.fly-fishingonline.com; full service fly shop, near Catharine Creek

TACKLE SHOPS

Hesselson's Sport Shop, Elmira Heights, NY

AIRPORT

Tompkins County Airport, 72 Brown Road, Ithaca, NY 14850 / 607-257-0456

Waterloo/Seneca Falls/Auburn/Skaneateles

HOTELS/MOTELS

Budget Inn, 61 State Street, Auburn, NY   13021 / 315-252-8969 / $-$$
Arbor House Inn, 41 Fennell Street, Skaneateles, NY 13152 / 315-685-8966 / www.arborhouseinn.com / $$-$$$

CAMPGROUNDS/RVS

Yawger Brook Family Campsite, Benham Road, Auburn NY 13021 / 315-252-8969
Sampson State Park, 6096 Route 96A, Romulus, NY 14541 / 315-585-6392

RESTAURANTS

Costello's, 13 Aurelius Avenue, Auburn, NY   13021 / 315-252-9778
Hilltop Restaurant, 813 West Genesee Street, Skaneateles, NY   13152 / 315-685-0016 / Open early
The Krebs, 53 West Genesee Street, Skaneateles, NY   13152 / 315-685-5714

FLY SHOPS

Les Maynard's Fly Shop, 1223 Hecker Road, Waterloo, NY   13165 / 315-539-3236 / Fly tying materials, accessories and gear
Royal Coachman Fly Shop, 1410 East Genesee Street, Skaneateles, NY 13152 / 315-685-0005 / www.skaneateles.com/royalcoachman, full service fly shop, guiding

AIRPORT

Tompkins County Airport, 72 Brown Road, Ithaca, NY 14850 / 607-257-0456

Syracuse

HOTELS/MOTELS

Ramada Limited-University, 6590 Thompson Road, Syracuse, NY   13206 /
315-463-0202 / 60-100 sites / $$

Red Roof Inn, 6614 North Thompson Road, Syracuse, NY   13206 / 315-437-3309
45-75 sites / $-$$

Embassy Suites, 6646 Old Collamar Road, North Syracuse, NY   13057 /
315-446-3200 / 150-160 sites / $$$-$$$$

CAMPGROUNDS/RVS

Foland's Trailer Park, Midler Avenue, Onondaga, NY / 315-463-1892 / No tents

RESTAURANTS

Mimi's Bakery and Cafe, 260 West Genesee Street, Syracuse, NY 13202 /
315-422-6630 / open 6:30a.m.

Danzer's Restaurant, 153 Ainsley Drive, Syracuse, NY 13210 / 315-422-0089

FLY SHOPS

*(Note: Syracuse is located between the Finger Lakes and the Eastern Ontario
Tributaries. Fly shops in the area will have equipment and information for both
regions)*

Nature's Best Flys, 504 Charles Ave. # 6, Syracuse, NY 13209 / 315-468-3749 /
http://members.xoom.com/NatsFlys/ primarily custom flies

The Serious Angler, PO Box 611, Jordan, NY, 13080 / 315-689-3864

The Troutfitter, 3008 Erie Boulevard East, Syracuse, NY 13224 / 315-446-2047 /
Full service fly shop

AUTO REPAIR

Fehlman Brothers Garage, 116 South Midler Avenue, Syracuse, NY 13206 /
315-463-5888

AIRPORT

Syracuse Hancock International Airport, 2001 Airport Boulevard, Syracuse, NY
13212 / 315-454-3263

HOSPITAL/CLINIC

University Hospital, 750 East Adams Street, Syracuse, NY 13210 / 315-464-5540

Western New York Trout Streams

The westernmost counties of New York are home to some outstanding trout fishing. Several of the best trout streams in the state are found here, including Oatka Creek and Wiscoy Creek. There are also a series of small tributaries on the Upper Cattaraugus that have very good populations of wild fish.

The streams in this region—especially Oatka and Wiscoy—are not undiscovered. In fact, anglers throughout the western part of the state fish them regularly. But they are probably less well known than their counterparts in the Catskills and Adirondacks and definitely worth visiting.

OATKA CREEK

Probably the top trout stream in the area, and one of the best in the state, Oatka offers excellent hatches and good fish, including a healthy population of wild fish in the prime section. Because of its proximity to Rochester and Buffalo, and the fact that the best fishing is in a relatively short stretch of a longer stream, it does see heavy pressure at times.

Oatka begins in Wyoming County and flows north and east until it meets the Genesee River downstream of Scottsville in Monroe County. The trout water runs roughly 14 miles from the village of Leroy to Scottsville within Genesee County. The renowned wild trout water is a subset of that—about five miles after Spring Brook brings in cool flows at Mumford. This section is not stocked, and while most of the wild browns are 6 to 12 inches, DEC surveys find fish in the 14- to 16-inch range, and a few as large as 18 inches. Browns are stocked above and below the wild section—about 10,000 fish, including a good number of two-year-olds—in Wyoming, Genesee and Monroe counties. Hard information is not available, but some of the stocked fish undoubtedly hold over.

In addition to good fish, the Oatka has a profusion of good hatches. The Hendricksons, which hatch from mid-April to the first week in May, are prolific and many anglers make a point of being on stream for these. Both dries and the rusty spinner are essential flies during this hatch. There are also good hatches of March Browns, as well as Sulphurs that follow the Hendricksons for about six weeks. Caddis are intermittent but important, with a green-bodied caddis and a good hatch of tan caddis around the end of May (sometimes called the Memorial Day Caddis).

Also around the end of May, an unusually colored mayfly appears that is unique to Oatka (and its tributary Spring Brook). Called the Coral Mayfly, this size 10-12 adult has yellow wings and a bright orange body. Carl Coleman, who operates a fly shop near Rochester and has been fishing the area since childhood, ties a dry fly with a yellow body ribbed with orange to imitate the fly's unusual color.

The big mayfly does attract big fish, but timing is essential as the hatch typically lasts less than two weeks (the first week of June is usually a good bet). Oatka also gets a good Trico hatch that begins by the end of July in most years.

Nymphing is frequently effective on Oatka Creek, and generic nymphs work well. These include the Gold-Ribbed Hare's Ear, Red Fox Squirrel and the Atherton series, with dyed blue wingcase. In early season, a size 12 will work, but drop down to 14 and 16 later on. For summer, local angler John Dwyer likes black ants as small as size 20. Scuds are also found in the cool, wild trout water of the Oatka.

In Monroe and Genesee counties, which encompass most of the good trout water, the stream is open to fishing all year and midge pupa along with larger nymphs such as Hare's Ears and Woolly Buggers are useful to intrepid winter anglers. In the other half of the year, water can get low and warm on Oatka in summer outside of the section cooled by Spring Brook. In addition, low flows bring on algae plumes, though these typically clear with the first rain.

Oatka Creek becomes a wild trout stream just below the mouth of Spring Brook.

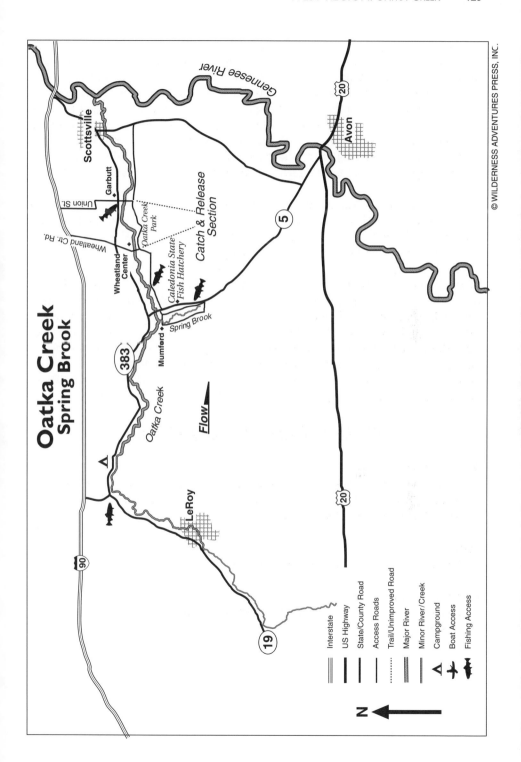

Oatka Creek
Spring Brook

Genesee River

Scottsville

Garbutt

Union St.

Wheatland Ctr. Rd.

Wheatland Center

Oatka Creek Park

Caledonia State Fish Hatchery

Catch & Release Section

Spring Brook

Mumford

383

Oatka Creek

Flow

LeRoy

90

19

20

Avon

5

20

© WILDERNESS ADVENTURES PRESS, INC.

Interstate
US Highway
State/County Road
Access Roads
Trail/Unimproved Road
Major River
Minor River/Creek
Campground
Boat Access
Fishing Access

N

Compounding problems of early season crowding, access on the Oatka is limited. For the prime section, access is available from Union Street in Garbutt and upstream near Wheatland Road. The stream can also be reached in this stretch from Monroe County Park (also called Oatka Creek Park). The park frontage includes a roughly 1.7-mile catch and release section just above Garbutt running from Wheatland Center Road down to Union Street. (This section replaced a longer artificials only, three fish per day section which extended past both ends of this catch and release section.) There is also a small stretch of public fishing rights near the intersection of Route 383 and Route 36, just below the junction with Spring Brook.

The Oatka Trail Road, though above Spring Brook, is a pretty good stocked area with limited access. There are reportedly a few unposted spots with pulloffs, and some public fishing rights at the upper end of this section at Hebbard Road.

As already noted, most of the stream is open all year, with the standard limit applicable except in the catch and release section. Anglers should note that revised regulations are expected for Oatka (and Spring Brook) starting in October 2002. For the wild trout section (between the mouth of Spring Brook and Bowerman Road in Scottsville) the proposed rules would make all off-season fishing—October 16 through March 31—catch and release only. During the normal season in this section, the limit would become two fish of 12 inches or longer. Above and below Oatka's wild section, five fish per day would remain the limit, but only two could be greater than 12 inches, to keep more of the two-year-olds in the stream. These changes are not final, so anglers should check the updated regulations.

Stream Facts: Oatka Creek

Seasons/Regulations
- Open all year, five trout of any size permitted (revised regulations expected in October, 2002). Catch and release only in 1.7-mile section below Wheatland Center Road (near the village of Garbutt).

Fish
- Mostly brown trout, mix of stocked and wild.

River Characteristics
- Freestone with substantial areas of smooth flow; subject to lower water and algae in summer.

Oatka Creek/Spring Brook—Major Hatches

INSECT	J	F	M	A	M	J	J	A	S	O	N	D	FLIES
Blue Winged Olives 14-20									●				Pheasant Tail Nymphs, Emergers, Comparaduns and Parachutes
Lt. And Dark Hendrickson 12-14				●									Light and Dark Hendrickson Parachutes and Comparaduns, Rusty Spinners
March Brown 12				●									Brown Nymph, March Brown Wets, Comparaduns, Rusty Sponners
Caddis Green, Tan 14-18													Lafontaine Deep Pupa and Emergent Sparkle Pupa, Soft Hackle Wets, Bead Head Nymphs
Sulphurs 14-20					●	●							Comparadun, Parachute, CDC Emergers, Compara-emergers, Pheasant Tail, Hares Ear Nymph
Coral Mayfly 10-12						●							Yellow and Orange Mayflies
Tricos								●					Small Dark Nymphs, Trico Spinners, Griffiths Gnats
Midges Light and Dark 18-24 (More important on Spring Brook)	●	●	●	●	●	●	●	●	●	●	●	●	Brassies, Light and Dark Pupa Imitations, Small Hackled Dries, Griffiths Gnats
Scuds Pink, Tan, Olive 12-14 (Primarily on Spring Brook)	●	●	●	●	●	●	●	●	●	●	●	●	Various Scud Patterns

Spring Brook doesn't offer much room,
but it does have big, wild fish.

SPRING BROOK

This small, short tributary to Oatka is a spring-fed creek whose steady food supply supports one of the densest populations of wild trout in New York. Ironically, these unstocked spring waters run alongside the Caledonia Fish Hatchery, once run by Seth Green and reportedly the first hatchery in North America.

The spring-fed flows on this stream maintain an almost ideal temperature range of high 40s to high 50s. This environment not only helps trout, it also supports a good insect population. As might be expected on a spring creek, this includes scuds and midges, and local anglers consider a pink scud imitation in 12-14 essential here. There are also caddis and mayfly hatches, including the Coral Mayfly and some Blue Winged Olives. The Olives are said to be particularly common near the hatchery. Given the brook's small size, it is worth having some ants and beetles ready when nothing else is going on. The constant temperatures make this a particularly good place for winter fishing with midge pupae and larger nymphs, and with midge dry flies during the occasional winter hatch.

The stream only runs about three miles, making solitude rare. Also, the stream's small size and clear water make stalking essential. Fishing is done mostly from just below the hatchery upstream, as swampy conditions and private land limit fishing below. Perhaps the best section, at least for big fish, is the area called the 900s—referring to the roughly 900 feet of public water below the hatchery property. This portion can be reached from the adjacent railroad trestle. Above the hatchery, access is available from a couple of road and railroad crossings along Route 5. Fishing is also permitted on the hatchery property (which includes access for the disabled) but only from 8 a.m. to 4 p.m., with three fish of 10 inches or better allowed and only from the bank (wading is not permitted). Elsewhere, a five fish, nine-inch limit applies and the brook is open to fishing all year.

As with Oatka, new regulations are in the offing that would make all fishing "catch and release" outside of the normal trout season. And from April 1 to October 15, limits throughout Spring Brook would become two fish per day, 12 inches or better. Check the new regulations after October 2002.

There is good fishing on the Wiscoy right in the village of Pike.

WISCOY CREEK

It's probably a toss up whether Oatka or Wiscoy is the best trout stream in western New York. Either way, the Wiscoy is one of the best trout fisheries in the state. The creek offers anglers cool water, good hatches and, most importantly, a healthy population of wild brown trout for most of its length.

The Wiscoy runs about 20 miles from its source to the Genesee River, but the prime trout fishing section is about a 12-mile stretch from the Wyoming County village of Bliss to the town of Hume in Allegany County. Only a short section at the lower end of the trout water is currently stocked, and even this small supplement might be eliminated. The rest is populated by self-sustaining brown trout. The fish are not large—most are less than a foot—but the number of fish in the 10- to 12-inch range is very high, and the fish are strong and beautifully colored. Anglers determined to catch bigger trout should concentrate on the lower end of the stream, where the population is thinner but the fish run larger.

The upper section of the Wiscoy is small water, as little as six feet across, and remains so almost to the town of Pike. Above Pike, there is a one-mile catch and release section where Hillside Road crosses the stream. Fishing is permitted year round here and there is public access through a narrow cow-proof gate. The stream

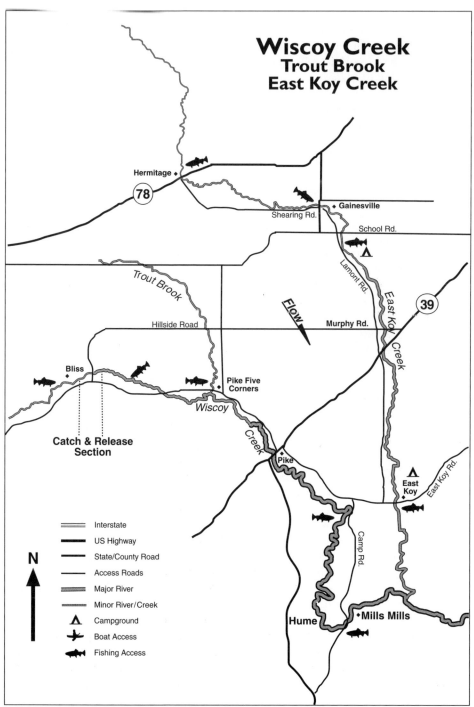

Wiscoy Creek
Trout Brook
East Koy Creek

Hermitage

78

Shearing Rd.

Gainesville

School Rd.

Trout Brook

Lamont Rd.

Flow

Murphy Rd.

Hillside Road

39

East Koy Creek

Bliss

Pike Five Corners

Wiscoy

Catch & Release Section

Creek

Pike

East Koy

East Koy Rd.

Hume

Camp Rd.

Mills Mills

N

	Interstate
	US Highway
	State/County Road
	Access Roads
	Major River
	Minor River/Creek
⛺	Campground
	Boat Access
	Fishing Access

has a series of bend curves that are reported to hold large numbers of fish—up to 300 pounds per mile, by some estimates—though they run small. Generally, it is the upper half of the catch and release zone that offers the best structure and fishing, but the entire catch and release section is heavily hit. If you're only fishing this smaller portion of the creek, a 4- or even 3-weight rod of no more than 8 feet will suffice.

The catch and release section gets a full array of Wiscoy hatches, and has particularly good Tricos starting as early as mid-July (from 8 a.m. to noon). The small size of the upper Wiscoy also begs for terrestrials in summer and fall. In addition to its size, the other challenge on the upper Wiscoy is its frequently murky water. The undercut meadow banks can quickly cloud the water during spring snowmelt or anytime it is running high. The Western New York Chapter of Trout Unlimited has done substantial bank stabilization here, making the problem less pronounced than previously.

Downstream, above Pike and near the village of Pike Five Corners, Trout Brook enters the Wiscoy, providing additional cool water and good spawning habitat. Trout Brook (discussed separately) is also widely known as a good place to fish for brookies and wild browns when the main creek is running cloudy. The pool at Route 39 where Trout Brook enters, made even more hospitable by bank supports, usually holds fish, but its location makes it heavily hit.

There is a dam within the village of Pike that offers good holding water, but it too is very heavily fished. There is parking and access at the Pike Fairgrounds (except during the fair in late August) and anglers can fish a long way up or down. Some of the Wiscoy's best fishing is found a few miles downstream of Pike. Beginning at the DEC access on Camp Road, sometimes called Susan's Acre, there is more than a mile of excellent holding water. Anglers can park at the DEC access and work downstream. In the alternative, a few parking spots are available at the Boy Scout Camp farther along Camp Road, if your willing to make the half-mile hike to the stream (visitors must park near the road). Anglers with two cars and enough time would do well to park in each location and wade the length of this run.

The water in this stretch is a classic series of runs and riffles, along with some deeper pools. There is a small dam near where you hit the stream from the DEC access, where a deep pool always holds fish, and if you're lucky enough to find it unoccupied, a beadhead nymph worked patiently can be effective. At the Boy Scout Camp, there is a bridge and stone retaining walls at the bank. Popular with spin fishermen, these walls are a good place to take fish on nymphs drifted tight to the bank. The water below the Boy Scout Camp begins to warm a bit; the lower end of the Wiscoy holds fewer trout (but some bigger ones) and isn't heavily fished.

Hatches are very good throughout the Wiscoy, including a very small black stonefly in early April, size 14-16. Hendricksons, Gray Foxes and especially prolific March Browns will take you through spring, In late spring and summer there are Sulphurs, Cahills, *Isonychia*, Brown Caddis and late summer and fall Tricos. Though some anglers have success with traditional ties, the lower-riding parachute and comparadun dry flies are probably a better choice for wild fish. Some local anglers use a double rig, such as an Elk Hair Caddis with a cream-colored pupa imitation tied to the bend.

As already noted, the one-mile catch and release section on the upper creek is open to fishing all year (an artificials only section was eliminated in the early 1990s). Elsewhere, the normal trout season applies. In addition, the Wiscoy is subject to a limit of three fish of 10 inches or better. Still, with wild trout so prized, catch and release is strongly recommended here. (Take a picture instead.)

Stream Facts: Wiscoy Creek

Seasons
• Normal trout season, April 1 to October 15, except one-mile catch and release section on upper stream open year round.

Special Regulations
• Three fish per day of 10 inches or more. One mile section at Hillside Road is catch and release only. Former special regulations section downstream has been eliminated.

Fish
• Wild brown trout and occasional brookies. A small stocking of browns at the lower end near Hume.

River Characteristics
• Small meandering meadow stream at upper end, growing wider and steeper downstream.

River Flows
• Low and clear in fall and late spring, can be high and dirty during early spring thaw or heavy rain, especially in upper section.

Wiscoy Creek—Major Hatches

INSECT	J	F	M	A	M	J	J	A	S	O	N	D	FLIES
Midges Dark 18-20			▓						▓				Bessies and small pupa, Griffith's Gnats; Sporadic, good in early season
Black Stonefly 16				▓									Small Dark Nymphs, Dark Elk Hair Caddis
Lt. And Dark Hendrickson 12-14					▓								Light and Dark Hendrickson parachutes and comparaduns, rusty spinners
March Brown 12					▓								Brown Nymph, March Brown Wets, Comparaduns, Rusty Spinners
Caddis Green, Gray, Tan 14-18					▓								Latontaine Deep Pupa and Emergent Sparkle Pupa, Soft Hackle Wets, Bead Head Nymphs
Sulphurs 14-20					▓	▓							Comparadun, Parachute, CDC Emerger, Compara-Emerger, Pheasant Tail Nymph, Hare's Ear Nymph
Tricos								▓					Small Dark Nymphs, Trico Spinners, Griffith's Gnats
Terrestrials					▓					▓			Dubbed and Foam Ants and Beetles, Letort Hoppers and Crickets

Trout Brook

In addition to providing an excellent pool on the Wiscoy, Trout Brook is fishable in its own right. It is a particularly good place to go when the Wiscoy is running high and dirty. Smaller than the Wiscoy, the brook also has heavy vegetation. Much of the upper stream is inaccessible due to posting, so it is the roughly half-mile of public access from Hillside Road to the mouth that is fished.

All the fish in Trout Brook are wild—Wiscoy browns are often born here—and there are quite a few small brook trout along with the browns. Plan on smaller flies and shorter rods when fishing Trout Brook. Normal trout season and regulations apply, but as on the larger stream, it is advisable to release wild fish.

East Koy Creek

Though this small stream offers some good trout fishing, it necessarily takes a back seat to the nearby Wiscoy. The East Koy begins north of Hermitage in Wyoming County and runs about 20 miles south until it meets the Genesee River. The best trout fishing begins below the village of Hermitage and continues for roughly seven miles to the village of East Koy. The stream is relatively small, smooth water with some good bend and bridge pools along the way. There is frequent access from crossing roads, including at Route 78 in the center of Hermitage, at Shearing Road just upstream of the Gainesville town center (along the railroad tracks), and downstream at School Road. More access is available on Lamont Road for several miles (with dedicated parking at Murphy Road) and at the easy to remember East Koy Road.

Unlike the Wiscoy, the East Koy is heavily stocked, primarily in the town of Gainesville. More than 14,000 brown trout are put in each year, including about 1,000 two-year-old fish. The stream is heavily pressured, especially in the early season. Supplementing the stocked fish there is some natural reproduction here, and unlike on many streams, this occurs not only at the headwaters but at various places along the creek.

Hatches are similar to those on the Wiscoy, including spring Hendricksons, Blue Winged Olives and Tricos—with the Tricos especially heavy around the village of Vermont (at the Murphy Road Access). Matching the hatch works, but so do basic flies like Wulff patterns on top and Prince Nymphs, Zug Bugs and Hare's Ears for subsurface work.

The standard trout season applies throughout the East Koy with no special regulations.

The East Koy at the School Road Access.

UPPER CATTARAUGUS AND TRIBUTARIES

Better known as the premier steelhead fishery on Lake Erie, the "Catt" actually has some good trout fishing upstream. It also has some excellent tributaries that offer the chance to catch a lot of wild fish in a small stream setting.

The Upper Cattaraugus actually divides just above Gowanda into main and south branches. A few trout are stocked on the South Branch in the town of East Otto, but this is primarily a put-and-take fishery. The trout portion of the main branch runs from the headwaters near the village of East Arcade to the Springville Dam, with stocked browns put in from the headwaters to below the mouth of Elton Creek. About 7,000 browns are added each year, including a substantial number of larger fish.

Probably the best fishing is from the village of Arcade upstream, where the stream is small to medium in size (becoming quite small above East Arcade). The stream has a good, gravelly bottom, with riffles, runs and pools, and a fairly steep gradient. The water is not well shaded and does warm in summer. Broken banks can also make it muddy. Also, more of a challenge than a problem, the gravel bottom shifts regularly, meaning the pool you fished last time may have moved when you return.

Upper Cattaraugus and Tributaries

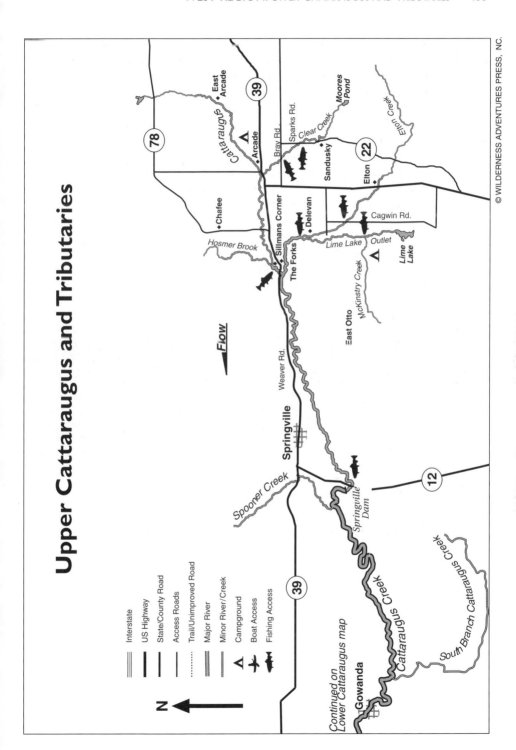

Legend:

- ═══ Interstate
- ─── US Highway
- ─── State/County Road
- ─── Access Roads
- ········ Trail/Unimproved Road
- ─── Major River
- ─── Minor River/Creek
- △ Campground
- ⚓ Boat Access
- 🐟 Fishing Access

N

Flow

© WILDERNESS ADVENTURES PRESS, NC.

78

39

East Arcade

Arcade

Chafee

Sillmans Corner

Hosmer Brook

The Forks

Weaver Rd.

Spooner Creek

Springville

Springville Dam

Gowanda

Cattaraugus Creek

South Branch Cattaraugus Creek

12

39

Continued on
Lower Cattaraugus map

Cattaraugus

Bray Rd.

Sparks Rd.

Clear Creek

Sandusky

Delevan

Lime Lake

Lime Lake Outlet

McKinstry Creek

East Otto

Moores Pond

Elton

Elton Creek

Cagwin Rd.

22

In addition to stocked trout, there are a few wild browns that spawn in the better tributaries. There are also rainbows, and these are all wild. The wild trout population fluctuates on the Cattaraugus, rising and falling with reproduction on the coldwater feeders. A prime spot to hit for these fish, and for good water, is the area near the mouth of Clear Creek in the center of Arcade. After Clear Creek enters, the river becomes noticeably larger, and while the fishing becomes uneven, it is a good place to try a streamer.

The Cattaraugus and its tributaries offer mayflies, including a good Sulphur hatch that begins in early May, along with some caddis. Many anglers who regularly fish in the area make an effort to match the hatch, including using low-riding parachutes and comparaduns. At the other extreme, anglers also have success with generic patterns like Elk Hair Caddis, Humpies and even the old fashioned Fan-winged Royal Coachman. For nymphs, Pheasant Tails and Gold-Ribbed Hare's Ears—with or without bead heads—are effective.

The Cattaraugus above Springville Dam is subject to the standard trout season and regulations.

Muddy water can make fishing difficult at times on the Upper Cattaraugus.

Clear Creek

Confusingly, there are two Clear Creeks that empty into the Cattaraugus. This, the eastern one of the pair, enters at Arcade and is probably the best of the Cattaraugus tributaries. The stream is short, running about five miles from Moores Pond north to the Cattaraugus, and averages about 15-20 feet wide.

Clear Creek is not stocked and holds both wild browns and rainbows. The fish are plentiful, but the rainbows in particular run on the small side, rarely getting to be more than 10-11 inches. (It is believed that the local rainbow strain lives only 3 or 4 years so the fish don't have time to grow very large.) Browns do get a bit larger: fish up to 16 inches are occasionally seen if not often caught. Surveys indicate browns make up more than half the trout, but flyfishers catch many more rainbows. During daytime, the browns seem to hide under tree roots and in other inaccessible places; anglers determined to catch them should probably fish at dusk and later.

Hatches and flies are similar to the Cattaraugus. Chuck Godfrey, who has been fishing here for four decades, uses an Elk Hair Caddis in size 16 with a gray or green body with considerable success. As on any small stream, terrestrials work well, especially in summer. Nymphs should be fished in any cut or hole, as there are not many deep pools on the stream.

The best section for flyfishing is from slightly upstream of the village of Sandusky downstream (north) to the mouth, with the roughly two-mile section between the Bray Road and Sparks Road crossings particularly good. Just below Sandusky the small tributary Cheney Creek enters and its mouth is also a good place to hit. There is access on most of the stream along Route 98 and from a couple of road crossings, and formal access at Bray Road (about a mile upstream of Arcade) and again at Church Street in Arcade itself. All of Clear Creek is subject to a minimum nine-inch size limit (designed to allow the small rainbows to spawn at least once); the regular trout season applies.

Elton Creek

Elton Creek runs west and north from the edge of Allegany County, passing through the village of Delavan, where Lime Lake Outlet enters, before meeting Cattaraugus Creek near a small village called The Forks. Elton runs more than 12 miles, but is only about 15-20 feet wide. The last few miles of the stream are not very productive and the uppermost stretch can be swampy. It is largely the portion from the village of Elton to below Delavan that offers the best flyfishing, with the roughly four-miles upstream of Delavan the best wild trout section. This section can be reached from the Cagwin Road/Weaver Road Bridge.

The fishing here is to browns, both stocked and wild, and all-wild rainbows. As on the other Cattaraugus feeders, the rainbows do not get very large, anything more than 12 inches is rare. The browns, both holdover and wild, occasionally get to 16 inches or more. Even for the smaller fish, stealth is important—perhaps because of a lack of angling pressure, the fish get startled easily.

There are a few hatches here. But as in most of these small wild streams, the fish, while spooky, are not terribly selective. It obviously pays to match whatever is

Clear Creek holds wild browns and rainbows.

hatching in size and color, but standard Adams, Coachman dries with peacock bodies and basic caddis imitations will cover most of your dry fly needs. Add a few generic nymphs, such as Pheasant Tails and Hare's Ears, and you'll be well armed. No special season or regulations apply to Elton Creek.

Lime Lake Outlet

This short tributary to Elton runs only about four miles north from Lime Lake to its mouth at Delevan. The stream starts out relatively flat and meandering, but picks up speed as it approaches the creek. Unlike Elton, the outlet is not stocked but has a thriving population of wild browns and rainbows.

There are a remarkable number of fish here, and while most—particularly the rainbows—are on the small side, there are definitely some bigger fish. A recent DEC survey of one large pool found a number of browns over 18 inches, and one specimen was fully two feet long. Admittedly, these are rarely caught, but an intrepid angler willing to fish at dark might hook one. Like most of the good Cattaraugus tributaries, this is lightly fished in summer, as local anglers turn to bass and walleye.

The stream can be very narrow and difficult to fish in its upper reaches. After McKinstry Creek enters about halfway to the mouth, the stream gets a bit wider. (McKinstry, which also holds wild browns and rainbows, is worth fishing as well.) There is formal access at the junction of the two flows, and some more near the mouth in Delevan.

Much of what applies to the fishing on Elton Creek is true also on Lime Lake Outlet: skittish fish that will take reasonable imitations like Adams dries and generic nymphs. The standard trout season applies to Lime Lake Outlet and to McKinstry Creek but Lime Lake trout must be at least nine inches to be kept.

Wild trout are plentiful in Lime Lake Outlet.

Hosmer Brook

Hosmer Brook is a short Cattaraugus tributary that runs south about four miles from its headwaters near the small village of Chaffee to meet the river near Sillmans Corner. Like several of the other tributaries, Hosmer is not stocked, offering a good supply of mostly small wild browns (and a few big ones). There is a decent hatch of Sulphurs here starting at the end of May, as well as some Cahills and caddis. The stream is narrow and brushy, which can make flyfishing difficult. There is formal access at the mouth, as well as informal entry at Route 39, Genesee Road, and Chaffee Road, which all cross going upstream. Hosmer Brook is subject to the standard season, but the minimum size is nine inches.

Mansfield Creek

This small to medium-sized feeder runs into the South Branch of Upper Cattaraugus Creek. While the South Branch itself is a marginal fishery, Mansfield hosts a good population of stocked and wild brown trout, along with some wild rainbows. The rainbows were established in the mid-1990s with small wild fish from nearby Clear and Hosmer brooks. Surveys indicate they have taken well and are reproducing in the stream. In fact, with both wild browns and rainbows present, it is possible that the small stocking of Mansfield may be ended in the future. This good quality water has been enhanced by the Red House Brook Chapter of Trout Unlimited. They have done bank stabilization work and fenced off banks to protect them from livestock (with the cooperation of local farmers).

Mansfield Creek fishes best in its first four miles or so—roughly from the headwaters to a bit below Eddyville Corners. Here the stream stays cold all year. Above Eddyville Corners, in the village of Maples, Elk Creek (sometimes called Hencoop Creek) enters and the pool it forms is a productive spot.

There is good access along Hinman Hollow Road and Route 13, including some dedicated access. The bed is mostly gravel and relatively easy to wade. Mayfly hatches on Mansfield Creek include good Cahill and Blue Winged Olive hatches in summer and excellent Tricos in late summer and fall. Caddis are also seen here, as is a large golden olive stonefly that hatches very sporadically. If you are lucky enough to be on the stream for the hatch, the stoneflies are said to run up to size 8. If not, a large brown stonefly nymph should be an effective searching pattern throughout the season. Like most small streams, terrestrials are generally effective and local anglers find that it is mostly the wild fish that hit small black ant imitations. No special regulations or season apply on Mansfield Creek.

Upper Cattaraugus Creek and Tributaries—Major Hatches

INSECT	J	F	M	A	M	J	J	A	S	O	N	D	FLIES
Midges Dark 18-20			━							━			Brassies and small pupa, Griffith's Gnats
Lt. And Dark Hendrickson 12-14				┃									Light and Dark Hendrickson Parachutes and Comparaduns, Rusty Spinners
Caddis Green, Gray, Tan 14-18					┃								Lafontaine Deep Pupa and Emergent Sparkle Pupa, Soft Hackle Wets, Bead-Head Nymphs, Elk Hair Caddis
Sulphurs 14-20					┃								Parachutes and Comparaduns, Soft Hackle Wets (Body color varies pale yellow to orange) Pheasant Tail Nymphs
Tricos								┃					Small Dark Nymphs, Trico Spinners, Griffith's Gnats
Terrestrials				┃									Dubbed and Foam Ants and Beetles, Letort Hoppers and Crickets

ISCHUA CREEK

A tributary to warmwater Olean Creek, Ischua Creek offers a good population of stocked browns supplemented by some wild browns and rainbows that mostly spawn in the feeder creeks.

Beginning in the Cattaraugus County town of Machias, Ischua Creek flows south 15 miles to Hinsdale where it meets Olean Creek. The trout portion of the stream is roughly down to the village of Ischua, but the better water is from the

*Ischua Creek at the start of the season, a good
time to fish the warmer downstream section.*

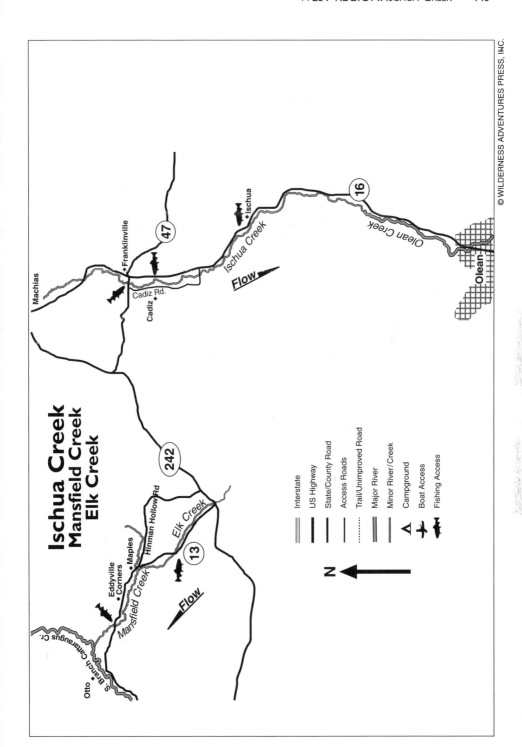

Route 16 crossing to about three miles downstream of Franklinville. And, within that shorter run, the couple of miles from the northern end of Franklinville to the village of Cadiz remains cool all season thanks to underground springs. By contrast, the lower half of the trout stretch warms in summer; it is best targeted at the start of the season, and then skipped later on.

Ischua is about 30 feet wide with a mixed gravel and silty bottom. There are decent mayfly populations, with a good Hendrickson hatch around mid-May followed by hatches of Sulphurs and Cahills. Green Drakes are virtually absent, despite the silty bottom that they would usually inhabit. In addition to mayflies, caddis are present too. Like many streams, the bigger fish tend to feed at night and local anglers recommend cutting back the leader and switching to a Woolly Bugger as the light fades. This is not the easiest kind of fishing, but big browns are occasionally taken this way in Ischua Creek.

The stream is heavily stocked with about 12,000 browns each year, but there is also some natural reproduction, particularly in the cool section around Franklinville. There is access along Route 16, including some formal access at Coony Road south of downtown Franklinville. No special regulations or season apply to Ischua Creek.

UPPER GENESEE RIVER

Above the steelhead portion of the river at Lake Ontario, and its long warmwater midsection, the Genesee offers pretty good trout fishing for stocked browns and the occasional stray brookie. South of the Pennsylvania border, the Genesee is composed of three branches, but by the time it crosses into New York it is a single flow.

The primary trout water on the "Gennie" (as it is often called) runs from the Pennsylvania border about 12 miles to Wellsville. Still, many local anglers target the first three or four miles to the village of Shongo. The water here offers a mix of riffles, runs, and pools for flyfishers, along with some mid-stream islands. By the time the flow hits the village of York Corners about another three miles downstream, it has become the wide, smooth flow that is popular with spin anglers. Heading away from the crowded bridge crossings in this section will offer solitude and a chance to catch trout on flies.

The fish in the Upper Genesee are almost entirely stocked browns, along with a few stocked rainbows. Over 20,000 trout are put in each year from the Pennsylvania border all the way to Amity. There isn't much natural reproduction, but despite high summer temperatures the fish reportedly find some deep holes and hold over well. In fact, tagged fish from the annual Trout Derby have sometimes been caught two years later. The stocked fish are also well distributed, since the Upper Genesee Chapter of TU has been float stocking the river for the last several years. (Fishing from a float tube or canoe would be possible when water is high early in the season, but it is difficult and not often done in the prime trout water.)

In addition to the stocked fish, a few brookies do make their way in from the feeder creeks (where they are wild) and from Pennsylvania, which stocks brook trout in its portion of the river.

The Genesee is arguably better know for caddis than mayflies, but is has both. There are a variety of caddis, and in addition to the obvious Elk Hair pattern, local angler Bill Fries notes that old-fashioned palmered patterns like the Vermont Caddis also work well. Black caddis and a version with a green body and brown wings are particularly common colors.

Mayflies include reliable Hendricksons and sporadic Green Drakes. Light colored flies seem to predominate on the Upper Genesee, with Sulphurs and Cahills both important. Mark Libertone lives near the stream and finds that soft hackles fished in the film work well on the Sulphurs, though he recommends an orange-tinged body to better imitate the naturals. In general, both winged and soft hackle wet flies are productive here.

Summer brings midges that even hatch all day and can be imitated with small brown and gray dries. Ants and grasshoppers are also important for summer. A few anglers have taken to fishing the stream at night with Mickey Finns and bucktail streamers.

Virtually the entire stocked trout water, from the border to the village of Belmont in Amity is open to fishing all year. In the prime trout water, a 2.5-mile section downstream from the Route 19 crossing in Shongo is catch and release only (also open all year) and has some very deep holes. Not many anglers fish in the dead of winter, but they do come out in March and continue fishing well into fall. For early season, Woolly Buggers and beadhead nymphs are useful, sometimes a sink tip will be necessary to get the flies down. Mid-summer fishing requires some care as the river can get dangerously warm for trout by mid-July. Bring a thermometer and fish the tributaries when the water reaches 70 degrees.

Smallmouth bass are also found on the Upper Genesee. Starting in Stannards, about 10 miles downstream from Pennsylvania, and picking up from Wellsville down, there are some good-sized smallmouth in the river. Flyfishers have started to target these, especially in fall. Marabou streamers and Woolly Buggers in dark colors are said to work well on the bass. Standard bass season and regulations apply.

UPPER GENESEE RIVER TRIBUTARIES

There are several good feeder creeks in the Genesee's trout section. All hold wild brook trout and some receive browns as well. These are small, but generally kept cool by shade; they are a good place to try when the main river is low and warm. All are subject to standard season and regulations.

Cryder Creek

This stream runs southwest and crosses the Pennsylvania border before meeting the Genesee. It receives about 3,000 browns a year—a fairly substantial stocking for its short length—and holds brookies in its upper reaches. Roughly six miles of the stream can be reached from Route 268A between Whitesville and the Pennsylvania border. There is no reciprocal fishing arrangement for Cryder, so be careful not to cross into Pennsylvania without that state's license.

Chenunda Creek

Downstream (north) of Cryder, Chenunda Creek runs west about 10 miles from its headwaters near the village of Independence to the Genesee near Stannards. Access is from Route 248 and from Stout Road upstream. Chenunda gets a small stocking of browns each year, and has some wild browns as well.

Dyke Creek

Dyke Creek meets the Genesee in Wellsville. The eight-mile run from Andover to the river—particularly where Indian Creek comes in—offers good fishing for wild brookies and about 1,500 small stocked browns. The stream gets very small in its upper reaches, no more than 3 or 4 feet across.

Vandermark Creek

This meandering stream runs through farmland before joining the Genesee at Scio. About 1,000 browns are put in, supplementing a wild populations of both brookies and browns. The fish can be stalked at the frequent undercut banks. Vandermark is better fished starting a mile or two up from the mouth; below there it lacks good holding structure. The upper section of the stream runs through some state forest land and most of it runs parallel to Vandermark Road, offering good access.

Ford Brook

A small stream which meets the Genesee River upstream of Stannards, Ford Brook is not stocked but has some wild brook and brown trout in its main (or north) branch and its south branch. Ford Brook Road conveniently has its own south and north branches, which parallel the respective parts of the stream.

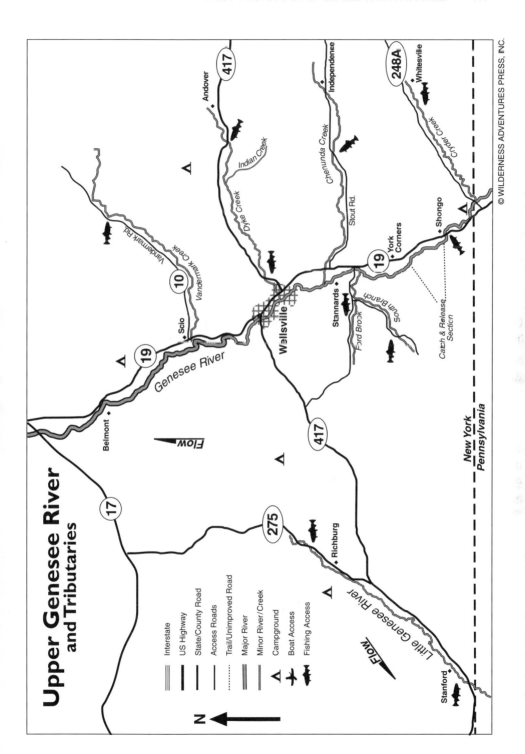

Upper Genesee River
and Tributaries

Interstate
US Highway
State/County Road
Access Roads
Trail/Unimproved Road
Major River
Minor River/Creek
Campground
Boat Access
Fishing Access

N

Belmont

Genesee River

Flow

Scio

Vandermark Creek

Vandermark Rd.

Wellsville

Indian Creek

Dyke Creek

Andover

417

10

19

19

Stannards

Ford Brook

South Branch

Stouf Rd.

Chenunda Creek

Independence

York
Corners

Shongo

Catch & Release
Section

Crybet Creek

Whitesville

248A

New York
Pennsylvania

417

275

Richburg

Little Genesee River

Flow

Stanford

17

© WILDERNESS ADVENTURES PRESS, INC.

Upper Genesee River—Major Hatches

INSECT	J	F	M	A	M	J	J	A	S	O	N	D	FLIES
Blue Quill 16-18					▮								Blue Quill Dry, Pheasant Tail Nymph
Lt. And Dark Hendrickson 12-14					▮								Light and Dark Hendrickson Parachute, Emergers, Spinners
Sulphurs 14-20					▮	▮							Comparadun, Parachute, Emergers; Smaller sizes more common
Green Drake 12					▮								Gray Fox Variant, Comparaduns, Compara-Emergers
Caddis Dark Gray, Green 14-18					▮	▮	▮						Lafontaine Deep Pupa and Emergent Sparkle Pupa, Soft Hackle Wes, Bead Head Nymphs
Terrestrials									▮				Dubbed and Foam Ants and Beetles, Letort Hoppers and Crickets

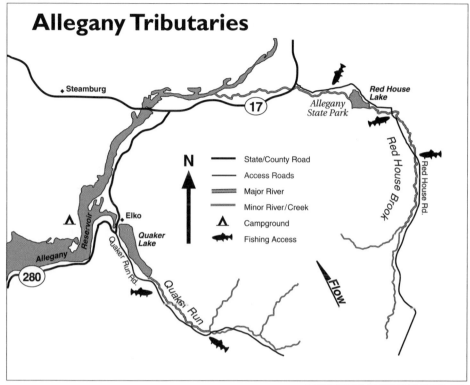

Allegany Tributaries

© WILDERNESS ADVENTURES PRESS, INC.

ALLEGANY TRIBUTARIES

There are a series of small tributaries to the Allegany River in New York and Pennsylvania. While most of these in New York are marginal trout streams that have little water by mid-summer, two are worth a look.

Quaker Run

Quaker Run flows about five miles to the Quaker Lake impoundment at Elko. The stream is stocked with brookies and rainbows in about a 2 to 1 ratio. There are also some small wild brookies in the stream that typically come from smaller tributaries. There are some pretty good hatches on Quaker Run, including Hendricksons, Sulphurs, Cahills and Olives. The best fishing is until July. The Red House Brook Chapter of Trout Unlimited, along with the DEC and State Parks Department, has begun a three year project to improve the flow and structure of the last portion of the stream above the lake. It is hoped that this project—which will include diverters, boulders and bank repairs—will improve fishing on the stream. Allegany State Park Road parallels Quaker Run and offers access.

Red House Brook

Red House Brook runs north of Quaker Run meeting Red House Lake near the entrance to the state park and flows a short distance out the other side to the Allegany. Like Quaker Run, the stream has good hatches, including a few Green Drakes. Unfortunately, the brook suffers badly from warm water caused by frequent beaver dams. As a result, the better fishing is the roughly three-quarters of a mile below the lake. Both rainbows and brookies are stocked here.

Both Quaker Run and Red House Brook are within Allegany State Park, which requires a free fishing permit. This permit can be obtained at the park administration building. Quaker Run and Red House Brook are currently subject to the normal fishing season, but anglers should check on any special rules set by the park (716-354-9121).

A portion of the streams are located on land belonging to the Seneca Indian Nation. A permit for fishing on Seneca land must be obtained from the nation (this is the same permit required for fishing parts of the steelhead section of Cattaraugus Creek.) The Seneca permit is available at some local tackle shops and gas stations in the area and at the Nation's Haley Community Building at 3502 Center Road in Salamanca. Additional information is available at 716-945-1790.

Little Genesee Creek

Despite its name, this stream, which runs south across the Pennsylvania border, is actually a tributary of the Allegany. Like some other area streams, it is a meandering meadow stream with undercut banks offering good holding lies. The fish in those spots are a combination of stocked browns and a few wild brookies. The brookies are more prevalent as you head upstream. Route 275 parallels the upper half of the creek's run in New York, with Route 417 running alongside the lower portion. Standard trout season and regulations apply. (See Upper Genesee River map.)

Little Conewango

This small feeder, near the Randolph State Fish Hatchery, enters the larger warmwater Conewango at the small village of Pope. Little Conewango is essentially a put and take trout stream, with about 3,000 small browns put in each year near the town of Conewango. No special regulations apply.

Western New York Trout Streams Hub Cities

Wellsville/Olean

(Also see Rochester hub)

ACCOMODATIONS PRICE KEY

$	Up to 60 dollars per night
$$	61 to 99 dollars per night
$$$	100 to 150 per night
$$$$	151 and up per night

HOTELS/MOTELS

Long-Vue Motel, 5081 Route 417 West, Wellsville, NY   14895 / 716-593-2450 / $$

Little Bit of Heaven Bed and Breakfast, 21 South Main Street, Silver Springs, NY 14550 / 716-493-2434 / $$

Castle Inn, 3220 W State Street, Olean NY / Restaurant / 716-372-1050

Hampton Inn, 101 Main Street, Olean, NY / 375-1000

CAMPGROUNDS/RVs

Breezy Point Campsite, 2749 Wolf Spring Road, Scio, NY 14880 / 200 sites / 125 full / 75 water/elec.

RESTAURANTS

Old Library Restaurant, 120 South Union Street, Olean, NY   14760 / 716-372-2226

Century Manor Restaurant, 401 E State Stree, Olean, NY / Great steaks and cocktails / 716-372-1864

L'Alcove Castle, Inc., 3230 W State Street / Fine dining in historic restaurant / 716-372-6141 / Also a branch at 501 Union Street, Olean NY / 716-372-3021

FLY SHOPS

Carter Hardware, 130 North Main Street, Wellsville, NY 14895 / 716-593-3550 / Good selection of reasonably priced flies

True Life Fly Co., 1005 W Main St, Smethport, PA 16749 / 814-887-1974

TACKLE/SPORTING GOODS

Mc Divitt's Sporting Goods, Bliss Road, Lawrenceville, PA 16929 / 570-827-2818 / White Tail Country, Olean NY

AUTO REPAIR

Master Automotive, 72 Railroad Avenue, Wellsville, NY 14895 / 716-593-2547

HOSPITAL/CLINIC

Jones Memorial Hospital, 191 North Main Street, Wellsville, NY 14895 / 716-593-1100

Lake Erie and Tributaries

Lake Erie offers very good migratory fishing in its tributaries, as well as some angling directly in the lake. While it doesn't have more than incidental salmon, there a number of good steelhead streams—from very large to very small—and plenty of fish.

LAKE ERIE TRIBUTARIES

New York's 70 miles of shoreline on Lake Erie, running from the Pennsylvania border to the southern end of the Niagara River, provide a fine steelhead fishery. Most of these fish are stocked—in the streams and directly in the lake. Natural reproduction is not possible in most Erie tributaries: the bedrock bottoms generally lack the necessary gravel for egg laying and the water is typically too warm in summer for the newborn steelhead to survive. A notable exception is Cattaraugus Creek—the most important fishery on Lake Erie—which has good natural reproduction. There is believed to be at least some steelhead reproduction on Chautaqua, Canadaway and Eighteenmile creeks as well, which an ongoing DEC study will try to quantify.

Despite the lack of wild fish, the Erie tributaries do see good returns. Straying is common, since smolts that are stocked often fail to "imprint" to their particular stream. This probably works to New York's advantage since Pennsylvania is known to stock heavily on its short Erie frontage and many of these fish undoubtedly make it into the New York streams, particularly those at the southern end of the Erie shoreline. On rare occasions, coho salmon stocked in small numbers by Pennsylvania will show up in New York streams, as will small pink salmon that survive in Lake Erie and spawn every other year. (New York eliminated its own salmon stocking in Lake Erie several years ago.) Perhaps because there is less forage, Erie steelhead aren't as large as ones in Lake Ontario. Size is usually 5 to 10 pounds, with anything over 10 a prize fish.

Erie steelhead have both fall and spring runs. A handful of 1- to 2-pound immature fish, known as "jacks," enter Erie tributaries in mid-September and the fall steelhead run peaks in October and November. Unlike spring spawning fish, the fall run fish are actively feeding and can be taken on streamers. Low water can be a problem for fall fishing on Erie tributaries. Bigger streams, notably Cattaraugus Creek, are more reliable for fall runs, particularly in late September and October. Anglers should take a look at water flows or ask local tackle shops.

Though there are fish in most streams throughout the winter, conditions can make it unpleasant for all but the most hardy anglers. Fly anglers will have a particularly difficult time as lines, reels and guides will freeze up quickly. If you do brave the elements, the Salmon Flea/Frammus is reputed to be a good fly for winter.

Come March and continuing through April, the spring run of steelhead from Lake Erie takes place. Catching fresh fish in early season chrome color—literally "bright"—is a main goal for fly anglers, as these fish put up the best fight. On longer streams, the steelhead move up the water in stages. This puts a premium on finding fish, as at any given time there are long stretches of dead water. Going with a knowledgeable angler or guide can save hours of wasted effort, especially if you are unfamiliar with the particular river. In general, look for fish in deep pools when the sun is out and in riffles and seams when it isn't. Also, the steelhead will rarely hold over the solid shale or slate common to Erie tributaries. Instead, seek out areas where broken shale and solid shale meet.

For flies, individual egg patterns and clusters, as well as the newly popular Sucker Spawn, in red, yellow, chartreuse and cheese, are good choices. As with all steelhead fishing, bring lots of flies and use patterns you can purchase cheaply or tie quickly (don't be afraid to use craft store pom-poms for egg imitations), as you'll lose many flies in a day. For high, discolored water—common on the Cattaraugus, in particular—try big Woolly Buggers or Zonkers in black and other colors (or head to a clearer flowing stream). By contrast, small stonefly nymphs work in low water.

The usual tactic is to drift the flies on a tight line, ticking bottom as you go. It is difficult to describe the take of a steelhead, but it's sometimes compared to flicking a finger against the tip of the rod. The best advice to beginners is obvious—if you see or feel the line hesitate, strike. In time, you'll learn the difference between bottom and a fish. Experienced anglers usually set the hook to the side, hoping to lodge the fly in the corner of the fish's mouth.

Fishing with West Coast steelhead patterns like the Silver Hilton, and even traditional salmon flies, is becoming more popular among Erie anglers. These flies are swung rather than drifted, which tends to work best in the warmer water of early fall and later spring.

Whether swinging or dead drifting, rods of 7- or 8-weight are usually sufficient for the smaller Erie steelhead. Longer rods, up to 10 feet, will help fight fish and mend line. Floating lines and a sink tip or two—either built in or the kind added with loop connections—will meet most flyfishing needs on the Erie tributaries.

The regulations applicable to Lake Erie and its tributaries up to the first impassable barrier allow fishing year round for trout and salmon, with three fish allowed in any combination (it is rare to catch any other species on Lake Erie), each measuring nine inches or better. From September 1 to March 31—which covers most of the two steelhead runs—some special regulations apply to virtually all Erie tributaries. These prohibit night fishing, the use of more than one hook or point, hooks with gaps more than one-half-inch wide and fly hooks with more than one-eighth ounce of weight. (Most standard fly patterns meet these restrictions.)

Cattaraugus Creek

More a river than a creek, Cattaraugus is undoubtedly the best Lake Erie steelhead stream in New York. It offers great length, sufficient water flows throughout the season and, most importantly, good runs of steelhead—including a sizable number of wild fish.

The Cattaraugus is amply stocked with about 90,000 fish each year. The creek—or more accurately its tributaries, including Clear Creek and Spooner Creek—also supports natural reproduction of migratory rainbows. The DEC is currently studying the Cattaraugus and other Erie tributaries to get accurate information on the numbers of fish born and returning, as well as their growth rates. Preliminary indications are that about 25 percent of the adult steelhead returning to the Cattaraugus are wild.

The Catt, as it is known to locals, runs along the borders of Erie, Chautauqua and Cattaraugus counties. The first impassable barrier in the stream is the Springville Dam, which allows fish to run nearly 40 miles upstream, far longer than other local steelhead fisheries. There is good if widely spaced access along the stream and in most water conditions anglers can cover long stretches of the stream up or down from the entry points.

There are accesses to the Catt at each of the eight major stream crossings up to the dam. In particular, Route 5 and Route 20 cross in the lower section and are popular places to fish. Upstream, there is also access off Versailles Plank Road. Aldrich Street and Point Peter Road in the town of Gowanda provide access as does the railroad trestle in town near Route 62. The area around Gowanda has gravelly substrate that attracts steelhead and anglers.

With so many miles to cover before hitting the Springville Dam, steelhead in the Cattaraugus move up the water in stages. The Cattaraugus is tough fishing for those without some knowledge of the stream, making it a good place to hire a guide or fish with someone who has been here before. In addition to its challenging size, the Cattaraugus drains from a large watershed and can run high and murky from rain or melting snow. In high water try a smaller local stream, including the creek's own tributaries.

As long as it is, the Catt could sustain an even longer run. The dam at Springville, which once produced electricity, is now dormant and there is some discussion of removing it or installing fish passage. This would give steelhead access to miles of excellent spawning habitat upstream. However, it won't happen soon. Careful analysis is needed first, including assessing the effect on resident trout on the Upper Cattaraugus.

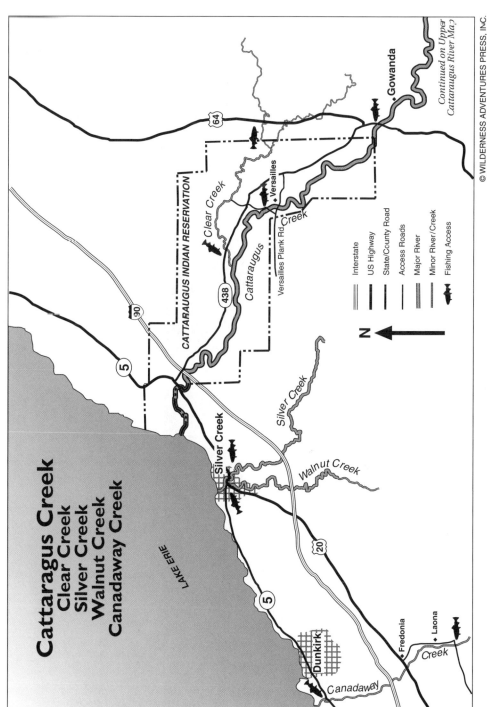

© WILDERNESS ADVENTURES PRESS, INC.

Cattaragus Creek
Clear Creek
Silver Creek
Walnut Creek
Canadaway Creek

LAKE ERIE

CATTARAUGUS INDIAN RESERVATION

Clear Creek

Cattaraugus

Versailles Plank Rd

Versailles

Creek

Gowanda

Continued on Upper
Cattaraugus River Map

64

438

90

5

Silver Creek

Silver Creek

Walnut Creek

20

5

Dunkirk

Fredonia

Laona

Canadaway

Creek

N

Interstate
US Highway
State/County Road
Access Roads
Major River
Minor River/Creek
Fishing Access

Seneca Land

Two long stretches of the Catt, totaling more than a dozen miles, are on land owned by the Seneca Nation of Indians. This water is open to fishing, but anglers must have a Seneca permit in addition to a New York State fishing license. The year-long Seneca license, currently $14.00 for non-tribal members ($10.00 for a three-day license), can be obtained at the Seneca One Stop Market near Gowanda, or at the Nation's general administration building at 1490 Route 438 in Irving, NY; 716-532-4900. The regulations, copies of which are available when you purchase your Seneca license, permit fishing only from 7 a.m. to a half-hour after sunset. Otherwise, they currently mirror New York State regulations for Erie tributaries, but it is worth checking before you fish. Note that any tribe member is entitled to ask for proof of a Seneca license and the Seneca Nation has its own enforcement officers who can issue fines and impound equipment of violators.

Cattaraugus Creek near Gowanda has the gravelly bottom that steelhead prefer.

Stream Facts: Cattaraugus Creek

Seasons
- Up to first impassable barrier (dam at Springville), all year for salmon, steelhead and trout.

Regulations
- Three fish in any combination, nine-inch minimum.

Fish
- Steelhead, mostly stocked with about 25 percent wild; very occasional pink or coho salmon.

River Characteristics
- Medium to large, mix of shale and gravel bottom.

River Flows
- Can be high and dirty during early spring thaw and after rains. Almost always has enough water for fishing.

The smaller water of Clear Creek can save the day when the Cattaraugus runs high.

CATTARAUGUS CREEK TRIBUTARIES

Clear Creek

As noted in the introduction, Clear Creek provides key spawning habitat for Cattaraugus steelhead. The creek also provides a refuge for steelhead anglers when the Cattaraugus is running high. Clear, which runs 10 miles to meet the Cattaraugus about 7 miles from the lake, is on the Seneca Reservation and requires the Seneca Nation permit. About 5 miles upstream from the mouth, the stream splits into north and south branches. The main stem can be reached where Route 438 crosses and from Versailles Plank Road. The two branches can be reached from various road crossings, including Route 62, which traverses both. (Clear Creek should not to be confused with the trout stream of the same name that joins the Cattaraugus far upstream at Arcade.)

Because of the creek's importance as spawning ground for steelhead, the North Branch of Clear Creek, from Taylor Hollow Road to Jennings Road, is closed to all fishing from January 1 to March 31.

Spooner Creek

The other major nursery on Cattaraugus, Spooner joins the main creek just a few miles downstream of the dam at Springville. It is both narrower and a bit shorter than Clear Creek. Spooner can be reached at the crossings of Concord Road and Route 39. All of Spooner Creek is closed to fishing from January 1 to March 31 to protect spawning fish. (See Upper Cattaraugus Creek map.)

Guide Joe Battaglia drifting a fly on a small Erie tributary.

SOUTH OF CATTARAUGUS CREEK

Chautauqua Creek

Chautuauqua Creek (pronounced "Sha Taw Kwa") has no connection to the lake of the same name. It is a medium-sized stream with a good run of steelhead and ample public access. The water emerges from a small dam in Westfield, with about three miles for the steelhead to run. The state stocks 50,000 small steelhead in Chautaqua Creek each year. There is access near the mouth at Barcelona, at the Route 5 crossing and farther upstream where the railroad crosses.

In addition, the upstream portion of the creek in the town of Chautauqua receives a small annual stocking of brown trout. This section of the stream can be reached from crossings at Lyons Road and Putnam Road.

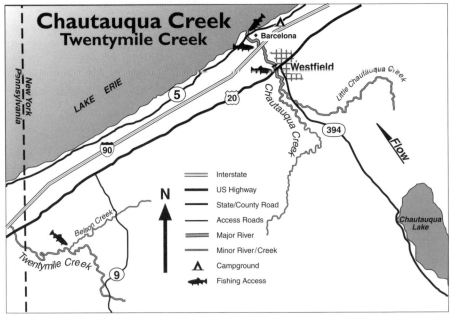

© WILDERNESS ADVENTURES PRESS, INC.

Canadaway Creek

Canadaway Creek (see Cattaragus Creek map) is fishable for steelhead for about three miles from the impassable falls in the town of Laona to the mouth outside Dunkirk. As with many area streams, the bottom is mostly shale, which puts a premium on looking for deep holes and areas where broken shale and the hard shale bottom meet.

There is access at the falls near Webster Street in Laona. The deep pool here is a productive spot but heavily hit by spin and fly anglers. There is additional access about halfway downstream where Route 20 crosses the stream and again at the nature sanctuary near the mouth. About 20,000 small steelhead are stocked in Canadaway Creek each year.

The Chautaqua at the Route 5 crossing near its mouth.

The mouth below the junction of Silver Creek and Walnut Creek gets a good run of steelhead.

Silver Creek and Walnut Creek

These two small streams merge just before entering Lake Erie in the village of Silver Creek a few miles south of the Cattaraugus. Both run a long way without obstructions, but they become quite small upstream. It is primarily the last few miles of the streams that are fished.

Both are stocked with about 5,000 steelhead a year and both get decent runs, provided they have sufficient water. These are good alternatives during high water or for anglers who prefer smaller streams. The area just above the mouth can be reached at the railroad trestle off Mechanic Street in Silver Creek, and the separate flows can be reached from the Route 5 crossings.

Twentymile Creek

This medium-sized steelhead creek runs through New York before crossing into Pennsylvania and emptying into Lake Erie; it is primarily fished across the border. A good number of fish do make it into the New York section, up to (and occasionally past) the barrier near the mouth of Belson Creek. However, the New York water requires a substantial hike from the road. It's easier to get a Pennsylvania license, start at one of the Pennsylvania access points and work your way upstream.

NORTH OF CATTARAUGUS CREEK

Eighteenmile Creek

Eighteenmile Creek (see Buffalo River map) runs about nine miles from Hamburg into Lake Erie (it is unrelated to the Ontario tributary with the same name). This Eighteenmile has a long unblocked run for steelhead from the town of Hamburg to its mouth. About halfway between Hamburg and the lake, the stream divides into a south branch and main stem. The South Branch adds about another five miles of fishable water and both parts get good runs of steelhead. Together the two branches receive about 40,000 steelhead a year.

The stream is medium-sized and prone to cloudy water, but it clears more quickly than big water like Cattaraugus. The most popular access point is probably the formal DEC access at the bridge on Versailles Plank Road. This stretch, known as Hobuck Flats, is productive but usually crowded with both fly and spin fishermen. For less crowded spots, get onto to the stream at the Route 5 crossing not far from the mouth or at the Conrail tracks upstream. For the South Branch, try the crossing of Belknap Road.

Cayuga, Buffalo, and Cazenovia Creeks

These three streams run independently then ultimately merge to form the Buffalo River. Though portions of these waters were once terribly polluted, they are now much cleaner and offer steelhead fishing right in the city of Buffalo and its suburbs.

Cayuga, the northernmost of the three creeks, runs near the Buffalo suburb of Cheektowaga, then merges with Buffalo Creek just east of Interstate 90, which is generally agreed to mark the start of the Buffalo River. Cazenovia enters the Buffalo River well downstream in the city, where the flow widens considerably.

Buffalo Creek gets steelhead from the barrier just east of Route 20/78 near the community of Blossom downstream to the mouth. (Some fish jump the barrier but under the regulations fishing upstream reverts to the normal trout season.) On Cayuga, fish cannot pass the barrier at Como Lake.

Buffalo and Cayuga each get a stocking of steelhead and they do get good returns. Cazenovia is also fishable, but the steelhead here are all strays. Access can be tricky in this urban/suburban setting. There is a formal access on Cazenovia Creek in West Seneca that is quite popular. Elsewhere access is more informal, including at road crossings and parking lots that back up on the streams.

Cayuga Creek offers steelhead fishing just outside of Buffalo.

Both streams can get fish as early as the third week in September and continue to hold them into April, or even May when there is spring rain. All the streams are relatively shallow, so anything more than a foot or two deep is potential holding water. Anglers use all the usual flies, including various egg patterns, buggers and leeches.

In addition to the three creeks, a few fly anglers do fish the short stretch of the Buffalo River upstream (east) of Route 90. Below that point the muddy bottom makes it mostly a spin fishing location.

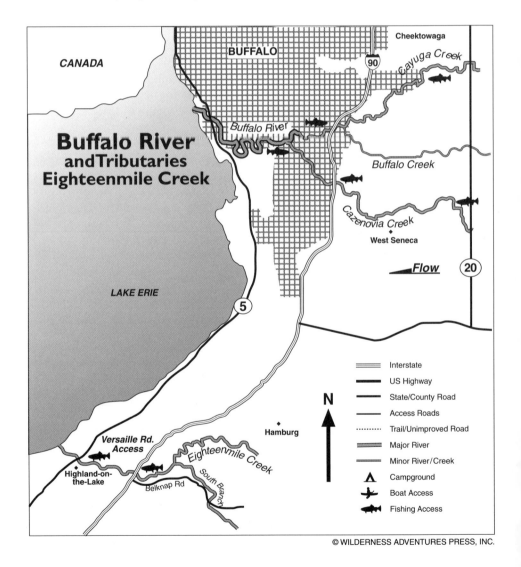

© WILDERNESS ADVENTURES PRESS, INC.

Lake Erie

Smallmouth

Smallmouth bass are plentiful in the lake and are just being discovered by fly anglers. Local outfitters, including Oak Orchard Fly Shop, have begun running boat trips for these fish. It is also possible to fish from float tubes and canoes.

The fishing is done in creek mouths and bays. Creek mouths are particularly good in early season, and there is an extended season for Lake Erie smallmouth beginning the first Saturday in May and running to the start of the third Saturday in June, when the regular season begins. During this early "trophy" season only one bass may be kept and it must be at least 15 inches. Trophy season is a good time to catch large bass as they can often be found in 4 to 8 feet of water during this period.

Cold water can be a problem with Erie smallmouth fishing—it needs to be near 60 degrees for the fish to be active. When the fish are moving, they will hit thin poppers on the surface and Clouser Minnows with top wings of gray, olive, chartreuse and occasionally blue. Large schools of emerald shiners swim in the lake, so slender streamers in green, silver and white should also be effective. Mornings and evenings are usually the best times to fish, in part because you'll avoid the heaviest boat and jet ski traffic.

By mid-summer, the better fish have gone deep, though they can still be taken with full sinking lines and long sinking tip or shooting head lines with about 300 grains at the head. In fall, fish will return to shallow water, with October a particularly productive month.

When flyfishing for bass, anglers should look for bottom with large boulders and rocks (these will be easy to spot in Erie's very clear water). Sharp drop-offs along the shoreline are also good spots. There are many creek mouths and bays worth trying, including the mouth of Eighteenmile Creek at the village of Highland-on-the-Lake, Sturgeon Point about five miles south (which has a boat ramp) and Bennett Beach a few miles farther down the shore.

As noted, the early season begins on the first Saturday in May with a limit of one fish of 15 inches or better. From the third Saturday in June through November 30—the standard bass season—five fish of 12 inches and up may be kept.

Steelhead

In addition to the tributary fishing, it's possible to catch steelhead directly outside creek mouths on the lake as they get ready to run upstream. On Erie this is limited to the fall run, since the lake is typically frozen over at spawning time in spring. Plan on using 8-weight rods with floating and sink tip lines and Clouser Minnows. The fish do feed aggressively and fight well, but don't expect large numbers; a couple of fish in a day is a good outing.

Trout (including steelhead) may be fished for all year in Lake Erie. Three fish in any combination are permitted, with a nine-inch minimum.

Lake Erie Hub Cities

Buffalo/Niagara Falls/Lockport/Medina

ACCOMODATIONS PRICE KEY
$ Up to 60 dollars per night
$$ 61 to 99 dollars per night
$$$ 100 to 150 per night
$$$$ 151 and up per night

HOTELS/MOTELS
Comfort Suites, 901 Dick Road, Buffalo, NY   14255 / 716-633-6000 / $$
Adam's Mark, 120 Church Street, Buffalo, NY 14202 / 716-845-510 / $$$-$$$$
Comfort Inn, 551 South Transit Street, Lockport, NY 14094 / 716-434-4411 /
   $$-$$$

CAMPGROUNDS/RVS
KOA Kampgrounds, 1250 Pletcher Road, Lewiston, NY 14092 / 716-754-8013
Beaver Island State Park, 2136 West Oakfield Road, Grand Island, NY 14072 /
   716-773-3271

RESTAURANTS
Old Man River, 375 Niagara Street, Tonawanda, NY 14150, 8 a.m.-11 p.m.
Saratoga Restaurant, 2694 Delaware Avenue, Buffalo, NY 14216 / 716-875-3015

FLY SHOPS
Oak Orchard Fly Shop, 5110 Main Street (Walker Center), Williamsville, NY
   14221 / 716-626-1323 / Full service fly shop, guiding and boat trips /
   www.oakorchardflyshop.com
Buffalo Outfitters (Reed & Son), 5655 Main Street, Williamsville, NY 14221 /
   716-631-5131 / Orvis

TACKLE/SPORTING GOODS
Galyan's Trading Co., 2 Walden Galleria, Buffalo, NY 14225 / 716-651-0600 /
   Mostly spinning gear, small flyfishing section

Canada
Wilsons Sporting Tradition, 26 Wellington Street East, Toronto, Ontario M5E 1S2
  / 416-869-3474 / Orvis / www.wilsonsorvis.com
Angling Specialties
   3251 Kennedy Road, Scarborough, Ontario, M1V-2J9 / 416-609-080
   2104 Highway 7 West, Concord, Ontario, L4K-2S9 / 905-660-9697
   325 Central Parkway, West, Mississauga, Ontario, L5B 3X9 / 906-275-4972
Le Baron Outdoor Products
   8365 Woodbine Avenue, Markham, Ontario, L3R2P4 / 905-944-0682
   1590 Dundas Street East, Mississauga, L4X2Z2 / 905-273-6434

Pollack Sporting Goods, 337 Queen Street East, Toronto, ON M5A-1S9 / 416-363-1095

Auto Repair
Nies Auto Service, 1115 East Ferry Street, Buffalo, NY 14211 / 716-896-5232

Airport
Lancaster Airport, 6100 Transit Road, Depew, NY 14043 / 716-683-7203

Hospital/Clinic
Sheehan Memorial Hospital, 425 Michigan Avenue, Buffalo, NY 14211 / 716-848-2000

Jamestown

Hotels/Motels
The Colony Motel, 620 Fairmont Avenue, Jamestown, NY 14701 / 716-488-1904 / $

Comfort Inn, 2800 Norht Main Street, Jamestown, NY 14701 / 716-664-5920 / $$-$$$

Campgrounds/RVs
Hidden Valley Camping, Kiantone Road, Jamestown, NY 14701 / 716-569-5433 / 215 sites, all w-e / Tenting, stream fishing

Restaurants
Vullo's Restaurant, 2953 East Lake Road, Jamestown, NY 14701 / 716-487-9568
Val's Place, 1103 Route 438, Irving, NY / On Seneca Reservation

Fly Shops
Ingersoll's Chautauqua Flyshop, 1227 Orr Street, Jamestown, NY 14701 / 716-665-2923 / flyshop@prodigy.net / Guided Trips
M & M Sports Den, 808 North Main Street, Jamestown, NY 14701 / 716-664-5400 / Orvis Dealer

PENNSYLVANIA
Fly Fishing Forever, Fairview Village, PA 19409 / 610-631-8990
Smith's Sport Store, 10 Erie Avenue, Saint Marys, Pa 15857 / 814-834-3701

Guides
Joe Battaglia, 716-763-5642, knowledgeable guide covering Erie Tributaries

Airport
Chautauqua County Airport, 3163 Airport Drive, Jamestown, NY 14701 / 716-484-0204

Hospital/Clinic
WCA Hospital, 207 Foote Avenue, Jamestown, NY 14701 / 716-487-0141

Lake Ontario and Tributaries

Lake Ontario and its tributaries are favored with four types of migrating fish: chinook and coho salmon, steelhead and large brown trout. Roughly from September through March, these fish enter streams on the eastern and southern shore of the lake, offering excellent fishing. Though there are similarities in flyfishing for these species, there are enough differences in timing and tactics to look at them separately.

Chinook Salmon

This huge Pacific species—sometimes called king salmon—can reach 40 pounds and is stocked in the prime streams on Lake Ontario, including the Black River, the Salmon River, the two Sandy Creeks and the Oswego River on the eastern shore, and the Genesee River and Oak Orchard along the southern side of the lake. There is only a modest amount of natural reproduction of chinook salmon; most of the fish caught are stocked. In addition to mature spawning fish two to four years old, some precocious one-year old chinooks also come upstream in fall. These males, called jacks, run six or seven pounds.

Because of their size, these fish are prized by anglers. Their spawning runs, which come in late September through October, can create an angling frenzy, making streams like Eighteenmile on the south shore, and the Salmon River on the east, shoulder to shoulder fishing.

There is a premium on getting salmon early in their spawning run. Chinooks don't feed while spawning and die soon after. Fish fresh to the stream are beautiful to look at and put up a good fight, but those toward the end of their stay become sluggish and discolored, with rotting fins.

Fly tackle for chinooks must be strong, 9- or 10-weight rods with disc drag reels and plenty of backing. Various drifted egg patterns will take chinooks, as will the very popular Comet patterns. There are various ways to tie Comets, but they usually have bead-chain eyes (allowing them to ride upside down), sometimes with chenille at the head, bodies of bright floss, braided mylar or chenille, and an optional tail of synthetic or natural hair.

Coho Salmon

Also native to the Pacific, cohos (or silvers) run smaller than the chinooks, typically weighing 10 pounds with fish up to 20 pounds are occasionally caught. Cohos are stocked in some of the same streams that get chinook salmon, including the Salmon River and Sandy Creek in the east and Eighteenmile, Oak Orchard and Niagara on the southern shore of Lake Ontario. The spawning run of cohos come a week or two after chinooks, but there is considerable overlap. They are sometimes a by-catch for anglers hunting chinooks, but a number of anglers actually prefer the smaller, feisty cohos.

Gear for cohos can drop down a notch or two, with 8 weight rods usually enough. Flies and tactics are usually the same as for chinooks.

Steelhead

The migratory version of rainbow trout, steelhead are stocked heavily in about 20 Ontario tributaries. They also stray frequently, so that many streams that don't get stocked still get decent runs of fish. Unlike the salmon, steelhead do reproduce well in Ontario tributaries and a number of streams, including the Salmon River, get good numbers of wild fish.

The steelhead have two runs, the first starting in the fall run in late September and reaching a peak in October and November. The spring run, when the fish spawn, typically begins in early March and tails off by mid-April. In fact, it is believed that the fall run is really just an early spawning run, a genetic holdover from the steelhead's Pacific origins in which months were needed to swim the hundreds of miles to spawning grounds deep inland. Whatever the explanation, Ontario steelhead streams see fish trickling in through the winter months, and many of these stay until spring. Determined anglers do fish in mid-winter, but the dual advantages of good numbers of hard fighting, fresh fish and much better weather make spring and fall the peak fishing periods.

Ontario steelhead are prized for their size—the biggest specimens get to nearly 20 pounds and fish in double-digit weights are common. Rods are 8- to 10-weight with plenty of backing; some Ontario anglers have taken to using spey rods on larger rivers. There is also a kind of hybrid rig, the "noodle rod," that is increasingly popular. This rod is long and very whippy and loaded only with lightweight monofilament. Noodle rodders sometimes use bait, but for non-purists it is also well suited for drifting egg imitations and nymphs.

The flies for steelhead vary somewhat by season. In the fall, they are actively feeding and streamers work well, as do big stonefly nymphs. In streams with salmon runs, the fall steelhead will eat the salmon roe, so egg and egg cluster imitations are also effective. The spring fish are spawners that don't feed; they hit flies only out of instinct. Egg patterns continue to work, as do flies like Zonkers and Buggers with natural action in the drift. Some local anglers go small, fishing with old-fashioned wet flies in sizes 8-12 with quill bodies in various colors and matching soft hackle.

Brown Trout

A number of streams, notably the Salmon River and Oak Orchard and Sandy Creek on the southern shore, see good runs of fall brown trout. These big browns, 5 to 10 pounds or more, do some spawning in the streams and also come up to feed on salmon eggs. They typically arrive in mid-October and often stay through the winter, dropping back in late March or early April, though most fishing is for a month or so after they arrive.

Five- to seven-weight rods are commonly used for the migratory browns, as are egg patterns (especially when salmon are in), small to medium-sized nymphs and various streamers. In the usually low, clear water of fall, the browns can sometimes be coaxed to the surface with dry flies. The autumn browns can be leader shy, so light tippets of 4- to 6-pound test are in order, and fluorocarbon is useful when fishing nymphs and eggs.

Landlocked Salmon

Since 1990 landlocked salmon have been stocked in several Ontario tributaries, including the Salmon River, Sandy Creek (eastern shore) and the Black River. Though this has the potential for an exciting new fishery, to date returns have been modest—at least from an angling perspective—and there is talk of reducing the stocking in some streams.

Gear

Angling for migratory fish, at least successful angling, often means getting flies right down on the bottom. Much of the fishing can be done with floating lines, but sink tips of 5 or 10 feet can often be useful. On big flows like the Salmon River, anglers often attach "slinkies" (netting filled with split shot) to the tag ends of their leader knots. Even more versatile is using split shot on such a tag, which allows weight to be quickly adjusted. Both setups will hang-up less often than split shot on the leader itself.

The risk of hypothermia, not to mention simple discomfort, is always present when fishing from fall through spring. Steelheaders, and salmon anglers too, remain devoted to neoprene waders—the thicker, the better. If you don't want to invest in a pair of neoprenes, which have become relatively inexpensive, make sure you have multiple layers on your legs and feet, including fleece pants and thermal underwear. Neoprene or fleece gloves, with or without fingers, are essential, too. Cleats of one kind or another are also vital, especially for icy winter fishing.

General Regulations

Lake Ontario regulations apply to the tributaries up to the first impassable barrier, with some additional rules. Fishing for all salmon and trout (including steelhead) is open all year. Three fish in any combination are permitted, with a 15-inch minimum (reduced to nine inches for the Salmon River, Lindsay Creek, Little Sandy Creek, Skinner Creek and the Black River on the eastern shore, and Irondequoit Creek on the southern shore). Except on a few streams, night fishing is prohibited. Also, with only a few exceptions, only one hook with no more than a half-inch gap and no more than one-eight ounce of weight directly on it may be fished.

The riffles and runs near The Trestle are a popular area on the Salmon River, especially for chinooks.

Lake Ontario Eastern Shore

SALMON RIVER

The Salmon River is the best-known migratory fish stream in New York. Anglers come from the entire Eastern Seaboard and beyond to fish for thick runs of chinooks and steelhead. The heaviest salmon and steelhead in the state are usually taken in the Salmon River. The stream has excellent access, a lengthy run of about 15 miles from the Lower Salmon Reservoir Dam to the mouth, and in recent years a reasonably steady flow.

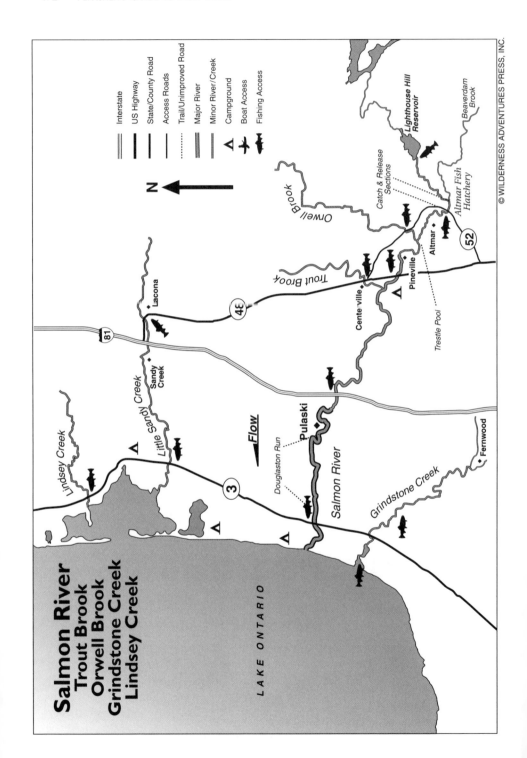

Salmon River
Trout Brook
Orwell Brook
Grindstone Creek
Lindsey Creek

Legend:
Interstate
US Highway
State/County Road
Access Roads
Trail/Unimproved Road
Major River
Minor River/Creek
Campground
Boat Access
Fishing Access

N

LAKE ONTARIO

Lindsey Creek
Little Sandy Creek
Sandy Creek
Lacona
Flow
Pulaski
Douglaston Run
Salmon River
Grindstone Creek
Fernwood
Centerville
Trout Brook
Pineville
Altmar
Trestle Pool
Catch & Release Sections
Orwell Brook
Lighthouse Hill Reservoir
Altmar Fish Hatchery
Beaverdam Brook

81
3
48
52

© WILDERNESS ADVENTURES PRESS, INC.

The village of Pulaski—which is at the heart of the Salmon River fishery—is the Las Vegas of salmon and steelhead fishing. It seems every block in and around the town has neon signs advertising tackle shops, smokehouses or fishing lodges—typically all three. Even simple convenience stores here sell split shot, wading cleats, and neoprene gloves.

The Salmon River receives enormous stockings of fish from the Altmar Hatchery near its upper reaches. Over 200,000 steelhead are put in each year, and there is good natural reproduction of steelhead as well. About 300,000 small chinooks are added, along with 90,000 cohos.

The length and character of the water is essential to the outstanding fishing here. The migratory section of the river runs from the dam on Lower Salmon Reservoir to the mouth. Along the way it encompasses good runs and riffles and terrific pools that provide great holding water and allow (or demand) every type of flyfishing tactic. These factors make it a good place to hire a guide, especially if you've never been here before.

Except for a long private pay-for-access stretch at the lower end (discussed below), virtually the entire river is open to public fishing. Unique among salmon and steelhead fisheries, the river has two short fly-fishing only, catch and release sections. Both are found in the smaller, upper portion of the river. The lower section runs less than half a mile, from the Route 52 crossing upstream to the mouth of Beaverdam Brook (signs mark the boundary). There is public parking nearby on Route 52. On this section, fishing is permitted only from September 15 to May 15, from 30 minutes before sunrise to 30 minutes after sunset.

The upper flyfishing section is slightly longer, running just over half a mile from a marked spot just upstream of the Altmar Hatchery to another marked spot farther upstream near the inflow from the Lighthouse Hill Reservoir. Fishing here is open during the same daylight hours, from April 1 to November 30. This season covers the tail end of the spring steelhead run and most of the fall runs of steelhead and salmon. It also encompasses the small run of summer Skamania strain steelhead that enter in June and July.

After a very wide section downstream, there is some good water at the Old Railroad Trestle, which has ample parking and a short walk to the stream. A series of major pools continue downstream to Route 81, with good access and parking. The Route 81 crossing creates the 81 Hole, a deep holding spot.

The last few miles to the estuary portion of the stream are on private property known as the Douglaston Run. Anglers can fish this section for a daily fee—currently $15 from September to November and $10 the rest of the year. About 300 people per day are admitted, and in prime season this limit is quickly filled. The appeal of the section, in addition to the limited number of anglers, is fresh, unpressured fish. The Douglaston Run is a particularly popular spot for chinook. Information on the Douglaston Run, including fees and fishing reports, is available at 315-298-3531.

Drift boat fishing is also popular on the Salmon River. Floating was limited somewhat by a 1997 decision by the New York Court of Appeals, the state's highest court, following a dispute between local guides and the Douglaston Property. The court held that Douglaston Manor, Inc. owns the streambed and has exclusive fishing rights on the water. Despite the limitations, floating is still possible on the river and can give access to more fish.

The Salmon River Fish Hatchery at Altmar, which stocks Lake Ontario and its tributaries, is open to the public and offers some interesting exhibits on aquaculture and good materials on the Salmon River, as well as a chance to see how salmon and steelhead are born and raised. The hatchery is located at 2133 County Route 22 in Altmar, NY, and open 9 to 4 daily from mid-March to the end of November. Call 315-298-5051 for more information.

Trout Brook

This tributary joins the Salmon River near the village of Centerville, in the upper half of the river. When it has sufficient water, salmon and steelhead come into Trout Brook and can be caught here. Access can be found at several road crossing, including Route 48 and Mattison Road.

Orwell Brook

Orwell enters the river from the north about two miles upstream of Trout Brook, between Pineville and Altmar. A bit tighter than Trout Brook, Orwell also gets runs when is has a sufficient flow. Access is available at the Tubbs Road crossing and downstream where Route 52 crosses near the mouth.

BLACK RIVER (LOWER)

The Black River is a good fishery for steelhead and salmon that runs through the city of Watertown on its way to Lake Ontario. The migratory portion of the Black River runs from the impassable Mill Street Dam in the center of Watertown downstream to the mouth. There are two dams downstream: one at the village of Glen Park west of Watertown, the other well downstream in the suburb of Dexter. These two lower dams both contain fish ladders installed in the mid-1990s that enable fish to go all the way to the Mill Street Dam. (The Dexter Dam ladder operates spring and fall, while the ladder at Glen Park is open year round.)

Unusual for Ontario tributaries, the chinook salmon are probably the strongest fishery in the Black River. They do well using the ladders in fall and can be taken all the way to Mill Street. Though this improves the fishery, it can make finding the fish more difficult—especially on such a wide river. A guide would be a big help, especially for anglers unfamiliar with the stream, but the base of the three dams is a good place to start.

For steelhead, reports are that in recent years there has been a drop in returning fish. Steelhead also successfully use the fish ladders, though local anglers report that the last segment below Dexter Dam is still a prime spot. This portion is very

Black River (lower)

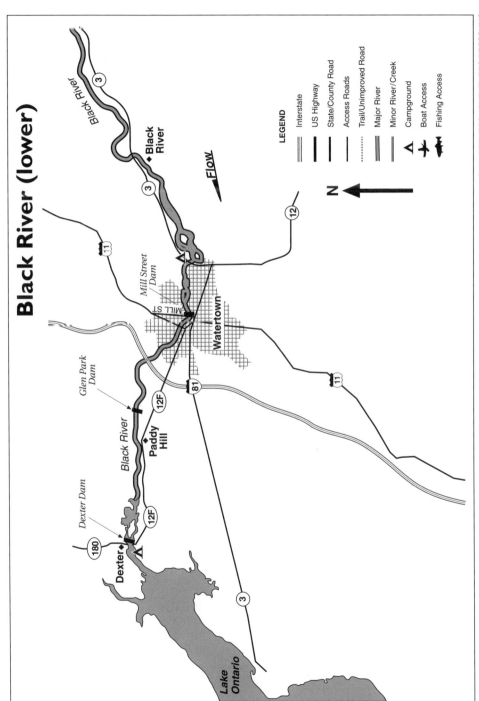

LEGEND

Interstate
US Highway
State/County Road
Access Roads
Trail/Unimproved Road
Major River
Minor River/Creek
Campground
Boat Access
Fishing Access

N

FLOW

Black River

Black River

Black River

Mill Street Dam

Glen Park Dam

Dexter Dam

Watertown

Paddy Hill

Dexter

Lake Ontario

© WILDERNESS ADVENTURES PRESS, INC.

wide and can be fished from canoes and kayaks; the public access at the dam permits such craft to be launched. When runs are strong, there is good natural reproduction of steelhead in the Black and the young fish can be caught. Even though some may meet the smaller nine-inch size limit, it is best to throw them back and try catching them again after they return fully grown.

In addition to steelhead and chinooks, landlocked salmon have been heavily stocked in the Black in recent years. Returns, however, have been spotty; in one year 200 fish were caught out of 75,000 stocked. In fact, the DEC is considering curtailing landlocked stocking here.

The typical patterns for salmon and steelhead will work on the Black River. Given the river's size, swinging a traditional salmon or steelhead pattern probably gives better odds than dead drifting a nymph. In general, long rods are the way to go on the Black River as its width can make it a challenge to flyfishers. In fact, this is an ideal place for spey casters.

The Black River up to Mill Street Dam is subject to the standard Great Lakes tributary regulations, with a few additions: The Black is subject to a smaller nine-inch limit, but only one steelhead per day is permitted (a limit applicable to all Jefferson County streams).

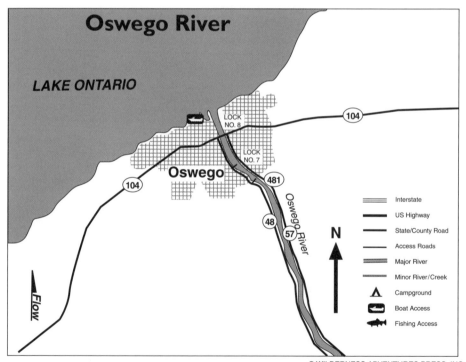

© WILDERNESS ADVENTURES PRESS, INC.

OSWEGO RIVER

This large river offers only a short run to migrating fish between its mouth and the impassable dam near Lock 7 in the city of Oswego. The modest length, a bit more than a mile, and its urban setting make it heavily fished at times. Much of the fishing is done from boats, which can be launched at the mouth and from a private fee-based launch area just below the dam. It can also be fished from shore at several parks in the city. In this big water, anglers should look for fish in seams and current breaks. Oswego gets good returns from a heavy stocking of chinooks and a moderate stocking of steelhead.

SMALLER EASTERN TRIBUTARIES

These smaller tributaries on the eastern shore of the lake all offer fishing for steelhead and Pacific salmon. While they won't have the same density of fish as the Salmon or the Black, they typically won't have as many anglers, either. They can also be a first choice when the larger rivers are running high. For the small streams it is usually low water, rather than high, that is a concern; decent runs—especially in fall—will depend on sufficient rain. At the tail end of the fall season these streams usually freeze, making fishing difficult if not impossible.

South Sandy Creek

Among smaller eastern shore Ontario tributaries, South Sandy arguably offers the best fishing for migratory trout. It receives good runs of fish, is readily accessible and offers the opportunity to fish from shore or boat. South Sandy is a particularly good place to fish for steelhead in the spring.

The fishable portion of South Sandy lies downstream of the village of Ellisburg in Jefferson County. The stream runs about five miles to the mouth, but it is the roughly three-mile run from the falls near Ellisburg to the Route 3 crossing that is best for flyfishing. There is good public access on the South Sandy along South Landing Road and at the bridge in the Village of Ellisburg. Small boats can be put in just below the old mill dam at Ellisburg and taken out at Route 3.

Sandy Creek (North Sandy Creek)

This stream, just north of South Sandy, is referred to on maps and stocking lists as Sandy Creek, but it is usually called North Sandy Creek by anglers. Like its neighbor to the south, it offers a short stretch of flyfishing—about six miles from the falls near the village of Hossington to Route 3. Access is available from Route 75 on the north bank and Allard Road and Shaw Road on the south bank.

Little Sandy Creek

Despite its name, this small stream runs well south of the other two Sandy Creeks—just about five miles north of the Salmon River. The creek is not stocked with steelhead or salmon, but both do ascend from the lake. As with many small lake tributaries, fishing depends largely on sufficient flows, especially in autumn.

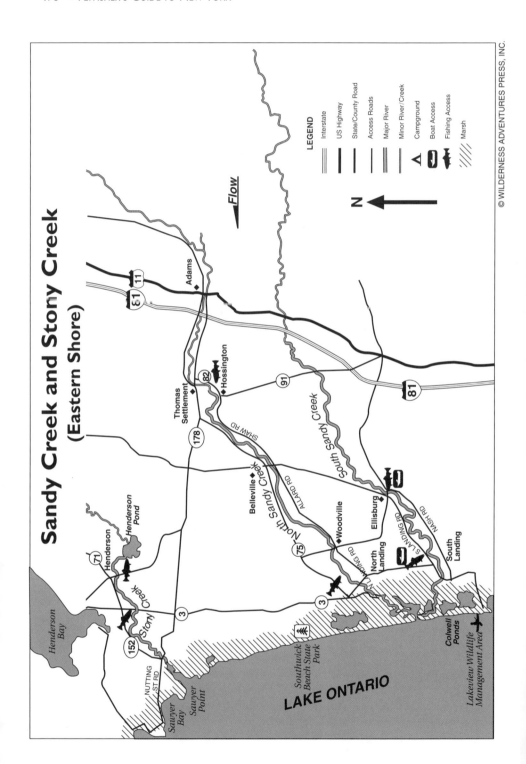

Sandy Creek and Stony Creek
(Eastern Shore)

Flow

LEGEND

Interstate
US Highway
State/County Road
Access Roads
Major River
Minor River/Creek
Campground
Boat Access
Fishing Access
Marsh

N

Adams

Hossington

Thomas Settlement

Belleville

Woodville

Ellisburg

Henderson

Henderson Pond

North Sandy Creek

South Sandy Creek

SHAW RD

ALLARD RD

N LANDING RD

S LANDING RD

NASH RD

North Landing

South Landing

Stony Creek

NUTTING ST RD

Henderson Bay

Sauyer Bay

Sauyer Point

Southwick Beach State Park

Colwell Ponds

Lakeview Wildlife Management Area

LAKE ONTARIO

© WILDERNESS ADVENTURES PRESS, INC.

The stream is small but runs a long way without any obstructions. There is a lot of posted land along Little Sandy, but access is available where Norton Road crosses and upstream in the villages of Sandy Creek and Lacona.

Grindstone Creek

Grindstone runs south of the Salmon River and receives a small stocking of steelhead. Both steelhead and a few salmon run into the stream, going as far as the barrier near the junction of the two branches in Fernwood.

Fishing here is complicated by the small size and overhanging brush. Posted land covers large parts of the creek, but access is available near the mouth, where it runs through Selkirk Shores State Park. There is also access upstream at the Route 28 and Salisbury Road crossings.

Stony Creek

This very small stream in the Jefferson County town of Henderson gets a modest stocking of steelhead. About four miles of the stream are fishable between Henderson Pond and the mouth at Henderson Harbor. Access is available where Route 3 crosses.

Lindsey Creek

Another small creek, Lindsey starts in Jefferson County and meets the lake just over the border in Oswego. No salmon or steelhead are stocked directly in the creek, but fish from the lake—including some that reproduce naturally—do come in. The runs are heavily dependent on sufficient flows, especially in fall.

Lake Ontario Eastern Shore Hub Cities
Pulaski/Oswego
(also see Syracuse Hub City)

HOTELS/MOTELS
Fox Hollow Salmon River Lodge, 2740 Route 13, Altmar, NY 13302 / 315-298-2876 / $

1880 House, (315) 298-3511, www.1880house.com / $

Driftwood Motel, Route 81, Pulaski, NY 13142 / 315-298-5000 / $

The Portly Angler Lodge, 24 County Route 2A, Pulaski, NY 13142 / 315-298-4773 / www.theportlyanglerlodge.com / $

CAMPGROUNDS/RVS
Stoney's Pineville Campground, 2904 Route 13, Pulaski, NY 13142 / 315-298-2325

Selkirk Shores State Park, West of Pulaski / 315-298-5737

RESTAURANTS
C & M Diner, Route 81 Pulaski, NY / Opens early

FLY & TACKLE SHOPS
Pulaski surely has more fly and tackle shops than any town its size. These shops all have flies, waders and at least some fly gear. Most can also arrange for guided trips.

Yankee Fly Shop, 4819 Salina Street, Pulaski, NY 13142 / 315-298-2466

Whitaker's Sport Shop and Motel, 3707 Route 13, Pulaski, NY 13142 / 315-298-6162

All Seasons Sports, 3733 Route 13, Pulaski, NY 13142 / 315-298-6433

Fat Nancy's Tackle Shop, Route 13 and Interstate 81, Pulaski, NY 13142 / 315-298-6357

Fish Inn Post, 2035 Route 22, Altmar, NY 13302 / 315-298-6406

Pulaski Sport Shop, 7676 Rome Road, Pulaski, NY 13142 / 315-298-6599

Steelhead Motel and Tackle Shop, 3178 Route 13, Pulaski, NY 13142 / 315-298-4371

Tony's Salmon Country Sports Shop, 3790 Rome Street Pulaski, NY 13142 / 315-298-4104

Malinda's Fly & Tackle Shop, 3 Pulaski Street, Altmar, NY 13302 / 315-298-2993

Oswego Outfitters, PO Box 86, Pulaski, NY 13142 / 315-298-6349

Tony's Salmon Country Sports, 3790 Route 13, Pulaski, NY 13142 / 315-298-4104

GUIDES
Most of the area fly and tackle shops, and many lodges, also offer guiding.

Pat Miura, 1417 State Street, Watertown, NY 13601 / 315-788-9571

AIRPORT
Syracuse Airport, About 35 miles from Pulaski and Oswego

HOSPITAL/CLINIC
Medina Memorial Hospital, 200 Ohio Street, Medina, NY 14103 / 716-798-2000

The Sycamore Pool is a prime spot on Oak Orchard Creek.

Lake Ontario Southern Shore

Oak Orchard Creek

Oak Orchard Creek offers outstanding fishing for steelhead and migratory brown trout in its short run from the dam on Lake Alice to Lake Ontario. Chinook salmon can also be caught and occasional cohos are found here, too.

Oak Orchard—the Oak to locals—runs about five miles from the small dam at Lake Alice to its mouth. However, for fly anglers, it is the first mile or so that is most important. After that, the stream widens and slows as it becomes an estuary. The prime flyfishing section begins just below the dam and ends at a pool in front of an archery club, commonly known as the Archery Pool.

There are two main access points on the flyfishing stretch, both on the eastern side of the stream: one at the dam and the other near the bottom off Park Road. Either will allow anglers to hike the entire stream. In most water conditions, anglers can find a spot to wade across and fish from the other side.

Like most Ontario tributaries, water flows are low and clear in fall and spring, higher and dirtier in late winter (March). However, dam releases obviously affect flows as well. Operated by Orion Power (which purchased it from Niagara Mohawk), the dam generates electricity and doesn't have a set flow regime. Orion does make an effort to keep water in the stream, but anglers are well advised to check on flows before making a trip, and to keep alert to rising water while fishing. When Lake Alice is full, anglers should be sure to check the secondary channel just below the dam on the western side of the river. This channel carries overflow and can offer great fishing for a day or two in high water conditions. (On the down side, fish inevitably get trapped in the back channel as the water recedes, and fall prey to animals as well as illegal snagging and netting.)

Anglers can sight fish on Oak Orchard when the water is low and clear. In high water the fishing becomes trickier and anglers need to look for key holes. While still well known, the Archery Pool has actually filled in over recent years and is not quite as productive as it once was. However, the Sycamore Pool just upstream (marked by a large, leaning tree on the east side of the stream) is productive for steelhead and browns. Farther upstream, there is a good pool where an old bridge abutment approaches the stream on the western bank. If you are on the stream in low water, make a mental note of pools for high water conditions. And even though it's a short stream, a guide can be helpful, especially in high water.

The migratory fishing on Oak Orchard begins with big chinook salmon and a few cohos that run into the creek starting at the end of September. Flies are typically individual eggs or clusters along with black Woolly Buggers. The salmon fishing lasts roughly a month.

The salmon are followed by big, migratory brown trout from Lake Ontario. These fish run 5 to 10 pounds, sometimes closer to 20, and come into Oak Orchard a week or two after the chinooks. The size of these fish and the pleasant fall conditions make this a very popular run. The peak for the browns is the second half of October and fishing continues well into November. The brown trout feed greedily on salmon eggs, and can sometimes be spotted directly behind spawning chinooks. Given their feeding, egg and egg cluster patterns are obvious fly choices.

The Oak's steelhead begin arriving in fall, with November probably the key autumn month. They remain, with additional fish trickling in, through winter and into spring. The spring run is at its best for five or six weeks in March and the first half of April. Fly choice for steelhead is as much a matter of personal preference as matching actual food. Marc Bierstine, who owns Orleans Outdoor nearby and fishes the river often, likes either single egg patterns or the Sucker Spawn.

Whether Sucker Spawn, egg pattern or nymph, the fly should be drifted on a tight line from shortly above the angler until it completes its swing. Steelhead are not feeding actively and must be enticed to strike, so plan to cast repeatedly to a spot before moving on. Plan as well to bring many copies of the same fly—if you aren't losing them occasionally, you're probably not fishing deep enough. When spawning steelhead are on the beds in lower water, a swinging presentation rather than a deep drift can be used. The fish aren't feeding, but they are much more aggressive in spawning mode.

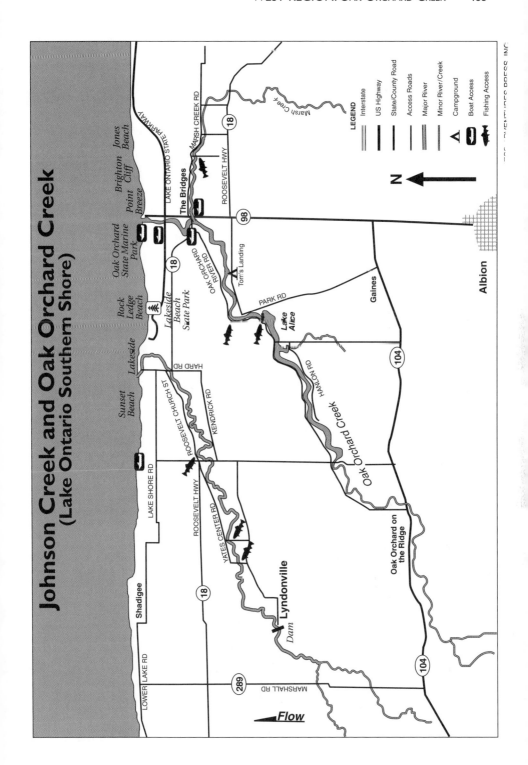

Johnson Creek and Oak Orchard Creek
(Lake Ontario Southern Shore)

Marsh Creek

This small tributary to Oak Orchard Creek can be fished for steelhead, salmon and some browns in fall and steelhead again in spring. (The stream should not be confused with the stream at the border of Orleans and Niagara Counties, which is not a trout or salmon fishery). The creek enters Oak Orchard well downstream from the main river's best flyfishing section near the mouth. Marsh Creek can be reached at various points along Marsh Creek Road.

Unlike the stream it enters, Marsh Creek does not receive dam releases, so the fishing is heavily dependant on having enough water at the right times. If it doesn't, angler's can simply head upstream to the prime water on Oak Orchard. Marsh Creek gets its own small stocking of about 4,000 steelhead each year.

Guide Mark Bierstine gets ready to release a big Oak Orchard steelhead.

Stream Facts: Oak Orchard Creek

Seasons
- Up to first impassable barrier (Orion Power Dam at Lake Alice), all year for salmon, steelhead and trout.

Special Regulations
- Up to first impassable barrier, Great Lakes regulations apply; three fish in any combination, 15 inches or more.

Fish
- Steelhead, migrating brown trout, chinook salmon, occasional coho salmon.

River Characteristics
- Small to medium-sized tailwater, influenced by runoff and snowmelt.

River Flows
- Low and clear in fall and late spring, can be high and dirty during early spring thaw. Fluctualtes with dam releases.

Though small, Keg Creek does hold some good-sized fish. This angler landed a steelhead a few minutes after this photo was taken.

WEST OF OAK ORCHARD CREEK

JOHNSON CREEK

Johnson Creek runs about seven miles from a dam in the town of Lydonville to its mouth on Lake Ontario. It is primarily the first third of the stream below the dam that is of most interest to fly anglers. The stream gets a good run of fall chinooks right up to the dam. There is access at the dam and the pool at its base is reportedly a good place to fish. There are also access points downstream off Yates Center Road that allow wading to pools and riffles. Because it runs through a well-settled area, Johnson doesn't always provide a bucolic fishing experience and suffers from streamside refuse as well.

In addition to the primary fishery for salmon, Johnson Creek gets a stocking of about 6,500 steelhead each year that can be targeted in fall and spring.

KEG CREEK

A small Ontario feeder in Niagara County between Johnson Creek and Eighteenmile Creek, Keg Creek offers some pretty good steelhead fishing; about 10,000 are stocked and there is some fall chinook fishing. There is formal access where Route 18 crosses the creek, less than a mile from the mouth. The large pool just below the bridge is ideal for drifting an egg pattern and can yield small but feisty steelhead on light fly tackle. If the pool is being fished, anglers can easily wade up or downstream. Above Swiggert Road, about two miles upstream of the access, the stream divides and becomes very small, but it can still hold fish if there is enough water. As with other free-flowing waters, Keg Creek fishing depends on adequate flows. If there isn't enough water, try a larger stream like Johnson or Oak Orchard.

EIGHTEENMILE CREEK

Though running only about two miles from the dam in the village of Burt to its mouth, Eighteenmile Creek can offer very good salmon fishing, and occasional steelhead as well. Access is at the docks near the mouth in the town of Olcott and upstream where the railroad trestle crosses.

The state plants a large number of chinook salmon in the Eighteenmile—more than 125,000 fingerlings each year—and about 25,000 cohos. Often it seems as if there are that many anglers here as well. While it is heavily hit by spin fishermen, fly anglers can have success with egg patterns and nymphs.

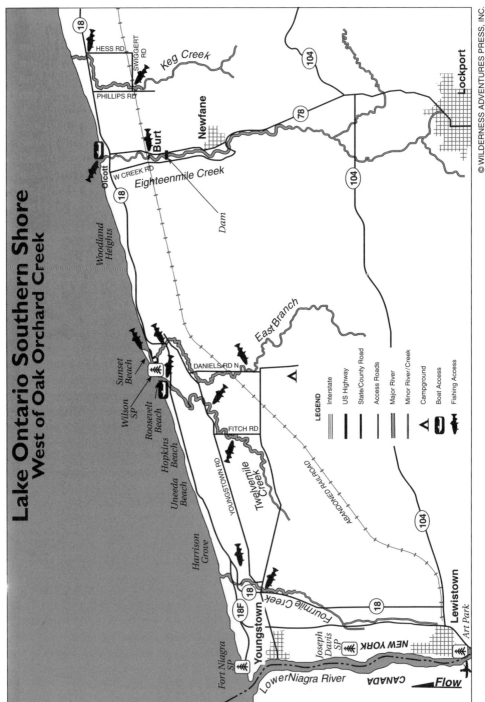

Lake Ontario Southern Shore
West of Oak Orchard Creek

© WILDERNESS ADVENTURES PRESS, INC.

LEGEND

Interstate
US Highway
State/County Road
Access Roads
Major River
Minor River/Creek
Campground
Boat Access
Fishing Access

ABANDONED RAILROAD

Keg Creek

Lockport

104

Newfane

78

104

HESS RD
SWIGGERT RD
PHILLIPS RD

Burt

Olcott

W CREEK RD

Eighteenmile Creek

Dam

Woodland
Heights

18

East Branch

DANIELS RD N

FITCH RD

Sunset
Beach

Wilson
SP

Roosevelt
Beach

Hopkins
Beach

Uneeda
Beach

Harrison
Grove

YOUNGSTOWN RD

Twelvemile Creek

Fort Niagra
SP

18F

18

Youngstown

Joseph
Davis
SP

NEW YORK

CANADA

Lower Niagra River

Fourmile Creek

18

18

104

Lewistown

Art Park

Flow

TWELVEMILE CREEK

True to its numerical designation, Twelvemile falls in between nearby Eighteenmile and Fourmile in size and significance. It does require sufficient water to make it fishable—primarily for steelhead.

This stream is actually two streams: the Twelvemile Creek that empties at Roosevelt Beach and the completely separate East Branch of Twelvemile that empties just east at Sunset Beach/Wilson-Tuscarora State Park. Each of the two "branches" is stocked with about 15,000 steelhead.

A long, lower section of the main stream is wide and slow, more suited to spin fishing. Starting downstream of Youngstown Road, the river narrows and speeds up (assuming it has water) and can be fished with egg patterns and other steelhead fare. Access can be had at Youngstown Road and Fitch Road upstream. The East Branch can be reached from the park, from a few spots on Youngstown Road, and farther upstream from Daniels Road north.

FOURMILE CREEK

A very small creek near the Niagara River, Fourmile can bring in salmon and steelhead when it has enough water. (No steelhead are stocked directly, but they do make their way in from the lake.) Even when it does, it is small enough to jump across, so careful stalking and wading are essential. Access can be had where Route 18 and Route 93 cross the stream.

Plan to fish Fourmile Creek from the bank.

Fishing from shore on the wide Lower Niagara is not easy.

LOWER NIAGARA RIVER

The Niagara flows out of Lake Erie into Lake Ontario. Wide and fast running, it is not ideal flyfishing water, but it is fished on occasion. Floating the lower end in the vicinity of Lewiston is popular with anglers, and a few people do use fly rods from boats. However, the modified rig needed to fish deep from the side of a boat barely resembles fly gear.

Fly anglers also cast from shore in the vicinity of Art Park in Lewiston. Shooting heads or long sink tips are required as is considerable patience and fortitude to learn where the fish will be in the very large flow. The quarry includes large steelhead and salmon from Ontario, as well as a good run of lake trout that enter the lower river in fall. Though steelhead anglers sometimes catch these fish in winter, the legal season for the lakers is January 1st through September 30.

EAST OF OAK ORCHARD CREEK

SANDY CREEK

Sandy Creek gets salmon and steelhead and is particularly good for migratory brown trout. (The stream should not be confused with the North and South Sandy creeks on the eastern shore of the lake.) Because there is no barrier to the fish, the creek can be fished all the way into its branches. Putting a canoe in the upper reaches and floating down is a little-used way to hit remote spots on the stream.

The wade fishing typically takes place in the shorter section below the junction of the two branches near Hamlin to the marshy section off the lake. There is good access in this stretch of the stream; Route 18 runs along the stream for several miles providing entry at several points. In addition, access can be had from Brice Road and the West Fork of Lake Road.

The same absence of barriers that allows fishing over much of the creek makes finding fish difficult. If you are in the wrong spot it doesn't matter how well or often you offer just the right fly—your chances of catching fish, especially steelhead, are slim. If you are in doubt, go with someone who knows the creek or hire a guide.

About 100,000 chinooks are stocked here, along with 25,000 cohos. Steelhead stocking is more modest given the stream's length—about 15,000 fish. Browns are not stocked but do come in from Lake Ontario in fall. These browns are known to winter over and Sandy Creek offers some of the best brown trout fishing through winter and early spring. However, mid-winter can be difficult as the river usually freezes. The period just after ice-out, around the last two weeks in March, is peak time for late-winter browns. After that, the browns drop back to the lake as the water slows and warms in spring. Normal egg patterns, including the Nuclear Egg with a bit of flash, are the typical offerings.

IRONDEQUOIT CREEK

Irondequoit Creek runs along the eastern edge of Rochester and offers some salmon and a good run of spring steelhead (it receives 25,000 fish a year). The prime fishing water is the seven miles or so between the village of Bushnells Basin upstream of Interstate 490 and Ellison Park on Landing Road. Access is available at the upper end from Linear Park, Ellison Park at the lower end and various bridge crossings in between. The lower end at Ellison has slow water, but if you know the right spots, good steelheading is available.

Allen Creek, which enters Irondequoit from the west in the town of Pennfield near Route 441, also has a good spring steelhead run when there is enough water. Both Allen and Irondequoit are good choices when larger streams in the area are running high; however, they are popular, especially on weekends.

Irondequoit also receives a substantial stocking of brown trout along much of its length, about 8,000 fish in all, including about 1,500 two-year-olds. This is primarily a put-and-take fishery due to low water in summer.

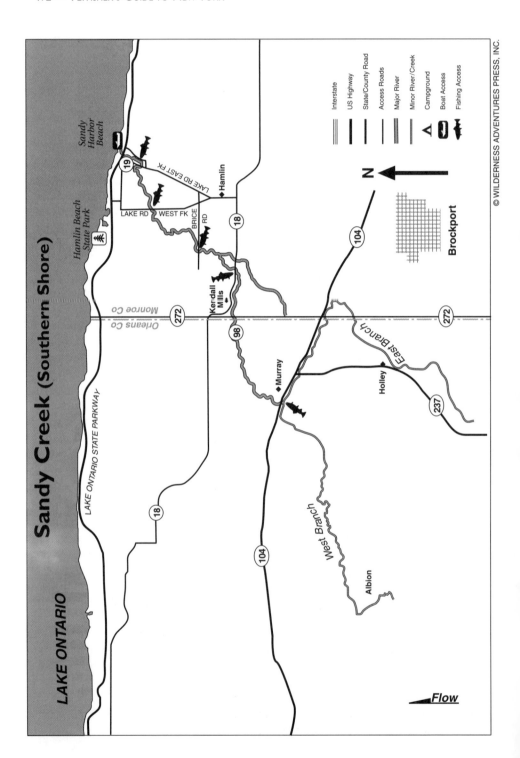

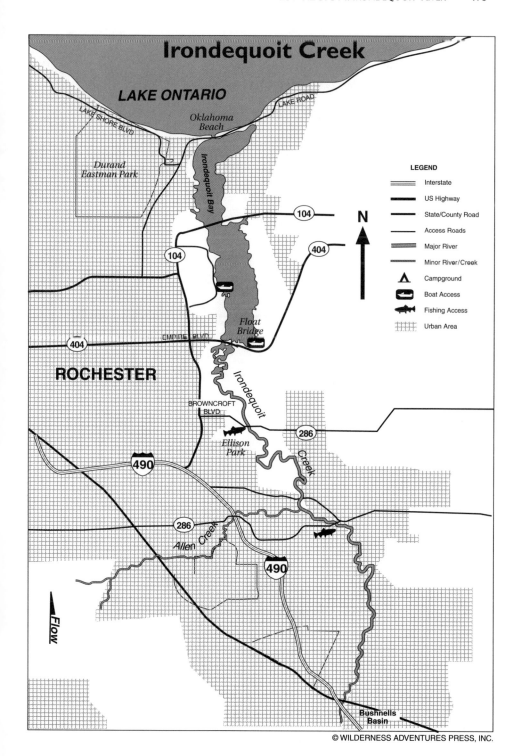

Irondequoit Creek

LAKE ONTARIO

LAKE SHORE BLVD

LAKE ROAD

Oklahoma
Beach

Durand
Eastman Park

Irondequoit Bay

LEGEND

Interstate

US Highway

State/County Road

Access Roads

Major River

Minor River/Creek

Campground

Boat Access

Fishing Access

Urban Area

104

404

N

104

Float
Bridge

404

EMPIRE BLVD

ROCHESTER

BROWNCROFT
BLVD

Irondequoit

Ellison
Park

286

Creek

490

286

Allen Creek

490

Flow

Bushnells
Basin

© WILDERNESS ADVENTURES PRESS, INC.

Fishing for brown trout that often spend the winter in Sandy Creek.

LOWER GENESEE RIVER

The Genesee's relatively short but wide migratory section gets runs of steelhead and salmon. From the first impassable barrier—a waterfall—the river runs about five miles to Lake Ontario.

The river's depth and width make it more appropriate for spinning gear, but the roughly one mile stretch below the dam is popular with fly anglers. There, rapids and pools will hold steelhead and can be hit with standard gear and flies for Lake Ontario fish. The stretch of the Genesee below the lower dam is accessible from steep trails on the west bank or from an access road on the east side.

The fall run of steelhead is especially strong. The river is often murky, and the fishing, especially the flyfishing, will be best when you can see 6-10 inches underwater. Due to flows and crowding, September and October are prime time for spinning anglers, November and December best for hardy flyfishers. One hybrid style of fishing that has caught on in this big water is the use of spey rods set up with monofilament.

Though low water can make many steelhead streams difficult or impossible to fish, the Genesee can get better under such conditions. Keith Nehrke, a biologist who lives in the area, recalls a dry season in the mid-1990s when fly angling became exceptional on the Genesee's low water. However, he notes these conditions required finesse fishing: four-pound fluorocarbon tippets and nymphs, generally stoneflies, in sizes 14-18.

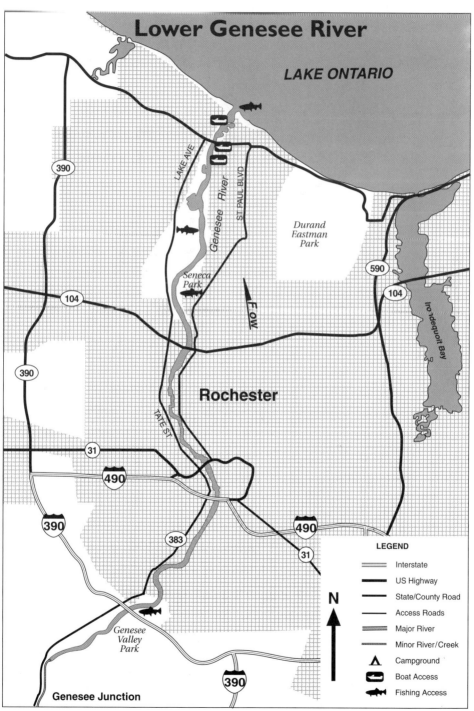

Lower Genesee River

LAKE ONTARIO

390

LAKE AVE

ST PAUL BLVD

Genesee River

Durand Eastman Park

590

104

Seneca Park

FLOW

Irondequoit Bay

104

390

Rochester

TATE ST

31

490

390

383

490

31

Genesee Valley Park

390

Genesee Junction

LEGEND

Interstate

US Highway

State/County Road

Access Roads

Major River

Minor River/Creek

Campground

Boat Access

Fishing Access

N

© WILDERNESS ADVENTURES PRESS, INC.

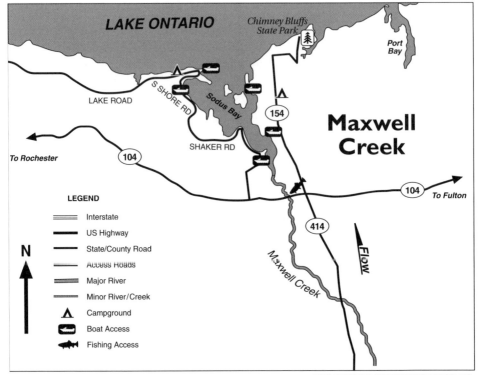

© WILDERNESS ADVENTURES PRESS, INC.

MAXWELL CREEK

This small flow, sometimes called Sodus Creek, runs a few miles into Sodus Bay in Wayne County. The stream is relatively narrow—not more than 20 feet wide—but does get good runs of steelhead in spring and fall, and fall runs of chinook salmon and browns. About 14,000 small steelhead are stocked in the stream, and chinooks are put in Sodus Bay.

Maxwell is a spatey stream, not worth fishing if it lacks water. The other challenge with Maxwell is access; the only ready access is where Route 104 crosses the stream.

LAKE ONTARIO

Trout and Salmon

While it is the Ontario tributaries that see most of the flyfishing for trout and salmon, a few hardy souls do fish for these species in the lake with float tubes or kayaks/canoes. The flyfishing is typically done right at the creek mouths, when the fish congregate for both their fall or spring runs. Autumn is probably the better time, as the fish are feeding then. Steelhead caught before they enter the streams are fresh and strong. Clouser Minnows and other streamers in gray/white, olive/white and other baitfish colors will take fish. Big browns that chase bait in the shallows are also caught this way, with late March and early April the prime times.

Obviously anyone launching a float tube or small boat in the lake needs to check weather conditions carefully and observe all safety precautions including the use of life vests.

Smallmouth

With all the attention on salmon and steelhead, it is easy to neglect the excellent warmwater fishing in Ontario. Recently, though, flyfishers have been going after smallmouth bass in the bays and shallow shorelines of the lake.

This fishing is generally done from boats, and except when confined to the bays, the boats must be sizable to handle the wind and waves on the lake. Anglers seek out shoal areas—places with a wide, rocky, shallow shoreline running from three or four feet deep gradually down to about 30 feet. There are shoals at various points on the lake, but the area near Rochester is particularly rich in this kind of structure. The roughly six-mile run from Irondequoit Bay to Nine Mile Point is a good section, as is the area farther east at Pultneyville. In addition to the shoals, the bays themselves can be productive, and are especially attractive on windy days or for those with less seaworthy boats. Inrondequoit Bay is good, as is Sodus Bay to the east.

Lake Ontario smallmouth anglers use 6- to 8-weight rods, usually leaning toward the heavier models. Lines are most often full sinking versions, except for floating or sink tip lines for bay fishing. Flies include Woolly Buggers in combinations of brown and olive (to imitate crayfish), Clouser Minnows, streamers and some saltwater slider patterns. The streamers are usually tied a bit brighter and shinier than the actual forage. It is important to put the flies where the fish are, so tying several copies with different amounts of weight is helpful. The fish are not huge, but do average 12-14 inches, with more than a few closer to 16 inches long. Flyfishers also report catching occasional large freshwater drum (sheepshead) when fishing for bass.

Water temperature is important as the bass will usually be found in water from the mid to high 60s. Time of day is less crucial, though sundown is reportedly a slow period. Smallmouth bass season begins the third Saturday in June, and the first few weeks are a good time to find fish in shallow water. However, flyfishers will continue seeking smallmouths until October.

Lake Ontario smallmouth are covered by the standard season and regulations: from the third Saturday in June to November 30, with five fish of 12 inches or better allowed.

Lake Ontario Southern Shore Hub Cities

Orleans County

ACCOMODATIONS PRICE KEY
$ Up to 60 dollars per night
$$ 61 to 99 dollars per night
$$$ 100 to 150 per night
$$$$ 151 and up per night

HOTELS/MOTELS
Fair Haven Inn, 14369 Ridge Road, Albion, NY 14411 / 716-589-9151 / Historic inn next to Tillmans / $-$$
Orleans Outdoor, 3 lodge rooms, with common lr and kitchenette / 50 double occ, $20 additional / $

CAMPGROUNDS/RVs
Hamlin Beach State Park, Lake Ontario Parkway (1 Camp Road), Hamlin, NY 14464 / 716-964-2462 / 264 elec / Tenting / May through mid October.
Green Harbor Campground, 12813 Lakeshore Road, Lyndonville, NY 14098 / 716-682-9780 / 135 sites, 30 full / April through October

RESTAURANTS
Carlton Grill Restaurant, 1750 Oak Orchard Road, Albion, NY 14411 / 716-682-4842 / 5 a.m. Sat-Sun
Gaines Family Restaurant, 14069 Ridge Road, Route 104, Albion, NY 14411 / 716-589-2160 / 7 a.m. to 8 p.m.
Tillman's Village Inn, Ridge Road, Rte 104 and 98 / 716-589-9151
The Cool Breeze-In', Point Breeze, NY 14477 / 716-682-0085 / On Lake Ontario / Good breakfast

FLY SHOPS
Orleans Outdoor, 1764 Oak Orchard Road (Route 98), Albion, NY 14411 / 716-682-4546 / www.orleansoutdoor.comFull service fly shop, spinning gear also, guiding (see above for lodging)

TACKLE SHOPS
Bait Barn & Tackle, Route 279, Albion, NY 14411 / 716-589-5004 / Fly and spinning gear
Narby's Superette & Tackle, 1292 Oak Orchard Road (Route 98), Kent, NY 14477 / 716-682-4624 / mostly spin, near mouth of Oak Orchard

AIRPORT
Rochester Airport, (About 50 miles from Oak Orchard Creek)

HOSPITAL/CLINIC
Medina Memorial Hospital, 200 Ohio Street, Medina, NY 14103 / 716-798-2000

Rochester and Vicinity

HOTELS/MOTELS

Hyatt Regency Rochester, 125 East Main Street, Rochester, NY 14604 / 716-546-1234 / SD 130-150 / $$$

Best Western Diplomat Hotel, 1956 Lyell Avenue, Rochester, NY 14606 / 716-254-1000 / SD 55-80 / $$

CAMPGROUNDS/RVS

Frost Ridge, Conlon Road, LeRoy, NY 14482 / 716-768-4883 / 116 sites, 15 full, 85 w-e,

RESTAURANTS

Phillips European, 1200 Brooks Avenue, Rochester, NY 14624 / 716-328-3390

Sullivan's Charbroil, 4712 West Ridge Road, Spencerport, NY 14559 / 716-352-5860

Village Coal Tower, 9 Schoen Place, Rochester, NY 14534 / 716-381-7866 / Opens 8 a.m.

FLY SHOPS

Rochester area fly shops cover both Lake Ontario fishing and nearby inland streams, including Oatka Creek.

Coleman's Fly Shop, 4786 Ridge Road West, Spencerport, NY 14559 / 716-352-4775 / www.colemansflyshop.com

Panorama Outfitters, Cliffside Common, 900 Panorama Trail, Rochester, NY 14625 / 716-248-8390 / www.panoramaoutfitters.com (Orvis dealer)

Up The Creek, 28 South Main Street, Pittsford, NY 14534 / 716-381-3550

AUTO REPAIR

Lefebre's Auto Service, 40 Stone Road, Greece, NY 14616 / 716-663-9632

AIRPORT

Rochester International Airport, 1200 Brooks Avenue, Rochester, NY 14624 / 716-464-6010

HOSPITAL/CLINIC

Rochester General Hospital, 1425 Portland Avenue, Rochester, NY 14621 / 716-922-4000

Some New York Flies

Fly recommendations are found in stream and lake descriptions, and in the hatch charts throughout this book. The following are some local specialties, which either originated on New York waters or have become especially popular here.

Compara-Emerger

Imitating vulnerable emergers and cripples is increasingly important when fishing over educated trout, especially in wild fisheries like the Delaware. This emerger/cripple imitation designed by Al Caucci is simple and effective. It has the added virtues of being sturdy and employing inexpensive materials. Body, wing and tail (shuck) colors can be varied to cover most mayflies. You may want to put some floatant on the wing when fishing.

- Hook: size 12-20 dry fly, extra long for largest flies
- Tail: sparse zelon or antron to match color of nymphal shuck (brown is common), no longer than length of shank
- Body: slim dubbing to match natural dun
- Wing: coastal or other deer hair tied at 45-degree backward angle; tips should not extend beyond hook bend
- Head: butts of deer hair strands, angled upright by loops of thread and clipped short

Ausable Wulff

This fly, designed by Fran Betters for the pocket water of the Ausable, is useful wherever a high floating and visible imitation is needed. It is primarily an attractor pattern, but the brown body does imitate a number of natural insects. Add the Gray Wulff and White Wulff and you'll cover many of your dry fly needs on fast, rocky streams.

- Hook: size 8-16 dry fly
- Tail: woodchuck
- Body: rusty brown (possum) dubbing
- Hackle: brown and grizzly hackle, wings
- Wing: white calf tail
- Head: orange or red thread

Other Wulff Flies

White Wulff (useful for White Fly hatches)

- Hook: size 10-14 dry fly
- Tail: white calf tail
- Body: white or cream dubbing
- Wing: white calf tail
- Hackle: white, badger or grizzly

Gray Wulff
- Hook: size 8-16 dry fly
- Tail: gray squirrel tail
- Body: gray dubbing (muskrat or synthetic)
- Wing: gray squirrel tail
- Hackle: dun

Sucker Spawn
This fly originated in Pennsylvania, but it has become popular with steelhead anglers on Lake Ontario and Lake Erie. Designed to imitate a cluster of the sucker's very small eggs, it should also work on the Finger Lakes tributaries, or any other lake feeders that see runs of spawning suckers.
- Hook: size 8-12 curved scud hook or straight nymph hook
- Tail: (optional) several short strands of flashabou
- Body: tying thread in color to match yarn
- Egg Loops: angora yarn in pink, chartreuse, orange, red and white
  (Note: angora yarn is strongly preferred and can be found at some craft shops; sparkle yarn or micro chenille/vernille can be substituted.)

Separate yarn strands and tie in at tail. Tie strands forward to eye in small loops (about 1/16 inch each), bunching loops so the fly is thickest at the middle. The result should resemble a small bunch of many small eggs (loops).

Grey Ghost
Though not "native" to New York (it was originated in Maine by Carrie Stevens) this smelt imitation can be used wherever the natural baitfish is found. It is usually the first choice for Lake Champlain landlocked salmon when they chase baitfish into the Saranac and Boquet in spring. It should be just as effective for the trout and salmon taking smelt in the Finger Lakes and their tributaries, or anywhere else trout and salmon feed on smelt.

This is slightly modified from the classic version, but is still a full-dress recipe. A quicker version can be tied omitting the jungle cock feathers and the golden pheasant crest.
- Hook: size 4-12 streamer hook, 4Xl to 6Xl
- Body: orange floss
- Rib: flat silver tinsel (with small tag of tinsel)
- Wing: a few strands of peacock herl, then four gray saddle hackles over that, all slightly past the hook bend
- Throat: golden pheasant crest tippets, with small sprig of white bucktail underneath, both roughly to point of hook
- Shoulders: silver pheasant body feather, one on each side
- Cheeks: jungle cock, centered over shoulder feathers

New York Game Fish

BROWN TROUT

Brown trout, a European import, were first introduced to New York waters in 1883. Since then they have become widely distributed throughout the state both by stocking and natural reproduction and are probably the most important trout species for New York fly anglers.

Identified by the large, dark, round spots on their backs and sides (but not on the tail), browns tend to like slower water and tolerate warmer temperatures than the brookies or rainbows. They are also more elusive than brookies or most rainbows, and wild browns are famous for being maddeningly particular about insect imitations and drag-free drifts. Like brook trout, browns spawn in autumn, and though difficult to catch, big spawning fish can be taken in the streams near lakes and reservoirs. Twenty pound brown trout are not unknown, particularly in big lakes and reservoirs, but 10-14 inches is a more common size for stream-caught fish.

Brown Trout

BROOK TROUT

The only trout native to New York State, the brookie is actually a member of the char family (which also includes lake trout). The pink and blue spots on their sides and the worm-like markings on their backs can readily identify brookies. (As with other char, and unlike true trout, these are light markings on a dark background.) Other notable brook trout features are the distinct white edges on the front of ventral (stomach) fins and the black interior on the mouths of larger specimens.

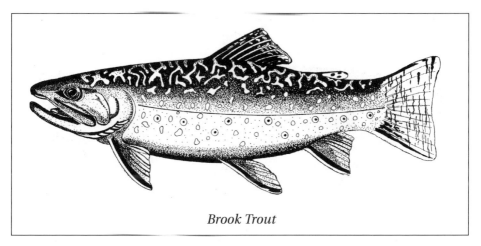

Brook Trout

Because of their shorter life spans—about five years at most—brook trout generally run smaller than rainbows or browns.

Brook trout need cold, clean water and this—along with competition from browns and rainbows—limits their range in New York. The state stocks some brookies, but most are naturally reproducing. The mountain streams and ponds of the Adirondacks are filled with usually small examples, and they are also found in many Catskill feeder creeks and in a famous wild population on Long Island's Carmans River. Particularly in small mountain creeks, brook trout are eager feeders, grabbing flies without much discrimination.

RAINBOW TROUT

Rainbows were actually stocked in New York waters about a decade before the brown trout, but today they are not as widely distributed as the other two species. They are stocked sporadically by the state and there are excellent wild populations in the Delaware River and Esopus Creek, in the Finger Lakes—most notably Seneca Lake—and in a number of small tributaries to the Upper Cattaraugus in the western part of the state.

Rainbows can be identified by the multitude of small black spots on their backs, sides and tail. The red stripe on the sides gives the rainbow its name, but the color is bright in some fish, barely visible in others. Unlike browns and brook trout, they are spring spawners. They are also more likely to be found in fast water than browns—in pools holding both species, look for the rainbows at the head, browns at the tail. Rainbows generally fall somewhere between browns and brookies in willingness to take flies, but the big, wild fish in the Delaware are as wary as any trout in the state.

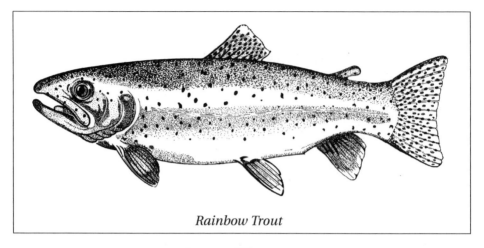

Rainbow Trout

Lake Trout

Like the brookie, the lake trout is actually a member of the char family, and it is also native to the state. Lakers live up to 20 years and can grow very large: the state record is nearly 40 pounds. Because they live and spawn in large, deep lakes they are not commonly taken on fly gear. The best chance for fly anglers to catch them is early season after ice-out when they inhabit shallow water, and by trolling with a fly rod from canoes or kayaks. Good populations of lakers can be found in the Great Lakes, the larger Finger Lakes and some Adirondack ponds. (A few Adirondack ponds also are stocked with splake, a hybrid of "speckled"(i.e. brook) trout and lakers.) Occasionally, lake trout can be caught in streams where they wash out of lakes like Otsego, Schroon and Owasco.

Lake Trout

STEELHEAD

It is generally believed that this migratory variety of rainbow trout is not truly a separate species. But its habitat and behavior are very different from the resident fish. Originating in Pacific coastal streams, steelhead have been successfully introduced to both of New York's Great Lakes, where they are sustained by a combination of stocking and natural reproduction.

In most respects, steelhead appears to be larger versions of rainbow trout, but their chrome coloring gives them the name (though they typically darken after entering streams to spawn). Steelhead up to 20 pounds are routinely taken in Lake Ontario tributaries—particularly the Salmon River—while fish from Lake Erie are typically about half that size. The fish spawn in spring and are most common in Great Lakes tributaries from February to March, but some fish move into streams in autumn and remain for the winter.

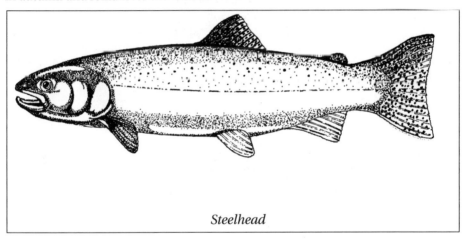

Steelhead

LANDLOCKED SALMON

Closely related to Atlantic salmon and often called that by anglers, these native New York fish are believed to have descended from migratory salmon that took up residence in inland waters. Overfishing, pollution and dam construction virtually wiped out New York's landlocked salmon by the turn of the last century. A restoration program was started in the 1950s and most fish in New York today are stocked by the DEC. The fish can grow to ten pounds or more and are usually silvery, bear scattered dark spots, and have noticeably more pointed profiles at the head than do trout. Like their ocean-dwelling relatives, they make spectacular leaps when hooked.

The best populations of landlocks in New York today are in Lake Champlain, a number of Adirondack lakes, the Finger Lakes and the Neversink Reservoir. They can be taken on flies cast or trolled in these lakes, but most of the flyfishing is done when the salmon enter the tributaries to these waters. Landlockeds head upstream to spawn in the fall, but can also be targeted in early spring when they enter stream mouths to feed on baitfish like smelt and alewives.

CHINOOK SALMON

Chinooks, also called kings, are found only in Lake Ontario in New York—a population sustained primarily by stocking. These giant Pacific salmon can grow to more than 40 pounds. In addition to their size, black mouths and black spots over the entire tail can identify chinooks.

These fish spawn in Lake Ontario tributaries in fall, with October the prime month. Like all Pacific salmon, chinooks die after spawning; so catching fish early in the run offers much better sport. With the reduction of stocking directly in the lake, strays are fewer; the tributaries receiving stocked fish offer the primary chance to land chinooks. The Salmon River on the eastern shore and Oak Orchard Creek on the southern shore are the two most famous spots, but South Sandy and (North) Sandy Creek on the eastern shore, the Genesee River, the Oswego River and Maxwell Creek receive substantial stockings as well.

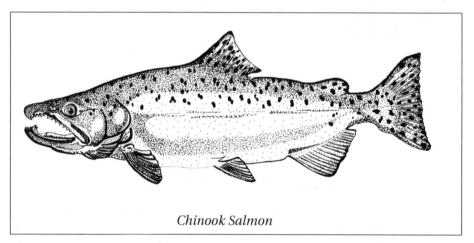

Chinook Salmon

COHO SALMON

Smaller than the chinooks, this is the other Pacific salmon stocked in Lake Ontario tributaries. Like chinooks, coho salmon, also called silver salmon, spawn in fall, though their runs peak a few weeks later. Despite their smaller size (typically half the weight of chinooks) these fish fight hard and acrobatically, and some fly anglers target them specifically. However, they are not stocked in as many streams, or in the same density, as the kings. In addition to the Salmon River and Oak

Orchard Creek, Sandy Creek on the south shore, Eighteenmile Creek and Maxwell Creek all receive cohos.

MUSKELLUNGE

Large, elusive and relatively rare in New York, muskellunge are the state's largest freshwater gamefish; the state record is a 69-pound trophy taken in the St. Lawrence River. A voracious predator, the muskie is hard to hook and equally hard to land—perhaps the toughest fish for freshwater fly anglers to catch. Many of New York's muskies are naturally reproducing, but some are stocked.

Much of the muskellunge fishing is done by spin and baitcasting anglers in New York lakes and big rivers like the St. Lawrence and the Alleghany, but fly anglers do catch these fish in stillwaters like Otisco and streams like the Grasse River. Heavy gear, big flies and bite tippets are all essential when flyfishing for muskellunge.

Tiger Muskellunge

TIGER MUSKELLUNGE

Sometimes called the norellunge, this hybrid of muskellunge and northern pike does not reproduce, but has been stocked by the state since 1967. Tigers are put in lakes such as New Croton Reservoir in Westchester, Otisco in the Finger Lakes region, and in big flowing waters like the Mohawk and the Susquehanna. These fish reach trophy size, but not as large as true muskies; they generally run two to three feet in length, and the state record is half that for muskellunge (a 35 pound fish taken in Tioughnioga Creek). Like muskellunge, the tiger's markings are dark on a light background, but they can be distinguished from true muskies by their smaller size and by the presence of scales on the lower half of the cheeks.

SMALLMOUTH BASS

A member of the sunfish family, these coolwater fish originated in the Ohio River Valley and reproduce naturally in many New York lakes and streams. As their name indicates, these fish can be distinguished from the related largemouth bass by the size of the mouth: the rear point of the jaw on a smallmouth does not go past the back of the fish's eye. They are also more brown rather than green—hence the nickname "bronzeback"—and usually have vertical bars on their sides.

Smallmouth can run up to six pounds in large lakes, but stream-bred fish are typically 10-14 inches. In prime rivers, particularly the Susquehanna, fish up to 20 inches long are taken on flies. In moving water, smallmouth bass are often mixed in with trout, the population getting denser as the water warms and the trout numbers decline. Smallmouth are usually found near structure: sunken timber, rocks and the downstream sides of islands. Though they do rise to hatches, crayfish, minnows and large nymphs like hellgrammites make up the bulk of their diets.

In addition to the fishing in the Susquehanna and its tributaries, good smallmouth fishing can be found in the lower Neversink. Both Great Lakes, Lake Champlain and the Finger Lakes also have good populations. In most lakes, flyfishers should try to fish early in the season, before smallmouth go deep. Lake Erie and the western Finger Lakes have an early smallmouth season that is ideal for targeting the fish in shallow water.

SHAD

This wild, anadromous fish—properly called the white shad or the American shad—lives in the Atlantic Ocean but spawns in coastal rivers. In New York, large numbers of shad spawn in the Hudson and Delaware, though the Delaware's smaller size makes it a better place to flyfish. The spawning fish enter New York waters in mid to late April and can be caught until early June, but the shad offer much better fishing when fresh from the sea. Egg-bearing females weigh up to six pounds, male "bucks" average a couple of pounds less. Their large silver scales, oval bodies, deeply forked tails and papery mouths easily identify shad.

Smallmouth Bass

Important Phone Numbers, Addresses, and Web Sites

GOVERNMENT

NEW YORK STATE DEPARTMENT OF ENVIRONMENTAL CONSERVATION
Headquarters: 50 Wolf Road, Albany, NY 12233; 518-457-2500 /
www.dec.state.ny.us
(See Regulations and Licenses for regional offices.)

NEW YORK STATE OFFICE OF PARKS, RECREATION AND HISTORIC PRESERVATION
(Operates state parks, state beaches, historic sites and other facilities) / New York
State Parks, Albany, New York 12238; 518-474-0456 / www.nysparks.com

NEW YORK STATE CAMPING/CABIN RESERVATIONS
(Reservations for both DEC campsites in the Adirondack and Catskill forest preserves and New York State Parks Department cabins and campsites in all state parks) / 800-456-CAMP (2267) / www.reserveamerica.com

NEW YORK CITY DEPARTMENT OF ENVIRONMENTAL PROTECTION
(Maintains and regulates use of Catskill and Croton reservoir systems) /see
Watershed Fishing Permit / DEC Headquarters, 59-17 Junction Boulevard,
10th Floor, Corona, NY 11368 / 718-337-4357 (DEP-HELP) /
www.ci.nyc.ny.us/html/dep/

UNITED STATES GEOLOGICAL SURVEY
(Various mapping, surveying and other activities, including monitoring stream flows and temperatures)
Regional Headquarters
Home page: www.usgs.gov
New York stream flow information: wwwdnyalb.er.usgs.gov/rt-cgi/gen_tbl_pg

Flyfishing and Conservation Organizations

TROUT UNLIMITED (NATIONAL)
(America's foremost coldwater fisheries conservation organization)
500 Wilson Boulevard; Suite 310, Arlington, VA 22209 / 703-522-0200 /
    Membership: 800-834-2419 / www.tu.org

NEW YORK STATE COUNCIL OF TROUT UNLIMITED
(Information on individual chapters may be found at this website.)
Web site: www.nyscounciltu.homestead.com /

NEW YORK CITY CHAPTER OF TROUT UNLIMITED
Web site: www.nyctu.org

NEW YORK STATE TROUT UNLIMITED CHAPTERS

- Art Flick
- Long Island
- New York City
- Ashokan-Pepacton Watershed
- Beamoc
- Catckill Mountians
- Croton Watershed
- Mid-Hudson
- Ray Bergman
- Ten MIle River
- Clearwater
- Columbia Greene
- Cooperstown
- Home-Waters
- Upper Delaware
- Upper Susuquehanna
- Adirondack
- Lake Champlain
- Black River Valley
- Mohawk Valley
- St. Lawrence Valley
- Al Hazzard
- Chenango Valley
- Colgate Red Raiders
- Fall Creek
- Iroquois
- Madison County
- Tug Hill-Salmon River
- Canadaiqua
- Catharine Creek
- Conhocton Valley
- Finger Lakes

FEDERATION OF FLYFISHERS
Web site: www.fedflyfishers.org
New York State Trout Unlimited

THEODORE GORDON FLYFISHERS
(New York City based fishing and conservation group)
Web site: www.tgf.org

JULIANA BERNERS ANGLERS
(New York City women's flyfishing club)
www.julianasanglers.com

NEW YORK RIVERS
(New York State River Conservation Organization)
PO Box 1460, Rome, NY 13442; 315 339 2097 /
www.newyorkriversunited.org

NATURE CONSERVANCY
(Preserves and manages natural sites, including on some key waterways)
Web site: www.nature.org
Web site: www.nature.org/states/newyork/

ADIRONDACK MOUNTAIN CLUB
(Not for profit group promoting hiking and camping in Adirondack Mountains, good source of maps and guidebooks for the Adirondacks)
ADK Headquarters, 814 Goggins Road, Lake George, NY 12845; 518-449-3870;
Membership & Information: 800-395-8080; www.adk.org

Fly Shops by Region

SOUTH

CATSKILLS

Al's Wild Trout, HC 89, Shinhopple NY / 13755 / 607-363-7135 / www.catskill.net/alstrout

The Beaverkill Angler, Stewart Ave, Roscoe, NY / 12776 / 607-498 5194 / www.beaverkillangler.com

Catskill Flies, Stewart Ave, Roscoe NY / 12776 / 607-498-6146 / www.catskillflies.com

Delaware River Club, HC1 Box 1290, Starlight PA / 18461 / 800-662-9359 / www.mayfly.com,

Fur, Fin and Feather Sport Shop, DeBruce Road, Livingston Manor, NY 12758 / 845-439-4476

Hornbeck's Sport Shop, 8 Pine St, Deposit, NY / 13754 / 607-467-4680

Joe McFadden's Fly & Tackle Shop, Route 97, Box 188, Hankins, NY / 12741 / 845-887-6000

Morne Imports, Main Street, Phoenicia, NY / 12464 / 845-688-7738

River Essentials, HC1 Box 1025, Starlight, PA / 18461 / 570-635-5900 / www.riveressentials.com

West Branch Angler, Route 17, Deposit, NY / 13754 / 607-467-5525 / www.westbranchangler.com

Wild Rainbow Outfitters, Route 191, Starlight PA / 18461 / 717-635-5983

WEST OF HUDSON

(These shops also serve the Catskills)

Ampro Sports, 743 State Route 28, Kingston, NY / 12401 / 845-331-9440

Blue River Anglers, Route 30 Middleburgh, NY / 518-295-8280 / www.northeast-flyfishing.com

Catskill Flies, 309 Mt. Cliff Road, Hurley, NY / 12747 / 845-434-268

Davis Sport Shop, Route 17, Sloatsburg, NY / 10974 / 845-753 2198 / www.davis-sport.com

Fishermans Corner, 183 Foxhall Avenue, Kingston, NY / 12401 / 845-340-1358

River Basin Sport Shop, 66 W Bridge St, Catskill, NY / 12414 / 518-943-2111

Thruway Sporting Goods, 78 Oak Street, Walden, NY / 12586 / 845-778-1400

NEW YORK CITY

(These shops serve Long Island, Westchester-Putnam and most of Southern New York)

Orvis New York, 522 Fifth Avenue (corner of 44th Street), New York, NY / 10036 / 212-697-3133 / National Orvis website: www.orvis.com

Urban Angler, 118 East 25th Street (3rd Floor), New York, NY 10010 / 212-979-7600 / www.urban-angler.com

(The following tackle and sporting goods shops have flyfishing equipment and related products)

Angler's World, 16 East 53rd Street, New York, NY 10022; 212-755-3400

Capitol Fishing Tackle, 218 West 23rd Street (7-8th Avenues), New York, NY 10011; 212-929-6132; e-mail: capcony@aol.com; www.captialfishing.com; flyfishing section

Paragon Sports, 867 Broadway (18th Street), New York, NY 10003; 212 255-8036; www.paragonsports.com; flyfishing section

Shooters and Anglers Sports Shop, 61-05 Grand Avenue, Maspeth (Queens), NY; 718-894-6122; flyfishing section

T. J. Huntsmon & Co., 36 West 44th Street, New York, NY 10036; 212-302-2463

WESCHESTER-PUTNAM COUNTIES

Bedford Sportsman Inc., 25 Adams St, Bedford Hills, NY / 10507 / 845-666-8091 / www.bedfordsportsman.com

CONNECTICUT

The Compleat Angler, 987 Post Road, Darien, CT 06820 / 203-655-9400 / www.compleat-angler.com

Fairfield Fly Shop, 917 Post Road, Fairfield CT / 06430 / 203-255-2896

Orvis, 432 Boston Post Road, Darien CT / 06820 / 203-662-0844

Orvis, 71 Ethan Allen Highway, Route 7, Ridgefield, CT / 203-544-7700

Sportsman Den of Greenwich, 33 River Rd., Cos Cob, CT / 06867 / 203-869-3234

Valley Angler, 56 Padanarum Road, Danbury, CT / 06811 / 203-792-8324

DUTCHESS AND COLUMBIA COUNTIES

Don's Tackle, 7396 So. Broadway Red Hook NY / 12571 / 845-758-9203 / www.flyfishdon.com

Orvis Sandanona, Route 44A, Millbrook, NY / 12545 / 845-677-9701

CONNECTICUT

Housatonic Meadows Fly Shop, 13 Route 7, Cornwall Bridge, CT / 06754 / 860-672-6064 / www.flyfishct.com

Housatonic River Outfitters, 7 Railroad St, West Cornwall, CT / 06796 / 860-672-1010 / www.dryflies.com

LONG ISLAND

NASSAU COUNTY

Orvis, 50 Glen Cove Road, Greenvale, NY / 11548 / 516-484-1860

SUFFOLK COUNTY
Camp-Site Sports, 1877 New York Ave., Huntington, NY / 631-271-4969 /
    www.campsite.net
Cold Spring Outfitters, 37 Main Street, Cold Spring Harbor, NY / 11724 /
    631-673-8937 / www.coldspringfly.com
The Fly Fishing Store, 4101 Sunrise Highway (Route 27), Bohemia, NY / 11716 /
    631-563-1323 / www.flyfishingstore.com

CENTRAL

EAST OF HUDSON (RENSSELLAER AND WASHINGTON COUNTIES)
A & P Custom Tackle, 155 Hidley Rd. Wynantskill, NY / 12198 / 518-283-5920
The Lower River, 4337 Route 22, Salem NY 12865 / 518-854-3138

VERMONT
Orvis, Historic Route 7A, Manchester, VT 05254 / 802-362-3622 /
    www.orvis.com

WEST OF HUDSON (MOHAWK VALLEY)
(These shops also serve the Southern Adirondacks)
Angler Essentials, 7 Glenwood Drive, Saratoga Springs, NY 12866 /
    518-581-0859
Goldstocks Sporting Goods, 98 Freemans Bridge Road, Scotia, NY 12302 /
    518-382-2037
Mad River Sports, 207 Clark Street, Canastota, NY 13032 / 800-231-9314
Nick's Field & Stream, 1511 Broadway, Schenectady, NY 12306 / 518-382-7908
Rising Trout Outfitter, 587 Main Street, New York Mills, NY 13417 /
    315-736-0353 / www.risingtroutoutfitter.com
Taylor and Vadney, 3071 Broadway, Schenectady, NY 12306 / 518-374-3030 /
    www.taylorandvadney.com
Walton's Sport Shop, 59 Lake Avenue, Saratoga Springs, NY 12800 /
    518-584-7151

NORTH

SOUTHERN ADIRONDACKS
(These shops also serve the other sections of the Adirondacks)
Beaver Brook Outfitters, Route 28 & Route 8, Wevertown, NY 12886 /
    888-454-8433 / www.beaverbrook.net
North Country Sports, Thirteenth Lake Road, North River, NY 12856 /
    518-251-4299 / www.lakegeorge-ny.com/northcountrysports

Peace Pipe Fishing Outfitters, 4375 Lake Shore Drive, Diamond Point, NY
518-668-9203 / www.fish307.com
VERMONT
Vermont Field Sports, 1458 Route 7 South, Middlebury, VT 05753 /
802-388-3572 / www.middlebury.net/vtfield/

NORTHEAST ADIRONDACKS
(These shops also serve the other sections of the Adirondacks)
Adirondack Sports Shop, Route 86 Wilmington, NY 12997 / 518-946-2605
Ausable River Sports Shop, Route 86, Wilmington, NY 12997 / 518-946-1250 /
www.ausableriversportshop.com / Fly shop, guide service
Blue Line Sport Shop, 82 Main Street, Saranac Lake, NY 12983 / 518-891-4680
Gordon's Marine, 1428 Route 3, West Plattsburgh, NY 12962 / 518-561-2109
Hook & Hackle Co, Kaycee Loop Road, #7, Plattsburgh NY 12901 / 518-561-5893
/ www.hookhack.com
The Hungry Trout, Route 86, Whiteface Mountain, NY 12997 / 518-946-2217 /
www.hungrytrout.com,
Jones Outfitters Ltd., 331 Main St, Lake Placid, NY 12946 / 518-523-3468 /
www.jonesoutfitters.com
Outfitters Plus, 1135 Cook Street, Dannemora, NY 12929 / 518-492-2006

VERMONT
The Classic Outfitters, 861 Williston Rd # 5, South Burlington, VT 05403 /
802-860-7375

CANADA
Ben La Mouche, 5926 Rue Hochelaga, Montreal, Quebec / 514-252-1225
Boutique Classique Angler, 414 Rue Mcgill, Montreal, Quebec / 514-878-3474
Boutique Salmo Nature, 110 McGill Street, Montreal, Quebec H2Y 2E5 / 514-
871-8447
Brightwater Flyfishing, 336 Cumberland Street, Ottawa, ON / 613-241-6798
Grand River Troutfitters, 790 Tower Street, Fergus, ON N1M 2R3 /
519-787-4359 / www.grandrivertroutfitters.com
Green Drake Outfitters, 342 Richmond Road, Ottawa, ON K2A 0E8 /
613-828-1915 / www.greendrake.com
Le Baron Outdor Products, 1 Stafford Road, Ottawa K2H9N5 / 613-596-4415

NORTHWEST ADIRONDACKS
Sandy's Custom Tackle, 10079 State Highway 37, Ogdensburg, NY / 13669 /
315-394-0308
Wear On Earth, 19 Market Street, Potsdam, NY / 13676 / 315-265-3178

WEST

LEATHERSTOCKING AND SUSQUEHANNA REGIONS
(Also serves the Catskills)
Timber Creek Sports Shop, 100 Rano Boulevard, Vestal, NY 13850 / 607-770-9112 / www.timbercreeksports.com

FINGER LAKES REGION
(Most of these shops also serve Ontario Tributaries)
Badger Creek Fly Tying, 1408 Hanshaw Road, Ithaca, NY 14850 / 607-266-0736 www.mwflytying.com
Community Fly Fisher, 1015 West Seneca Street, Ithaca, NY 14850 / 607-697-0053 / (Shop run by a non-profit organization promoting fly fishing to youngsters, refer to listing in index for more on this program)
Les Maynard's Fly Shop, 1223 Hecker Road, Waterloo, NY 13165 / 315-539-3236
Nature's Best Flys, 504 Charles Ave. # 6, Syracuse, NY 13209 / 315-468-3749 / http://members.xoom.com/NatsFlys/
Nehrke's Fly Shop, 34 Robie Street, Bath, NY 14810 / 607-776-7294 (by appointment)
Pinewood Flies, 185 Pine Valley Road, Pine Valley, NY 14872 / 607-739-4348 / www.flyfishingonline.com
Royal Coachman Fly Shop, 1410 East Genesee Street, Skaneateles, NY 13152 / 315-685-0005 / www.skaneateles.com/royalcoachman
The Serious Angler, PO Box 611, Jordan, NY / 13080 / 315-689-3864
The Troutfitter, 3008 Erie Boulevard East, Syracuse, NY / 13224 / 315-446-2047 / Full service fly shop
The Wayfarer Company, 5125 Route 174, Camillus, NY 13031 / 315-672-9691

WESTERN NEW YORK TROUT
Carter Hardware, 130 North Main Street, Wellsville, NY 14895 / 716-593-3550 Pennsylvania
True Life Fly Co., 1005 W Main St, Smethport, PA 16749 / 814-887-1974

LAKE ERIE AND TRIBUTARIES
(These shops typically also serve Southern Ontario Shore Tributaries)
Oak Orchard Fly Shop, 5110 Main Street (Walker Center), Williamsville, NY 14221 / 716-626-1323 / www.oakorchardflyshop.com
Buffalo Outfitters (Reed & Son), 5655 Main Street, Williamsville, NY 14221 / 716-631-5131
Ingersoll's Chautauqua Flyshop, 1227 Orr Street, Jamestown, NY 14701 / 716-665-2923
M & M Sports Den, 808 North Main Street, Jamestown, NY 14701 / 716-664-5400

PENNSYLVANIA
Fly Fishing Forever, Fairview Village, PA 19409 / 610-631-8990
Smith's Sport Store, 10 Erie Avenue, Saint Marys, PA 15857 / 814-834-3701

CANADA
Angling Specialties,
   3251 Kennedy Road., Scarborough, ON M1V-2J9 / 416-609-0801
   2104 Highway 7 West, Concord, ON L4K-2S9 / 905-660-9697
   325 Central Parkway, West, Mississauga, ON L5B 3X9 / 906-275-4972
Le Baron Outdoor Products,
   8365 Woodbine Avenue, Markham, ON / L3R2P4 / 905-944-0682
   1590 Dundas Street East, Mississauga / L4X2Z2 / 905-273-6434
Pollack Sporting Goods, 337 Queen Street East, Toronto, ON M5A-1S9 /
   416-363-1095
Wilsons Sporting Tradition, 26 Wellington Street East, Toronto, ON M5E 1S2 /
   416-869-3474 / www.wilsonsorvis.co

LAKE ONTARIO AND TRIBUTARIES
EASTERN SHORE
All Seasons Sports, 3733 Route 13, Pulaski, NY 13142 / 315-298-6433 /
   www.allseasonssports.com
Fat Nancy's Tackle Shop, Route 13 and Interstate 81, Pulaski, NY 13142 /
   315-298-6357 / www.salmon-river.com/fatnancy
Fish Inn Post, 2035 Route 22, Altmar, NY 13302 / 315-298-6406
Malinda's Fly & Tackle Shop, 3 Pulaski Street, Altmar, NY 13302 / 315-298-2993
Oswego Outfitters, PO Box 86, Pulaski, NY 13142 / 315-298-6349 /
   www.flyfishingnetwork.com/ffn/gregliu.html
Pulaski Sport Shop, 7676 Rome Road, Pulaski, NY 13142 / 315-298-6599
Steelhead Motel and Tackle Shop, 3178 Route 13, Pulaski, NY 13142 /
   315-298-4371
Tony's Salmon Country Sports Shop, 3790 Rome Street Pulaski, NY 13142 /
   315-298-4104 / www.tonyssalmoncountry.com
Whitaker's Sport Shop, 3707 Route 13, Pulaski, NY 13142 / 315-298-6162, /
   www.whitakers.com
Yankee Fly Shop, 4819 Salina Street, Pulaski, NY 13142 / 315-298-2466

SOUTHERN SHORE
(These shops also serve Lake Erie and Western New York Trout)
Orleans Outdoor, 1764 Oak Orchard Road (Route 98), Albion, NY 14411 /
   716-682-4546 / www.orleansoutdoor.com
Coleman's Fly Shop, 4786 Ridge Road West, Spencerport, NY 14559 /
   716-352-4775 / www.colemansflyshop.com
Panorama Outfitters, Cliffside Common, 900 Panorama Trail, Rochester, NY
   14625 / 716-248-8390 / www.panoramaoutfitters.com
Up The Creek, 28 South Main Street, Pittsford, NY 14534 / 716-381-355

Index

T

NOTES

NOTES

NOTES

WILDERNESS ADVENTURES GUIDE SERIES

If you would like to order additional copies of this book or our other Wilderness Adventures Press guidebooks, please fill out the order form below or call **1-800-925-3339** or *fax 800-390-7558.* Visit our website for a listing of over 2000 sporting books—the largest online: **www.wildadv.com**   *Mail To:*

Wilderness Adventures Press, Inc., 45 Buckskin Road • Belgrade, MT 59714

☐ **Please send me your quarterly catalog on hunting and fishing books.**

Ship to:
Name _____

Address _____

City _____ State_____ Zip_____

Home Phone_____ Work Phone_____

Payment: ☐ Check   ☐ Visa   ☐ Mastercard   ☐ Discover   ☐ American Express

Card Number _____ Expiration Date_____

Signature_____

Qty	Title of Book	Price	Total
	Saltwater Angler's Guide to Southern California	$26.95	
	Saltwater Angler's Guide to the Southeast	$26.95	
	Flyfisher's Guide to the Florida Keys	$26.95	
	Flyfisher's Guide to Colorado	$26.95	
	Flyfisher's Guide to Idaho	$26.95	
	Flyfisher's Guide to Michigan	$26.95	
	Flyfisher's Guide to Montana	$26.95	
	Flyfisher's Guide to Northern California	$26.95	
	Flyfisher's Guide to Northern New England	$26.95	
	Flyfisher's Guide to Oregon	$26.95	
	Flyfisher's Guide to Pennsylvania	$26.95	
	Flyfisher's Guide to Washington	$26.95	
	Flyfisher's Guide to Minnesota	$26.95	
	Flyfisher's Guide to Utah	$26.95	
	Flyfisher's Guide to Texas	$26.95	
	Flyfisher's Guide to New York	$26.95	
	Total Order + shipping & handling		

Shipping and handling: $4.99 for first book,
$3.00 per additional book, up to $13.99 maximum